Afghanistan Under Siege

Afghanistan Under Siege

The Afghan Body and the Postcolonial Border

Bojan Savić

I.B. TAURIS
LONDON • NEW YORK • OXFORD • NEW DELHI • SYDNEY

I.B. TAURIS
Bloomsbury Publishing Plc
50 Bedford Square, London, WC1B 3DP, UK
1385 Broadway, New York, NY 10018, USA
29 Earlsfort Terrace, Dublin 2, Ireland

BLOOMSBURY, I.B. TAURIS and the I.B. Tauris logo are trademarks of
Bloomsbury Publishing Plc

First published in Great Britain 2020
This paperback edition published in 2021

Copyright © Bojan Savić, 2020

Bojan Savić has asserted his right under the Copyright, Designs and
Patents Act, 1988, to be identified as Author of this work.

For legal purposes the Acknowledgements on p. x constitute an extension
of this copyright page.

Series design by Adriana Brioso
Cover image: Afghan residents ride a motorcycle past soldier from
the US Marines in Garmser, Southern Afghanistan on February 23, 2011.
(© ADEK BERRY/AFP via Getty Images)

All rights reserved. No part of this publication may be reproduced or transmitted
in any form or by any means, electronic or mechanical, including photocopying,
recording, or any information storage or retrieval system, without prior
permission in writing from the publishers.

Bloomsbury Publishing Plc does not have any control over, or responsibility for, any
third-party websites referred to or in this book. All internet addresses given in this
book were correct at the time of going to press. The author and publisher regret any
inconvenience caused if addresses have changed or sites have ceased to exist,
but can accept no responsibility for any such changes.

A catalogue record for this book is available from the British Library.

A catalogue record for this book is available from the Library of Congress.

ISBN: HB: 978-1-7883-1526-5
PB: 978-0-7556-3755-3
ePDF: 978-1-7883-1793-1
eBook: 978-1-7883-1794-8

Typeset by Deanta Global Publishing Services, Chennai, India

To find out more about our authors and books visit www.bloomsbury.com and
sign up for our newsletters.

Contents

List of abbreviations	viii
Acknowledgements	x

Part I Questions, Who Is Addressing Them and How		1
1	Introduction: The Abnormal of the Afghan War on Terror	3
	The Troublesome Herati Subject	3
	Herat at the Limit: Between the Postcolonial Frontier and Security Unbound	5
	Herat at the Limit: Between Afghanistan and Iran, Pashtunistan and Persia, Sunnis and Shias	6
	Herat at the Limit: Between Peace and Resistance on the Frontier	9
	Global Stability in Herat	13
	Critiques of Security in Afghanistan and Herat	13
	Herati Encounters of Class, Race and Geography: Seeing Like the Subject	15
	The Roadmap	17
Part II Why Does Postcolonial Security Care about Herat?		19
2	Mapping Out Tools of Critique: A Conceptual Framework	21
	Introduction: Governing the Ungovernable	21
	Strategies of Power	22
	Strategies of Sovereign, Disciplinary and Governmental Power	25
	The Body and Power: The Many Axes of Afghan Vulnerabilities	29
	Conduits of Power: Security Apparatuses and Uncertainty	34
	Postcolonial Power and the Afghan Body	35
	Government through Experimentation	38
	Nonviolent Everyday Resistance: Power as Power Struggle	40
	Conclusion	44
3	Spaces and Forces of Pacification and Containment	46
	Introduction	46
	Brown Bodies and Lands: Violent, Dirty, Fantastic and Risky	47
	Representations of Afghanistan: Background and Proximate, from Instability to Filth	48
	Background and Proximate: Imaginations of Herat as Decline and Risk	53

The Global Defining Itself as Imperilled	58
Who Is At Risk and What Must Be Defended?	59
Afghans in Global Security: The Necessary Threat	64
Heratis at Risk	69
Whose Risk Matters?	73
Three Sets of Apparatuses: Governing through Spatial Enmeshments	74
Security Apparatuses and Experimentality	79
The Rationality of Government through Experimentation	81
Conclusion: Herati Hearts and Minds	85

Part III Power over Heratis and Resistances to It: Three Case Studies   87

4 How Pacified Heratis 'Milk the Cow': Nonviolent Resistances to Global Security   89

Introduction	89
Herat at the Limit of Power and Resistance	92
Ambivalence in Herat	93
Ambivalent Employment as Counter-exploitation of Security Governance	94
Ambivalent Resistances through Knowledge and Skills	103
Conclusion	110

5 Banished by Culture, Violated in Its Midst: Managing Musalla's Homeless between Minarets, Development and Security   112

Introduction	112
The 'Otherness' of the Homeless and the Study of It	115
'What is Splendour?' Culture as Population Management	116
'Police' in the Study of Afghan Law Enforcement's Management of Musalla	117
The Cultural Apparatus and the Cultivation of Splendour	118
Musalla and 'Its' Homeless: Visible Neglect	120
How Do Visible Misery and Violence, and Invisible Pain Work?	127
Three Questions	127
Patterns of Representation of Musalla's Homeless and the Conditions of Their Pain	132
'Better Not Talk to Them': Pathologizing Musalla's Homeless	137
Becoming a UNESCO World Heritage Site: Herat's Cultural Apparatus and its Noble Cause	138
Conclusion	143

6	Experiencing Self as the Periphery: Heratis at the Iranian-Afghan Border	146
	Introduction	146
	Afghans in(to) Iran	150
	Conceptual Reflections	154
	The Periphery in the 'World as a System'	154
	The Body as a Peripheral Space: Experiencing Self as the Periphery	157
	The Periphery and the Frontier at Islam Qala	159
	Islam Qala: Thinking and Encountering the Periphery at the Border	159
	Being a Child, Being Afghan, Being a Woman at Islam Qala	164
	International Agencies and Their Spatial Effects on the Normalization of Islam Qala	171
	Islam Qala's Fluctuating and Inflated Spatiality	172
	The Exceptionality of Commerce. Commerce as a Window into Border Surveillance	174
	The Fragmentation and Inflation of a 'Fine' Violent Border	179
	Manoeuvring the Periphery by Evading, Co-opting and Counter-Surveilling the Border	180
	Conclusion	192
Part IV Conclusion		197
7	On Postcolonial Power Equilibria	199
References		203
Index		237

Abbreviations

AAF	Afghan Air Force
ABP	Afghan Border Police
AFN	Afghani (currency)
AHRO	Afghanistan Human Rights Organization
ANA	Afghan National Army
ANP	Afghan National Police
ANSF	Afghan National Security Forces
BEIC	British East India Company
CDC	Community Development Council
DAFA	French Archeological Delegation in Afghanistan
EU	European Union
HUDA	Herat Urban Development and Housing Department
IDP	internally displaced person
IFRC	International Federation of Red Cross and Red Crescent Societies
IMF	International Monetary Fund
ISAF	International Security Assistance Force
ISMEO	Instituto Italiano per il Medio ed Estremo Oriente
LOFTA	Law and Order Trust Fund for Afghanistan
NATO	North Atlantic Treaty Organization
NDS	National Directorate of Security
NGO	nongovernmental organization
NSP	National Solidarity Program
NPP	National Priority Program
OEF	Operation Enduring Freedom
OFS	Operation Freedom's Sentinel
PRT	Provincial Reconstruction Team
SMAF	Self-Reliance through Mutual Accountability Framework
TAAC-W	Train Advise Assist Command – West
UAE	United Arab Emirates

UK	United Kingdom
UN	United Nations
UNAMA	United Nations Assistance Mission in Afghanistan
UNESCO	United Nations Educational, Scientific and Cultural Organization
UNDP	United Nations Development Program
UNHCR	Office of the United Nations High Commissioner for Refugees
UNODC	United Nations Office on Drugs and Crime
US	United States
USAID	United States Agency for International Development
WMD	weapon of mass destruction
WSA	World-Systems Analysis

Acknowledgements

I will forever remain indebted to my informants in Herat, Kabul and North Carolina. Much of what I have learned about the lives of ordinary Heratis in the midst of global insecurity – I owe this to you. Thank you, Toorialey, Zabiullah, Barialay, and Wasel for patiently answering my questions and for sharing with me your experiences of daily life and politics in Afghanistan. You made my research in Herat and Kabul possible and you treated me like your guest and friend. And to dozens of other informants named and unnamed in this book: thank you. I hope I did your voice justice.

I also want to thank my colleagues and mentors who have offered invaluable advice and encouraged me to persist in this research. Tom Casier, Amanda Klekowski von Koppenfels, Betty Morgan, Gerard Toal and Maria Mälksoo, thank you for your support and critical feedback over the past five years. I am also grateful to the American Political Science Association whose annual meetings have helped me develop the ideas and arguments presented in this book. I owe a great deal of gratitude to my editor, Tomasz Hoskins, for his endless patience and faith in this project.

To Bridget: thank you for reading the entire manuscript and for helping me make it better. And to Crina: our long conversations about everything and nothing have found their way into this book. I expected nothing less of us. Miša and Kosta, my fellow travellers through the oddities of this long-distance friendship, thank you for the years of care and love.

It is safe to say that finding the faith and strength needed to complete this book would have been impossible without you, Stanley. Thank you for changing my life, Mr Pinnix. Noemí and Momchil, thank you for being there for Stanley while I was away on fieldwork. Moreover, you have been a second home to me. I owe you.

Finally, I am grateful to my brother and my whole family for their warm support. *Tata*, I will never forget your sacrifice. And to my *Mama*: I wish I could tell you how much your love and faith in me still inspire me every day. You are my hero.

Part I

Questions, Who Is Addressing Them and How

1

Introduction: The Abnormal of the Afghan War on Terror

The Troublesome Herati Subject

My first visit to Afghanistan was in December 2014. Truth be told, it did not take long before I realized that years of preparation for fieldwork had not done enough to dispel my subliminal notions of Afghan modernity as 'different' and 'not quite familiar'. As I walked around Kabul's international airport looking for Zabiullah – my guide, interpreter and key informant in the city – I realized that the little I knew about him was comically inadequate. '*Tall, in his mid-twenties, usually wearing very modern clothes*' is the person I was looking for. Alas, nearly every young man I saw around the airport looked just like that. The male Afghan body presented itself to me in the manner most bodies do – as unremarkable and everyday. It took us about an hour until we finally found each other based on the photos and verbal descriptions that we had been given. At any rate, the conversation unfolded easily and I was soon sharing with Zabiullah my first experiences of Kabul. I remember being both unsettled and entertained by a brief interaction I had had with an American security contractor at the airport arrival hall. I jokingly told Zabiullah that she had warned me against leaving my 'secure compound' while in town. He responded by bemoaning the separation of 'Westerners' from 'real Kabul', and added: '*This idea of escape is false. Afghans make their compounds possible. There would be no compounds without us.*'

Ordinary Afghans have been thrust into security and economic relations that privilege foreign development professionals and security personnel. Yet, while deprived of safe compounds, Afghans are indispensable to the operation of the US/NATO governance apparatus as farmers, police officers, private security recruits, construction workers, trash collectors, pharmacists, language interpreters, etc. They appropriate exclusion into fodder for endurance. Throughout my fieldwork, numerous interviewees iterated these power relations as reminiscent of Afghanistan's colonial experience during the nineteenth and twentieth centuries. This book critiques the post-2001 US, NATO, and UN-led governance of Afghanistan by going beyond the recurring debates on its failures and errors (Bizhan 2018, Fairweather 2014, Coburn and Larson 2014, Johnson and Leslie 2004). Instead, it scrutinizes the strategies and social effects of Afghan reconstruction against the backdrop of pervasive imaginations of Afghan populations as risky and threatening. How and by what means have global security priorities affected Afghan lives? This book argues that global governance targets the Afghan *body as a space of power*, a risky landscape to be monitored and governed. This targeting works through combinations of security and development interventions that betray the postcolonial logic of governance: one that reproduces hierarchies in the social utility of humans along racial, class, cultural and other lines. Few regions in Afghanistan have experienced the diversity of post-conflict reconstruction and security programmes like Herat, the country's westernmost province of around 1.9 million residents. On average, Herat has been the sixth largest recipient of foreign aid among Afghanistan's thirty-four provinces (Afghan Ministry of Finance 2012, Afghan Ministry of Finance 2011) and a historical 'trading' and 'economic hub' in Central Asia (Leslie 2015). Based on original fieldwork carried out in Kabul and Herat (in December 2014 through January 2015 and May through June 2016), this monograph studies Herati encounters with postcolonial security. I embed Herat in the 'postcolony' – a space of entangled temporalities, discontinuities, and inertias mired in the legacies of exploitative colonial power (Young 2015, 135–148, Mbembe 2001). To paraphrase Joshua Lund's discussion of race, postcolony is the '*racialization of space*' and the '*naturalization of segregation*' (Lund 2012, 75) on trans-social and trans-corporeal ('global') scales.

Justified by ritualized invocations of September 11 and alarming migration statistics, postcolonial governance targets dangerous populations everywhere. Brown, dispossessed, physically isolated from the neighbouring nations and the wider world, and poorly protected, Afghan bodies are easy targets that reflect the pain of Muslims violated worldwide. Postcolonial security heightens Afghan vulnerabilities by murdering them, constraining their 'free' movement, or incentivizing only acceptable work and religious practices. While cultivating 'normal' conducts, power represses the *abnormal* of Afghan terror wars: those eccentrically religious, poor, desperate, and ominous to 'global stability'. Moreover, postcolonial governance utilizes security and development interventions to surveil the constricted Afghan body and develop lessons about its behaviour purportedly reflective of global 'extremism'. Throughout, governance apparatuses re-test hypotheses about what 'works' in 'combatting terror'. Yet, this book also tells stories of how power generates its own resistances. It is a narrative of Heratis who counter-exploit postcolonial interventions to maximize their own life chances in ways deemed corrupt or dangerous by the governance apparatus.

Media reporting, punditry, politicians, military brass and dominant International Relations, Development and Security Studies scholarship portray Afghanistan and Afghans as risky for the 'world' in terms of security, migration, opium production, public health, organized crime, etc. They casually depict Afghans as a financial and human drain on global governance institutions: as a space of sparse success or outright failure of reconstruction, development and state-building efforts. A 2013 public poll found that eight in ten Americans had an unfavourable opinion of Afghanistan, making it the sixth least popular country in the world among US respondents (Newport and Himelfarb 2013). These representations seem uninterested in the everyday experience of insecurity, loss of life and welfare, systemic surveillance, neglect, and marginalization of ordinary Afghans subjected to the priorities and instruments of regional and global 'stability'. This book addresses this *representational gap* by drawing attention to a fuller experience of life in Herat as one of Afghanistan's more prosperous cities, a mere 125 km from the Afghan-Iranian border. I invite the reader to think of perilous bodies as lives in peril. Furthermore, in contrast to simplifications of Afghan resistances as the *violent*, cannibalistic and anti-civilizational Taliban or Daesh insurgencies, this book highlights *nonviolent* everyday rejections and evasions of the US, EU and NATO-funded security apparatus and governance more broadly.

The critiques and stories presented here aim to achieve several purposes. My primary goal is to counter journalistic, policy and scholarly caricatures of Afghans as violent, religiously fanatic, tribal and expendable, and instead draw attention to Afghan lives as vulnerable to oppression by enmeshed 'external' ('Western' and 'Oriental') and 'domestic' actors. In articulating Herati vulnerabilities, this book underscores the unequal life chances and experiences of security stemming from class, racial, ethnic, gender and other divides typically invisible to the white, male, middle-class expert and analyst. I hope that this monograph will help intensify discussions on the impact of global security on Afghan lives and well-being by injecting vocabularies of social justice and global race-class inequalities into the conversations on governance, security and reconstruction.

Dominant scholarship on Afghan security and state-building is trapped in success/failure debates and metrics shaped by international donors (Felbab-Brown 2013, Jones 2008). Instead, this book analyses how Afghan governance subjects the lives it claims to empower and, paradoxically, empowers them in ways it does not intend to. Furthermore, in departing from the literature on Empire (Hopkins 2018, Chomsky 2012, Mann 2003, Hahn and Heiss 2001), this book argues that security governance in Afghanistan serves to protect an evasive norm of 'global stability' more so than the US or her NATO allies. Likewise, I argue that postcolonial power subjects the racial, cultural, and gendered 'abnormal', regardless of whether 'Western' or 'liberal' actors are involved. Iranian, Emirati, Russian, and other non-Western 'core' actors treat the Afghan body as the global 'periphery': the abnormal that is only conditionally useful and otherwise dangerous. Finally, this book uniquely argues that winning Afghan 'hearts and minds' is compatible with ignoring them as the 'collateral damage' of counterterrorism: both strategies objectify Afghan bodies as resources in the war on terror. To both counterterrorism and counterinsurgency, Afghan populations are means deployable in defence of global security.

The rest of this chapter situates Herati bodily geographies within broader global security. Thereafter, I position this monograph in the field of critiques of security and development in Afghanistan, and reflect on the reward and difficulty of researching the quotidian practices of Herati life in the context of postcolonial security. Finally, I outline how the remainder of the book will proceed.

Herat at the Limit: Between the Postcolonial Frontier and Security Unbound

An inquiry into the social-corporeal effects of security on Heratis should perhaps begin by situating Herat Province and Herat City historically and geopolitically, particularly vis-à-vis the logic of *global security governance*. This will help explain why Herat is a place and a population *at the limit* of competing and overlapping power relations.

Herat at the Limit: Between Afghanistan and Iran, Pashtunistan and Persia, Sunnis and Shias

Speaking to Heratis over the years, my understanding of *where Herat is* has shifted. Chapter 2 will expound upon territory and population as subjectivities or 'selves' that are neither one's conscious choice nor simple facts of genetics and geography. Rather, they are products of broader social truths and power struggles. I have come to see Herat's subjectivity as *liminal* (rather than Afghan): as 'in-between', 'both' and 'neither' (Bhabha 1994) in relation to dominant population-territories that have delineated it through history.

The imaginations and descriptions of Herat have varied over time, and Chapter 3 will explore some of that history. Yet, whichever descriptors are applied to the city and its wider region, the vitality of the Harirud (Herat River) and its fertile valley has been credited with breathing life into the city and the whole Province.[1] Historical and contemporary accounts (Henty 1902, Doubleday 2006, Lamb 2002) romanticize Herati life as a historical force that has willed itself upon an arid geomorphology and climate, surrounding dominions and plundering tribes of lesser sophistication. Its 'strategic' location, *'not quite on the Silk Road, but close enough to profit from its trade'* (Gammell 2016, 5), has been credited with sustaining that force. Rather than seeing Herat as battling to maintain its integrity and heroically pushing back against invading empires and tribes, this book is inclined to see it as constituted *by*, and constitutive *of* the forces around it and in its midst. Herat's geopolitics has been tied to the wider geo-cultural area of (Greater) Khorasan, a plateau co-influenced and inhabited by shifting (and often enmeshed) Persian, Turkic, Mongol, Pashtun, Hazara and other populations. The name *Khorasan* ('sunrise' in Middle Persian) most likely came about during the Sassanian Empire (probably in the AD sixth century), designating a fluctuating space east of 'Iraq Adjami' (Persian Iraq), and vaguely extending through the Transoxiana region (modern-day Uzbekistan and Tajikistan) and Hindustan. In historiography, the region was typically associated with its key cities, centres of trade, urban culture, and elite politics, including Balkh and Herat (now in Afghanistan), Mashhad and Nishapur (in modern-day northeastern Iran), Bukhara and Samarkand (in Uzbekistan), and Merv and Nisa (in Turkmenistan) (Daryaee 2012, Beckwith 2009). Presently, the toponym 'Khorasan' designates a northeast Iranian administrative province. Given the politics of geography, naming and historiography, positioning Herat as liminal is not a historical compromise, but a summary of the in-betweenness of Herati life and subjectivity.

My intent is not to recount histories around the Harirud dating back to the Assyrian and Achaemenid (First Persian) empires or the conquests of Alexander the Great. Instead, I point to the liminality that has shaped Herat's modern (used here very

---

[1] For instance, see Chapter XXIX of *The Lands of the Eastern Caliphate* by G. Le Strange, published in 1905 by Cambridge University Press.

loosely) history, which can tentatively be tied to 1717, when a confederation of Pashtun families – the Abdali Sadozai – expelled Herat's last Persian Safavid governor from the city. Moreover, the eighteenth century marked the point of Herat's transformation into a more Pashtun and 'Afghan' political space. In eighteenth-century British colonial vocabularies, *Afghan* meant *Pashtun*. Prior to 1717, Herat's slice of Khorasan was controlled by various iterations of the Persian Empire, including the Sassanian dynasty (from the early third through the fifth century) and the Safavids (in the sixteenth and seventeenth centuries), as well as the Tajik Kartid dynasty (thirteenth and fourteenth centuries) and the Mongol Empire (through the rise of the Safavids in the sixteenth century). Speaking to the cultural, geopolitical and self-representational eclecticism over centuries, both the Kartids and the Il-Khan Mongols adopted Persian legal, juridical and administrative codes, cultural practices and imperial notions of power. As a cobweb of Tajik families, the Kartids spoke Persian, and the Il-Khans adopted it as well, situating their courts in various Persian cities (Morgan 1988, 68).

When the Pashtun Sadozai rose to power in 1717, it was the culmination of their century-long ascent as a prominent Pashtun family in Herat (having moved west from Kabul). As their ascent led to the foundation of the Pashtun Durrani Empire in Kandahar (1747), the 'eastern' Pashtun-dominated Sunni and the 'western' Persian-Shia spaces began to shape Herat's geopolitics. In practice, however, the Durranis mimicked the Persian courtly customs, social hierarchies, artistic and legal practices. The first Durrani king, Ahmad Shah, thought of himself as 'King of Khorasan' (rather than 'Afghanistan' or 'Cabul', which will be used later on) (Martin 2014, 17–19, Ahmed 2013, 199). Moreover, Herat often enjoyed a measure of political autonomy and simultaneous ambivalent affiliation with Kandahar, Mashhad, Tehran and Kabul, as well as with the British East India Company (BEIC) and the British Raj (post-1858).

In 1808, Mountstuart Elphinstone, an administrator at the BEIC, described two-thirds of Herat's population as '*Herautees, or ancient inhabitants of the place, who are all Sheeahs*' and only '*a tenth of the whole population*' as Pashtuns ('Dooraunees') (Elphinstone 1815, 216). Elphinstone described rural areas around the city as predominantly Sunni 'Taujik' and, to a smaller extent, 'Afghaun' (Pashtun) and 'Mogul' (Mongol) (Ibid). Since Afghanistan's Central Statistics Organization presently avoids studying the country's ethnic divides, even a simplified map is hard to construct and critically compare to Elphinstone's picture. An overwhelming majority of my informants described Herat's population as predominantly Tajik and Farsiwan (Persian-speaking Herati urbanites with vague or no prominent ethnic identities), with smaller Pashtun and growing Hazara groupings. While most Tajiks describe themselves as Sunni and most Farsiwans practice Shia Islam (like Iranians), my informants described the city as predominantly Sunni in a confessional and cultural sense. Most interviewees showed discomfort with the topic of ethno-religious divisions in Herat, especially in the context of increasing insurgent attacks on Shia temples since 2014.

Remarkably, Charlie P.W. Gammell dates Herat's in-betweenness as far back as '*the Achaemenid era (c. 550-330 BC)*', when the city became '*a liminal outpost in a contested region*' (Gammell 2016, 3). While this portrayal might itself be an essentialization and 'fixing' of history, it captures Herat's location as 'neither' and 'both'. Historical examples of modern liminal eventfulness of Herat abound.

Between the late eighteenth century (the rise of the Persian Qajar dynasty) and the 1860s, Herat was a place of heightened tensions between pro-Persian/anti-Pashtun partisans and those who opposed Persian-Shia domination. However, both currents valued Herat's distinct position and political uniqueness (Gammell 2016, 178). Likewise, Herat's Pashtun Sadozai rulers pledged loyalty to the Persian Qajars in the nineteenth century, minting coins and ordering Friday prayers to be sung in their name, while doing little to hide aversion towards the Persians. The Barakzai dynasty also claimed Herat through ethno-genealogical (Pashtun) ties and conquests, and enjoyed some local support in the process (Ibid, 227). According to Gammell, Herat was *'too far from Qajar Tehran to be a meaningful part of that state'*, however, the city's *'distance from Afghanistan's feuding capitals, Kabul and Qandahar, rendered it independent by accident and default'* (Ibid, 179). The Sadozai resistance to the Barakzai expansion continued through 1863, when Dost Mohammad Khan Barakzai subdued the city militarily, tying it to a unified 'Afghan' (Pashtun-dominated) kingdom. In 1885, Charles Edward Yate of the Afghan Boundary Commission described Herat's liminal place through its residents' strong anti-Pashtun and anti-Kabul sentiments, regardless of faith, which curiously paralleled their distrust of the Qajars (Yate 1888, 14). When the Soviet client government was overthrown in 1992, Ismail Khan, a Mujahedin warlord from a small Herati town of Shindand, seized the Province, further cultivating its political and security separation (if not independence) from Kabul (Giustozzi 2009, 207–213, 267–280). The Heratis' disdain for, and nonviolent resistance to the Taliban (1995–2001) made palatable tactical alliances with Tehran. This reinforced Herat's politics as different and defiant (Rashid 2010, 31–40). To Heratis, their land is Persian-Khorasani, but not Iranian. It is Afghan, but not Pashtun. Following the US invasion in 2001, the wartime tactical cooperation with Iran (and Tehran's financial support to Ismail Khan) made Herat untrustworthy in the eyes of the United States and the government in Kabul, highlighting Herat's positioning as 'not quite anything' or 'anyone's'.

Perhaps Herat's liminality can be correlated to a transnational conception of the 'Persianate world' (Green 2019). This notion of space acknowledges how Persian dialects encounter languages *'from the Balkans to Bengal, or even China'* (Ibid, xiv) to shape specific sociocultural, juridical and political discourses. Framing the Persianate world as transnational deconstructs Iran as its privileged centre and *'decouple[es] the [Persian] language from the exclusive heritage of any particular people or place'* (Green 2019, 2). Thus, it is a departure from Hamid Dabashi's Iran-centred conception of Persian 'literary humanism' (Dabashi 2012) and Marshall Hodgson's Persianate geography of 'Iranian highlands' (Hodgson 1974, 60). After all, as Nile Green argues, *'For the Ottomans, it was Timurid Herat that served as the primary model of Persianate culture, while for the Mughals it was Timurid Samarqand'* (Green 2019, 7). Following Green's paradigm, Herat can be understood as part of

> an interregional or 'world' system generated by shared knowledge of religiosity, statecraft, diplomacy, trade, sociability, or subjectivity that was accessed and circulated through the common use of written Persian across interconnected nodal points of Eurasia. (Green 2019, 9)

Pushing this liminal and transnational geography yet further, this book highlights Herat's history as one of (post)colonial power relations, of 'global peace' and resistances to it.

Herat at the Limit: Between Peace and Resistance on the Frontier

Jef Huysmans has argued that the practice of security has become 'unbound' through the work of anxiety, insecurity and suspicion upon wider society. This has reshaped politics into a proliferating government of life, risk, and uncertainty in spaces as different as migration and network surveillance (Huysmans 2014). Post-Cold War risk management has come under the guise of 'liberal interventionism' (Duffield 2009) and 'liberal peace' (Duffield 2001), or life based in orderly, non-fanatical politics and capital-friendly economics. The need for orderliness after decades of nuclear tensions, imperial proxy wars, and alignments with 'nonaligned' tyrants has enabled power to regulate whole new classes of conduct across the globe. The scope of necessary interventions has expanded to the physical safety and health of Western/Northern populations, the fiscal stability of their welfare states, swelling poverty across the 'Third World', and the cultural homogeneity of 'normal' societies (as opposed to 'failed' or 'fragile' states). The correlation of these insecurities has perpetuated the 'security-development' (or security-development-*migration*) nexus. Pacification of unstable populations, their containment, state-building, and aggressive border controls (Duffield 2001) are prescribed to alleviate global anxieties. To understand Herat's *other kind* of liminal politics, constituted by security and resistances to it, I outline here the logic of the world's effort to govern and pacify Afghan volatility. I do so by critiquing the practice of post-Cold War *global security governance* predicated on multilateralism, cooperation and market-driven security. While some of their technologies appear new, attempts to put a lid on Afghanistan are not unprecedented. Through three Anglo-Afghan wars, Britain's role in the 1863 solidification of a Pashtun Afghanistan (contra Persian ambitions in Herat), the Anglo-Russian Convention (1907), and economic interventions into Afghan power hierarchies, the British Empire had long attempted to colonize and 'conduct the conduct' (Foucault 2009) of Afghan politics (Rahimi 2017, Gammell 2016).

I focus on security governance since it claims to practice the kind of politics I intend to critique as postcolonial: that of 'stability' and 'security provision'. Dominant International Relations (IR) and Security Studies scholarship, as well as international institutions portray security governance as socially beneficial and inclusive (Ehrhart, Hegemann and Kahl 2015, Kirchner and Dominguez 2011). Yet, it is important to question the limits of inclusivity of liberal peace. Couched in pleas for '*major power security cooperation*' (Kirchner and Sperling 2007, xiii), the governance discourse is both aspirational and seductively commonsensical. As I aim to reassess what 'major powers' are cooperating over, I focus on seven assumptions and normative biases in the discourse of security governance. This will enable the ensuing chapters to study Afghan governance as power and, in fact, as a power *struggle*.

Drawing on liberal and neoliberal traditions in IR (Bellamy 2011, Ikenberry 2009, Keohane 1984, Krasner 1982), the 'governance school' differentiates security governance from government or state-based security practices (Krahmann 2008). Within the dichotomy, governance is seen as state and non-state cooperative security *provision* (rather than 'imposition'), apparently necessary to tackle 'new' post-Cold War risks (e.g. climate change, migration, terrorism, organized crime, etc.). Provincial Reconstruction Teams (PRTs) in Afghanistan (2002–2014) – which combined military forces, post-conflict 'reconstruction experts' from NATO and non-NATO countries, and private contractors – are the archetypes of multilateral cooperation targeting 'societal' sources of 'instability' (Hameiri and Jones 2015). PRTs reinforced the notion that non-state or 'private' actors[2] are indispensable to peace because governments and intergovernmental organizations (the UN, NATO) purportedly lack expertise (technological, linguistic, cultural, etc.) and face prohibitive financial and political costs to governing Afghanistan (Krahmann 2003, Krahmann 2005). This warrants a cooperative management of cross-border risks to *global* stability – as the security of life *everywhere*. The problems of interpretation and representation of 'everyone' and 'everywhere' arise immediately. Robert Latham noted how the 'global' as 'unbounded' captures hegemonic urges to govern the '*totality of human existence*' (Latham 1999, 28), leaving no place for 'outside' forms of life that '*can challenge or resist it*' (Latham 1999, 36). But where do the truths that underpin the notions of 'risk', 'threat', and 'stability' come from, and whom do such conceptions speak for?

The *diversity of interests* and *actors* involved in 'stabilizing' Afghanistan supposedly guarantees a more cooperative and inclusive conduct of security beyond hegemonic states alone. Private security companies provide physical security in Afghanistan for commercial motives. They are not driven by national security concerns, but they have cooperated with NATO-ISAF (NATO-Resolute Support since 2015), UN bodies, US Operation Enduring Freedom (Operation Freedom's Sentinel since 2015), US agencies in Afghanistan, the Afghan government, communal and religious bodies, etc. Rather than the vague felicity of global peace, it is the diversity of interests that explains cooperative security. Claiming that anyone can be harmed by Afghan instability, governance discourses suggest that the combined logics of *efficiency* and *legitimacy* shape the cost-benefit calculus of 'coordination' (Keohane 1984) over peace. Efficiency is temporal, political, and financial *cost reduction* (Sperling and Webber 2014, Krahmann 2005), while (input) legitimacy emerges through *multilateral cooperation* (Blavoukos and Bourantonis 2014, Krahmann 2003) among the various types of actors (Lucarelli 2014, 76). Transnational risks induce market-driven security provision, demanded perpetually and everywhere in the Global War on Terror (Krahmann 2003). Risk mobilizes collaborative and non-hierarchical structures where, supposedly, no single actor can exercise veto power or control the process (Duffield 2001, 12). Paradoxically, when no one can veto 'cooperative security', anyone can be excluded from it. This applies to the UN, too, and explains the rise of ad-hoc 'coalitions of the willing'.

Security governance fosters a liberal world view, whereby global uncertainties compel cooperation needed to defend progressive order (opposed to 'barbarism',

---

[2] Here, 'private' is synonymous to 'non-state' and involves transnational corporations, nongovernmental organizations, private military-security companies, etc.

'tyranny', 'terrorism', etc.). This supposition captures at least seven conceptual biases and implications for everyday politics. First, governance uses a *functionalist logic* to justify itself: it satisfies self-evident social needs (e.g. defence, retribution, peace, etc.). Portrayed as self-evident, these needs also appear *legitimate* and *non-ideological*, and the politics that produce them are obscured, making governance seem 'post-political' (Latham 1999, 43). Thus, interests neglected by international institutions, the 'cooperative' Afghan government, and NGOs are key to upending the hidden politics of Afghan (in)security. Second, governance functionalism is *market-based*: demand for security (presented by 9/11, 'migration crises', etc.) generates its own supply by agents who are said to provide it at comparatively lower cost (hence the privatization of security overseen by Northern/Western governments). Third, while security governance describes itself as innovative, it is committed to the stability and survival of *the existing global*. This makes it status-quo-oriented, conservative, and *repressive* of 'dysfunction' (Latham 1999, Cox 1981). Fourth, security governance claims legitimacy based on 'intersubjective consensuses' (Rosenau 2009, 9) and 'coordination' (Latham 1999). Invoking Gramsci, Craig Murphy shows that, to manage life, governance needs to appear non-ideological, as that '*minimizes the use of force*' (Murphy 2004, 172). Fifth, the ambition of security governance is *universal*: peace is preferable everywhere and demand for it is globalized through imaginations of cross-border risks. The rhetorical iteration of terror is key to universalization. Narratives of 9/11 – which showcased the lethality of non-state actors and a new world politics that '*is not going away*' – abound among think-tank pundits (Mansoor 2016, Spencer and Nguyen 2003), NATO analysts (Rühle 2011, Steinhäusler 2007), opinion pieces (The Telegraph 2017, Brill 2016), and politicians eager to entertain the ubiquity of terror. Ultimately, universality makes certain threats appear naturalized and fighting them seems, *again*, apolitical or untethered to partial interests.

Sixth, security governance in Afghanistan suppresses its internal contradictions and social tensions (Demmers, Jilberto and Hogenboom 2004, 5). This reinforces liberal peace as non-ideological and merely technical. For instance, NATO supports a stronger central government, while relying on regional 'powerbrokers' and local militias (Coffey 2017, Carati 2015). Likewise, counterinsurgency commitments to poverty eradication, improved healthcare, and education are at odds with fiscal controls (mandated by the IMF). Finally, security governance reduces politics to narratives of power diffusion (away from the state) or power circulation through collaborative and horizontal (rather than egalitarian) networks (Avant and Westerwinter 2016, Krahmann 2005). This narrative draws on liberal-realist binaries of 'power *over*' (realism) and 'power *with/to*' (liberalism). Yet, how cooperation dominates Afghan populations through diffuse networks (as 'power *with* X *over* Y') is ignored.

As a problem-solving approach to international relations, security governance offers an interest-based, yet hopeful, progressive, and 'forward-looking' account of politics (Rosenau 2009, 17). Critiquing the hegemonic effects of governance, Jörg Friedrichs identifies in it an '*optimistic … viewpoint of liberal-minded people*' (Friedrichs 2009, 120). Simultaneously, security governance purports to merely *describe* for the security consumer how cooperation (already) works and how conditions for more collaboration abound in international politics (Kavalski 2008). Seductive *descriptions* of cooperation obscure the *normativity* of hope: state and non-state actors are included, diverse interests can converge, everyone has something to contribute, and security can be cheaper (for the sacrosanct 'taxpayer'). Even the stubbornly 'ungovernable' becomes merely 'dysfunctional' (Latham 1999, 38) and decipherable. Consequently, Afghan 'traditional society' actors are also accorded a governance role. Jirgas (Pashtun tribal councils), shuras (tribal-religious councils), and 'community' elders are involved in institutions and consultative forums that blur the foreign/domestic divide. But deliberative performances of empowerment also marginalize anti-hegemonic resistances. Ultimately, not everyone has to participate in peace as long as their defiance is governable. *Involvement*, however, yields the benefits of stability. Some of those involved (NGO professionals, private security, agricultural corporations, etc.) also profit financially. The storyline is appealing because it is demonstrable. The charm of cooperative security is that it seems commonsensical. Who can say *no* to peace?

Nonetheless, who *is involved*? Latham claims that global governance represents 'no political signified' (Latham 1999, 29). Moreover, security governance in Afghanistan cannot represent itself as inclusive to the civilian victims of night raids, drone attacks, bombing campaigns, violent US-allied warlords and the Afghan National Security Forces (ANSF), or to the subjects of 'conflict-related' arbitrary detention and 'responsible' fiscal policies. Nor can it be 'rational' to their families. The 'involvement' of those labelled 'collateral damage' is violent and nonsensical in terms of cooperative security. The homeless, migrants abused at Afghan borders, disabled veterans, and women are used to justify security and economic interventions cobbled together by 'domestic' and 'international' actors (UN agencies and programmes, the EU, NATO, Western universities, NGOs, Afghan provincial governments, bilateral donor agencies, etc.). Yet, Afghan lives have grown more precarious since 2001. When security networks promote 'participation' and delegitimize vetoes to cooperation, their silence on power makes the meaning of cooperation ambiguous. No single interest or resource is indispensable enough to obstruct peace-via-cooperation. Global security may at once speak through the Iranian government, an Afghan NGO or a UN body, only to discard them if they impede a certain vision of peace or are useless to it. Governance '*even rolls over the vested interests*' (Ibid, 37). If peace can preempt any voice, can its Herati victims upset the governance of, not so much Afghanistan, but of lives and bodies confined to it?

Security governance presents itself as commonsensical, apolitical and beneficial. This book focuses on its arbitrariness, political bias, controlling normativity (rather than mere descriptiveness), and the unequal benefits it delivers across class, racial, geographic, gendered and other axes of difference. Security governance has failed Herat's 'weak' (Scott 1985), but I contend that it has done so by design rather than omission. If cooperative security is based on self-evident needs, *whose* self-evident needs matter? If the markets of security are apolitical, why do certain bodies pay for peace disproportionately through diminished life chances? While global stability *enjoys* the benefits of counterterrorism and counterinsurgency, how are those benefits imposed and '*enjoyed upon*' the subjects of pacification in Afghanistan?

Throughout 2017, President Trump considered handing Afghan security (and *lives*) over to private military contractors led by Erik Prince (formerly of Blackwater) and

Stephen Feinberg, CEO of Cerberus Capital Management (the parent company of DynCorp, already a major contractor in Afghanistan) (Gray 2017). As academics reject their plans as 'neocolonial' (McFate 2017), Prince's blueprint for Afghanistan draws entirely on the discourse of security governance. He promises to 'strengthen' the central government in Kabul, '*minimize [US] causalities*', '*mitigate political risk*', and 'reduce costs' of 'security provision' (Prince 2017, Gray 2017). Occupation couched in market rhetoric shows the compatibility of cooperative security with capitalism, 'liberal', and 'illiberal' politics alike. Latham argues that the '*global governance conceptualization is open for anybody's business*' (Latham 1999, 39). As long as governance is 'effective' in averting risks, '*anyone can define what the inside is*' (Ibid).

If security governance is violent despite agreeable multilateralism, what makes it work in Afghanistan? Furthermore, why is Afghan life a thorn in its side? I aim to show that the ordinary human, while neglected and violated, is the indispensable subject of global terror wars and postcolonial security.

Global Stability in Herat

Employment opportunities, safety, and access to education and healthcare in Afghanistan have faltered since the decline in foreign aid in 2013. Ordinary Heratis struggle to defend own life chances while their province continues to be victimized by global geopolitics. Once the '*highway of conquest*' (Fletcher 1965), Herat has been the highway of migrations since 2002 when the (in)voluntary repatriation of Afghan refugees in Iran intensified. Hundreds of thousands of Afghans pass through Islam Qala (a Heriti checkpoint at the Iranian-Afghan border) every year on their way from and to Iran. Thousands criss-cross Herat and Iran trying to reach Turkey, Greece, Germany and other places of hope. The UN Security Council sanctions against Iran (2006) undermined the livelihoods of Heratis working in Iran's formal and informal economies. They also undercut the lives of their families in Afghanistan, now vulnerable to cuts in remittances. After the United States abandoned the 2015 agreement on Iran's nuclear capabilities and re-imposed sanctions on the country, the wages of Afghan migrants in Iran declined again. Thousands of precarious jobs have been erased in the process (Bezhan and Parsa 2018). Consequently, over 500,000 undocumented workers returned to Afghanistan from Iran between January and September 2018 (International Organization for Migration 2018). The sanctions also undermine Afghan exports to Iran. Given the inelasticity of demand for Afghan exports (partially due to trade barriers), alternative markets are hard to come by. Such are the benefits of Afghanistan's 'enduring partnership' with the United States and NATO (Group of Experts and Former US Officials on Afghanistan 2016).

Critiques of Security in Afghanistan and Herat

Scholarship in Critical Security Studies, Political Geography, Political and Economic Anthropology and Postcolonial Studies offers detailed accounts of what it means for racial, class, and cultural 'Others' to be targeted by security, trade and aid – globally and in Afghanistan particularly. However, critical approaches have paid almost no attention to Herat in spite of its economic, historical, cultural, and geopolitical importance within Afghanistan and regionally (vis-à-vis Iran, Central Asia and the Gulf states). Moreover, Herat has experienced an extraordinary variety of development, civil society, reconstruction, 'good governance', and security interventions by international donors. Yet academic analysis has not kept up with this extensive policy interest. Therefore, this book addresses a *paradoxical gap* in the literature: while much global attention is paid to the issues of security and development in Afghanistan, a key region in the country has been neglected by the academia, both 'mainstream' and 'critical'. Perhaps this is due to Herat's recurrent descriptions as relatively safe and frontier/peripheral compared to the rest of the country. But this should not obviate the interest of critical scholarship in the lives exposed to multifarious policy interventions. On the contrary, if a geography is fixed as 'relatively stable', yet still attracts 'stabilization' measures and continues to be seen as 'threatening', these tensions in spatial representation need to be unpacked.

Charlie P.W. Gammell's *The Pearl of Khorasan: A History of Herat* (2016) stands out as a rare in-depth treatment of the city's social and political *history in the present*, particularly in his portrayal of life at the intersection of colonial and imperial powers. Beyond Gammell's work, there are five key strands of literature that critique the work of power in the US-led intervention in Afghanistan. I have particularly benefited from the monographs that investigate the *everyday practices* of security, development and reconstruction in Afghanistan.

First, among reflections on (post)colonial power in Afghanistan, Derek Gregory's analysis of colonial 'imaginative geographies' (2004) shows how they enable specific strategies of normalizing and regulatory power through Afghan reconstruction and state-building. Moreover, Gregory reinforces the import of the conditional and contingent agency of ordinary people in colonial spaces. Mark Duffield's work (2001, 2007) expounds upon the links between colonial power, liberal governance and liberal warfare. He explores postcolonial governance as 'population containment' (Duffield 2001, 4) and '*pacification of the global borderland*' (Duffield 2007, 137), and analyses the security-development nexus as social 'experimentation' (Duffield 2001 264; 2007). I broaden Duffield's criticism to argue that strategies of postcolonial power are untethered to 'Western' actors or liberal discourses. Postcolonial security does not require US, EU or NATO involvement to exclude and marginalize Afghans. Iranian, Emirati, and other state and corporate actors employ postcolonial differentiations in the utility of humans and treat the Afghan body as the racial, class, gender, and sexual abnormal (or Lacan's 'Other') that is only conditionally useful and otherwise ominous. They do so without any pretence of liberalism.

Countering the narratives of 'never-colonized' Afghanistan, a distinct cluster of works has studied histories of colonial formation of the Pashtun state in the context of eighteenth- and nineteenth-century British (global), Russian (Eurasian), and Persian (regional) empires. Shah Mahmoud Hanifi studied nineteenth-century trade across Peshawar, Kabul, and Kandahar as a '*consortium of colonial frontier markets*' (Hanifi 2008, 6), and their interactions with Durrani and British colonial-economic policies. Nivi Manchanda (2018), B.D. Hopkins (2008), and Mujib Rahman Rahimi (2017) have highlighted the colonial construction of the 'tribe' as a premodern lens used to imagine and contain the congealing Pashtun monarchy, as well as modern Afghanistan.

Second, ethnographies of power in Afghanistan – exemplified by Noah Coburn's work (2016, 2011) – have shaped the microphysical focus on security governance. Coburn narrates how everyday lives (of potters, businessmen, an ambassador, etc.) articulate power struggles in locales close to Kabul (the Bagram Airbase and town of Istalif). Mike Martin's research (2014) shares a similar approach to the everyday and routine quality of negotiation of power in Helmand. Third, a canon of critical gender and feminist works addresses reconstruction and security in post-2001 Afghanistan. Jennifer Fluri and Rachel Lehr (2017) and Synne Dyvik (2017) offer micro-spatial analyses of everyday geopolitics and its underlying gendered imaginations. Robin Riley (2013) points to 'transnational sexism' in the racialized and gendered use of Muslim women (and men) as fodder in the war on terror. Using ethnography, Julie Billaud (2015) highlights the paradoxical entrenchment of gender inequalities in attempts to foster democracy, reconstruction, and gender rights in the 'Afghan postcolony' (Ibid).

Fourth, among Critical Theory conversations (beyond postcolonial and feminist analyses), contributions to the 2011 volume *Globalizing Afghanistan: Terrorism, War, and the Rhetoric of Nation Building* (edited by Zubeda Jalalzai and David Jefferess) explore representations of Afghanistan among liberal Western feminists, the US government and Western media, and the neighbouring Iranians and Pakistanis. Furthermore, Volha Piotukh (2015) analyses the biopolitical discourses of care in post-2001 Afghan reconstruction, concentrating on the securitization and militarization of aid and 'new' humanitarianism. Fifth, a body of literature counters dominant representations of Afghan resistances to military interventions throughout history. For instance, Rob Johnson (2011) disassociates warfare in Afghanistan from the caricatures of tribalism and fanaticism. Conversely, while Carter Malkasian (2013) shares some of Johnson's sociological focus on Afghan narratives and micro-geographies of conflict, he remains visibly committed to 'international security'.

Herati Encounters of Class, Race and Geography: Seeing Like the Subject

James C. Scott identified the rationality of statecraft in making social spaces *legible to the state* and *standardized for* the conduct of government (Scott 1998). This book is an attempt to 'counter-see' postcolonial power and statecraft from the perspective of the postcolonial subject and her/his vulnerability. This entails deconstructing the homogeneity of the subject and portraying Heratis as complex populations with a plethora of desires, social positions and differentiations.

Following the precepts of Grounded Theory (Urquhart 2013), the collection and processing of data for this book has been an ongoing and overlapping process. Throughout, my research focus, conceptual lens and argumentation have shifted. My fieldwork in Afghanistan began in Kabul in December 2014 and continued in Herat and Islam Qala through mid-January 2015. I returned to Herat the following year (May–June 2016) to follow up on specific site visits and conversations that felt previously unfinished or again relevant due to unfolding events. Specifically, fieldwork experiences led me to shift and expand my research focus from the possibility of security and postcolonial *power* to an analysis of postcolonial power *struggles* and everyday maximizations of life chances by ordinary Heratis, especially those relegated to risky jobs, homelessness and abuse by law enforcement.

Whatever I have learned about these struggles was profoundly shaped by long conversations and (over eighty) semi-structured interviews with informants in Kabul, Herat, and Islam Qala, including three Skype interviews conducted from North Carolina. Interviews included 'civil society' informants (NGO employees and activists, business entrepreneurs, academics and journalists); Afghans who worked with NATO (via private subcontractors), a UN agency or a private security company in Herat; civilian government officials in Kabul and Herat working on reconstruction and 'good governance'; military officials in Kabul and Herat in charge of, or familiar with ANSF recruitment and training practices; Afghan intelligence (National Directorate of Security-NDS) officers, and two former PRT-Herat employees (Slovenian and Italian, both civilians). Conversations with informants whose daily lives revolved around the sites I visited (e.g. shopkeepers around the Musalla Complex, small-business owners at the Islam Qala checkpoint, etc.) were instrumental to my understanding of everyday lives of the vulnerable. Overall, the scope of informants included individuals professionally and personally (through varieties of felt kinship) associated with the security-development apparatus in Afghanistan. Participant observation of how spatial arrangements interact with social conducts was key to my understanding of the 'microphysics' (Jessop 2008) of security and postcolonial inequalities. This was particularly relevant during my visits to the Musalla Complex and the Islam Qala border crossing.

Collecting primary and secondary data has also involved relevant colonial and postcolonial state (Afghan and otherwise) and 'civil society' (non-profits, research institutes, corporations, academia, media, etc.) *statements* on place-specific histories, statecraft, economic and other sociocultural practices that reproduce Afghan and Herati subjectivities and spaces. Two criteria have driven data collection in this sense: *strategic* (whether a statement points to the methods and techniques power uses to shape its subjects) and *thematic* relevance.

Concerning data processing, narrative inquiry was key to interpreting qualitative data in interview transcripts, field notes and photos taken in the field. This meant reading data as stories reflexively embedded in my experiences of textuality, both thematic (synchronic) and chronological (diachronic). I captured my experience of interview transcripts, field notes, and photos through Foucauldian narrative inquiry (Tamboukou 2013), whereby I explored (1) how narratives reinforce the productivity of power and designate its subjects, (2) how security apparatuses work through narratives, and (3) how narratives operate as technologies of sovereignty, discipline, and government, including the '*care of the Self*' (Foucault 1990). Throughout, I embedded fieldwork and other primary and secondary data in Foucauldian and critical discourse analysis (Jager 2001). Specifically, to critique the representations, controls and normalizations that reproduce Afghan vulnerabilities, I analysed discourse as material, embodied in practice, performative, con-textual, and extra-textual or social and historical, rather than merely linguistic and textual. I employed Foucault's key 'methodological demands' of discourse analysis, focusing particularly on *exteriority*, or the external conditions of possibility of truth and power rather than mere interpretations of meaning and truth from within the text (Foucault 1972, 229–230). Unfortunately, due to the low quality of photos taken with my cell phone camera, some key visuals (e.g. of an archaeological complex and graffiti on the fence wall of a local high school) have not been included in this monograph.

Finally, I have tried to base my research and writing in an attitude of reflexivity and recognition of own positionality in Afghanistan. This has entailed continuous reflection upon the power relations between the researcher, interviewees and passers-by, always cognizant that I am, as Spivak put it, one of the '*white boys talking postcoloniality*' (Spivak 1999, 168). This book nonetheless attempts to engage the entangled vulnerabilities and privileges of the various research participants. It shows how the participants are unevenly subject to felt racial, gender, and class disparities or affinities, proximate or distant personal geographies, distinct or analogous linguistic mannerisms, gendered conducts, and (un)comfortable sexualities. I have emphasized situational caution in interactions with my informants and research participants. This was critical, since various social cleavages (class, gender, sexuality, ethnicity/race, etc.) shaped our interactions, incurring a certain risk upon the informants, bystanders and myself. At times, these divides made fieldwork tactically more feasible, enabling me to challenge my expectations. On other occasions, they made me feel troubled by the limitations of research (including, for instance, the constraints I grappled with while studying homelessness in Herat). Most importantly, these cleavages have made me reconsider the impact and contradictions of activist scholarship, and the extent to which I have been unwittingly empowered by Herat's 'subaltern' – the migrants, homeless, low-rank police and military recruits, human rights activists, etc. Creating room for the experiences of the ignored, silenced and marginalized is inextricably linked to the pitfalls of *representing them* as *speaking for* them. In a way, the aporia of white male research about the postcolonial subject (Spivak 1999) never fades: the researcher records the voice of the excluded just to see it colonized by the researcher's own narrative mere hours after the native informant has uttered her words. My work and subjectivity, too, inhabit the postcolonial frontier: privileged by the risk I have experienced (and been rewarded for) and elevated by the postcolonial *difference* that I critique.

The Roadmap

This book is divided into four key parts, each developing a distinct narrative point. This introductory chapter has outlined the topic, its core puzzle, guiding questions and argument. It has also explained how I have collected and analysed data in the course of this research, including how I have come to study what postcolonial security has done to ordinary Afghans. Second, in Chapters 2 and 3, I move on to shed light on why and how postcolonial power shows its 'care' for Afghanistan, Herat, and 'the world', as well as how Herati populations become its targets through security and development. I focus on how they become a 'multiple body' (Foucault 2003a, 245) that needs to be surveilled, disciplined, regulated, and contained away from the normal (and within Afghan borders). Part II achieves this goal by showing how a set of postcolonial, Foucauldian, and other conceptual tools enable a study of social and corporeal effects of governmental power at the postcolonial frontier. Part II studies the strategies and effects of power across mutually constitutive spaces of Herati life, particularly the politically dominant binaries of the external/domestic and public/private. Such binary spaces articulate the rationality of postcolonial power: to monitor, control and contain the ubiquitous socioeconomic, biological, and behavioural abnormal that threatens 'global stability' everywhere. Moreover, binary geographies extend postcolonial rationality to the most intimate and elemental spaces: onto the exposed, exoticized, primitive, hazardous, surveilled, abandoned, and unstable brown body and its various population aggregates (the homeless, farmers, insurgents, etc.). Nevertheless, Part II concludes by showing how these enmeshments inadvertently empower Heratis to utilize the weight of postcolonial governance and pacification (rather than peace) as fodder for resistance.

Therefore, in the third part (Chapters 4, 5, and 6), I continue to draw on my fieldwork and secondary data to explore Herati resistances to postcolonial security. I also continue to detail how postcolonial governance targets Herati populations. Part III analyses the effects of security-development interventions through the vulnerabilities they heighten and the resistances they provoke. Part III surveys the experience of power among lower-level police and military recruits, language interpreters, entrepreneurs, farmers, travellers and emigrants to Iran, and Herat's homeless. Their entanglements with 'global stability' show the micro-spatiality and pervasiveness of postcolonial power, as well as the paradoxical ways in which power fuels the practices of life it deems corrupt, dangerous and worth eradicating.

Part IV (Chapter 7) concludes the monograph by arguing that postcolonial power and Herati resistances to it have achieved an uneasy balance of *mutual* exploitation, surveillance, and normalization; an equilibrium riddled with contradictions and inequalities. In it, ordinary Heratis are the strategically indispensable objects and subjects of postcolonialism, while their ability to counter-exploit and appropriate postcolonial power remains constrained and mostly tactical. Moreover, the strategies, apparatuses, and discourses of postcolonial governance circulate globally and can therefore be reinvigorated against the locality of Herati resistances, outliving them in the long run. Conversely, resistant brown bodies have largely themselves and, paradoxically, postcolonial forces to draw on. While both power and resistance reshape one another in the process, the conclusion warns against relegating Postcolonial Studies to romantic and conciliatory dialectics of postcolonialism. Therefore, it continuously draws attention to lives oppressed, jolted and lost, as they attest to the inherently unequal, racialized, classist and gendered operation of the postcolony.

Part II

Why Does Postcolonial Security Care about Herat?

2

Mapping Out Tools of Critique: A Conceptual Framework

Introduction: Governing the Ungovernable

This chapter proposes a method of critique of postcolonial power in Afghanistan. Since the method is constructed by questioning power practices predicated on 'stability' and 'security provision', I draw on the summary of security governance in Chapter 1 and the self-representation of security as 'cooperative'. Chapter 1 reassessed '*major power cooperation*' (Kirchner and Sperling 2007, xiii) as cooperation over the control of vulnerable populations. I extend this critique by, first, pointing to the complex governance strategies of sovereign, disciplinary and governmental regulation of bodies and populations. Second, I revisit this inquiry through a postcolonial lens, which focuses on the differential treatment of populations as classed, racialized, gendered and sexed subjects. Third, I introduce the concept of experimentality to capture how postcolonial subjects are governed through policy experimentation (in security, economic planning, development, etc.). Finally, I refine this model of power by conceptualizing everyday resistances to postcolonial government. This enables a view of power as a power *struggle*.

Casualty figures and images in the Afghan chapter of the War on Terror tend to raise concerns about Afghan sovereignty. Hence, they privilege a state-centric lens of critique. This is understandable for human rights organizations who work to assign responsibility for violations of International Humanitarian Law. Yet, even lucid attempts to overcome state-centrism prioritize sovereignty in the critique of death (Gregg 2016, Shawki and Cox 2009). Andrew Neal argues that '*modern state sovereignty is only one [historical] articulation of a sovereign 'regime' of truth and power*' and, rather than a 'positive reality', it is a '*set of normative claims about … how the world and human life 'must' be shaped and ordered*' (Neal 2010, 32). Therefore, moving beyond the 'fragility' and 'failure' of sovereignty in Afghanistan enables critiques of what sovereignty – as a claim about ordered life – does *to* Afghans through security and development. It also enables critiques of other forms of power. The Afghan state is only one conduit of power that subjects Afghan life and it need not be privileged to understand the operation of security upon the brown body. To explore the *social effects* of security – as effects on Afghan *lives* and *populations* – a more intimate framework of critique is required. To understand why the most vulnerable Afghans – women, children and the homeless – are disproportionately exposed to airstrikes as 'collateral damage' (UNAMA Human Rights Service 2018a), or how the weak are reproduced through migration and economic policies, this chapter moves past state-centrism and the benevolent multilateralism of governance scholarship. I point to how power must *produce* the weak as *perilous* to be able to kill it, win its 'heart and mind' as spoils of war, or exploit it as cheap labour and a dangerous savage that must be saved from *him*self, and from whom the brown woman must be protected.

Overall, the toolbox outlined here rejects 'state failure' and the 'failure of governance' as the sources of Afghan vulnerability. It points to how intertwinements of sovereignty, discipline and corporeal regulation control Afghans as threats to global stability. To understand the precariousness of Afghan life, one must ponder the treatment and worth of a *dispossessed brown body*. As I have argued, the governance school remains agnostic about such vocabularies of power.

Strategies of Power

The concept of strategy used here draws on the work of Michel Foucault. He employed it to examine how relations of domination are reproduced from within society. While Foucault never offered a singular definition of strategy, some commonalities stand out throughout his research programme.

In *The Archeology of Knowledge* (1972), Foucault refers to strategy as 'discursive'. It involves 'possibilities' (Ibid, 37) of competing and mutually constitutive '*options and choices*' (36) or '*different ways of treating objects of discourse (of delimiting them, regrouping or separating them, linking them together and making them derive from one another)*' (69). All such choices and options make it '*possible, with a particular set of concepts, to play different games*' (37). Therefore, understanding how discourses (e.g. 'global stability' or 'security-development nexus') work entails studying '*how [discursive strategies] are distributed in history*' (64) – by 'necessity', 'chance encounter', or some specific 'regularity' (Ibid).

Consequently, explaining how global stability operates as a socially legitimate, truthful, and conduct-shaping discourse entails identifying the *options* and *choices* deployed in reproducing its objects (threat/defence, risk/opportunity, utility/uselessness, ally/foe, etc.). Strategy is the *how* of discourse maintenance, an account of the means by which discourses work. That a discourse can draw on multiple such options, and assign, stabilize or reverse their probabilities is precisely how strategy reinforces its own effectivity. In other words, strategy is the productive uncertainty (or 'possibility') that reinforces social truths and knowledges.

In *Power and Strategies* (1980), *Security, Territory, Population* (2009), and *The Birth of Biopolitics* (2010), Foucault speaks of strategy in terms of social power and refers to '*strategies of resistance [to domination]*' (Foucault 1980a, 138). Thus, he recasts strategy as a probabilistic, conditional, or aleatory (chance-based) exploitation of material possibilities and options in the exercise of power that is '*dispersed, heteromorphous, (*and*) localized*' (142). Strategy is *a strategy of power*, a diffuse force that circulates through society. Common to the conceptualizations of *strategy* as *discursive* and *power-based* is Foucault's interest in the operation of social control, subjection, counter-conduct, and power practices linked to *'material arrangements of force'* (Hook 2001, 530) across social spaces. What correlates these conceptions of strategy is Foucault's notion of discourse as more than a linguistic expression of reason and desire. Discourse is a *productive force* in society. It works through material wealth inequalities, skin colours, body parts (such as the hair, the hands, or the genitalia), or nuclear stockpiles. In turn, material force becomes meaningful through discourse. Foucault saw discourses as contingent and unstable formations and affiliations (Said 1983, 212) of *text* and *con*-text, as social *practices* that perform and constitute realities (e.g. race, gender, or social-economic status) rather than express them (Hook 2001, Foucault 1972, 79–106, Foucault and Gordon 1980b). A linguistic event (e.g. calling civilian victims of an airstrike 'collateral damage') occurs within a material context (e.g. the ability of US and Afghan air forces to target humans from afar; the fact that the US funds, equips and trains the Afghan Air Force, etc.). Linguistic statements and physical-spatial dispositions make one another meaningful and produce dominant knowledge (e.g. credible justifications for civilian casualties embedded in the truths and priorities of international security). Power and truth work through and legitimize one another, which makes them co-dependent and indistinguishable. Therefore,

> power and knowledge directly imply one another, ... there is no power relations without the correlative constitution of a field of knowledge, nor any knowledge that does not presuppose and constitute at the same time, power relations. (Foucault 1995, 27)

To summarize, strategies are situational 'manoeuvres' aimed at the maintenance, displacement, broadening, or dislocation of *'a certain relation of forces'* (Foucault 1977, 206) circulating through the textual and con-textual. But how do strategies work? Upon whom do they operate as they reinforce power relations and social truths?

In prefacing the performative (productive) effects of power, I have underscored that power/discourse strategies constitute own *objects* and *targets* through 'dividing practices' (Foucault 1982, 777–778) or delimitations, re-combinations and hierarchies across elements of reality. *Objectifying* strategies of power go beyond mere negation, destruction, or repression (Foucault 1982). Objectification matters because it *subjects* humans and their relations to the very power/knowledge regimes (*'regimes of truth'*) that have targeted them in the first place. For instance, being objectified under drone surveillance, the Cartesian-optical sciences that underpin it, and the field of knowledge which one might call 'counter-terrorism' (or inter/national security), implies a categorization of humans. It means that Afghans are reproduced as terrorist suspects, part of a suspect's support network, otherwise suspicious individuals, potential 'collateral damage', etc. In other words, humans become subjects of the discourses/power that target them. The discourse of surveillance does not only entail the mere action of 'watching over'; it also invests its objects with a meaning. This diffuse and intimate process of subjection leads to the final step of control, or *subjectification* (Rabinow 1984, 11). Subjectification includes the subject's practices of 'self-care', her work on 'own' body, soul, and conduct (Foucault 1986), or *'an exercise of the self on the self* (Foucault 1997, 282). If the object of surveillance knows that she could be observed, she will *internalize* this possibility, the fear, the caution and the need to maintain low visibility and will behave as if she is being observed continuously. To survive and avoid pain, she will become a *docile body* shaped by an 'unequal gaze' of disciplinary power. 'Unequal', since, unlike her watcher, she does not know whether or when she is being watched (Foucault 1995). For Afghans accustomed to drone attacks, night raids and bombs, even a distant possibility of being inspected from afar is tangible, thereby informing their daily conduct.

Often, power strategies produce *subjectivities* (conceptions of *Self*) by organizing them into *hierarchical binaries* (Foucault 1986) or 'violent hierarchies' (Derrida 1981, 41) (e.g. problematic/unproblematic, safe/unsafe, or normal/abnormal). *Subjection* works by *privileging* one end of the binary and relegating its opposite to a dominated position, even if the divide is unstable and resisted (Foucault 1997, 283). For instance, in the binary between 'legal' and 'illegal immigration', the penal code, law enforcement, courts, and the wider public will sympathize with, and legitimate the former, while seeking to punish the *transgression* of the latter (Simons 2002). To punish 'an illegal', power must first produce him, and must do so by upholding punitive *desires* and *truths* throughout society (Foucault and Gordon 1980b, 62). The notion that power produces social realities through observation, categorization, description and by responding to pre-existing realities helps understand three key propositions. *Security governance* is consequential because its strategies (productive choices):

(1) describe cooperative security as a response to the threat of terror;
(2) purport to care for and protect Afghans (from themselves) and the world, and
(3) reproduce Afghan vulnerabilities.

This governance trifecta helps contain and control Afghan bodies, populations and their circulations.

This raises the question as to what animates power strategies. That may be chance (the 'aleatory') or 'necessity' (Foucault 1972, 64) and 'nonsubjective intentionality' (Foucault 1978), rather than the will and interest of the Sovereign Subject (the individual, class or the state). While a minimal sense of intentionality and purpose directs relations of power, that pull is not owed to any one subject's discrete design; hence its designation as 'nonsubjective'. Goals, tactics, and logics of social practices might be 'intelligible', 'perfectly clear', and 'decipherable', and *'yet it is often the case that no one is there to have invented them, and few who can be said to have formulated them'* (Foucault 1972, 95). This dismantlement of the Sovereign Subject, 'Author', King, and Agent permeates Foucault's work (Foucault 1981). The body is invested with numerous, often-conflicted subjectivities because multiple, dispersed, and microphysical discourses/power relations shape its conduct, truths and desires. One can be a Farsi-speaking Shiite struggling with feelings of kinship with Iran after being deported from the country or recruited in Syria's war. When Iranian police officers arrest, detain and deport Afghan migrants, they need not have coherent notions of why people are being deported or what *raison d'état* stimulates this policy. The notions that they do have are difficult to compare against a 'master source' of the repatriation policy. This is because its single creator is hardly singular and, instead, reflects a cobweb of concepts, procedures, interpretations, histories, strategies, (inter)personal and organizational agendas, oral and written exchanges, etc. Therefore, isolating the 'original intent' or 'interest' that informs a consistent cost-benefit calculus is both impractical and unlikely. However, officers involved in arrest, detention, and deportation will have a reasonable sense of *what* they are doing and will have a stake in executing their tasks. Subject to power, people experience '*strategies without a strategist*' (Flynn 2005, 36). The repatriation policy has worked with cruelty since 2002 because the calculus of arrests and deportations circulates through Iranian society as part of the discourses of 'the Afghan' (Olszewska 2015, Monsutti 2008, Adelkhah and Olszewska 2007, Tober 2007, Monsutti 2007).

Strategies of Sovereign, Disciplinary and Governmental Power

I utilize the lessons of power performativity, its micro-spatial distributions and non-subjective intentionality to argue that security targets Afghan bodies across multiple spaces and subjectivities. In doing so, power is untethered to the United States, the 'West', or any coherent plan of Afghan neo-colonization and exploitation. Deprived of a master plan, power nonetheless expands and exploits with persistence, if not consistence and effectivity, if not success. *How* then can the strategic work of power over Afghans be analysed?

In *Security, Territory, Population* (2009), Foucault outlines a threefold model of sovereign, disciplinary and governmental power, whereby their strategies are enmeshed and mutually contingent (Foucault 2009, 11). Strategies are entangled because, like sovereignty, discipline and government are interested in *spatial control*, and sovereignty relies on discipline and government to manage the *multiplicity* of *subjects* and *forces* (Ibid., 12). Foucault understands *sovereignty* as juridical, territorial power relations formed through the monarchic-medieval and bourgeois-Enlightenment eras. Sovereignty works to maintain hierarchical and Hobbesian order (survival from '*all against all*' warfare), as the central will of the metaphorical and empirical *King* flows through subordinate institutions, laws, and decrees upon subjects circumscribed by said laws (Foucault 1980c, 121). Sovereignty works towards an internal/external *dualism* of order/law/peace *within* and war *without* (Neal 2004, 384). Its normativity seeks to '*subordinate [internal] war to politics*' (Ibid., 379), silencing struggles across races, classes, genders, etc. Thus, sovereignty reproduces domination, for imposing a narrative of order on histories of '*pillage and exaction*' (Foucault 2003a, 109) is oppression masquerading as progress. Sovereignty's historical entrenchment (post-French Revolution) lies in its subjectivity as a neutral hierarchy *for everyone* and *by everyone*, even if its history is *by* and *for some* (the capitalist bourgeoisie). Therefore, as a *pacifying force*, sovereignty informs the apolitical claims of security governance that multilateral cooperation yields peace. Yet, peace is 'provided' by overcoming contradiction, including by violating the weak.

The Leviathan-like sovereign gaze is totalizing and hierarchical, which complicates the circulation of multiplicity: of goods, people, ideas, diseases, crime, etc. Foucault claims that the rigidity of sovereignty ('*the territorial state*') and the need of the '*commercial [mercantilist] state*' for capital circulations clashed in the seventeenth century (2009, 15). Therefore, the work of sovereignty hinged on refashioning the treatment of *space*, so that it would '*not be conceived or planned according to a static perception*' (Foucault 2009, 20). Instead, it would '*open onto a future that is not exactly controllable, not precisely measured or measurable*', since a useful '*plan takes into account precisely what might happen*' (Ibid). The natural functioning of multiplicity generates risk and undermines the predictability of social flows that sovereignty wishes to control. Therefore, the role of the sovereign is challenged and sovereignty adapts by relying on new forms of power and strategy (Ibid, 23). According to Foucault, these necessities led to the emergence of *disciplinary*, *governmental* and *biopolitical* forms of power between the seventeenth and nineteenth century, allegedly in Northern and Western Europe.

While these configurations of power are historically coterminous and have productive effects, their approaches to managing 'multiplicity' differ. *Discipline* extends social control beyond sovereignty and targets the body-soul, the physical-ethical elements of life through the practices of *individuated* inspection, observation, and surveillance (Foucault 1995). I have illustrated this process earlier in exemplifying the moves of objectification-subjection-subjectification in drone warfare. Surveillance broke with the sovereign's exaction of revenge on the deviant body via torture, since torture proved to energize resistance and generate sympathy for the delinquent. Surveillance shifted '*the point of application of this power*', which is

> no longer the body, with the ritual play of excessive pains, spectacular brandings in the ritual of the public execution; it is the mind or rather a play of representations and signs circulating discreetly but necessarily and evidently in the minds of all. (Foucault 1995, 101)

While still a corporeal strategy of punishment, discipline introduces control that appears less theatrical and less objectionable. It manages individuated subjects in arrays of micro-spaces: prisons, schools, military barracks, factory floors, hospitals, etc. Surveillance produces subjects by compelling body-souls to internalize control and become agents of self-management. Such internalizations and interventions upon the 'soul' (Foucault 1995) improve the cost effectiveness – or 'the economy' – of power. Namely, to survive, subjects renegotiate own conduct, as an important condition for resistance is deflated: the visibility and grotesqueness of power's operation. Surveillance methods enable '*the meticulous control of the operations of the body*', imposing upon it a '*relation of docility-utility*' (Foucault 1995, 137). Discipline is not aimed '*only at the growth of [the body's] skills, nor at the intensification of its subjection*' (Ibid, 137–138), but at making it '*more obedient as it becomes more useful*'. In other words, discipline '*increases the forces of the body (in economic terms of utility) and diminishes these same forces (in political terms of obedience)*' (Ibid, 138). Chapters V and VI address the correlation between the body's docility and utility to power, as I explore *how* cultural conservation in Herat (in function of development) and spatial arrangements of Islam Qala (an Afghan-Iranian border checkpoint) heighten Afghan vulnerabilities by compelling the population to be useful to security and progress.

Thus, power permeates relations beyond juridical compliance to include a calculus of the body's habits, desires, anatomy and cognition in service of an order that can be extended and optimized. The problem of multiplicity/optimization helps Foucault identify the formation of *governmentality* between the sixteenth and eighteenth centuries. Two points of divergence from disciplinary and sovereign powers stand out.

First, while the individuating strategies of discipline aggregate subjects into 'disciplinary society' (Foucault 1995), they cannot tackle *populations* as irreducible political objects/subjects with their own risks of optimal functioning (Foucault 1995, 42). Rates of ANSF recruitment in cities as opposed to districts (or overall); trends in the uptake of certain agricultural production techniques, seeds or breeds; rates of homelessness; temporal and spatial trends in migration flows; the economic impact of small-business programmes; Afghan birth, literacy or child mortality rates, etc. These processes occur at the level of the population and being able to shape them collectively is critical to the functioning of power. Such is the task of governmentality.

Second, sovereign strategies reinforce juridical hierarchies and police the external/domestic divide. However, their coercive instruments make them inept at intervening into the 'stubbornness' and '*natural course of things*' (Foucault 2009, 344) beyond one's compliance with law. Command and prohibition are limited in shaping collective desires, beliefs, and practices of 'good life'. Foucault defines governmentality as '*regulation based upon and in accordance with the course of things themselves*' rather than '*regulation by police authority*' (Ibid). Likewise, global governance promises security *provision* (driven by human needs and natural demand-and-supply forces) rather than *imposition*. Governmental power optimizes the production of subjectivities, desires, and truths beyond territorialized top-down coercion (sovereignty) and targeted individuation (discipline). Power dispersion throughout the population marks the spatial quality of *government* (as the *practice* of governing). Governmental strategies target capillary spaces, micro-interactions, and truths *from within*, or as mere responses to their 'natural' and 'free' functioning (Ibid, 382). Their objective is to optimize good and useful social forces and relations (as opposed to those threatening or idle). Rather than command a vision of social growth, governmentality incites it, cultivates and encourages it by shaping the actions of its subjects, i.e. by acting upon their actions. Governmental power works to '*to arouse, to facilitate, and to laisser faire, ... to manage and no longer to control*' (Foucault 2009, 352). Therefore, Foucault sees governmentality as the '*conduct of conduct*' of populations and bodies (Foucault 1982) through indirect guidance. Instead of disciplining the body into desired economic, moral and cultural behaviour, contemporary power regulates the parameters of social practice and makes it desirable to its subjects.

I discuss governmental practices in Chapter 3 as I outline how security governance involves Afghans in enmeshed external/domestic social spaces that enable the operation of power *from within* everyday realities and lives, or as mere responses to them. Chapter 3 will also discuss the notion of government through experimentation. Chapters 5 and 6 will examine how the discourses of growth, stability, progress and security operate upon Afghan populations and shape their experiences of the economy, culture, safety and freedom of movement.

Critiqued through the lens of governmentality, the promise of security governance to foster global peace and integrate Afghanistan into this project resurfaces as a strategy that incentivizes practices useful to stability, while neglecting those that are useless, costly or dangerous. Thus, governmentality recasts the governance strategy of *pacification* via *inclusion* as *exclusionary*. The oppressive character of security hides in plain sight, as security is at stake whenever power defends its claim to orderly expansion: '*Security therefore involves organizing, or anyway allowing the development of ever-wider circuits*' (Foucault 2009, 45).

If security serves certain power relations, how does it *affect Herati life*? This question creates an opening for critiques of *biopower* and *biopolitics*. In *The History of Sexuality* (*The Will to Knowledge*), Foucault defines biopower as a complement to sovereign power. Sovereignty, as '*power of life and death*' or '*power to* take *life or* let *live*' (original emphasis) (Foucault 1978, 136) extends into power that '*foster[s] life or disallow[s] it to the point of death*' (138). In *Society Must Be Defended*, Foucault indicates that biopower both extends sovereignty and breaks with it in that it constitutes the right to '*make live and let die*' (Foucault 2003a, 241). In other words, it is a form of power that targets biological life and cultivates, incentivizes and maximizes its desirable forms, while discouraging and minimizing life that undermines power and is therefore 'costly'. Biopower works '*to incite, reinforce, control, monitor, optimize, and organize*' life and thereby articulates techniques '*bent on generating forces, making them grow, and ordering them, rather than … impeding them, making them submit, or destroying them*' (Foucault 1990, 136). This point highlights Foucault's conception of power as productive rather than merely coercive and destructive. Modernity does not merely murder, for that alone would, according to Foucault, be self-debilitating. Rather, it governs life through disincentives to the point of *natural vanishing* that appears unobjectionable. If peace and security (as 'public goods') can be unfavourable to certain forms of Afghan life, then sovereignty does not have to murder (as often) and show the 'darker side' of power (Mignolo 2011).

Foucault argues that biopower operates upon two mutually constitutive 'poles': the body and the population. The body is also disciplined through the strategies of 'anatomo-politics' that produce 'docility' (Foucault 1995). In other words, the body's biological functions, capacities, postures, and spatial circulations are all of interest to strategies that deploy corporeal forces in service of maintaining and expanding certain power relations. The other pole, the population, is subject to a form of 'biopolitics' (Foucault 1990, 139) that regulates the forces of the 'multiple body' (Foucault 2003, 245) and nurtures its utility to power (28). Regulating a population reinforces *economies* of power, i.e. its cost-efficient functioning. This implies overlaps between the concepts of biopower and governmentality, but one can differentiate them in two ways. First, biopolitics targets humans *as a species* and regulates its social-material functions, needs and processes. This makes it visible in public health, medicine, ecology, the 'welfare state' (as it shapes the population's life chances), sexuality, gendered policies, etc. Second, one can think of governmentality as the '*art of government*', 'governmental mentality', or a general method of administering populations through 'soft' and 'indirect' regulation (or the *conduct of conduct*) beyond the biological. Yet, both governmentality and biopower work through internalized truths and desires rather than sovereign punitive domination (which is often unavailable; e.g. to NGOs, corporations, etc.). Biopower and surveillance both work upon the body by shaping self-care, desire and truth, yet their strategies differ: biopower 'massifies' by intervening into the 'multiple body' or the population (Foucault 2003, 242), while surveillance individuates. Domination is fostered when one is unable to distinguish between the enforced (discipline) and the wanted (biopower).

Most important, the *body* and the *population* are always context-specific. How they identify, what they know, and desire (their subjectivity) is not exhausted in an ahistorical *Man* endowed with a core universal rationality. For Foucault, power does not work upon predetermined individuals, groups, or 'actors' (Foucault 1990, 95). Instead, out of the necessity of self-optimization, power shapes space- and discourse-specific bodies by administering the productive abilities of life. Power reproduces its subjects (bodies and populations) by investing them with discourses of desire, truth, knowledge and identity. Therefore, a (multiple) body is never a pre-discursive or ahistorical agent. Rather, it is an unstable target and space of control, cultivation, quantification, regulation and learning. It is at once a rich migrant 'investor' and a 'dirty Afghan' (Christensen 2016); a behaviourally or sexually deviant 'illegal alien' and an abused youth worthy of compassion, medical and psychiatric care. The population can be a healthy workforce or a terrorist hotbed. What one *is* depends on the discourse/power structure that she is embedded in, i.e. on the kind of politics she is subjected to.

Foucault's ideas allow us to study the body as a landscape of power and eventfulness, and deconstruct the strategies that target it. That does not imply the body's passivity; on the contrary, the body is a bustling location of resistance and counter-conduct that constitutes power itself (Foucault 2009). A disparaged 'mute' and 'analphabet' can tactically use his/her apparent lack of linguistic skills or speaking ability to elude harsh interrogation by customs officers. An aspiring migrant can use his Hazara background to promise to fight in the Iranian-run Fatemiyoun Division in Syria just to be allowed into Iran. Otherwise, joining the Taliban camps in Iran – endorsed by the government in Tehran – could serve the same purpose. Across discourses, docile bodies are more than just compliant objects. Power is always power *struggle* or 'agonism' (Foucault 1982, 790).

The Body and Power: The Many Axes of Afghan Vulnerabilities

Surveying the body as a place of power relations requires a further specification of its ontology. I integrate scepticism of universal human nature (e.g. *homo oeconomicus*) into narratives of corporeal politics by drawing on intersections of postcolonial, critical-feminist, cultural-anthropological, and Foucauldian analyses (Crampton and Elden 2007, Stoler 2002, Rhodes 1998, Callard 1998, Stoler 1995, Jones and Porter 1994, Csordas 1994). This book retains scepticism of the body as indivisible individuality, as 'nature' (juxtaposed with 'culture'), or as a counterpoint to the (rational) mind. I question the universal human, partly because this abstraction congeals the images of white, heterosexual, middle-class, and cisgender men (Ammaturo 2017, Salamon 2010, Butler 1990). Instead, I approach the body as *spatial subjectivity*, or a concrete *site of politics*. The body is an intimate micro-space of power struggles and 'agonisms' that reproduces, reflects, toys with and co-opts sovereign, disciplinary and regulatory interventions. The body is oppressed, constrained, enabled, as well as oppressive, transgressive, resistant, and transformative (Mbembe 1992). It is the *'inscribed surface of events (traced by language and dissolved by ideas), the locus of a dissociated self ..., and a volume in perpetual disintegration'* (Foucault 1984, 83).

Constituted by power/discourse, and being a site of struggles, the body is also interpreted and written as a *text* of domination and transgression (Lefkovitz 1997). It is a location of inscription, renegotiation, and recodification of social discourses (meaning and values interlocked with power). Insofar as they can be understood as discursive subjectivities, bodies are constituted through *'images, symbols, metaphors and representations'* (Gatens 1996, viii). Yet, following Foucault's notion of discourse, I argue that the discursivity of the body does not entail a phenomenological textuality. On the contrary, Foucault's work on discipline and biopower addresses politics as palpable, gory and subject to touch. In *Nietzsche, Genealogy, History*, Foucault aspires to reveal *'a body totally imprinted by history and the process of history's destruction of the body'* (1984, 83). Frantz Fanon captures the corporeality of the text in *Black Skin, White Masks* (1986) as he exclaims: *'The white man ... had woven me out of a thousand details, anecdotes, stories'* (84). Trinh T. Minh-ha considers the corporeal as political by *'writing the body'*, i.e. by critiquing power relations (gendered, raced, classed, and, therefore, postcolonial) through their everyday 'physicality', 'tactility', and 'vocality' (Minh-Ha 1989, 44). *Writing the body* entails politicizing it as a space of 'contradiction' instead of privileging the obvious sites of struggle, such as state institutions (Minh-ha and Morelli 1996, 13–14).

I want to both concretize this discursive-power ontology of corporeality and give it latitude that can reflect fieldwork insights. How do discourses of race, social-economic class, ethnicity, gender, religion, geography, legal/citizenship status, ability, and other axes of (ascribed) identity, subjectivity, and *inequality* condition the *life chances* and conducts (Rose 2007) of ordinary Afghans? *Intersectional* approaches advance research into these dimensions of subjectivity, even, or especially, if the axes are at odds with one another (Crenshaw 1991). In applying intersectionality, at least two conditions stand out. First, compounding subjectivities should be understood as mutually relational and 'positional' rather than separate (May 2015). Second, they should be analysed as products and conditions of power strategies, not as either 'innate' or 'imagined' traits, or as merely chosen identities (Jiwani 2006). What is the limit of utility of upper-class Afghans to capitalism, and when do they become racial and cultural Others? How are socioeconomic class and gender inequalities inserted into the broader management, containment and marginalization of Afghan lives *as racial Others*? How do certain ethnic-tribal subjectivities in Afghanistan (e.g. being a 'Kuchi nomad') correlate with class and ability? What are the lived implications of these intersections? Intersectionality addresses these questions by engaging fieldwork carried out in Kabul and Herat. Therefore:

> When it comes to social inequality, people's lives and the organization of power in a given society are better understood as being shaped not by a single axis of social

division, be it race or gender or class, but by many axes that work together and influence each other. (Collins and Bilge 2016, 2)

In refining the ontology of the body/population, intersectionality unpacks experiences of marginalization, domination and vulnerability. '*Rather than seeing people as a homogenous, undifferentiated mass*', intersectionality explains how different 'social divisions' (of race, citizenship status, etc.) '*position people differently in the world*' (Collins and Bilge 2016, 15). Chapters III-VI consider how the governance of Afghan security reproduces socioeconomic, gender, confessional and other inequalities. Here, I clarify my understanding of socioeconomic class and race since I argue that these axes of division critically underwrite the constricted and controlled space of what it means *to be Afghan in global stability*.

While notions of socioeconomic class abound, I draw on Jacques Bidet (2016) and try to correlate Marx and Foucault's concepts of class. Although Foucault's view of class fluctuated, both him and Marx associated it with social hierarchy, income and privilege, and Foucault agreed – at least through the mid-1970s – that class is inter alia tied to the divides in the ownership of means of production. Whereas Marx saw collective and individual beliefs about economic regulation and class belonging (Marx 1906) as subjective class-consciousness, Foucault tied them to wider regimes of truth that work through material disparities. Bidet differentiates two '*poles of privilege*' and class division: property-power and knowledge-power, associating them with Marx and Foucault's notions of domination, respectively (2016). According to Bidet's interpretation of Foucault, '*strategy forms class (as Althusser says: class struggle precedes classes)*' (Ibid, 153), but not as a 'pre-given entity' (Foucault and Gordon 1980b, 203) or a dominating agent of history (Ibid). To Foucault, power relations do not serve an '*economic interest taken as primary*' (Foucault 1980a, 142). For Marx, class relationship is a 'divisor': it separates and generates classes, which '*exist as fluctuating groupings, or historical actors*' (Bidet 2016, 136). Given the situation of my argument in enmeshments of sovereign, disciplinary and biopolitical power, I adopt a view of class that is *transnational*, rather than state-centric (Wallerstein 2004, Cox 1981). Moreover, I treat class as *subjectivity*, an *axis of division* and a *space of struggles*, rather than as an agent who struggles.

Likewise, this book views race and ethnicity in spatial-strategic rather than essentialist terms. Eduardo Bonilla-Silva points to race as a recent (post-Second World War) academic concept, and argues that race/racism needs to be seen as more than just irrationality or prejudice. Moreover, race should not be ideologically reduced to other, more 'real' social cleavages, such as class (Bonilla-Silva 1997). The first, 'idealist' approach generates individual-level social-psychological analyses and disciplinary (educational and mental health) solutions directed at 'curing' racism. It implies that '*(1) social institutions cannot be racist and (2) studying racism is simply a matter of surveying the proportion of people in a society who hold 'racist' beliefs*' (Ibid, 467). Bonilla-Silva also summarizes the shortcomings of the second ('reductionist') approach, championed by (neo-)Marxists: '*When racism is regarded as a baseless ideology ultimately dependent on other, "real" forces in society, the structure of the society itself is not classified as racist*' (Ibid). In other words, letting racism off the hook by homogenizing inequality as socioeconomic trivializes the strategies of hierarchy. Furthermore, Bonilla-Silva understands racial politics as a form of rationality (as opposed to dismissing racism as irrational), i.e. as place and history-specific calculi of social utility of different population categories. Herein, *utility* is any context-specific calibration and assessment of objectives, interventions, and subjectivities that serve the maintenance and expansion of power relations (Brunon-Ernst 2016, Foucault 2009, Foucault 2010).

While Foucault's concepts of governmentality and biopower help understand the rationality of racialized power, his treatment of race has been critiqued as transient, absent (Young 2001, 395–396), and Eurocentric, especially by postcolonial authors (Loomba 2005, Kaplan 1995, Said 1988, Spivak 1988b). Nonetheless, *Society Must Be Defended* (2003a) helps adopt an understanding of race as subjectivity and a space of power relations, particularly biopolitical 'race wars' and 'race struggles'. Foucault quotes Marx's recollection that he and Engels '*found [their] idea of class struggle*' in '*the work of French historians who talked about the race struggle*' (Ibid, 79). This points to the lived intertwinements of class and race, but also to a genealogy of race as a marker of struggles over vitality '*within the social body*' (Ibid, 231), over deserving and superior life. Foucault traces the modern use of racism to enmeshments of the nineteenth-century 'ethnic racism', colonialism, medical 'degeneracy' theory, eugenicism, social Darwinism and the penal theory of 'social defence', '*which in the nineteenth century developed techniques for identifying, isolating, and normalizing "dangerous" individuals*' (e.g. through ethnic cleansing and labour camps) (Fontana and Bertani 2003, 285). In *The Abnormals*, Foucault concludes that the praxis of psychiatry stimulated the emergence of racism (Ibid, 286). Chapter 3 in this book argues that the governance of Afghan security is precisely enabled by imaginations of Afghan spaces and lives as aberrant and abnormal. Foucault defines race and racism as '*introducing a break into the domain of life that is under power's control: the break between what must live and what must die*' (Foucault 2003a, 254) to promote and defend society as a whole. Racism is a technology that creates '*the hierarchy of races*', a way of '*fragmenting the field of the biological that power controls*', '*separating out the groups that exist within a population*', and '*establishing a biological-type caesura within a population that appears to be a biological domain*' (Ibid). Thus, the population becomes '*a mixture of races*' and a space of '*subspecies known, precisely, as races*' (Ibid, 255). This resonates with Bonilla-Silva's (1997) and Omi and Winant's (1986) contentions that racialization practices produce racial categories and realities. Racism is '*the precondition that makes killing*', as the 'death function' of biopower, 'acceptable' in defence of society (Ibid, 256, 258). Most importantly, Foucault's account of race focuses on '*every form of indirect murder*' or '*exposing someone to death, increasing the risk of death for some people, or, quite simply, political death, expulsion, rejection, and so on*' (Ibid, 256). Viewing race as biopolitical helps to explore how security governance heightens Afghan vulnerabilities and undermines their life chances. While Foucault surveyed the genealogies of European 'internal wars' against the abnormal (2003a), my understanding of racialized security and peace is by necessity trans-social insofar as I study the enmeshments of 'external'/'domestic' spaces, technologies and subjectivities in the pacification of Afghanistan. Although Foucault acknowledges that the techniques, models, and '*political and juridical weapons*' of colonization – including the production of race – had a 'boomerang effect' on racial conceptions in the West (Ibid, 103), this point remains underdeveloped in his work. I return to racial subjectivities in postcolonial contexts shortly.

I treat racialization as one of the strategies that produce social hierarchies in the intrinsic utility of humans to civilization, the world 'as a whole', and global stability. Therefore, the insidiousness of race in biopolitics is that it refashions the pain of white/coloured divides and reinvents their content (e.g. to allow the Irish, Italians, and Poles to become white in the United States, or to conceive of Pashtuns as racially superior in the nineteenth century as the '*sons of Alexander the Great*'). I argue that in the current racializations of Afghans (and Muslims worldwide), skin colours play a *limited role* in a *global/brown* racial hierarchy. The 'global' is imperceptibly white, self-fashioned as colourless, colour-neutral and colour-blind as it disguises its racial genesis. The 'global' even employs and deploys brown and black bodies (both 'Western' and 'local'/'indigenous') to *manage the risks of colour and class* across the postcolonial world. (This is reminiscent of the colony's use of black and brown tribal chiefs, administrators and militias to maintain order.) The 'global' is normal; it is the space, face and agency of *peace, progress* and *security*. The brown is represented as unstable, risky, backward, troubled, and hazardous in ways that range from public health and 'culture' to the economic demography of the Northern/Western welfare state. Spivak reconfigures race when she claims that 'epistemic discontinuity' – or the gap in conceiving of certain knowledges as socially useful and legitimate – is what separates the 'top' and the 'bottom' of postcolonial hierarchies, '*not skin color or national identity crudely understood*' (Spivak 2004, 527). Drawing on Etienne Balibar (1991), Duffield similarly contrasts 'biological racism', which '*did not survive the cataclysm of the second world war*' (Duffield 2006, 71), with 'sociocultural racism' (Ibid), or the notions of incompatibility of cultures, of economic habits of different populations, of their healthcare practices, social norms, etc. Sociocultural racism '*now plays the classificatory role that biological difference once did*' on a 'planetary scale' (Ibid, 69). Sociocultural racism connects population anxieties to migration and development policies to pacify threatening bodies and contain their movements. Duffield relays Balibar's qualification of 'new racism' as '*racism without races*' (1991, 21) and Sivanandan's contention that 'xeno-racism' is '*a racism that cannot be colour-coded*' (Sivanandan 2001, 2). My rendering of the global racial hierarchy as *global/brown* aims to acknowledge the range of class, cultural and sociobiological discourses invested in the subjectivity of race in terror wars, where '*poverty is the new black*' (Sivanandan 2001). Moreover, this understanding of the contemporary racial 'caesura' acknowledges that religion subject to power forms a '*second axis of race*' insofar as Muslims are believed to '*harbor enemies of the body politic*' (Medovoi 2012, 44). According to Medovoi, the racialization of Muslims goes beyond skin colour. It is '*a fluctuating, geopolitically motivated judgment about Islam*' (Ibid), a theme I continue to explore in Chapter 3.

Finally, if Bonilla-Silva is correct in asserting that '*both class and gender are constructed along racial lines*' (1997, 473), I want to stress that race is also intersectional – gendered and sexualized. The Northern/Western media, academics, and nativist fringe groups privilege the representations of brown and black migrants as overwhelmingly male (BBC News 2018, Hudson 2016, Melchior 2015). Saving brown women from brown men and 'educating girls' is deployed as the rationale of humanitarian and state-building interventions (Thobani 2007, Spivak 1988b). Yet, the women being saved are also pitied as culturally weak and compliant *Muslims*, complicit in their own oppression (King 2009, Ayotte and Husain 2005). Even as Western liberals, conservatives, and feminists claim to speak for, and defend postcolonial queer (particularly Muslim) populations, they portray their condition as one of timid, feminine, and primitive weakness (Bracke 2012, Puar 2007, Richter-Montpetit 2007).

Conduits of Power: Security Apparatuses and Uncertainty

In addition to the lives lost, governmental and biopolitical critiques question *how* lives are lived. The coercion of air and night raids, drone strikes, ground attacks, and aid conditionalities undermine the populations that are being persuaded to disavow the Taliban or unlawful economic practices. Funding, supervising, training, and equipping ANSF, instilling concepts of their tasks, building schools and an 'open' national economy are tools used to homogenize Afghanistan. Strategies to secure Afghanistan constrain Afghan lives before any attempts at winning their hearts and minds are even made. Chapter 3 expounds upon the import and operation of these spatial strategies. Here, I outline tools of their analysis by drawing on the *rationality* (Foucault 2009) and *apparatuses* (Foucault 1977, 194–228) used to sustain pre-existing models of security and the economy.

In spite of the temporal, organizational and regional variance in the operation of NATO, EU, UN and US missions in Afghanistan, a common logic of security/stability stands out. Chapter 3 critiques the governance logic of *cost efficiency* as excluding the life chances and body counts of ordinary Afghans, privileging instead metrics private to NATO allies (Pusateri, et al. 2004). Foucault uses *rationality* to designate reasoning practices, including the use of statistical tools and the '*calculus of probabilities*' to govern society (Foucault 2009, 59), 'medical rationalities' (Ibid, 199), '*type of thought*' and 'calculation' that governs 'men' (Ibid, 232), the *raison d'état* as the governing rationality of the state (Ibid, 237–238), etc. I use the concept to denote ways of framing, designation and mapping of social relations. Those include the intuitively capitalist *homo oeconomicus*, competing models, as well as their rejections and ambiguities, including the Foucauldian resistance to a universal *He* endowed with enlightened Reason.

Strategies of power draw on specific *rationalities* and methods of social evaluation. To understand the vehicles, tools and techniques that power deploys in the government of life, this book uses the concept of *dispositif* or (security) *apparatus*. Foucault defines it as an '*ensemble of discourses, institutions, architectural forms, regulatory decisions, laws, administrative measures, scientific statements, philosophical, moral and philanthropic propositions*' (Foucault 1977). Their purpose is not to merely defend the physical integrity of persons and objects, but to secure configurations of power relations. Distinguishing security apparatuses from discipline and sovereignty, Foucault claimed that dispositifs '*respond to a reality in such a way that this response cancels out the reality to which it responds – nullifies it, or limits, checks, or regulates it*' (Foucault 2009, 69). He adds:

> The smallest infraction of discipline must be taken up with all the more care for it being small. The apparatus of security, by contrast, ... 'lets things happen'. Not that everything is left alone, but *laisser-faire* is indispensable at a certain level. (Foucault 2009, 45)

For instance, Foucault refers to marginal price hikes that are allowed for to avoid the '*general scourge of scarcity*' in commodities. He also points to how the body is cured or kept healthy through immunization and inoculation, i.e. by injecting pathogens into bodies under controlled conditions.

As I have relayed in relation to governmental power, security apparatuses intervene into social reality 'from within', acting upon the expected tendencies in human conduct at the level of the population. Foucault concludes: '*This regulation within the element of reality is fundamental in apparatuses of security*' (Foucault 2009, 69). This book correlates security apparatuses and the population consistently: from asking why NATO and the United States remain engaged in the training, equipping and funding of ANSF in spite of insurgent infiltration and corruption; to exploring how the marginalization of the homeless in Herat results from the operation of cultural/security apparatuses and the bourgeois discourses of economic growth, culture, civilization, beauty, hygiene, etc.

Postcolonial Power and the Afghan Body

I have cited postcolonial critiques of Foucault's work on race as Eurocentric. Likewise, Timothy Mitchell emphasizes Foucault's silence on the colonial genealogies of power (particularly discipline) and argues that the geopolitical imaginary of 'Europe' partially emerged in 'colonial India' and the '*colonial frontier with the Ottoman Empire*' (Mitchell 1988, 35). Similarly, Derek Gregory identifies Foucault's Eurocentrism in analyses of how '*European modernity constructed the self – as the sane, the rational, the normal – through the proliferation of spacings*' (Gregory 2004, 3) or the multiplication of othering distances. Yet, '*these were all spacings within Europe*' (original emphasis) and due to Foucault's attention to '*these interior grids – the clinic, the asylum, and the prison among them – the production of spacings that set Europe off against its exterior "others" ... was lost from view*' (Ibid). Therefore, Foucault's conception of power/discourse strategies needs to be rethought for postcolonial geographies. What makes power relations postcolonial? Who are their subjects?

To paraphrase Stuart Hall, postcolonial politics reflect '*the crisis of the uncompleted struggle for "decolonisation" and the crisis of the "post-independence" state*' (Hall 1996, 244). For Herat, this crisis has involved tussles with 'own' dynasties, empires and racial, class and economic hegemonies since the eighteenth century. While the prefix 'post' in 'postcolonial' implies a temporal 'after', Elleke Boehmer points to its critical connotation, as postcolonial analysis '*subversively scrutinizes the colonial relationship*' and privileges voices that '*resist colonialist perspectives*' (Boehmer 2005,

3). Similarly, Peter Hulme defines the postcolonial as a '*process of disengagement*' from the colony (Hulme 1995, 120). Summarizing the thrust of postcolonial critiques, Hall differentiates what postcolonial *is* and *is not*. It is not '*one of those periodisations based on epochal "stages"*' or a time in which '*all the old relations disappear for ever and entirely new ones come to replace them*' (Hall 1996, 247). Moreover, '*it does not mean ... that what we have called the "after-effects" of colonial rule have somehow been suspended*' and '*certainly does not mean that we have passed from a regime of power-knowledge into some powerless and conflict-free time zone*' (Ibid, 254). However, politics can '*no longer be mapped completely back into, nor declared to be "the same" in the post-colonial moment as it was during the period of the British mandate*' (Ibid, 248). Rather, colonization '*so refigured the terrain that, ever since, the very idea of a world of separate identities, ... self-sufficient cultures and economies, has been obliged to yield*' to more enmeshed geographies (Hall 1996, 252–253).

Therefore, the postcolonial is '*not only "after" but "going beyond" the colonial*' (Ibid, 253). This challenges the ideas of nation-state realism (and responsibility for 'own' politics) as improbable geopolitical conceptions at odds with power relations that both maintain and scramble external/domestic dichotomies (from extrajudicial killings of terror suspects to microfinance projects). The enmeshed, yet distinguishable, and the trans-social, yet disjointed, are substantively different in colonial and postcolonial artefacts (e.g. the British Empire had no NATO to draw on in its regulation of Afghanistan's foreign policy in the late nineteenth and early twentieth centuries). Yet, the rationalities of geopolitical penetration and control reproduce themselves in *postcolonial pacification*. They travel through the strategies of civilizing what was once unenlightened to the development of what is nowadays unstable and risky. Moreover, the '*mechanisms of 'otherness', alterity and exclusion*' and '*the tropes of fetishism and pathologisation*' (Ibid, 252) of the Other have invested themselves in the contemporary controls of Afghan life, as Chapter 3 argues. Therefore, the *postcolonial* reconfigures power as spatially and temporally '*transnational and transcultural*', 'decentred' rather than '*nation-centred imperial*' (Ibid, 247). Postcoloniality speaks to Foucault's notion of power as a transversal and dispersed relationship, and identifies the genealogy of Europe's wealth, whiteness and creativity throughout metropolitan and colonized-peripheral spaces. Transversality reinforces Bhabha's invitation to the postcolonial scholar to practice a '*critical ethnography of the West*' (Bhabha, Bennett and Collits 1991, 54): an analysis of spatially dispersed subjectivities and truths produced through violence, ambivalence, hybridity and uneven mimicry between the colonizer and the colonized.

Similarly, Robert Young charges postcolonial theory with three tasks: (1) to investigate how European and US history, culture, and knowledge were complicit in '*the practice of colonization and its continuing aftermath*'; (2) to identify '*the means and causes of continuing international deprivation and exploitation*' and analyse their '*epistemological and psychological effects*', and (3) to transform '*those epistemologies into new forms of cultural and political production*' that '*enable successful resistance to ... the degradation and material injustice*', which continue to subject people worldwide (Young 2001, 69). Therefore, Young aligns postcolonial analysis with wider critical theories committed to subverting structural inequalities (Hoy and McCarthy 1994, Cox 1981).

Embracing the normative focus on the disempowered and intersectional subject, I refer to postcolonial relations as geopolitically diffuse sovereign, disciplinary and biopolitical struggles. Moreover, I argue that *security governance* works as a *postcolonial power apparatus* precisely because of how its strategies affect the marginalized, their bodies and life chances. Aníbal Quijano underlines social classifications between population segments as constitutive of colonial and postcolonial societies, and identifies them around the axes of *race* and *role in capitalist production* (i.e. class) (Quijano 2000). Racial distinctions and divisions between slaves, capitalists, and wage labour were interrelated and implicated in the expansion of colonialism and still condition inequalities in postcolonial societies. Therefore, what connects the colony and the postcolony is a '*coloniality of power*', or a specific rationality that refashions and reutilizes colonial-era strategies, apparatuses and raced, classed, sexualized and gendered imaginations of the Other. In the postcolony, dispossessed brown and black Muslims are made vulnerable globally, but further biopolitical hierarchies apply (depending on gender, sexuality, citizenship, skin tone, etc.). Coloniality intertwines race and class in '*the "racial" distribution of work*', '*new "racial" geocultural identities*', and a '*capitalist colonial/modern world power*' (Ibid, 218). Postcolonial power differentiates the corporeal utility of humans in transnational hierarchies of labour, whereby bodies are admitted into the practices of government, disciplining, and control based on their utility to virtuous life and 'world capitalism' (Quijano 2000). In reference to race as the crux of (post)colonialism, Daniel Nemser describes racial hierarchies as the '*uneven distribution of vulnerability*' and unequal '*forms of humanity*', which operate as lopsided life chances and unequal proximities to '*premature death*' (Nemser 2017, 11–12).

In the era of global terror wars, this basic hierarchy works as a *global/brown* differentiation, and the good life and society to be defended are captured in vague references to 'global stability' and 'security'. Security governance is productive (and contested) insofar as it reinforces the deceptive metonymic association between *global* and *all/everyone*, thereby entrenching the seduction of its own democratic potential. While domination is resisted and refashioned beyond the elegant dominant/dominated binary, postcolonial power assigns the 'global' and the 'brown/black' inverse positions in relations of subordination. Apparently, black and brown bodies cannot 'do' stability and peace due to their natural flaws. Thus, *the global* is called upon to *secure* and redefine security in the process.

This book's approach to marginalization and oppression is rooted in intersectionality and Foucault's understanding of subjectivity. Additionally, Chapters 3-6 will refer to these experiences as *subalternity*, and to the bodies wounded and violated to make subordination work as *subalterns*. In *Prison Notebooks*, Antonio Gramsci uses subalternity to connote positions of subordination: from lower-lever '*non commissioned military officers*' (Gramsci, Buttigieg and Callari 2011, Volume 1, 157) to 'classes' who are '*subject to the initiatives of the dominant class*', since '*even when they rebel, they are in a state of anxious defense*' (Ibid, Volume 2, 21). He also referred to slaves, subjugated races, women, peasants, and the proletariat as subalterns (Green 2011, 69). While Gramsci essentializes certain groups as subaltern, Ranajit Guha and the Subaltern Studies Group use the term to refer to a *relationship* of subordination, a non-elite position of difference '*expressed in terms of class, caste, age, gender and office or in any other way'* (Guha 1988, 35). This framework speaks to intersectionality, but requires further refinement.

Sceptical of the concept's inflation and spurious claims to victimhood, Spivak asserts that 'subaltern' should not be a 'classy word' for those who are *'not getting a piece of the pie'*, but are *'within the hegemonic discourse'* (de Kock 1992, 45–46) or in the game for the pie. The American white working class is oppressed, but not a subaltern (Ibid). Subalternity is a relational condition, a congealed experience of social inability to portray, describe, and *represent* (darstellen) one's Self through own practices. It is also a relationship of exclusion that requires an-*other* subject to *re-present* (vertreten) and speak *for* the oppressed. In all, the subaltern herself *'cannot speak'* (Spivak 1988b). This is because power silences the experiences of subalternity unless the West/North is the representing Subject: the listener, interpreter, and speaker of the subaltern reality in terms meaningful to 'normal' audiences. In postcolonial conditions, the *'benevolent* Western *intellectual'* (original emphasis) (Spivak 1988b, 292), well-meaning as *he* may be, profits financially and culturally from 'talking postcoloniality' (Spivak 1999, 168). Therefore, when the subaltern attempts to speak, she merely reinforces colonial discourses that have rendered her weak, pitiful, primitive, dangerous and abnormal in the first place. This contradiction (Spivak 1988b, 306) and the exploitation of subaltern representations have already appeared in Chapter 1, when I discussed the role of informants in this research. I will revisit the condition of subalternity (of 'below-otherness') to discuss how homelessness in Herat is driven by the discourses of culture, civilization and economic growth, as well as to describe the periphery experienced by Heratis at the Afghan-Iranian border. Here, I continue to conceptualize Afghan life in the postcolony by considering how Afghan populations are governed through experimentation, and how 'experimentality' advances the governance of 'global stability'.

Government through Experimentation

For decades, governance discourse has insisted on the novelty of security through multilateral cooperation and 'public-private partnerships'. The discourse of demand-driven security *provision* (versus *imposition*) accounts for some of the intuitive appeal of security governance as 'non-traditional'. Yet, the very strategy of governing through newness, tests, trials and errors has been understudied in postcolonial literature. This is unusual, since trialling out reconfigured (not entirely 'old' or 'new') policies through social engineering 'overseas' has been the hallmark of (post)colonial power relations and a core critique in Postcolonial Studies.

Paul Rabinow highlights the utility of the colony by referring to it as a *'laboratory of experimentation for new arts of government'* (Rabinow 1989, 289) – from urban planning to military strategy. Similarly, Towghi and Vora define the experiment as a *'technology of truth-making'* based in observation and hypothesis testing (Towghi and Vora 2014, 2). The colonial laboratory (through the mid-twentieth century) was used to rejuvenate and reinvent the 'decadent' metropolis by exploring and generating *'a new political, social, and spiritual system'* (Rabinow 1989, 289). While the rationality of testing new social relations *elsewhere first* has travelled into postcolonial government, I argue that the purpose of experimentation is not so much to reinvigorate metropolitan societies anymore, as it is to govern risk and contain danger *everywhere*. This logic is at work regardless of the threat and its (im)probability. Therefore, postcolonial experimentation is less about *elsewhere first* and more about *everywhere*. It is a ubiquitous strategy of administering life rather than improving metropolitan societies (although some of that rationality is still at work in the correlations between development *abroad* and welfare programmes *at home*). I frame this mentality of postcolonial power as government through experimentation, or *experimentality*. This approach to governmental power recognizes experimentation as '*a subjective orientation toward the world and toward society in everyday practices*' (Towghi and Vora 2014, 2). It is a mode of rationality that conceptualizes social relations in probabilistic terms, as trial-and-error policy iterations that serve larger public goods, such as 'global stability'.

Experimentality features in critiques of surveillance, data collection and regulation in public health, pharmaceutical research, population control, epidemiology, etc. (Towghi and Vora 2014, Nguyen 2009, Petryna 2009). The concept draws on Foucauldian governmentality and biopower, and Bruno Latour's sociological work on the scientific laboratory (Latour 1983). Anthropologists have extended the metaphor of the scientific manipulation of reality to critique state-building and 'humanitarian governance' as a '*laboratory of intervention*' (Pandolfi 2008) predicated on '*a "right to intervene" in the name of saving lives*' (Nguyen 2009, 201). Nguyen identifies experimentality in colonial histories, 'military occupations', population control (Ibid, 207), and corporate capitalism, where a public authority 'subcontracts "providers"' and fulfils '*the need for efficiency*' (Ibid, 203) as the animating rationality of security governance.

Experimentality reveals the contingent, trial-and-error, and probabilistic normalization of Afghan conducts via development and security interventions, and sheds light on the practices of knowledge production and circulation. By viewing postcolonial spaces as laboratories of racialized and classed government, I identify probability-based strategies across domains. Those include the limits and drivers of insurgent infiltration into ANSF, the elasticity of preferences for opium production, lessons about insurgent disarmament and reintegration, warlord co-optation, the timelines and volumes of reconstruction and aid projects, etc. Moreover, experimentality shows that learning about brown populations entails global circulations of knowledge. Scores of quasi-scientific hypotheses are borrowed from elsewhere in the world, or are circulated within larger bureaucracies (e.g. USAID), and retested in Afghanistan. This is because the universalist rationality of governance assumes that knowledge '*can "travel" to inform practice far away from where the evidence was generated, allowing "modularizing" successful programmes*' (Nguyen 2009, 210). These hypotheses and datasets circulate across issues and knowledge 'disciplines': from violent insurgencies, post-conflict reconstruction, counterinsurgency and counterterrorism to legal and judicial reforms, migration management, agriculture, fiscal and monetary policy and other problems of modernity. Once confirmed, revised or rejected, the hypotheses about what 'should work' in security, development and 'state-building' become part of the globe's knowledge about Afghanistan and the racial, class, 'underdeveloped', or 'failed' Other.

Postcolonial laboratories make ample use of notions that '*one can only 'learn by doing', and doing is synonymous with knowing'* (Nguyen 2009, 210). After all, producing 'evidence', 'best practices', and 'lessons' is useful on its face (Ibid). According to Nguyen, experimentality 'enrols' postcolonial populations '*to keep them alive and to generate evidence that [it is] doing so*', for '*without a population to manage, [it] cannot generate the desired outcome*' (Ibid, 207). Returning to Foucault's concept of security apparatuses, experimentality works within social uncertainty, since the uncertain is the predicate of experimentation. Finally, evoking intertextual connections across postcolonial and intersectional narratives, Towghi and Vora ask how the experiment shapes '*differences of gender, race/ethnicity/caste, class, religion, and nationality*' (2014, 4). I pose this question to focus on the precariousness of Afghan life.

Nonviolent Everyday Resistance: Power as Power Struggle

While the subsequent chapters refine the analysis of Herati resistances, this section focuses on the *possibility* of resistance in the postcolony. It frames resistance to postcolonial power as *tactical* and *ambivalent*.

To study relationships between postcolonial power and resistances *to it*, I embed resistance *in* power and analyse them as mutually constitutive. Through Homi Bhabha's notions of *ambivalence* and *hybridity* (Bhabha 1994), I argue that resistance and power, the dominated and the dominant are entangled and that their relationships are muddled rather than neatly oppositional. They involve the subjects' imitation of, and tactical and opportune cooperation with power as techniques of its exploitation, weakening and destabilization. Furthermore, 'rereading' *security governance as postcolonial power* sheds a different light on the legitimacy of governance apparatuses. To be seen as legitimate and cooperation-driven, security governance has to open up spaces for interaction with ordinary Afghans. This necessity, in turn, enables Heratis' tactical engagements with security apparatuses and counter-exploitations of their lethal, economic and financial assets.

Revisiting security governance as postcolonial power raises certain questions. If its operation is as pervasive as suggested throughout this chapter, how are nonviolent resistances and maximizations of local life possible? According to Foucault, '*to say that one can never be outside power does not mean that one is trapped and condemned to defeat no matter what*', nor does it '*entail the necessity of accepting an inescapable form of domination*' (Foucault 1980a, 141–142). Moreover, Foucault posits that power relations '*don't take the sole form of prohibition and punishment, but are of multiple forms*' whose '*interconnections delineate general conditions of domination*' (142). He asserts that '*dispersed, heteromorphous, localized procedures of power*' are '*accompanied by numerous phenomena of inertia, displacement and resistance*' (Ibid). Therefore,

> one should not assume a massive and primal condition of domination, a binary structure with 'dominators' on one side and 'dominated' on the other, but rather a multiform production of relations of domination. (Ibid)

In other words, power does not operate in the single direction of oppression. Domination does not have to entail slavery or tyranny. Rather, power is effectuated and experienced through the resistances it inevitably induces. Moreover, power and resistance are not straightforwardly binary. Michel de Certeau formulates the difficulty of power by rejecting its binary elegance: '*I shall assume that plurality is originary, that difference is constitutive of its terms*' (de Certeau 1984, 133). Likewise, Foucault hypothesizes that the necessity of resistance lies in unstable distributions of power relations:

> There are no relations of power without resistances; the latter are all the more real and effective because they are formed right at the point where relations of power are exercised; resistance to power does not have to come from elsewhere to be real, nor is it inexorably frustrated through being the compatriot of power. (…) Hence, like power, resistance is multiple and can be integrated in global strategies. (Foucault 1980a, 142)

Therefore, while postcolonial power itself induces defiance, everyday resistance does not always operate as wholesale rejection. It often resembles tactical cooperation and complicity that gradually undermine the ambition and weight of power. Taking advantage of the activities of entangled international/Afghan security apparatuses and misappropriating security resources and reconstruction aid are just some practices that can maximize Afghan life chances. De Certeau exemplifies such subversions by invoking resistances to Spanish colonialism:

> The spectacular victory of Spanish colonization over the indigenous Indian cultures was diverted from its intended aims by the use made of it: even when they were subjected, indeed even when they accepted their subjection, the Indians often used the laws, practices, and representations that were imposed on them by force or by fascination to ends other than those of their conquerors; they made something else out of them; they subverted them from within – not by rejecting them or transforming them (although that occurred as well), but by many different ways of using them in the service of rules, customs or convictions foreign to the colonization which they could not escape. (1984, 31–32)

If power and resistance are enmeshed, one can hypothesize similar motions and tactics in how Heratis have coped with governance apparatuses and the Taliban. My hypothesis on Herati everyday resistances focuses on how ordinary people absorb, make use of and counter-subject postcolonial governance to tactics of survival, both stabilizing and weakening power in the process. Living *under* Them involves painful and dangerous mimicries of living *as* and *with* Them.

Speaking to Foucault's notion of power as a spatial relationship, de Certeau captures the routine, stubborn and unexceptional character of everyday resistance through a distinction between *strategy* and *tactic*. A strategy is '*the calculation (or manipulation) of power relationships*', whereby power delimits own space and uses it to manage '*relations with an exteriority composed of targets or threats*' (de Certeau

1984, 218). The Cartesian ambition of power is to structure space by fixing inside/outside boundaries, thereby reinforcing '*the typical attitude of modern science, politics, and military strategy*' (Ibid). Furthermore, strategy is *experimental* insofar as it seeks to master the future '*variability of circumstance*' through surveillance and 'areas' of knowledge (cities, institutions, laboratories, etc.) (Ibid, 218–219). Therefore, strategy lies in the domain of power. Its rationale is to manage uncertainty by controlling space and producing knowledge. This correlates de Certeau's notion of strategy to Foucault's governmentality as risk management. Conversely, tactic is '*a calculated action determined by the absence of a proper locus*' – its domain is delineated by power (Ibid, 219). De Certeau quotes von Bülow to define tactic as '*a maneuver "within the enemy's field of vision"*' or '*within enemy territory*' (Ibid). Tactic does not have '*the options of planning general strategy and viewing the adversary as a whole*'. Being conditioned by strategy makes tactics operate '*in isolated actions, blow by blow*', dependent on 'opportunities' outlined by power, chance, and contingency (Ibid). To de Certeau, '*this nowhere gives a tactic mobility..., but a mobility that must accept the chance offerings of the moment*'. Tactics '*must vigilantly make use of the cracks*' created in the operation of power. Capturing the deception and ambivalence of resistance, de Certeau calls it '*a guileful ruse*' (Ibid).

In conceptualizing tactics as improvised by necessity and circumscribed by power strategies, de Certeau – much like James C. Scott – concludes that tactic is '*an art of the weak*' (de Certeau 1984, 219). While power claims *strategic* latitude, resistance is constrained, responsive to power and chance, and *tactical*. If Foucault is right to claim that power generates its own resistances, that undermines (post)colonialism as unchallenged tyranny. But, according to de Certeau, it also implies that power circumscribes the space and scope of struggles. Kimberlé Crenshaw articulates everyday resistance as tactical when she claims that '*prevailing structures of domination shape various discourses of resistance*' (Crenshaw 1991, 1243). Power already shows how it should be resisted:

> People can only demand change in ways that reflect the logic of the institutions they are challenging. Demands for change that do not reflect ... dominant ideology ... will probably be ineffective. (Crenshaw 1991, 1243)

Embedding resistance in power calls for an account of the resisting subject. Understanding the resisting body through the lens of subjectivity and intersectionality explains the many dimensions of resistance amid global security and violent conflict. Drawing on the works of Foucault and de Certeau, I have asserted that subjectivity complicates the dominant/dominated or occupier/occupied binary. Specifically, the intimacy and infinitesimal entanglements of postcolonial power and resistance can be understood through Homi Bhabha's idea of ambivalence (Bhabha 1994) and its appropriations in political geography, development, and security:

> Rather than represent the colonized subject as simply either complicit or opposed to the colonizer, Bhabha suggests the coexistence of complicity and resistance. The hegemonic authority of colonial power is made uncertain and unstable because

the ambivalent relationships between colonizers and colonized are complex and contradictory. (Blunt and Wills 2000, 187)

Ambivalence points to relationships that otherwise remain obscured through convenient binaries (e.g. colonizer/colonized). It explains how ordinary Heratis seize fortuitous opportunities, enabled by the pressing demands of compliance with, loyalty to and participation in security apparatuses. Government ministries, Provincial Reconstruction Team-Herat (PRT-Herat), and Train Advise Assist Command – West (TAAC-W) have been subjected to numerous tactics of exploitation by ordinary Heratis. Ambivalence helps excavate the 'liminal' and 'in-between' spaces and histories of indigenous survival, toying with and complicity in the amplification, maintenance, weakening and exhaustion of security governance. Ambivalence is a fluid maximization of local life, a simultaneous or quickly alternating process of *against and with*, of dissidence and alliance, conflict and companionship, contradiction and cooperation, of confusion and re-composition of the internal/external, Afghan/foreign, occupied/occupier, and employee/employer relationships. In other words, then/now, public/private, and Them/Us – much like the colonial/postcolonial – '*develop an interstitial intimacy*' (Bhabha 1994, 19) or an experience of enmeshed difference that Bhabha calls *hybridity*. Thereby, the subject of power '*inhabits the rim of an "in-between" reality*' (Ibid): she both desires and detests certain qualities of the colonizer and works to renegotiate this tension as logical. According to Bhabha, '*the analytic of ambivalence questions dogmatic and moralistic positions on the meaning of oppression and discrimination*' (1994, 95) and counters condemnations of resistances that tactically accommodate power. Bhabha suggests that the critical '*point of intervention should shift from the ready recognition of images as positive and negative*' to understanding how the 'stereotypical discourse' of heroic resistance further oppresses the subject. If this 'stereotyped image' of resistance is to be 'displaced' rather than 'dismissed', critique must tackle the 'effectivity' of power (Ibid), or what power compels us to desire, believe and do to maximize our life chances.

Ambivalence offers insight into the subjectivities of the developed and secured; into her wiggle room for creative, playful and dangerous resistances that are not all fulfilled or heroic in confrontations with power. Ambivalence casts aside the 'stereotypical discourses' of peace and security as indisputable social values. It complicates maximalist and 'Utopian' (Bhabha 1994, 29) notions of resistance as radical rejections of power, allowing us to see structural privilege behind one's request for blanket repudiations. Ambivalence helps appreciate how resistance inelegantly and artfully dances and wrestles with power strategies and counter-exploits their burden. As moves of governance and resistance electrify each other in theatres of war and development, ambivalence helps avoid seductive dichotomies between the 'dominant' and 'dominated'. According to Bhabha, ambivalence reconfigures resistance as '*a negotiation (rather than a negation) of oppositional and antagonistic elements*' (Ibid, 33). It challenges all that which trivializes the granular and quotidian subtlety of struggles to live.

Correlating de Certeau and Bhabha, I understand ambivalence as the 'originary' process of othering; as a dividing practice (Bhabha, 1994, 110) that produces the subject herself. This is because it captures the mutual contingence of Self/Other and life as unsettled, as agonistic desire and repulsion, affiliation and difference. Heratis experience both admiration and resentment through geopolitical imaginations of 'Iran', 'the West', 'Dubai', etc.

To capture how Heratis have expressed ambivalence and subjected governance to localized resistance, I analyse security and development as locations of power. The ensuing chapters deconstruct security governance into micro-economic relationships of employment and micro-spatial surveillance. These relationships reflect contextual intertwinements of the 'international' and 'local' from ANSF compounds and checkpoints to government offices, interstate borders and historical monuments. They capture the operational necessity of postcolonial power to work *from within* Afghan populations and the opening that this need creates for Heratis to engage in ambivalent counter-exploitation. Within these relations, Heratis act as both employers and employees in various security bodies and agencies (ANSF, PRT-Herat, TAAC-W, etc.), as both transgressors and defenders of order, as threatening and threatened lives. Heratis are both the delegates of power and the performers of elusive resistance. Beyond Foucault and de Certeau's associated reflections (de Certeau 1982, 257–265), a 'micro-physics' of power (Jessop 2008) that engages specific spaces and bodies remains understudied. Analyses of micro-power acknowledge the spatial rootedness of control, regulation and resistance. They also acknowledge that said spatiality is *uneven* and *disrupted*. Bhabha's account of the hybridity and liminality of the postcolonial experience captures this unevenness:

> Such cultures of a postcolonial *contra-modernity* may be contingent to modernity, discontinuous or in contention with it, resistant to its oppressive, assimilationist technologies; but they also deploy the cultural hybridity of their borderline conditions to 'translate', and therefore reinscribe, the social imaginary of both metropolis and modernity. (Bhabha 1994, 9)

To govern rather than enslave, power works from within. Likewise, to resist means to resist from within. This book is about how the enmeshed strategies and tactics of power struggles are gauged, ascertained, and practised micro-physically: in recruitment centres, households; government, NATO or UN offices; bazaars, checkpoints, etc.

Conclusion

This chapter has established an approach to seeing security governance as postcolonial power: a differentiation in the utility of entire classes of humans to global stability. I have assembled a lens that enables the reader to focus on how postcolonial security deploys racial, class, gendered and geopolitical discourses to circumscribe Afghans as destitute brown bodies, *different* from the virtuous and normal globe. The chapter has also asserted that such valuations of Afghan populations are not specific to any one nation-state, class or geopolitical entity – such as the proverbial West – but rather operate as trans-social necessities of myriad dispersed subjects to dominate 'cost-efficiently'. In other words, postcoloniality is indebted to trans-corporeal necessities to govern life and risk in any social context marked by tension and *agonism*. The following chapters will elaborate on how postcolonial security produces the object/subject of its anxiety, ire, pity, sympathy and fear – the threatening Afghan. I will also discuss how ordinary Heratis take advantage of this subjectivity, straddling it as both a constraint and energy of life.

3

Spaces and Forces of Pacification and Containment

Introduction

Mandy Turner and Florian Kühn have argued that security, development, and state-building interventions work to '*integrate the periphery into the capitalist system*' (and global security) while '*protecting itself from the conflicts emanating from transformations in this periphery*' (Turner and Kühn 2016, 6). In other words, the integration, pacification and containment of peripheral populations are ostensibly dissonant effects of one set of sovereign, disciplinary and governmental strategies. This chapter draws on the conceptual framework outlined in Chapter 2 and the critique of functionalist (needs -> institutions) and market (demand -> supply) logics of security governance. It seeks to understand what makes postcolonial governance *possible* and *necessary* as a project of pacification and containment (Kienscherf 2011, Duffield 2007) of the global abnormal. In doing so, the chapter investigates how postcolonial government describes, measures and shapes Herati subjects and their geographies. Since my conceptual lens frames security as the encouragement of good life and global risk management, I raise four questions pertinent to Herati calculations of risk. First, in asking who is portrayed as risky in international politics, I identify four clusters of historical imaginations of Afghans/Heratis as *unstable, pathological, exotic* and *backward*. This leads to the second question of what or whom they pose *risk for*. To identify the value that is purportedly at risk, I survey a series of American, French, British, UN, NATO and EU strategic declarations produced since 2001. Therein, I observe *seven paradigmatic discourses* that reinforce an opaque notion of 'global stability' vulnerable to particularism, tribalism, fanaticism, poverty, etc. Third, the chapter reverses the focus to study *how Heratis experience risk* and highlights the very corporeal, classed, gendered and racialized vulnerability of Herati populations. Finally, I examine *whose risk* in this relationship *is acted upon* and addressed as a social priority. This question enables a critique of postcolonial security apparatuses that target and use Herati bodies to defend the vague norm and space of 'global stability'. Overall, the chapter reinterprets postcolonial security as unequal risk and population management that increases Afghan vulnerabilities and diminishes their life chances through sprawling security apparatuses.

Brown Bodies and Lands: Violent, Dirty, Fantastic and Risky

Western/Northern *representations* of Afghanistan as threatening and abnormal make its management and containment appear necessary. British, American, French, Imperial Russian, Soviet, and other historiographies, travelogues, government and media reports, etc. describe 'Afghans' (an ever-shifting designation) and their territories as risky, distant, vast and needing order and pacification. Moreover, as I argue below, such imaginations inform the post-2001 postcolonial governance apparatus. In other words, how social woes and threats are conceptualized affects how they are tackled and contained. Articulating Foucault's conception of productive power – and echoing Said's *Orientalism* (1978) – Doty claims that (post)colonial

> encounters between the North and the South were (and are) such that the North's representations of 'reality' enabled practices of domination, exploitation, and brutality, practices that probably would have been considered unthinkable, reprehensible, unjustifiable were an alternative 'reality' taken seriously. (Doty 1996, 13)

For Doty, '*analyzing [representational] practices*' is not meant to

> reveal essential truths that have been obscured, but rather to examine *how* certain representations underlie the production of knowledge and identities and *how* these representations make various courses of action possible. (emphasis added) (Doty 1996, 5)

This book is interested in a range of such 'actions': from the global funding and US-led training of the Afghan National Security Forces to the creation of development, reconstruction, and 'small and medium enterprise' arrangements appropriated from UN, IMF, USAID, and World Bank global reports and 'lessons learned'. Dominant discourses of the Afghan (as a Southern/Oriental subject) enable such interventions. I map them out through two criteria: their *temporal* and *subject specificity*. In temporal terms, I divide tropes and descriptions of Afghanistan/Herat into *background* and *proximate*. The former encompass geographic, environmental, anthropological, economic, etc. portrayals in media, personal, academic, popular, and government archives through the end of the Cold War (and dating back to the early nineteenth century). The latter include depictions of Afghans/Heratis as violent and unhealthy during the 1990s civil war and following 9/11. The proximate discourses arouse, inform and justify the 2001 invasion and continuous experimentation with security and development in the country. Yet they are also re-articulations and re-enactments of broadly permissive colonial and Cold War imaginations of Afghan populations and spaces as treacherous, filthy and threatening. Regarding the subject specificity of these representations, I identify four core images of Afghanistan/Herat as (1) *unstable*, (2) *pathological*, (3) *exotic/unknown*, and (4) *backward*. For reasons of parsimony, I will not rehash the extensive literature that treats historical imaginations of Afghanistan/Herat in detail (see Chapter 1 for more). I will merely spotlight key images and descriptors that continue to reproduce '*a desolate, inward-looking, and isolated place*' (Crews 2015, 3).

I underscore the stubbornness of these representations to shed light on the work that they do in enabling and justifying the protracted global military and administrative presence in Afghanistan. They make possible ritualized invocations of 9/11 imaginaries and the strategic use of opium, migration and conflict statistics. They also make associations of Pashtun insurgents with weapons of mass destruction look plausible (Toukan and Cordesman 2009). In all, they make postcolonial interventions meaningful and operative.

Representations of Afghanistan: Background and Proximate, from Instability to Filth

The modern 'rediscovery' of Afghans by the globe is tied to Mountstuart Elphinstone's ethnographic observations made in 1808-1809. He represented the British East India Company at the court of King Shah Shuja, the ruler of what colonial lexicons called the '*Kingdom of Caubul*' (Smedley, Rose and Rose 1845, 185–192, Elphinstone 1815). Elphinstone's notes about the lands of the 'Afghauns' (confederations of Pashtun tribes) and the Pashtun Durrani monarchy were published in 1815 as *An Account of the Kingdom of Caubul*. They capture present-day Pakistani Khyber Pakhtunkhwa, Kabul, Kandahar, Herat, Hazarajat, Baluchistan, Sistan, and Turkic and Tajik populations north and northeast of Kabul (along the Amu Darya and Panj rivers). At the time of Elphinstone's travels across the Durrani monarchy, it was loosely held together through Durrani kinship ties, intermittent military coercion and subsidies to non-Durrani Pashtuns and other groups. Elphinstone's descriptions, tropes and vocabularies shaped the Anglo-American and European colonial knowledge of Pashtuns, Hazaras, Tajiks and others so profoundly and consistently that B. D. Hopkins referred to this system of meaning and designation as the 'Elphinstonian episteme' of Afghanistan. Within it, the Durrani realm and its dependent territories (such as Herat) were homogenized as *Afghan* (at the time synonymous with 'Pashtun'), *Kabul-centric*, and *tribal* (based on primordial kinship and genealogies) (Rahimi 2017, Hopkins 2008, Hanifi 2008). These descriptors were reductive insofar as they silenced non-Pashtun, non-Sunni and nontribal discourses and subjectivities. As such, they were at odds with 'dialogical' Indo-Persian accounts of the Durrani and Barakzai monarchies, written in the eighteenth and nineteenth centuries in Dari Persian, Pashto, Urdu, Uzbek, and Arabic (Green 2016, Noelle-Karimi 2016). Nonetheless, Pashtun-centric and 'racialized [tribal] typologies' (Crews 2015, 4) became essential to how Afghanistan was imagined in highbrow magazines (e.g. *The Scots Magazine and Edinburgh Literary Miscellany*, 1815), travelogue ethnographies (e.g. in Arthur Conolly's *Journey to the North of India*, 1838, or Alexander Burnes' *Travels into Bokhara*, 1839), lexicons of lesser-known things (e.g. *Encyclopaedia Metropolitana*, 1845), geographic almanacs (e.g. *The Treasury of Geography*, 1860), and British Company and government reports – to name but a few textual trajectories of the Elphinstonian episteme. According to Hopkins, key anthropologists of South and Central Asia '*have been at least partly beholden to Elphinstone's tribalization of Afghan society*' (Hopkins 2008, 31), enabling the circulations of neo-Elphinstonian tropes of a 'segmentary', tribal, and ethnically fragmented Afghanistan among contemporary anthropologists (Barfield 2010, 4, 8, 10).

Therefore, Elphinstone demarcated key *background* representations, which inform *proximate* post-Cold War descriptions and cover a range of themes. To show how they enable interventions into Afghan lives, I focus on descriptions of Afghan lands and peoples as (1) *unstable and dangerous*, (2) *pathological*, (3) *exotic/unknown*, and (4) *backward*. In Chapter 1, I have prefaced Herat's subjectivity as 'liminal', 'in-between', 'neither', and 'both' in relation to (1) the Pashtun-dominated Durrani monarchies and the Afghan republic, and (2) Persia/Iran. Herat's liminality has been shaped through the representational politics of a wider, Pashtun Afghanistan, which gradually extended to non-majority Pashtun parts of the modern Afghan state (such as Herat). To global audiences and policy-makers less familiar with Afghan political geographies, Herat is just a part of Afghanistan, placed within a neatly bounded picture of a nation. To most Heratis (in particular those speaking Farsi), this picture has never been uncontested or unproblematic.

First, Elphinstone's descriptions of Afghan tribalism convey images of unstable, dangerous and threatening populations occupying swaths of hardly controllable land. In Foucault's terms of strategic analysis, Afghanistan's *security, territory and population* are grasped as ungovernable. To Elphinstone, Pashtuns were so aggressive that '*scarce a day passes without a quarrel*' (Elphinstone 1815, 20). In such instances, '*swords are drawn, and wounds inflicted, which lead to years of anxiety and danger*', and all '*ends in assassination*' (Ibid). Even minor violence habitually escalates as '*each injury produces fresh retaliation*', leading to '*attacks in the streets, murders of men in their houses, and all kinds of suspicion, confusion, and strife*' (Ibid). Elphinstone reifies this picture as ordinary tribalism and a '*state of anarchy*' (Ibid, 23), which paradoxically allows certain tribes to be democratically egalitarian, albeit 'turbulent' and violent (Ibid, 22–23, 65, 86). To him, Afghanistan's volatile and subsistence-level life nurtures '*brave, but quarrelsome*' people (Ibid, 3). Elphinstone rearticulates the colonial tropes of the lying and cunning native (Memmi 1991), labels certain tribes as '*bigoted and intolerant*', and indicts them for being '*under the influence of their Moollahs*', '*vicious and debauched*' (Elphinstone 1815, 3), and 'repulsive' (Ibid, 33). *An Account of the Kingdom of Caubul* invokes civilizational hierarchies to conclude that Afghans '*appear to have united the ferocity and craft of savages with the moderation of a more advanced stage of civilization*' (Ibid, 13). Afghan volatility compelled Charles Masson to call for their 'Anglicization' in the nineteenth century (Hopkins 2008, 17).

Unsurprisingly then, such not-quite-civilized people live in either '*the absence of all government*' or 'despotisms', depending on the tribe (Elphinstone 1815, 18). They are free, but divided (Hopkins 2008, 19). Fear of Afghan tribalism (as unruliness, volatility, and aggression) compelled a British colonial administrator to warn that 'one word' from the Afghan Emir could trigger entire tribes to intervene in the Indian Mutiny (1857) '*in a wave of fanatical irredentism*'. Afghans could '*overrun and possess the rich valley of Peshawar and the Derajat*' (Barfield 2010, 129). In the late nineteenth century, the British Indian colonial apparatus '*saw Afghanistan as a land of 'tribal' disorder*' (Hopkins 2008, 1). The British '*view of Afghanistan was largely limited to its violence, which they neither understood nor cared to*' (Ibid, 4). The more proximate 'Western' portrayals of Afghanistan as unstable and backward – and therefore in need of stabilization and modernization – abound in ways that surpass the limitations of this chapter. In 1999, Ahmed Rashid wrote about 'Talibanization' as '*the destabilizing export of Afghan-style radical Islam*' (Rashid 1999) aided by Afghanistan's 'porous borders' (Ibid). If left uncontained, the threat will grow. The same year, Afghanistan was also described as '*the archetypal failed state*' and a 'volatile environment' (Newberg and Newland 1999). A year into the Western intervention, Anthony Hyman reiterated the conceptualization of Afghanistan as tribal, sectarian, fragmented, and 'broken-backed' (Hyman 2002, 299), with '*a large, volatile constituency of young men and women*' (Ibid, 305). In 2018, Fareed Zakaria described Afghan society as tribal, whose domestic and international relations are based in an esoteric notion of 'honor' rather than 'national interest' (as is the implied normal). Zakaria also expressed concern that Iran and Pakistan can '*ensure that Afghanistan stays unstable forever*' (Zakaria 2018). Yet, few phrases capture better the imagination of Afghan roughness, treachery, and violent pride than the trope of Afghanistan as a '*graveyard of empires*' (Jones 2010), an 'unconquerable' (Heath and Zahedi 2011) and historically 'ungovernable' space (Malkasian 2013, xx–xxii).

Second, Elphinstone's descriptions conjure up images of corporeal and micro-spatial pathology, of troubled populations living in subpar conditions. Expressing racial associations of skin colour, cleanliness and conduct, he describes the members of one Pashtun tribe as '*small, black, and ugly*', '*barbarous in their manners, and rude and squalid in their general appearance*' (Elphinstone 1815, 178) and refers to Durranis as '*so unpolished a people*' (Ibid, 114). Elphinstone relays that poor Durranis '*only change their clothes on Fridays, and often only every other Friday*', but adds: '*They bathe once a week at least*' (Ibid, 119). (This was exceptionally frequent compared to British bathing habits at the time (Eveleigh 2002).) Elphinstone found it curious that even though the poor lived in subpar tents, they still showed hospitality to their guests (Elphinstone 1815, 124). Alexander Burnes, like Elphinstone, portrayed many Afghan lands as 'needy', 'poor', and 'miserable' (Burnes 1839, 82, 235, 326). Arthur Conolly remarked that Turkic tribes were 'dirty people' (Conolly 1838a, 162) and described his lodging in Herat as a '*dark and filthy hole ..., which smelt so abominably that it was distressing to be in it*' (Ibid, 327).

However, sweeping portrayals of Afghan spaces as unclean, unhygienic and medically dangerous to the colonizer's body did not become commonplace until the late nineteenth century. I underscore Maximilian Drephal's research on how British diplomats stationed in India experienced Afghanistan from 1922 to 1947, since their reports shaped corporeal conceptions of the country (Drephal 2017). According to Drephal, '*Afghanistan was regularly cast in anti-Indian terms spatially, meteorologically, and with regard to physical comforts, hygiene, and civilizational chronology*' (Ibid, 11). British diplomats reported on '*depressing and harassing conditions*' in Kabul (Ibid, 12), which required their premises to be '*at some distance from the more densely populated part of Kabul City*'. This would make them '*habitable according to European standards*' (Ibid). Staff accounts describe Kabul as 'insanitary', 'notoriously unhealthy', and '*a health hazard*', where '*the method of sewage disposal is crude in the extreme*' and people supposedly *'prefer 'dirty water' from streams and drains to the tap water coming from nearby hills'* (Ibid, 12-13). Kabul is mired in enteric fever and occasional cholera, and the *'immediate surroundings and neighbourhood of ... the Legation are insanitary to such a degree as to baffle description in ordinary language'* (Ibid). Historically more proximate pathologizations of Afghans span governmental and intergovernmental policy documents, popular media narratives and academia. The United States' 2015 National Security Strategy refers to *'upheaval across the Middle East and North Africa'* and asserts that *'fragile and conflict-affected states incubate and spawn infectious disease, illicit weapons and drug smugglers, and destabilizing refugee flows'* (President of the United States of America 2015, 1). Afghanistan shares in the destiny of postcolonial spaces constituted through travel advisories and country profiles as disquieting geographies of general health and safety risks.[1] As British media outlets ponder the descriptions of Afghan and other refugees as 'vermin', 'rats' and 'cockroaches' (Williams 2015, Grenoble 2015), Poland's Interior Minister Mariusz Błaszczak echoes Orientalist pathologization when he compares immigrants from the Global South to 'a bomb' that needs to be 'defused'. Jarosław Kaczyński, Poland's Law and Justice party leader, warns of oriental migrants carrying *'all sorts of parasites and protozoa, which, while not dangerous in the organisms of these people, could be dangerous here'* (Cienski 2017). Across centuries, such representations have enabled governmental power to mobilize migration, development and security policies of population containment and control.

A third discourse portrays Afghans as less civilized than the peoples of the British Isles or, more recently, as being premodern. In Elphinstone's *Account*, Pashtun and other lands dependent on 'Caubul' are backward, anachronistic, and reminiscent of Europe's distant past (1815, 4, 116). Few Afghan settlements *'even merit the name of a town'* (Ibid, 129). Likewise, Conolly differentiated Turkic tribes and the *'inhabitants of [Khorasani] deserts'* (including Heratis) from *'[more] civilized people'* (Conolly 1838a, 52, 131, 137). Emir Sher Ali Khan (1863-1866, 1868-1879) may have internalized the notions of Afghan backwardness when he concluded that *'all people are advancing in the arts of peace and civilization. It is only we Afghans who remain the ignorant asses we have always been'* (Barfield 2010, 138). The colonial gap in progress and modernity inevitably correlated with emphases on power/knowledge gaps. In 1886, Rudyard Kipling contrasted the Pashtuns with the advances of the British Empire by juxtaposing 'the Yusufzaies' (a tribe) and 'our "ologies"' ('European' sciences). Similarly, he compared *'two thousand pounds of [British] education'* with a 'ten-rupee jezail' (an Indian and Central Asian musket). In Kipling's poem, *Arithmetic on the Frontier*, the 'hillsides' of the risky and vast British Indian frontier 'teem' with 'home-bred hordes'. This picture reflected a legacy of two Anglo-Afghan wars and the gory memories of British civil servants, military personnel, and (mostly Indian) troops who died in them. Over a century later, the 2002 US National Security Strategy claimed that *'weak states,*

---

[1] For instance, see the US Center for Disease Control and Prevention webpage on Afghanistan (at https://wwwnc.cdc.gov/travel/destinations/traveler/none/afghanistan/), the UK 'Foreign Travel Advice: Afghanistan: Health' page (at https://www.gov.uk/foreign-travel-advice/afghanistan/health), or the Afghanistan 'Passport Health USA' page (https://www.passporthealthusa.com/destination-advice/afghanistan/).

like Afghanistan can pose as great a danger to our national interests as strong states', since 'poverty, weak institutions, and corruption' make them 'vulnerable to terrorist networks and drug cartels within their borders'. Therefore, intervening in Afghanistan and 'rebuilding' it is 'necessary ... so that it will never again abuse its people, threaten its neighbors, and provide a haven for terrorists' (President of the United States of America 2002). The picture of an anachronistic terrorist 'hotbed' justifies occupation. Likewise, the widespread oppression of Afghan women has become indispensable in the litany of Afghanistan's 'medieval' defects that the emancipated, enlightened, and respectful West/North needs to correct (Berger 2011, Chishti and Farhoumand-Sims 2011). Yet, the paradoxes and contradictions in 'women's rights' and 'freedoms' since the 'liberation' of Afghan women in 2001 have not received much global attention (Wimpelmann 2017, Billaud 2015, 13–15, Rostami-Povey 2007).

Fourth, the Elphinstonian episteme abounds with portrayals of an exotic and attractive, but never quite knowable or fathomable Afghanistan. Elphinstone, Burnes, Conolly and later chroniclers revel in the lush mountains and gardens, rivers, orchards, valleys and other memorable geographies of Afghanistan. However, those memories are embedded in imaginations of Afghan spaces and populations as alien and different from 'Our' familiar geographies, from 'Europe' and 'home'. Elphinstone had to 'confess' that he was *unable to explain* the politics of the Pashtun Yusufzai (Elphinstone 1815, 4) or how it was possible that *'few possess[ed] any knowledge'* of their history (Ibid, 8). While the history of the Yusufzai and wider 'Caubul' are *'mixed with ... fables'* and *'superstitious and romantic notions'*, Elphinstone claimed the expertise and ability to separate *'an appearance of truth and exactness'* (note the caveat) from fiction (Ibid, 9). The exotic and spectral nature of Afghan histories and politics, the Afghans' notable physiques (Ibid, 44, 121, 220, etc.), and striking landscapes correlate with descriptions of Afghanistan's non-human biosphere, where *'all the fruits and flowers of Europe grow wild'* (Ibid, 5) or *'none ... are found'* (Ibid, 8). The remoteness of Afghan spaces is abridged through comparisons with quintessential Europeanness, thereby preserving Afghanistan's impenetrable exoticism. Europe is associated with cultivation and Afghanistan with wilderness. The use of tropes of exotic and bestial wilderness (Ibid, 5) had long been perpetuated in colonial encounters to connote *difference* as *ambivalence*: fantastic and attractive, yet risky and threatening. More recently, Western/Northern audiences have exoticized the noble suffering of women in the oppressive 'Afghan culture' (Khan 2014, Billaud 2015, 10) and the media have marvelled at ceasefires as a *'rare, goodwill gesture in Afghanistan'* (where, apparently, only 'ill will' reigns) (Domonske 2018). In 2018, the BBC sentimentalized the 1970s Afghanistan as still 'there' – a *'landscape with fertile valleys and desolate plains, burned-out Russian vehicles and bombed buildings, with roads full of huge holes'* (BBC 2018).

Notably, these representations are at odds with self-empowering, agential, and exceptionalist imaginations and practices of another 'global Afghanistan'. This other land and people are integrated into biblical and early Islamic histories, transnational arts, trade flows, sciences, leisurely travel, innovation, diplomacy, urban cosmopolitanism, religious pilgrimage, and Eurasian multiculturalism (Crews 2015). Foregrounding the mobility of 'Afghan' bodies and their creative role in imperial and transnational politics advances histories of Afghans as *global actors* who are more than victims, objects, or mere bystanders (Ibid, 15).

Background and Proximate: Imaginations of Herat as Decline and Risk

In all, by the mid-nineteenth century, the British objectified Afghanistan into an unstable and ungovernable space instrumental to the Anglo-Russian 'Great Game'. The Durrani Kingdom and its dependencies became a *'highway of conquest'* (Fletcher 1965) to the British – one perilously vulnerable to the Russian Empire fixated on India (Gammell 2016, 12). From those dependencies, Herat stood out as the *'Key to India'* (Ibid, 183). The Elphinstonian episteme, however, treats Herat as an appendix on the tribal and Pashtun-centred map of Afghanistan. Elphinstone describes Herat as one of merely few places to *'even merit the name of a town'* in the 'Dooraunee country' (Elphinstone 1815, 129). In fact, Elphinstone saw it as *'one of the most ancient and most renowned of all the cities of the East'* (Ibid, 215), blessed with *'a fertile plain'* (Ibid, 216), *'mosques, tombs, and other edifices, intermixed with numerous trees and gardens with which it is embellished and from the lofty mountains by which it is surrounded'* (Ibid). Herat was an Afghan/Durrani place embedded in a nascent colonial imaginary of Afghanistan as tribal, pastoral, backward and dangerous. Nonetheless, Elphinstone grapples with Herat's liminal subjectivity when he asserts: *'Heraut is included within the Dooraunee limits ..., but it was always a distinct government, and is now almost an independent state'* (Ibid). He adds: *'The Prince at Heraut always exercised an authority almost uncontrolled by the [Durrani] King'* (Ibid, 218).

British colonial servants saw Herat, much like the Durrani Kingdom, as a risky and dangerous place for anyone, and particularly for 'outsiders'. George Foster of the East India Company admired Herat's 'religious edifices', but also wrote about the personal risk he assumed trying to *'slide into the Mahometan community'* (Forster 1798, 134), including being physically intimidated and threatened with circumcision by a local mullah (Ibid, 133). In Foster's account, he sacrificed himself to gather intelligence and advance colonial knowledge, risking his life to the Sunni oppression of the Hindus, Christians, and Jews in the city (Ibid, 134–135). Before Elphinstone's *Account* was published in 1815, Captain Christie (whom Elphinstone references) had already described Herat's citadel – the city's architectural and defence treasure – as 'contemptible' (Gammell 2016, 184). In 1834, Arthur Conolly portrayed Herat as *'one of the dirtiest [towns] in the world'* (Conolly 1838b, 2). Vaulted Old City streets formed *'low dark tunnels, containing every offensive thing'* (Ibid), including trash and *'dead cats and dogs ... lying upon heaps of the vilest filth'* (Ibid). Elsewhere *'lay for many days a dead horse, surrounded by bloated dogs'* (Ibid, 3). Conolly called the Heratis 'bestial', blaming their pathological customs for poor public hygiene (Ibid). However, his account of Herat beyond the city limits differed, for *'without the walls all [was] beauty'* (Ibid) of *'little fortified villages, gardens, vineyards, ... corn-fields'* and *'many small streams of shining water'* (Ibid). To Conolly, unadulterated natural beauty only highlighted Herat's pathological human geography. Writing in 1833, Mohan Lal

(Burnes' guide and translator) described Herat as a gloomy and dirty city that had declined since its glory Timurid days (Lal 1846, 213-277). Gammell describes Lal's attitude as one of *'mystification at the chaos of what went on within [Herat's] walls'* (Gammell 2016, 190-191). In 1837, Lieutenant Eldred Pottinger described Heratis as *'a poor and oppressed people'*, *'dirty and ill-clad* (Ibid, 197). The city felt *'hardly safe for a stranger'*, with *'no protection for life, liberty or property'* (Ibid). Joseph Pierre Ferrier, French military officer and author, witnessed Herat's physical destruction in the wake of the Persian siege of 1838. He described crumbling houses and ruins of mosques and mausoleums that littered the city (Ferrier 1856, 144). He derided the Heratis' backward medicine (Ibid, 149) and mocked their admiration for European culture, referring them to *'humanity, civilization, political economy, and the rights of man'* instead of 'alchemy' to explain Europe's 'riches' (Ibid, 149-150). He reiterated the Orientalist tropes of shrewd and greedy natives, highlighting *'the true Afghan feeling'* that *'he who gives an egg expects an ox in return'* (Ibid, 150). Nonetheless, his virtue would not allow him to give in to the *'cupidity of the Afghans, whose natural and national propensity is to lay hands upon other people's property'* (Ibid). To him, the Heratis and Afghans were disingenuous, hypocritical on religion, mindlessly hedonistic, and uncivilized (Ibid, 151-152). By the 1840s, Herat and Afghanistan were integrated into the colonial motifs of the Orient: the Heratis were invested with an intrinsic 'nature' in a 'nation' of alien 'them' (Ibid, 154). They became fully 'Asiatic': lagging behind Europeans and *'full of illusions which could not be dispelled'* (Ibid, 156). All in all, *'there was nothing'* in *'the province of Herat'* (Ibid). Ferrier did observe the *'extraordinary security of the public roads of Herat'* (Ibid, 158), but this, too, came with a caveat. Security existed only in relation to *'Central Asia, for the most part infested with thieves and bandits'* (Ibid). In Herat, security was the work of an iron fisted 'Vezir'; the locals *'had never before enjoyed such security for life and property'* (Ibid).

Gammell quotes Sir Henry Rawlinson, *'the British diplomat and noted Afghan expert'*, when he assesses the political and security situation in Herat (in 1880) as 'anarchy' (Gammell 2016, 230). Visiting Herat in the summer of 1885 as part of the British Afghan Boundary Commission, Charles Edward Yate showed appreciation for the Province's natural environment, but recast the area as underdeveloped and underutilized. He noted: *'Much might be done in the way of arboriculture in this country under proper supervision'* (Yate 1888, 14). However, Yate's confidence in the British ability to improve Herat's condition dissipated when he visited the Musalla Complex (Ibid, 16), previously destroyed to aid the British troops against the Russian infantry (I discuss this further in Chapter 5). Yate describes the once famed Herat bazaar as a large, but *'very poor affair'* where over half the shops are closed (Ibid, 20, 25). Everything about the city *'betokens the poverty of the people'* (Ibid, 20). Moreover, like most 'Eastern cities', Herat is *'not inviting-looking'* (Ibid, 25). Many houses were *'practically nothing but a mass of ruins'* (Ibid, 27). Likewise, the streets were *'dirty crooked lanes'* (Ibid). Yate goes on to describe the homeless, beggars, dilapidated ancient monuments, unkempt courtyards, mud, and a general atmosphere of decay (Ibid, 34-35, 39-40). Due to a decline in Herat's population (to *'under 2000 [families]'*) and the state of its public infrastructure, Yate concluded that calling Herat a city was a 'misnomer' (Ibid, 21). Gammell quotes a Persian diplomat who, in 1929, described Herat as 'deplorable'

(Gammell 2016, 262) and dangerous for a Shia like himself (Ibid, 261–262). To him, Herat was a dirty health hazard, a crumbling place of *'boredom, disorder, idleness and gloom'* (Ibid, 263–264).

Before I show how the representations of Herat as pathological and dangerous travelled through the 1990s civil war era, I pause to mention the Herat of an English travelogue writer and architecture aficionado, Robert Byron. Byron visited the city in 1933 and 1934 and admired its cultural, artistic and social history marked by poetry, sacral and secular architecture and Islamic scholasticism. To him, Herat was *'Asia without the inferiority complex'* (Byron 1982, 86). Yet, he noted that Herat had been isolated for centuries, without railways or major roads to connect it to travellers other than the Persian, British, Russian, Pashtun and Turkic conquerors. Byron's Herat was not quite Asian. He compared Herat's notables to Dante and the Medici, and its sophisticated atmosphere of 'Timurid Renaissance' to Italy's cinquecento (Ibid, 88–89). Yet Byron also marvelled at the violent Herati: ferocious, carrying *'rifles to go shopping as Londoners carry umbrellas … in a country where the law runs uncertainly'* (Ibid, 86). Gammell summarizes the rare personal, diplomatic, and journalistic descriptions of Herat through the world wars as a *'God forsaken city' with the air of a 'lesser capital"* (Gammell 2016, 270).

Stories of socioeconomic and urban improvement and *'vibrant cultural life'* in Herat dominated in the 1960s and 1970s (Gammell 2016, 276). This was upended in 1978 when the Saur Revolution – a Soviet-aided coup d'état – brought to power the People's Democratic Party of Afghanistan and its Khalq faction in particular. Western reports out of Herat highlighted Khalq's oppressive practices: *'threats to families, electrocuted limbs, savage beatings, … broken limbs'* and prison abuse (Ibid, 288). Herat and Afghanistan were again portrayed as violent, dangerous, inhumane and chaotic. With minor substantive discontinuities, this portrayal still dominates the Western media and academia (Ibid, 290–300). Following the Soviet invasion of Afghanistan in December 1979, the communist-controlled news media in Kabul and Moscow evoked the images of the primitive Mujahedeen and regressive Islamists to describe Herat (Ibid 302–303), dismissing them as disorganized 'thieves' and 'bandits' (Kakar 1995). Afghanistan's 'backwardness' and 'savagery' seemed commonsensical to the Russian press fluent in the Communist Party's developmentalist Marxist worldviews (Braithwaite 2011, 5, 11, Snesarev 2014). Conversely, media outlets and scores of academics in the United States, Britain, and elsewhere in the 'West' slowly started sympathizing with the Heratis and their anti-Soviet resistance. Notions of volatility and violence remained, and Afghanistan was still depicted as 'backward', 'primitive', and 'unspeakable' in the United States (Nunan 2016, 147). However, popular geopolitical narratives were shifting and Afghanistan 'became' oppressed by the Soviets (Ibid, 147–148). Rather than solely pointing to Afghanistan as naturally dangerous and chaotic, descriptions of Afghan spaces in the 1980s identified an external force that was culpable for Afghanistan's misery. As the Soviets withdrew from Afghanistan, Herat's political divisions and infighting in the early 1990s captivated UN rapporteurs and the occasional NGO observer. While attributing power struggles to primordial social cleavages, they memorialized the politics of tribal and ethnic belonging, religion, class, and pro- and anti-government allegiance (UNHCR 1992, Jawad 1992, Human Rights

Watch 1991, UNHCR 1990). As the Cold War ended, the world looked away from Afghanistan and '*both the conflict and the people*' became '*forgotten*' (Ermacora 1990).

When Ismal Khan, the wealthy Herati warlord and Mujahedeen militiaman, took control of the Herat Province, close observers learned about the '*veiling of women and the beating of those who refused to wear a long beard*' (Gammell 2016, 326). Herati politics were not only volatile; they came to be seen as fanatical. In a rare in-depth take on the Afghan politics of security and statehood in the mid-1990s, Heratis and Afghans are portrayed as deprived of historical agency, powerless, and naturally dependent on foreign hegemony and aid (Rubin 1996). The Taliban takeover of Herat in 1995 solidified this image through IGO, NGO, and media reports on 'Islamist' violence against competing militias and civilians (particularly women). To the world, Herat was poor, divided, and victimized by the Taliban, Iran, and Pakistan (United States Institute of Peace 1997, CNN 1996, Khalilzad 1996, Immigration and Refugee Board of Canada 1995). The Taliban repression became infamous for its lethality, bodily violence and restrictions upon the everyday lives of women, their movement and clothing. In rare reports out of the city, Herat subsisted as a former enclave of urban life that was sinking into the rural backwardness of the Pashtun-dominated Taliban (Colville 1996).

Visual, written, and audio accounts of Herat surged in the months and years following the Taliban withdrawal in November 2001. One of the early testimonies came from Christopher de Bellaigue, who described Herat as '*the lost city*' amid clouds of dust and an air of exhaustion. He conveyed widespread destruction and neglect throughout the city, and – channelling Byron's Occidentalism – contrasted this gloom with Herat's fifteen-century heyday under the 'Oriental Medici' (the Timurid dynasty). While Herat made de Bellaigue feel like a liberator, the city was still swarming with '*men with Kalashnikovs and handheld grenade launchers*'. Unsafe and isolated from the world, Herat was 'free', but its liberation was 'precarious' (de Bellaigue 2002). A year later, Grant Podelco reported that being a journalist in Herat 'exhausted' and 'intimidated' him (Podelco 2002). The city projected fear, disjunctive backwardness, and the premodernity of 'donkey carts' and 'omnipresent' burqas (Ibid). Herat seemed neo-medieval in Podelco's portrait: part lawless, part dominated by Ismal Khan, his '*large private army*' and 'enormous wealth'. Echoing the colonial tropes of perilous native duplicity, Podelco described a Herat of 'paranoia' in which '*no one [was] to be trusted*'.

As Ismail Khan received US support and regained control over Herat, two Human Rights Watch reports cemented the portrayal of life in the Province as violent, oppressive and risky. *All Our Hopes Are Crushed: Violence and Repression in Western Afghanistan* (2002a) outlined the inhumanity of Ismail Khan's paranoid regime: the violent muzzling of journalists, the intimidation of perceived political opponents, arbitrary arrests and prison torture, restrictions on women's mobility, and a '*climate of fear and pessimism*' (Human Rights Watch 2002a, 45). While the report accused the United States for its complicity in funding, aiding, and legitimizing the violence (Ibid, 11), it also essentialized it as 'medieval' and permanent (Ibid, 4). Violence is not complex or US-enabled – it is 'Afghan' and 'local'. Afghanistan is not a 'post-conflict' (or whichever) society: it is a '*fractured, undemocratic collection of 'fiefdoms*'' (Ibid). '*We Want to Live As Humans*': *Repression of Women and Girls in Western Afghanistan* (2002b) further detailed gendered inequalities in the Province: from mobility restrictions and arbitrary detention to abusive gynaecological examinations. The report described gendered and religious tyranny as endemic to Herat, but did not indict the United States for its role in its perpetuation. Instead, it underscored the role the United States should play in liberating women (Ibid, 48).

Since 2001, Herat has been locked in a Western/Northern discourse of risk. It is portrayed as an Iranian spying outpost along the Afghan frontier, a vehicle for Iran's cultural and political influence close to US troops, a corridor for desperate westward migrants, a passageway of illegal trade and terrorist recruitment, a vortex of Taliban-dominated rural roads, and a hub for kidnappers and gangs. Each of these abnormalities supposedly transcends Herat and generates risks for *the global*, whether it is a foreigner visiting the city or a EU Member State's welfare system tested by immigrants.

Western policy analysts and journalists have identified Herat as a conduit of Iran's political and social influence in Afghanistan. They focus on Tehran's cultivation of friendly warlords, the local Shia, and Farsi-speaking populations (Nader, et al. 2014, Johnson 2004), or the funding of mosques, schools, roads, railways, and other infrastructure projects (Koepke 2013, King 2010). Herat has been labelled the geopolitical 'model' of Iran's 'soft power' (Toscano 2012, 7–8). *The New York Times* describes Herat as 'Little Iran', where '*people ... speak with Iranian accents*' and '*Iranian schools, colleges and bookshops line the streets*' (Gall 2017). The article leaves no pore of Herati life unaffected: the women's 'black chadors' match those '*favored in Iran*', the shops are '*full of Iranian sweets and produce*', the 'air' of Iranian '*intrigue infuses Herat*' through '*bribery, infiltration or violence*' (Ibid). Herat is '*filled with Iranian spies, secret agents and hit squads*' and '*plagued by multiple assassinations and kidnappings in recent years*'. Iran funds '*militant groups and criminal gangs*' and '*is sponsoring terrorism*' (Ibid). Rediscovering colonial medicalization, the article describes Iran's influence as malignant, spreading 'aggressively' (Ibid). Herat is sick and Iran is the virus. Yet, it is the cultural affinity of Iran and Herat that enables the disease to spread, allowing Iranian spies to infiltrate Herat's government (Radio Free Europe-Radio Liberty 2018). *The Wall Street Journal* echoes Herat's natural complicity as a place of Iran's 'Afghan clout' (Abi-Habib 2012). Even if a victim of external power politics, Herat is not off the hook.

Furthermore, Herat is recast as a corridor of illicit trade in drugs, consumer goods, US dollars, and humans (Karimi 2018, UN Office on Drugs and Crime 2008, Kreutzmann 2007). It aids the Taliban insurgency (McCoy 2016) and enables the spread of infectious diseases (Ruiseñor-Escudero, et al. 2014). Western journalistic, academic, and policy reports have also identified Herat as a corridor for desperate Afghans trying to reach 'Europe's shores' (Dimitriadi 2017, Koelbl 2015). Moreover, the Taliban and Islamic State insurgencies in Herat's rural districts threaten everyone: migrants, visitors from abroad, NATO and US troops, foreign NGOs, government employees, ordinary Heratis, etc. The insurgency causes 'shock', 'terror' and 'fear' (Sharifi and Adamou 2018, Human Rights Watch 2018), threatens the US and Indian consulates (in 2013 and 2014 attacks, respectively), and targets Shia mosques. Wealthy locals, middle-class international professionals, and travellers are not safe either (Mahr 2014, Sieff 2013). '*Kidnapping for ransom*' has been called

Herat's *'top security concern'* (Radio Free Europe-Radio Liberty 2017) and *The Washington Post* fears for the city's *'burgeoning middle class'* (Sieff 2013). On August 4th 2016, the 'West' was reminded that Herat is a threat when the Taliban ambushed twelve American, British and German tourists, leaving seven injured (Karimi 2016). Their trip was organized by a British tour operator whose website describes Western Afghanistan as 'desperately poor', with 'diabolical' roads and *'history ... scattered everywhere, from Buddhist remains to burnt-out tanks'* (Rasmussen and Harding 2016).

The Global Defining Itself as Imperilled

The 'securitization' of Afghanistan predates September 11, 2001. Even a cursory survey of background and proximate discourses about Afghans shows that (post)colonial power had rendered Afghanistan knowable through the calculi of security and risk decades before Al-Qaeda struck the Twin Towers and the Pentagon. However, 9/11 made it possible to repurpose these calculations for a new *global war*: not a 'world' or a 'cold' one, but one *'on terror'*. What has been defended in this war from the scourge of Afghan volatility, *'an archaic threat to be contained'* (Crews 2015, 10)? What is Herat's role in this imagination? Since Afghanistan and Herat are the apparent location of *ab*normalities, this section counter-inspects the *normal* that is putatively threatened by the abnormal brown body. I scrutinize the normal in two steps.

First, I critique US, British, French, NATO, EU, and UN discourses on the threatened by surveying key national and intergovernmental strategic concepts and declarations since 2001. These include post-9/11 US (2001, 2002, 2006, 2010, 2015, 2017) and British national security strategies (2008-2011), French 'white papers' on security and defence (from 2008 and 2013, including a 2017 strategic review); NATO's 2010 Strategic Concept, Wales Summit Declaration and Wales Summit Declaration on Afghanistan (2014a, 2014b), Warsaw Summit Communiqué, and The Warsaw Declaration on Transatlantic Security (2016); EU security strategies (2003 and 2016, including the Council conclusions accompanying the latter), EU 'global strategy' document (2017), a joint NATO-EU declaration (2016), as well as fifty-three UN Security Council resolutions on Afghanistan (from September 12, 2001 to March 8, 2018). While the scope of texts could be wider (e.g. to include non-NATO troop contributing nations), I have narrowed them down for parsimony. At the level of government publications, I focus on the strategic statements of some of the largest (troops and funding-wise) contributors to NATO, EU and UN missions in Afghanistan. Regarding the level of intergovernmental statements, I have privileged NATO, UN Security Council, and EU declarations due to their political, organizational and financial dominance in the governance of Afghanistan. While other UN bodies (e.g. UNDP or UNHCR) can be examined, their descriptions of what should be defended within and without Afghanistan are (1) referenced in UN Security Council resolutions, and (2) focus on narrow policy agendas. Broader surveys of discursive representations could include 'non-Western' regional organizations (e.g. the Organisation of Islamic Cooperation) and transnational

NGOs active in Afghanistan since 2001. The selection offered here is not exhaustive, but it illustrates core hegemonic conceptions.

Second, this section questions from a critical strategic perspective (Rosén 2016, Porter 2009) the risk posed by ordinary Afghans, the Taliban and Al-Qaeda for the United States and its allies. In all, how does Afghanistan threaten the world and what does the world do to defend itself?

Who Is At Risk and What Must Be Defended?

To identify that which claims to be threatened by a volatile Afghanistan, I focus on representations drawn from American, British, French, EU, NATO and UN strategic declarations produced since 2001. Specifically, I highlight paradigmatic descriptors of the threatened in the Global War on Terror. Following the precepts of Foucauldian discourse analysis, I emphasize the political subjectivities the discourses of risk and threat work to produce. While individual governmental and intergovernmental texts within this sample differ spatially, temporally and thematically, I highlight seven discourses common to them all.

First, security and defence declarations reproduce a distinct *global* space as the privileged vantage point of evaluation of politics and life. For instance, as the 2003 EU security strategy posits, '*state failure ... undermines global governance*' (European Council 2003, 4). *The global* is apparently valuable in its own right and needs no justification throughout the document. Moreover, it is beyond the reach and reproach of nation-states, even as its values and precepts are framed as intelligible to everyone. Thus, the UN Security Council invites 'all parties' to '*comply with their obligations under ... international humanitarian law and human rights law*' and emphasizes the '*importance of the ongoing monitoring and reporting to the United Nations Security Council*'. The global is neutral, superior (to be reported to), and logical since its ostensibly underlying principles are 'universal' and 'fundamental' (freedom, justice, rule of law, fair elections, free media, etc.). Likewise, in 2013, the French government explained its civilian and military intervention in Afghanistan as '*defending universal values*'. Referencing universalism whitewashes French and European security practices, since fighting for a public good makes it '*difficult ... to imagine that [Europe] might be the source of a major conflict*' (President of the French Republic 2013, 13). One might quibble over what it means to be 'the source' of conflict, but European weapons sales to Afghanistan and civilian 'collateral damage' complicate the correlation between globalism and peace. Yet, to reassure billions worldwide, international institutions are referred to as 'rules-based': the global is not lawless. For instance, in 2016, the European Council claimed that a '*rules-based global order*' is one of '*the vital interests underpinning [EU] external action*' (European Council 2016a).

Second, the global communicates through national and international security strategies replete with First-person Plural speaking positions. The 2002 US National Security Strategy promised: '*We will defend the peace by fighting terrorists and tyrants*' (President of the United States of America 2002) and the British 2010 National Security Strategy vowed: '*We will tackle the causes of instability overseas*' (Government of the United Kingdom 2010, 10). The *we* in official publications claims to speak for individual governments and populations (an already problematic power game). Yet, coupled with iterations of 'universal' and 'fundamental' values, *we* takes on a more ambitious quality of '*all of humanity*' (UN Security Council 2001a), '*the whole world*' (European Council 2016a, 5), or '*the entire planet*' (President of the United States of America 2017, 7). Altogether, this renders the global apolitical, representative and neutral; it situates it spatially 'above the fray'. This quality of impartiality, in turn, makes the globe inspirational and worthy. Finally, while the global seems coterminous with the West/North, the two are never equated. National governments and the UN Security Council do not claim to *be* the globe (the politically marginalized General Assembly makes such claims). This maintains the globe's status of a disinterested benchmark in a world of partial interests and nationalist bias, the vaunted dispassionate voice that signals the standards of good life everywhere and for everyone. The global remains the space of possibilities, opportunities, and aspiration (on issues as diverse as trade or scientific knowledge circulation), i.e. a space worthy of defence. Alas, pandemic diseases, climate change, 'violent extremism', financial crises, '*the continuous high level of violence*', and the '*security situation in Afghanistan*' (UN Security Council 2018) threaten this esoteric space. The necessity of defence is heightened by the 'fact' that some threats – like '*transnational criminal organizations*' – infiltrate the prized space from within through '*global supply chains*' (President of the United States of America 2017, 13).

Third, strategy documents reinforce the spatiality of the global by objectifying Afghans at corporeal and population levels. Thus, NATO declares to be concerned with defending Afghan children (North Atlantic Treaty Organization 2014a) or with '*preventing conflict-related sexual and gender-based violence*' in Afghanistan (North Atlantic Treaty Organization 2014b). Similarly, the UN Security Council demands certain rights and protections recognized '*regardless of gender, ethnicity or religion*', remains interested in regulating the use of anti-personnel landmines (UN Security Council 2001b), and requests that Afghan institutions be constituted as 'multi-ethnic' (UN Security Council 2001c). Extending the globe's care to the body reinforces Afghan life as a rightful concern of the global (rather than merely subject to the 'local' or 'national'). Globalizing the body and Afghanistan (Jalalzai and Jefferess 2011), in turn, reinforces how they should participate in society (as gendered, ethnic, sexed, age and religion-specific subjects of 'democratic' politics).

Fourth, through *binary differentiations*, the global is reproduced *as threatened by the regional* and particularistic. Insofar as the global is marked by risks and threats, they come from specific regions (Afghanistan, Central Asia, the Middle East, North Africa, Europe's 'southern' and 'eastern' neighbourhoods, etc.). The regional is a place of deterioration that needs to be addressed through '*an inclusive political process*' (North Atlantic Treaty Organization 2014b) in order to contain and reverse its 'growing instability' (Ibid). Aberrant local politics '*threaten regional and our own security*' (Ibid). For the world to be safe, the remedy is '*peace, stability, and development in Afghanistan, the region and beyond*' (UN Security Council 2014). Circumscribing regional politics as threatening the United States and the world, the 2006 National Security Strategy refers to Iraq and identifies '*a* region that for decades has been a source of instability and stagnation' (President of the United States of America 2006, 13). The region does not need specifying: a mere reference to a 'problematic' and different place triggers the reader's anxiety. While most surveyed documents contrast ('global/international') 'stability' with 'regional instability', there are no allusions to US, French, British, international, or global 'insecurity' and 'instability'. The location of threat is in the particular (e.g. Afghanistan).

Fifth, in addition to claiming to defend the globalized body-population from the risks of particularism, the global is reinforced by colonizing the local and micro-spatial. This takes place when local and global ontologies are used to define one another. Security strategies and UN Security Council resolutions do this by correlating localities through contagious security risks. The 2006 security strategy of the United States connects life across spaces by invoking the postcolonial trope of overflowing instability across 'neighbours': '*If America's nearest neighbors are not secure and stable, then Americans will be less secure*' (President of the United States of America 2006, 37). The United States approximates global and national security by linking up localities through risk flows. Self-defence makes the globe America's legitimate concern. Similarly, America's 2017 National Security Strategy makes the politics of security in Europe its business and claims that '*instability in the Middle East and Africa*' triggers '*the movement of millions of migrants and refugees into Europe, exacerbating instability and tensions in the region*' (President of the United States of America 2017, 48). Echoing this logic, a British security strategy asserts: '*Domestic security cannot be separated from overseas security issues*' (Government of the United Kingdom 2009, 38). While the global transcends the local, multiple correlated localities approximate the globe, which is narrated as both natural and risky. Thus, the stable individual (the US or the UN Security Council) integrates itself into the globe, which enables it to claim to be at risk and needing protection. The solidification of the global comes full circle when it underwrites and protects the local. For instance, the UN Security Council encourages '*the international efforts to assist in setting up the new Afghan Parliament and ensure its efficient functioning*' (UN Security Council 2005).

Sixth, strategic statements use a finite set of terms to denote the quality of the global that is threatened. They typically enumerate 'order', 'security', 'stability', 'prosperity', and 'peace' and seem to use them interchangeably. Each element contributes to the imagination of a balanced global that can be lost to nuclear proliferation, 'violent extremism', the Taliban, or simply – 'Afghanistan'. Whether it is '*international/global order and security*', '*stability and security*', or '*peace and stability*', repeatedly clustering these spaces congeals them into a supranational equilibrium of good life. This harmonious imagery effortlessly merges with universal values, impregnating global life with the qualities of moderate, inclusive, and normal (as opposed to 'radical', 'extreme', and 'abnormal') politics (North Atlantic Treaty Organization 2014b), fairness (UN Security Council 2004), functioning infrastructures (Government of the United Kingdom 2010, 10), cooperation (North Atlantic Treaty Organization 2014b), '*our way of life*' (Government of the United Kingdom 2010, 10, President of the United States of America 2017, 7), international society (European Council 2003, 8, 9), the international community (European Council 2003, Ibid), common resources (European Council 2016a, 8), rule of law (North Atlantic Treaty Organization 2014b), development (UN Security Council 2005), etc. The global is iteratively correlated with orderly, normal, prosperous, peaceful and agreeable life.

Seventh, global stability, security, peace, and order are described and reified through enumerative series and specifications: stability can be 'political' (President of the United States of America 2010, 44), 'nuclear' and 'strategic' (President of the United States of America 2015, 11), 'economic', 'financial', (Government of the United Kingdom 2008, 20), commercial (President of the United States of America 2010, 33), or related to oil and gas (Government of the United Kingdom 2010, 27), high seas, outer space (President of the United States of America 2010, 31, European Council 2016b, 5), cyberspace (President of the United States of America 2001, 7), and other sites. While the itemization of stability helps to identify that which is to be defended, it also proliferates its meanings and reproduces it as integral to nearly every aspect of life. The need for global stability is everywhere.

Overall, global stability stands for a distinct and prized space that provides politics everywhere with a sense of ultimate worth – it constitutes a value to be upheld and defended. Security is felt through experiences of (de)stabilization, which all surveyed documents use to underscore the linearity of peace. Peace can be lost through 'destabilization', but it can also be recovered through its linear opposite – 'stabilization'. This linearity is a quasi-quantitative lens that summarizes the eventfulness of the world. Global stability has its balanced state – an equilibrium between stabilization and destabilization. It can be 'restored' (President of the United States of America 2002, 9) and instability can be 'reversed' (President of the United States of America 2010, 26) and 'controlled' (President of the United States of America 2001). Global stability has its 'factors' (President of the French Republic 2013) and an internal mechanics. Nonetheless, its trajectory is *'difficult to predict'* (Ibid) and stability can be preserved only through the monitoring of risk. Since stability is a matter of degree, anything can be risky. *'The maintenance of a secure environment'* (UN Security Council 2002) requires that *everything* be subject to risk calculus and observed out of defensive necessity.

National and international strategic statements use *global stability* (rather than merely 'national security') to explain why Western/Northern populations should still think of 9/11 as an immediate experience and why organized crime in Afghanistan should concern them as a matter of self-defence. The productivity of this discourse is astonishing given its artificiality, at least as outlined here. At what point can one empirically describe the global as stable and secure, or the world as 'peaceful'? No single strategic document defines this and even questioning how global stability would look like sounds glib. Yet, precisely because of this unquestioned status and implied solemn meaning, and due to its lack of any definable core, global stability is invoked as the goal and engine behind prudent diplomacy, military spending, international alliances, development aid, state-building and peacekeeping. Unlike national security, *global stability* makes it possible to think of all of these security and defence practices as both self-interested and selfless. That global stability has no empirically testable content makes it all the more productive as a discourse: it can be invoked with few constraints upon the speaking subject, while conveying a both felicitously and perilously interconnected world where '*instability in the Middle East and Africa*' can cause '*instability and tensions in [Europe]*' (President of the United States of America 2017, 48). In other words, it is a low risk-high yield stock in power relations. In axiomatic set theory, global stability/security would be the 'empty set', yet one that does the productive work of allying together the UN Office on Drugs and Crime, the Iranian government, EU member states, Europol, Interpol, NATO's Resolute Support mission, and US Operation Freedom's Sentinel in monitoring and containing the lives and everyday movements of ordinary Afghans within and without Afghanistan.

Therefore, global stability/security has '*an anchoring role*' and operates as a master signifier, or a '*privileged discursive element*' (Laclau 2000, 70). Its content is assumed to be obvious, but – upon cursory scrutiny – it cannot be discerned. While its meaning is vague, global stability 'anchors' and structures security practices and makes meaningful the claim that the normal subject in New York, London, Tehran, Moscow or Beijing must be defended from the destitute brown body, whether it comes from beyond 'our' borders or it resides in the metropolis. Thus, global stability does the work performed elsewhere – concurrently – by other master signifiers such as 'freedom', 'progress', and 'civilization', overlapping with them in the proliferation of valuables that can be lost to racialized, classed and gendered Others. Empty as it may be, global stability is protected and prized for its work in demarcating the normal from the abnormal, the safe from the unsafe, the virtuous from the wretched, the developed from the failing. Global stability dominates transnational politics because both the normal and the abnormal wish to inhabit it, yet few can safely call themselves its permanent residents. Even relatively affluent Afghans get deported from Europe and Iran, or lose investment privileges in Dubai.

Most insidiously, this powerful signifier only works in relation to that which it debases and targets as a threat. In interpreting Franz Neumann, Jef Huysmans articulates this paradox through a lucid proposition that '*security is about securing against insecurities*' (Huysmans 2014, 3–4). In other words: '*There is no way of doing security without foregrounding insecurities*' (Ibid, 4). Without the ritualistic repetition of ossified phrases in UN Security Council resolutions about the '*situation in Afghanistan*' (even before 9/11) or the promises of UK, French, EU, NATO, and US aid to Afghanistan to fight extremism, organized crime, population displacement and poverty – the audience would be at pains to imagine the need for global stability, let alone to internalize its obviousness. Yet, global stability can produce both normal and abnormal subjects (and shape their conducts) because it conveys that to be stable means *not* to be *of* or *in* Afghanistan. Thus, being stable and *in the global* might even include the pariah Iranian government (depending on the context). Since Afghan '*women and girls*' (in UN parlance) remain the designated victims of Afghan cruelty and instability, global stability represents itself as racialized, classed and gendered in reference to its racialized, classed and gendered Other – the brown man. However, as Afghan women show inability for self-defence, weakness and even complicity in own oppression, they, too, need to be corrected, empowered and educated to become global citizens. Even so, it is best if they become and remain global in Afghanistan. Judith

Butler highlights these spatial and distancing effects of the global and universalism, for their cleanliness, normality, and virtue *must be defended*:

> Universality is an 'emergence' [*Entstehung*] or a 'non place', 'a pure distance, which indicates that the adversaries do not belong to a common space'. (Butler 2000, 37–38)

Thus, the meaning of global stability as *distance* is impossible without iterative references to the threat that is said to eclipse it. Like 'peace' and 'freedom', the repeated and vague invocations of global stability reify it into an obvious policy goal with a deceptively commonsensical meaning. Once unpacked, peace and stability reveal ambiguous or no content beyond, paradoxically, imaginations of risk and threat. That which is to be defended is whatever is *threatened by* the racial, class and gendered abnormal, which itself is made meaningful by that which it *threatens*. The threatened Self is exhausted *in* the threatening Other, a circular paradox that echoes David Campbell's analysis of American foreign policy (Campbell 1992). Such circularities, tautologies, and self-referential 'empty-set' ontologies inform the taken-for-granted value of instruments used to serve 'global security', a point to which I return in the conclusion of this chapter.

Afghans in Global Security: The Necessary Threat

This chapter has mapped out how (post)colonial discourses constitute Afghans as aberrant and ominous. Since 2001, those representations have helped construct a global stability threatened by a violent population that rejects order. I will briefly consider the application of global security strategies in Afghanistan in relation to other 'security events' to highlight internal contradictions in the cordoning off and pathologization of Afghanistan. On one hand, the military strategy does not visibly correlate to the insurgency's capabilities on the ground. On the other hand, there is no plausible causal link between Afghanistan's alleged abnormality and the policies enacted against it in defence of Western/Northern populations. Ordinary Afghans can barely navigate one of the most restrictive visa regimes against any country in the world, and many struggle to access arable land, potable water, electrical power, schoolbooks and healthcare. Yet, based in the imagery of two passenger planes slamming into the World Trade Center on 9/11, national and intergovernmental security strategies highlight global 'interconnectedness' (President of the United States of America 2017, 45) as the vehicle and amplifier of risk originating in Afghanistan. A people and a land cordoned off from their neighbours and the wider world are thought to be dangerous for the globe because they have experienced modernity.

Brutalizing as global stability has been to ordinary Afghans, does targeting them militarily and economically serve its ends anyways? Can nearly two decades of military 'assistance', occupation, and economic remodelling of Afghanistan stamp out terrorism 'at home' and 'globally'? None of the 9/11 plane hijackers were from Afghanistan. While the presence of Al-Qaeda in the country dates back to the 1980s, the financial and organizational network that has supported it originated elsewhere (in the Gulf, the United States, and Pakistan) (Gerges 2011). Bin Laden was crucial to the organization and funding of foreign fighters against the Soviet Union and its client Afghan government until 1989. He was also based in Afghanistan between 1996 and 2001, and Al-Qaeda has run training camps in the country since the 1980s. According to intelligence reports, the Taliban and Al-Qaeda have cooperated as anti-Western insurgents, although their relationship has been unstable since October 2001 (Ibid, 177–187). Therefore, one might argue that the continuity of operation of terrorist and insurgency networks in Afghanistan requires NATO's long-term and open-ended presence there.

However, even after the numbers of Al-Qaeda combatants dwindled in 2009, NATO and the United States did not start pulling out troops until 2012. Conversely, the organizational and financial recovery of Al-Qaeda since 2013 (McNally and Weinbaum 2016) has not compelled the international coalition to boost ground troops back to 2009-2012 levels. Neither did the steady expansion of the Taliban since 2015. The insurgency controls or contests around 70 per cent of Afghanistan's territory (Sharifi and Adamou 2018) and President Trump's deployment of an additional 3,500 troops has not reversed the trend. Although the United States has intensified the bombing campaign in Afghanistan in 2017 and 2018, that has not reduced areas under Taliban control. Yet, no change in US strategy is in sight. In other words, 'battleground' developments do not correlate to the strategies of military interventionism in Afghanistan. Moreover, terrorists do not need Afghanistan to plan and conduct attacks against Western targets – Al-Qaeda's Hamburg cell and Daesh's cell in Brussels illustrate that.

Nonetheless, in solidifying Afghanistan as a place of risk, two terrifying threats have been merged: Americans, Europeans, Indians, and others are being warned about Afghan terrorists with nuclear bombs, or chemical, biological, and radiological weapons (Gerges 2011, 6–7, President of the United States of America 2010, 4, President of the French Republic 2013, 41, Allison 2004). By injecting weapons of mass destruction (WMDs) into the imaginations of global terrorism (Levi 2007, Stern 2001), both threats become inflated. This makes the surveillance, pacification, population containment and military control of Afghanistan appear necessary and inevitable. A US government report from 2003 asserted that there was '*a high probability that al Qaeda [would] attempt an attack using a CBRN [chemical, biological, radiological, and nuclear] weapon*' within 'two years' (Mowatt-Larssen 2010, 9). In 2004, Graham Allison claimed that a nuclear terrorist attack on America was likely in the coming decade (Allison 2004). Time has shown that these warnings were exaggerated, much like President Obama's similar missive from 2010. While American neoconservatives and some WMD proliferation experts pointed to Al-Qaeda's alleged anthrax and chemical weapons capabilities prior to October 2001 (Phillips 2016, Mowatt-Larssen 2010), this argument seems overstated. After all, the fall and winter of 2001 would have been the opportune moment for Al-Qaeda to deploy these arsenals against the invading US troops. Most analysts argue that Afghan insurgency networks do not currently possess nuclear or other WMD capabilities (Hummel 2016, Mowatt-Larssen 2010, Toukan and Cordesman 2009, Jenkins 1998). Finally, even if Al-Qaeda or the Taliban took over Pakistan's allegedly poorly guarded nuclear missiles, this would not make NATO's presence in Afghanistan more consequential. First, barred the unlikely prospect of a Taliban nuclear assault on NATO bases in Afghanistan, Pakistan does not possess the nuclear capacity needed to target the United States or Europe – the country's longest-range missiles are of only medium range. Second, a nuclear-powered Taliban state could behave like any other actor in bilateral nuclear confrontations and use its nuclear capacity for deterrence. Regarding the scenario in which a terrorist organization could detonate a nuclear or radiological weapon on US soil, Brian Jenkins summarized a straightforward counterargument:

> The fact that, despite nearly three decades of intense world-wide terrorist activity and more than 25 years of warnings, nuclear terrorism has not occurred suggests that nuclear terrorism is neither attractive nor as easy as it is often imagined. (Jenkins 1998, 243)

Another two decades have passed since this remark. Moreover, the attention paid to the threat of 'Islamic terrorism' (particularly that tied to Afghanistan) and foreign policy, defence, and financial resources dedicated to 'fighting' it well exceed its effects on Western populations relative to other security preoccupations. The commonly mentioned terrorist groups kill many more people in the Middle East, North and sub-Saharan Africa and Central and South Asia than in Europe or North America. In fact, 85 per cent of all incidents caused by 'Islamist extremists' occurred in majority Muslim societies over the 2011-2016 time period (Cordesman 2017). Alex Nowrasteh shows that '*from September 12, 2001, until December 31, 2015, 24 people were murdered on U.S. soil by a total of 5 foreign-born terrorists*', whereas '*80 people were murdered in terrorist attacks committed by native-born Americans and those with un-known nationalities*' (Nowrasteh 2016, 6). While the imagery of 9/11 is invoked as the reality of the 'Global War on Terror', '*the foreign-born terrorist murder rate of 1.047 per 100,000 in 2001 is 176.3 times as great as the next highest annual rate of 0.0059 in 2015*' (Ibid). In fact, '*the statistical mode (meaning the most common number) of the annual murder rate by foreign-born terrorists is zero*' (Ibid). The probability of an American dying at the hands of a terrorist immigrant is one in 3.6 million (including the outlier effect of 9/11) (Ibid). Moreover,

> assume for a moment that one 9/11-like event killed 3,000 Americans per year, and indefinitely ... the typical American is still far more likely to die walking out the door, getting into a car, jumping into a pool, or simply standing up. (Mosher and Gould 2017)

Business Insider drew on Nowrasteh's statistics, National Security Council, National Center for Health, and other sources and concluded that an American is more likely to be killed by a local police officer than a foreign-born terrorist. An American has a higher chance of being killed by an asteroid than a 'refugee terrorist' or an '[undocumented] migrant terrorist' (Mosher and Gould 2017). Furthermore, there have been '*301,797 firearm-related deaths*' in the United States in the 2005–2010 period. Conversely, only seventy-one Americans died in combined 'domestic' and 'international' terror attacks carried out on US soil by both American and foreign-born individuals over the same period (Qiu 2015). While 'jihadist' terrorism is a likewise extremely rare event in Europe, annual and overall casualty statistics in the EU are higher than in the United

States (excluding 9/11). In 2017, sixty-two people were killed in the EU in 'jihadi' terror attacks (Europol 2018, 23). By comparison, an average of 1,000 EU citizens die in homicides each year (Flemish Peace Institute 2015). There have been fewer than two-dozen terror incidents in Europe and North America correlated with Al-Qaeda, ISIS and Al-Shabaab since 2014. Only four perpetrators (out of dozens of attackers) were non-US or non-EU citizens (most were French, Belgian, and American) (Lister, et al. 2018). This further complicates restrictive immigration practices and justifications of EU and US armed presence in the Middle East, North Africa and Afghanistan. Only two perpetrators – Omar Mateen and Riaz Khan Ahmadzai – had any connections with Afghanistan, however immaterial.

Nonetheless, Western law enforcement and defence expenditures justified by the 'security situation in Afghanistan' have ballooned since 2001. The United States has spent over a trillion US dollars on the Afghan war since 2001, $45 billion in 2018 alone (Pennington 2018). USAID has pledged $62.5 billion since 2006 to Afghan development, governance, and state-building (ForeignAssistance.gov 2018), adding to a litany of donors who work to fund and defund their way to a pacified Afghanistan. Rather than argue that the West is not getting its money's worth, I question the rationality of security and development interventions. Why control populations in the name of global security if they are already victimized by it? While both global stability and its 'extremist' enemies undermine the life chances of ordinary Afghans, the weak remain designated as spaces of risk, terror, social-economic desperation and disease. This representation persists even if no causality has been shown to link the surveillance of everyday life in Afghanistan with population safety in the terrified North/West. The UN Special Rapporteur of the Human Rights Council confirmed as much when he found '*little evidence ... that terrorists take advantage of refugee flows to carry out acts of terrorism*' (Emmerson 2016, 4). I emphasize that because migration 'crises' are regularly invoked to justify open-ended population management in Afghanistan (Hammerstad 2014, 271–289).

Likewise, it is difficult to argue that the presence of US and NATO troops in Afghanistan is indispensable to countering opium production and trade. Alarming opium and heroin production statistics enable 'global governance' institutions as the obvious leaders in the 'war on drugs'. In 2007, the UNODC reported that Afghan producers supplied 93 per cent of the '*global opiates market*' (UN Office on Drugs and Crime 2007, iv). From 2016 to 2017, the total area of Afghanistan used for opium poppy cultivation grew by 63 per cent (UN Office on Drugs and Crime 2017, 5) following a 70 per cent increase between 2011 and 2014 (UN Office on Drugs and Crime 2015, 12). Thereby, Herat is a 'smuggling route' and a 'trading gateway' that threatens Europe's youths and the sick (Peters 2009). Such statistical representations enable the maintenance of power that associates international troops to the vague imperatives of global stability. The United States supported drug-dealing warlords in the 1980s and prior to the 2001 invasion of Afghanistan (Scott 2003). In post-Taliban relations of governance, the US has used drug lords as allies to gather intelligence and pacify localities across the country. In return, it has allowed them to conduct their business undisturbed. Moreover, United States defence and private security contractors benefit from the 'public-private partnership' in a war on drugs that treats differently American allies and foes (McCoy 2016, Ackerman 2015). A UNODC executive director has pointed to NATO's ambivalence in the eradication of the opium poppy, since the Alliance is '*wary of making enemies out of opium farmers*' (Costa 2007). Furthermore, he has maintained that '*money made in illicit drug trade has been used to keep banks afloat in the global financial crisis*' (Ibid). The image of an aberrant, violent, and dysfunctional Afghanistan makes it possible to forget that opium and heroin production have exploded since the US invasion of the country, and that opium is not natural to Afghanistan.

Overall, there are at least two gaps in the discourse of global stability threatened by Afghan abnormalities. First, Afghans have little or no agency in the construction of a West/North at peril and, in fact, can be hardly shown to affect it. The only association of ordinary Afghans with 'global risks' is their racialized, classed and gendered subjectivity, which recasts them as desperate brown men and compliant brown women. Thus, they look like a convenient cast of villains and victims of the '*Greater Middle East*' – the central geopolitical code of modern global governance (Güney and Gökcan 2010). Second, strategies deployed in Afghanistan hardly correlate with the basic goals of European and US national security in the country, whether it is the uprooting of the insurgency or the eradication of the opium poppy. If so, why are the United States, NATO, EU, UN and others present in Afghanistan at various levels of life and government?

The narrow debate over the successes and failures of security governance in Afghanistan obscures a broader dynamic. Postcolonial security does not defend so much the 'West' or the Afghan people. No internally consistent narrative can be recovered on how any of the strategies of Afghan security governance make the proverbial 'world' or the 'West' safer. However, this has not made the discourses of global security any less productive. Out of them, there emerges an Afghanistan of uncertainties, risks, possibilities, and threats: a place where new forms of governance are possible because they are in demand. In other words, the defence of normal life everywhere is necessary as a natural response to disorder anywhere. Saving 'global' lives matters to the balance sheet of postcolonial security (it is its axiom that their sovereignty cannot be endangered). Conversely, brown lives are treated as more expendable. But if that axiom were all that mattered, global security would be exhausted in racialized violence.

The calculus of postcolonial security is more intimate: it is about how lives – both 'global' and 'brown' – are lived. Postcolonial power relations stimulate the production of entrepreneurial and peaceful middle-class life through development and state-building strategies that exclude and inhibit volatile and useless elements of society. This makes global stability transnational, trans-corporeal and intimate in its ambition. It perpetuates the anxiety of the global body over its survival. It enables security and development 'solutions' for anxiety – interventions that cannot be shown to defend the global body even if the claims of 'Middle Eastern' threats are taken at face value. It constricts the movement and worth of all brown bodies, but improves the life chances of those who can still be redeemed and normalized through orderly politics, microloans, export opportunities, non-threatening religious practices and subsistence-level jobs. Both ends of the racial hierarchy – 'global' and 'brown' bodies – are subject to global stability, albeit in disparate ways. This spatial disconnect privileges the voice of global security – an empty signifier safeguarding the rationality of normal life.

Heratis at Risk

Tackling the third underlying question of this chapter, I reverse the privileged focus on the professed normal and instead examine *risk felt by Heratis*. This section zeroes in on the effects of 'global security' and the War on Terror on Heratis. While Herat is typically categorized as one of the safest provinces and cities in Afghanistan, I scrutinize safety and security in it as a social discourse. I do so to argue that (in)security is contingent upon one's bodily experience of space, gender, class, ethnic/tribal belonging, ability, sexuality, health, etc. These markers make it difficult to homogenize Herat as (un)safe. Instead, they indicate contingencies, uncertainties and probabilistic experiences of corporeal integrity. Bodily subjectivities become vulnerabilities useful to the expansion of postcolonial power.

Herat Province has been redrawn as an administrative, cadastral, political and economic space of power contestations since 2001. While exposed to lower degrees of violence compared to provinces such as Kandahar, Helmand or Uruzgan, it has experienced the violence of the coalition forces, the Taliban, smaller insurgent groups, the Islamic State, gangs and regional warlords. This, along with the presence of high-value military assets (e.g. the Shindand airbase), distinguishes Herat as a space of development and security. Across Herat, conflict is simmering and roadside bombs, kidnappings, suicide attacks and armed clashes are regular. A 2006 US government report described Herat as an environment '*where instability precludes heavy NGO involvement, but where violence is not so acute that combat operations predominate*' (Morris, et al. 2006, 23). A US government (SIGAR) report from 2018 designated Herat City as 'controlled' by the Afghan government and most of the Province under '*Afghan government influence*' (Sopko 2018a, 71). According to NATO's statistics on civilian casualties from January through mid-August 2018, Herat had the thirteenth lowest fatality count out of the country's thirty-four provinces (Ibid, 81).

Therefore, the grids of armed control and authority contestation in the Province are in flux. ANSF, the central government and the provincial governor are largely in control of Herat City and bigger towns like Ghourian. Typically, such towns and their immediate surroundings are also marked by more extensive governance agendas, larger budgets, and more assertive governing bodies (e.g. provincial development councils) supported by Kabul and international donors. Unlike the larger urban spaces, Herat's rural districts are more heavily affected by the insurgency. There, the 'state structure' has altogether collapsed in parts of the Province (Dorronsoro 2009, 28) and has been substituted by the Taliban, other insurgency groups, or individual strongmen (National Directorate of Security Employee No. 1 2014). However, rural-urban distinctions only partially capture the Herati experiences of security. Herat's power matrix is more ambiguous and its (in)security more contingent. Real levels of felt (in)security vary across places, bodies and time. They are also contingent upon the intensity, spatial distributions and frequency of insurgent attacks, local ANSF conduct, clashes between strongmen and wider crime. Thus, a district (e.g. Shindand or Kushki Kuhna) nominally controlled by the government may often be only partially, even marginally controlled by ANSF, and tax collection may be disrupted, defunct or colonized by the Taliban or smaller insurgent factions. The government often controls only majority portions of the town of Shindand with US and NATO troops monitoring the airbase, while certain frontier territories across the Province switch hands over time. Furthermore, 'grey zones' have been subject to regular insurgent attacks and IED explosions (Marty 2015, TOLOnews 2015), rendering them loosely governed. According to Obidullah Yari, deputy head of Herat's Craftsmen's Union (Yari 2015), and Shah Mohammad, an Afghan National Army (ANA) instructor (Mohammad 2015), the contingency of (in) security makes it difficult for ordinary Afghans to gauge where 'they' (often left vague upon my insistence to clarify) will attack. While certain places (e.g. remote country roads and flee markets) are deemed less secure and riskier on average, the contingency and fluidity of authority and security undermine the predictability of threats for ordinary people, as well as their calculus of personal responsibility. For instance, even as private security and volunteers have been recruited to protect Shia mosques and gatherings in the city, the Shia body is treated as inherently alien. This intensifies their experience of risk: *'The feeling of anti-Shia threat is always there, especially for women*,' which *'the Taliban and the Islamic State despise as fickle infidel whores'* (Herati NGO Activist No. 2 2018). In fact,

> since they [the Taliban and the Islamic State] see the Hazara and the Farsiwan Shia as weak and feminine, I've heard that they sometimes joke about how Shia mosques and Ashuras are just a bunch of unaccompanied women, which is immoral and should be banned. (Ibid)

Therefore, places such as ANSF checkpoints or mosques are both heavily secured and vulnerable to insurgent attacks or clashes between warlords (Ghanizada 2014). Conversely, locations considered continuously threatened by insurgent attacks (e.g. the Iranian, former US, Indian and Pakistani consulates) are targeted comparatively rarely (less than once a year). Classified UN *'residual risk accessibility'* studies and maps of Afghanistan (Trofimov 2010) hint at this fluidity. Two such maps that leaked to the public trace changes in security between March and October 2010 and convey Herat's ambiguous status: parts of the Province shifted from 'high' to 'medium' risk within six months, while most of it was labelled 'low' risk. No part of Herat was deemed 'free' of risk.

Furthermore, certain macro-social statistics available for Herat and Afghanistan call attention to two interrelated themes. First, they point to the precariousness of life for ordinary Heratis and Afghans who struggle to sustain own life chances, often against the pressures of postcolonial security. They redirect attention from the fragile globe to populations whose fragility has been reproduced by global (post)colonial forces. Second, even aggregate statistics can illustrate population discrepancies and can begin to elucidate that security is *not overall*, but population and body-specific. At the level of national poverty and inequality statistics, the World Bank has reported that, in 2016-2017, 54.5 per cent of all Afghans lived below the national poverty line of approximately $1 a day, up from 38 per cent in 2012 (Haque, et al. 2018, 5). In Herat, 48 per cent of the provincial population lives below the poverty line (NSIA 2018, 72) and over 50 per cent of all Heratis experience protein deficiency in their nutrition (CSO 2018, 130). While rural poverty has been seen as the Achilles heel of Afghan welfare, urban poverty, too, has doubled since 2007 (Haque, et al. 2018, 5). The growth of the urban poor has particularly affected Herat, more than almost any other city in Afghanistan (CSO 2018, 111). Poverty is negatively correlated to education (Ibid, 5–6) and this accentuates the socioeconomic vulnerability of girls and women. Namely, in Herat, the Gender Parity Index in education has collapsed between 2011-2012 and 2016-2017 from 1.02 (primary education), 0.9 (secondary education), and 0.69 (tertiary education) down to 0.02, 0.06, and 0, respectively (the latter figure indicating that the number of women in universities is negligible) (NSIA 2018, 71). Furthermore, children from better-off families (the highest income quintile) are twice as likely to attend school than children from the country's poorest households (Haque, et al. 2018, 32). While employment rates have declined across the board since 2011-12, the decline has been the sharpest for rural women, as around 130,000 jobs have been lost in Herat's rural districts (Ibid, 6). In Herat's urban milieu, single women, widows, and female-headed households suffer more from food and job insecurity (Hall 2014), and often experience workplace verbal and physical (including sexual) harassment. Socioeconomic and physical insecurity compel them to rely on relatives for financial assistance and protection (Ibid), which, in turn, reinforces their vulnerability. Moreover, the share of Heratis who live in overcrowded households (of more than three persons per room) has jumped to 34.7 per cent (from 25.9 per cent in 2007-08) (NSIA 2018, 72), which disproportionately affects the quality of life for women and girls.

An important aspect of housing inequalities in Herat is the situation of internally displaced persons (IDPs), mostly from the neighbouring provinces (Ghor, Badghis, and Farah) or the rural districts of Herat. They are, by and large, constrained to living in informal settlements around Herat City. While the number varies over time, around 2,000 IDPs have lived in Shaidayee, Maslakh, and Minaret (main informal settlements) as of 2017 (European Asylum Support Office 2017, 18), down from 6,500 families in 2011 (Redaelli 2011, 16). There, most live in overcrowded tents or shacks and struggle to access education, health services, electrical power, sanitation, and potable water (European Asylum Support Office 2017, 63–64). Less recent IDPs (i.e. those who have lived in Herat City for about a decade) tend to enjoy marginally better conditions: they live in mud-and-brick sheds and have established social networks that allow them to access or create more stable jobs. While the IMF and the World Bank pressure the government in Kabul to 'balance' the national budget and cut social spending (International Monetary Fund 2018), the impact of such measures on the life chances of the homeless, disabled, underemployed, IDPs and repatriated refugees does not seem to be a top priority. In a 2018 IMF country report, it is the 'financial sector' that is 'vulnerable', not the Afghans (Ibid). The relationship between public spending and the population's quality of life is trivialized as merely one inscrutable indicator – 'pro-poor spending' (Ibid). The global neglect of, and restrictions upon the social safety net in Afghanistan undermine the well-being of Heratis across the socioeconomic, tribal, geographic and ethnic spectrums, but particularly affect women, children, the homeless, the disabled, war veterans, IDPs and returnees. Herat ranks among the provinces most affected by *idiosyncratic household shocks*, which include sudden bankruptcies of family businesses, incapacitating illnesses, accidents or deaths of working household members; loss of house or land, sudden loss of employment of a household member, etc. (Ibid, 258). In 2017, Afghan poverty indicators were worse than immediately after the fall of the Taliban (CSO 2018, 97–116).

Diminishing the life chances of ordinary Afghans, 'weapons releases' by US manned and unmanned aircraft have soared since early 2017, reaching monthly spikes as high as 200 per cent compared to the fall of 2016 and 2015 (Woody 2018). In March 2018, more *'bombs and other munitions'* were dropped on Afghanistan than Iraq and Syria *combined*, an ignoble first since the US-led anti-ISIS intervention began in 2014 (Wellman 2018). The United States has deployed advanced surveillance and ground-attack jets with unparalleled destructive capability to kill resilient, yet technologically inferior insurgent troops who live and operate in makeshift conditions. The disproportional show of force has increased environmental destruction and civilian casualties. In 2017, 631 civilians were injured or killed in US and US-supported aerial bombings (including drone strikes), which was a 7 per cent increase over the 2016 baseline, and another sixty-nine civilians died in targeted killings (as 'collateral damage') by US and US-aligned forces. Civilian casualties in 'ground engagements' of insurgents reached nearly 3,500 in 2017 (UNAMA Human Rights Service 2018a). Yet these figures were dwarfed by the trends observed between January and June 2018. *'During the first six months of 2018'*, the UNAMA mission *'recorded a 52 percent increase [in civilian casualties] from the same period in 2017'* (UNAMA Human Rights Service 2018b, 5).

Herat was the seventh deadliest region for Afghan civilians in 2017, with a 37 per cent increase in civilian casualties compared to 2016 for a total of 495 (238 deaths and 257 injured) (UNAMA Human Rights Service 2018a, 67). Specifically, thirty-eight deaths and twenty-nine injuries came from counterinsurgency 'ground engagements' (Ibid, 21). Some casualties were also women murdered by the Taliban for supposed moral transgressions (Ibid, 10). On August 28, 2017, Afghan Air Force killed nine children and eight women, and injured three women in Herat's Shindand district (Ibid, 46). An Islamic State suicide bombing attack on Herat's Jawadia mosque (a well-frequented Shia site) on August 1, 2017 killed thirty-three and injured sixty-six civilians. On March 25, 2018, another Islamic State suicide attack occurred outside a Shia mosque in Herat (Nabi Akram), killing one and wounding seven. This was one of at least seven attacks on Shia mosques since 2016 (Clark 2018). The escalating politics of insecurity have led to a government-sanctioned recruitment of volunteer vigilante guards around Shia houses of prayer (Ibid). A Herati Shia-Hazara neighbourhood has been repeatedly targeted in the 'sectarian' violence blamed on the Islamic State (UNAMA Human Rights Service 2018a, 41).

This dizzying slew of statistics is meant to re-centre the reader's concern away from the globe threatened by a volatile country of brown tribesmen. Rather than provide a finite map of Herati vulnerabilities, I want the Herati to be seen without caveats, as a complex subject of postcolonial security. My goal is to invite the reader to abandon an empty signifier ('global stability') and, instead, look to the corporeality of postcolonial subjects for clues about the inequity of life chances in an era of global security. Thus, the contingency of (in)security in Herat is more than temporal, *macro*-spatial and situational. Real and felt security is also *micro*physical and embodied. It reflects and constitutes one's subjectivity: what it means to suffer an 'idiosyncratic shock' or not, have a home or be homeless, be a Sunni man, a Shia woman, straight or queer, a wife or a widow, a Pashtun, Tajik or a Hazara, etc. While the ensuing chapters touch only on some of these divides, I try to make a general appeal to situate security in corporeal subjectivity and study it as intersectional.

Whose Risk Matters?

Finally, whose bodily protection is prioritized in postcolonial Herati geographies? To address this question, it is useful to unpack how risk is managed around brown and global bodies in their shared spaces. Therefore, I study security and development programs that enable Herati encounters with the UN, NATO, EU, NGOs, etc. These encounters blur dominant spatial binaries (e.g. international/national, external/internal, foreign/domestic, public/private, etc.) without erasing them. Spatial enmeshments that *preserve* the external/domestic *boundary* enable Afghan state-building and reinforce Afghanistan's contested sovereignty. They also make brown bodies useful to the operation of postcolonial power. The insertion of Afghan populations into the external/domestic divide enables their subjection through surveillance and normalization. And while surveillance extends the operation postcolonial power, it also makes it more visible and more vulnerable to critique and counter-exploitation. It is, therefore, a risk worth taking. I develop this argument through Foucault's notion of security apparatuses (introduced in Chapter 2), which I use to study various security-development interventions, including NATO's Provincial Reconstruction Team in Herat, Herati Community Development Councils, and ANSF (the former two having been discontinued). I show how they have served to create 'the local community', engaging Afghans in non-coercive normalization processes. In addition to shaping Afghan conducts (e.g. via small-business financial grants or former-insurgent reintegration programmes), such interventions serve to develop lessons about individual and group Afghan propensities for aberrant, risky and threatening behaviours. They also redevelop metrics of 'success' of various pacification techniques (e.g. diversion of farmers away from poppy production to cultivating wheat, saffron or pomegranates). Overall, the necessity of governmental power (global stability) to normalize 'from within' results in mutual enmeshments of the 'external' and 'domestic', 'public' and 'private'. This is crucial to the expansion of power with minimal resistance within the population. I argue that such interventions ultimately *mitigate risk* for global stability (by observing, pacifying, confining, and knowing the threatening Afghan), while ignoring or escalating the risk felt by Heratis.

It is precisely the consistent portrayals of Afghans as perilous for global security that enable administrative, security and economic interventions into Afghanistan. The 'truths' about the Afghan that I have outlined in this chapter normalize and make necessary the external funding, training and management of apparatuses that are meant to pacify Afghanistan. Yet, these apparatuses are both 'external' ('foreign', 'international', etc.) and 'domestic' ('national'); both 'public' ('state' or 'sovereign') and 'private' ('non-state', 'corporate', or 'civil society'). To understand how the merger of these spaces (external/domestic and public/private) matters, I return to Foucault's notion of governmental power as a management of *things*, of enmeshed human and non-human elements of social reality. I focus on government as 'conducting the conduct' of reality by acting upon it 'from within' its natural course. According to Foucault, this strategy captures '*a synaptic regime of power, a regime of its exercise* within *the social body, rather than* from above *it*' (original emphasis) (Foucault and Gordon 1980b, 39). This view of power mobilizes security apparatuses as vehicles and spaces within, and through which power acts upon, manages and normalizes unruly reality.

Governing *within* Afghan populations creates spaces of more controlled contact with them. It incentivizes Afghans to participate in security governance instead of coercing them to be peaceful (which also occurs through sovereign and disciplinary strategies). Thereby, governmentality (government from within) minimizes Afghan resistances to security by rewarding their cooperation with *internationally supported domestic institutions*. (The stilted language hints at the paradox of 'Afghan sovereignty'.) Why would anyone resist jobs, orderly public institutions, reconstructed national monuments, business loans, the rule of law, and, ultimately, peace? Governing from within the problematic and threatening space allows the retesting of globally circulating hypotheses on how to improve and replicate 'sustainable development' and 'good governance', and how broader lessons can be learned and circulated elsewhere, in other 'troubled regions'. Therefore, governmentality is indispensable to globalized knowledge production.

Three Sets of Apparatuses: Governing through Spatial Enmeshments

Arrays of development, security and stabilization programmes, funds, institutions and bureaucratic mechanisms introduced into Afghanistan since 2001 are overwhelming. Therefore, I consider three such apparatuses to understand how postcolonial power works through them to pacify Afghans and defend global stability. Specifically, I analyse how postcoloniality defends itself through biopolitical distinctions between useful and useless – or *dangerous* – social practices and populations.

First, I briefly introduce three apparatuses of global security in Herat: the Afghan National Security Forces (ANSF), the Provincial Reconstruction Team (PRT-Herat) (non-operational since 2015), and the National Solidarity Program (NSP) (phased out in 2017). Second, I explore them as conflations of external/domestic and public/private spaces. This explains how the strategies of spatial hybridity surveil Afghans, test stabilization hypotheses on them, generate knowledge about them and enable global circulations of knowledge about volatile populations and failed states.

Eighteen years into the world's intervention in Afghanistan, the formation of NSP, PRT-Herat and ANSF seems interrelated and rapid. The PRTs' predecessor, the first Coalition Humanitarian Liaison Cell in Islamabad (Pakistan) was established in early 2002, followed by attempts to reboot the ANA the same year and the Afghan National Police (ANP) in 2003. ANA and ANP became the backbone of ANSF, which now also includes the Afghan Air Force, Afghan Local Police, Afghan Border Police, and the National Directorate of Security (NDS) (the country's key intelligence agency).

The 207th *Zabar* (Victory) *Corps* is the foundation of ANSF in Herat. The NSP was launched in 2003 as a micro-spatial and rural apparatus of 'self-governance' through small 'community development' projects, including irrigation, water supplies, school and road construction, education, etc. NSP project design and implementation engaged transnational NGOs and UN-Habitat (as 'facilitating partners'), bilateral donor agencies, the World Bank, and 'Community Development Councils' (CDCs) made up Afghan town residents. While ANSF has security, safety and law enforcement tasks and NSP was focused on development and reconstruction, PRT-Herat combined the two missions. However, all three apparatuses shared a common rationality: to expand sovereign, disciplinary, and governmental power in Afghanistan (against the ungoverned spaces and the insurgency) and 'stabilize' the social landscape (Jochem, Murtazashvili and Murtazashvili 2016, Davids, Rietjens and Soeters 2011). They have been tasked with monitoring security within the population and with creating spaces of 'peaceful' legal, political and economic order. 'Order' is reflected in the acceptance of one sovereign Afghanistan and one central government in Kabul, if not of the specific 'balance of power' among political parties and 'power brokers'. To paraphrase Foucault, order is achieved when '*everything that is prohibited has in fact been prevented*' (Foucault 2009, 46). In Afghanistan, the prohibited includes the warlords' rejection of Kabul's sovereignty, anti-global politics and the insurgent control of Afghanistan's large population, telecommunications, administrative, and industrial centres, transportation routes and border crossings. Therefore, security apparatuses are tasked with protecting the space and limit within which the circulation of life makes sovereignty meaningful and 'real'. If violence against a unified Afghanistan is inevitable, then postcolonial government can contain it to some tolerable degree of territorial contestation (e.g. around 30 per cent of rural Afghanistan controlled by the Taliban, ISIS and others). This allows for an equilibrium between more and less stability instead of a more costly suppression of any armed dissent (through a closer involvement of foreign troops akin to the 2009-2012 period).

How have the external and the domestic, the public and the private constituted and sustained each other in the operation of PRT-Herat, ANSF and NSP? Their hybridity is made possible through *at least two strategies*. First, all three apparatuses have been predominantly funded by external sources. Herat's first (US-led) PRT (2003-2005) was funded by the Department of Defense, Department of State, and USAID (Petrik 2016, 168, Perito 2005, 10). Italy's Ministry of Defense, Ministry of Foreign Affairs, and Cooperazione Italiana (governmental aid agency) funded its successor, the Italian-led PRT (2005-2014) (Ruzza 2013). ANSF is funded by over thirty NATO and non-NATO nations (e.g. Australia, South Korea, Japan, Russia, Saudi Arabia, etc.) that call themselves the 'International Community' and contribute to the ANA Trust Fund and the Law and Order Trust Fund for Afghanistan (LOTFA). The United States maintains a separate Afghanistan Security Forces Fund (ASFF) (NATO Public Diplomacy Division 2018). Finally, NSP was funded through the World Bank's International Development Association (itself a pot of transnational capital), the UK Department for International Development, the Danish International Development and Assistance Agency, the Canadian International Development Agency, and USAID (Beath, Christia and Enikolopov 2015, Sohail 2014). In NATO, US, Italian, and World Bank publications.² these funding schemes are portrayed as boosting the legitimacy of the Afghan government, as (re)constructing *one* national economy, and fostering a version of security that legitimizes the Afghan nation-state. Moreover, the variety of funding sources (state and non-state, Western/Northern, and Eastern/Southern) captures the transversal and heterogeneous (rather than 'Western' or 'American') geography of security governance. It shows that the discourse of global stability electrifies desires and anxieties from Moscow, Baku, Tbilisi, Beijing and Riyadh to Washington, realigning geopolitical foes into 'partners' in Afghanistan.

Second, ANSF, PRT-Herat and NSP have aimed to involve Heratis, engage their experience and employ their time, careers, aspirations, skills, knowledge and very bodies in the mission of Afghan 'stabilization'. ANSF recruits and officers are all Afghans – it is *them* (rather than foreign troops) who should '*take the lead*' and 'assume responsibility' for physical security in Afghanistan (NATO Public Diplomacy Division 2013). The recipients of NSP projects and development interventions were Herati 'rural communities', the explicitly invoked Afghan 'men', 'women', and 'children' (Beath, Christia and Enikolopov 2015). PRT-Herat (both US and Italian) prided itself on the inclusion of '*local civilian staff*' in logistics, conflict mediation, reconstruction project implementation, and service provision (Zajc 2014, Afzaly 2015). PRT-Herat used 'inclusion' and 'participation' as vehicles for local employment, a way to legitimize foreign intervention, as a growth and a 'hearts and minds' strategy. Thereby, the Italian PRT was predicated on reconstruction and population welfare more so than narrow security (Aresu 2014, La Piscopia and Croci 2012, Coticchia and Giacomello 2009). Furthermore, a governing trifecta of (1) prolonged training supervision, 'assistance', 'care', and 'advice' (O'Connel 2017), (2) constitutive documents and teaching manuals,³ and (3) monitoring practices extends the work of postcolonial management. It enables at least *two effects*.

First, the governing rationalities of PRT-Herat, ANSF and NSP foster hierarchical employment relations and surveilled livelihoods. In doing so, they create 'locals' logically contained to 'Afghan' land, households, and towns in a way that appears driven by Heratis themselves and their desire to improve own life chances. Postcolonial population deterrence through opportunities and choice dissuades Afghans from pursuing lives in Europe, Iran, Dubai or Australia, and pacifies them away from the financial and anti-imperial lure of the armed insurgency. Such incentive-based governing strategies of spatial containment have been tested elsewhere for decades, including Afghanistan in the 1990s (Duffield 2007, 133–158). As the postcolony exploits the population's natural wants, the faces of coercion and discipline are minimized, even as they remain embodied in multilayered spaces of control. Governmental power manages Afghan conducts through external funding schemes that can be – and have been – withheld, or through American and Italian supervisors who '*train, advise, and assist*' ANA's 207th Corps and ANP's 606 Zone in Herat. The

---

² For instance, see: Aresu, Emmanuele (2014). Il Provincial Reconstruction Team (PRT) in Afghanistan. *Informazioni della Difesa*. June: 5-13

³ For instance: *Community Development Council By-Law* (2006/7), *United States Plan for Sustaining the Afghanistan National Security Forces* (2008), consecutive *ISAF Provincial Reconstruction Team Handbooks*, etc.

postcolonial management of Heratis has worked through the conditional transfer of NSP funds to 'rural communities' or the contingent renewal of NSP based on geographic criteria, needs assessments (Nixon 2008), and any such 'community's' strategic relevance to the counterinsurgency (Sohail 2014, Mamundzay 2014, Yama 2014, Azizi 2014). In the process, the 'communities' remain excluded from funding decisions. Postcolonial mentoring and surveillance have worked through the ongoing procedures of instruction, training, and monitoring of project (in fact, population) performance by the NSP Steering Committee (composed of Afghan government and international donor representatives), two corporate 'oversight consultants' (German GIZ and American DAI Global), and the international NGOs who acted as NSP 'facilitating partners' on the fetishized 'ground' of development interventions. Overall, training and monitoring, formative documents and operation manuals bind Afghans to spatially definite livelihoods. They circumscribe Afghan movements to confined geographies, while portraying containment as non-coercive, non-hegemonic and self-driven.

Second, these instructional and mentoring practices recast security and development as Afghan, Heratic, and local rather than foreign, 'Western', or 'American'. This is because the body that an ANSF recruit or NSP CDC member most often encounters is brown and vaguely native, even if their language, accent, clothing, facial features or personal narratives are not always intimately familiar. The brownness of the more immediate hierarchy and supervisory relations obscures the global trajectories of funding, training and rulebooks that constitute these security apparatuses. With brown bodies explaining and monitoring how NSP joint accounts and CDC sessions should work, how software should be used on PRT-donated computers at the Herat Airport, or how physical fitness should be attained at ANA training camps – the progress of 'local' and 'regional' stability, the jobs, the industrial parks for 'local entrepreneurs', and bank loans feel, sound and look like they are from, by, within and for Herat. Therefore, as foreign public and private aid started declining in 2013 (Joya, et al. 2017, 2), Afghans were regrettably diagnosed as having (again) failed to create a sustainable economy and take responsibility for their country (Bandow 2017). The ledger of blame and failure has been reflected in the 'remedies' recommended to manage the declines in aid and Afghan macroeconomic indicators: the challenge has been framed as one of 'responsible' governance by the Afghan state (Islamic Republic of Afghanistan 2015). Thus, Afghanistan received a SMAF ('Self-Reliance through Mutual Accountability Framework') from the UN, IMF, EU and others. Despite its 'mutual accountability' rhetoric, SMAF's 'priority areas', 'indicators', and 'short-term deliverables' place the burden of effectiveness and responsibility on Afghan ministries and government agencies. For instance, '*accountability to the Afghan people*' is defined in terms of *Afghan government* accountability (Islamic Republic of Afghanistan 2015, 1), thereby remaining silent on how bilateral and multilateral donors are to be held accountable. Moreover, SMAF states: '*The [Afghan] government's delivery of the mutually agreed commitments will be key for sustained international support*' (Ibid). Thus, it relieves the donors of any agency (and responsibility) in the 'delivery' of 'commitments', while failing to acknowledge how Afghan lives have been conditioned through economic and military interventionism. Whereas benevolence is external, failure is domestic. If one doubts the assignment of merit and fault, all they need to do is look around and recognize the brown faces in charge of development and security 'on the ground'.

This is not to say that the effects of postcolonial government and containment always amount to either 'success' or 'failure'. It is not to say that people accept security and development as 'Afghan' or reject them as a foreign 'ruse'. As Barialay – my guide, interpreter and informant – noted in December 2014 during one of our long conversations:

> Some development money that circulates around here is USA dollars, but a lot of it is in Afghanis. And it mostly circulates from one Afghan to another, that's what most people see. And most bosses and employees in NGOs and the security forces are Afghans; mostly from here, from Herat. We sell, trade, go to work, and a lot of people risk their lives to work at the army, the police, even the Red Crescent. People often forget that 'stabilization' [uses air quotes] is us. But people also forget that all that stuff, that whole life can go away, and is going away. It's not really ours.

It is us, but not ours. Everyday life in Herat goes on because the necessity to work, start a business or have a family is not driven by any one development or security project. Much of Herati life is neither *due to* nor *in spite of* global security/development. Yet, many parameters and forces that have come to shape Herati lives are in flux and this has deepened Herati vulnerabilities. Global stability murders some, leaves others disabled, homeless or orphaned and provides livelihoods – only to take them away as foreign policies shift or one's politics become 'destabilizing'. Whether it is recent university graduates who have lost 'civil society' jobs that mushroomed post-2001 or farmers whose opium poppy production became a 'threat' overnight – the unpredictability, contingence and unaccountability of security governance has toyed with Afghan lives.

Do Heratis think about their lives (that feel 'local' and 'theirs') as affected by something global and foreign, both detached and ubiquitous? Barialay says that the political instability of life is always '*in the back of everyone's mind*' and that '*everyone knows that a lot of what happens to us doesn't depend on us*'. Heratis seem to be integrated into security and development interventions at nearly every step of their execution. Nonetheless, it is difficult to see friends, relatives, neighbours and acquaintances as embodiments of postcolonial power. Even if one knows that local jobs are often funded from somewhere else and that '*no one just gives money away without wanting some outcome*' (Afzaly 2015), it is inconceivable that Self is a postcolonial subject, nurtured just so he/she would not become desperate or radicalized, and thus perilous to the *Other*'s life. If we allow the disappointing possibility that power has no face, and yet that subjection is a bodily reality, then it becomes clearer why the postcolony can look and sound Herati, *brown*. For postcolonial government to work, Afghans need *not* legitimize 'the economy' and 'security' as *their own*. For the external and the domestic to be in each other, Heratis merely need to enact these shared spaces through 'participation', incomplete, resisted and discordant as it is. These entwinements have remade Herati spaces – from freshly painted facades of public institutions and large billboards advertising the beneficence of foreign donors to mundane sites of everyday life. One such site is the Herat International Airport. Blue plastic chairs in its departure hall bear pictures of fading Afghan flags with labels that read: *'This project has been implemented by Italian PRT in Herat.'* They echo the normalization, banality, and capillarity of Western/Northern presence in the Province.

Security Apparatuses and Experimentality

The centrality of the postcolony *being in the intimate*, of traversing the body, cannot be overstated. It is the flipside of the postcolonial subject's desire *to be in the modern and civilized*. Assuming the brown face and creating shared spaces with Heratis makes postcolonial power vulnerable and opens it up to critiques and resistances (as the ensuing chapters discuss). Nonetheless, spatial conflation is how the postcolony learns the strategies and tactics of living on – not as coerced upon life, but as an ally to 'stability' and 'progress'. In Chapter 2, I have described this practice as experimentality, or government through experimentation and probabilistic trial-and-error learning. The range of experimental programmes about how to govern and pacify the subject is as broad as the spectrum of apparatuses deployed to enable experimentality. Learning curves include macroeconomic growth strategies on how to combine fiscal discipline (controlling public spending) and NSP-style 'community-level development' (Mukherjee, Baird and Nabi 2008), ultimately resulting in the Heratis' heightened dependence on global financial forces. Likewise, they include 'lessons learned' on the methods and pace of liberalizing foreign trade in counterinsurgency conditions (Sopko 2018c), as well as the programming of economic privatization and 'private sector development' in conditions of 'state fragility' (Ibid). There, wealthy warlords and foreign companies keen on investment subsidies and facilitations undermine the prized project of building a 'capable' central government. Overall, macro and micro-economic experimentality favours the scientific, cultural and financial-lending hegemony of the IMF, the World Bank, and, to a lesser extent, the Asian Development Bank and UN bodies. According to the Special Inspector General for Afghanistan Reconstruction (SIGAR), the World Bank, which manages the largest Afghan reconstruction fund (ARTF), *'restricts donor and public access to how it monitors and accounts for ARTF funding'*, therefore *'leaving donors, and their taxpayers, without important information necessary to understand the activities they fund'* (Sopko 2018b, 6). While critical of the World Bank's leadership, SIGAR fails to recognize that Afghan 'program recipients' and ordinary people may also want to understand development and reconstruction 'activities' in Afghanistan. Afghanistan features in SIGAR's equation insofar as its government can be indicted for its (well-documented) complicity in the obscure management of aid (Ibid). SIGAR's 'lessons learned' include the need to increase donors' project surveillance, as well as their ability to abandon Afghan reconstruction, regardless of who is at fault for its lack of transparency or implementation failures (Sopko 2018b, iv).

Further in the field of aid, international agencies and contributing governments have used PRTs, NSP, and National Priority Programs to gauge the 'moral hazard' in deciding how to incentivize stabilization (from entrepreneurship to education and healthcare), while maintaining control over the agendas and conduct of Afghan civil servants and 'civil society' institutions (European Commission 2015). PRT-Herat devoted its 'learning curve' to tinkering with the extent and target populations for its 'quick-impact projects', including a swift education of Heratis about their city's cultural history (La Piscopia and Croci 2012). Coupling reconstruction and humanitarian projects with physical security through PRTs and US-led OEF often overshadowed the supposed need to protect civilians. Instead, it devolved into disputes over the security of humanitarian workers, or the prudence and modalities of merging development and military tasks alongside development agencies (USAID and Cooperazione Italiana) and NGOs (Petrik 2016, Mitchell 2015, Maley and Schmeidl 2015). Furthermore, Afghanistan has served as another testing ground for 'tied aid' and aid conditionality, leading to new data about the balance between conditional and unconditional aid, as well as new 'insights' about the improved use of aid conditionality (rather than its abandonment) (Gilmore 2011, Goodhand and Sedra 2007). Donors have also been retesting ways to coordinate aid, increase its effectiveness and study the impact of antipoverty, reconstruction, and alternative livelihood interventions (ATR Consulting 2018, Ward, Mansfield, et al. 2008). In addition, global donors and defence planners continue to evaluate the axiom that opium poppy production and insurgency recruitment are economic problems with global security and health implications. They keep exploring the hypothesis that financial and employment incentives can alter the behaviour of farmers, dealers and insurgents. Yet, the lack of strategic consensus results in hybrids of coercive opium poppy eradication, governmental incentives to abandon the production 'voluntarily', and delays in implementing either approach (Felbab-Brown 2010). Disarmament, Demobilization and Reintegration (DDR) strategies (for insurgency fighters) also continue to rely on this logic. While civilian-military apparatuses pretend to be testing the effectiveness of these approaches individually, they are unwittingly evaluating them *simultaneously* in an environment saturated with military, economic and administrative interventionism. That merely reinforces the marginalization of Afghan subaltern voices (e.g. agricultural wage labour) in the process.

This whirlwind of assumptions, hypotheses and programmes being tested *on* Afghanistan is just a sliver of experimental practices unfolding in the country. Since Afghanistan has been 'opened up' (Johnson and Leslie 2004, 99) in 2001, it has become a field of bodies utilized to calibrate how peace and stability are to be maintained in 'unstable regions' and 'failed states'. The constructed 'volatility' of Afghanistan calls for being experimented upon, since it is an acute problem yearning to be solved. Julian Reid has explored the biopolitical expansion of the UN-sanctioned 'Oil for Food' programme in Iraq, which started in 1995 as '*aiding the provision of food and medicine*' (Reid 2005, 245), only to grow by 2002 so far to include '*construction, industry, labour and social affairs, youth and sports, information, culture, religious affairs, justice, finance, and banking*' (Ibid). Likewise, Alan Ingram outlines the breadth of the decades-long health, development, and security interventions by the United States initially predicated on countering the HIV/AIDS across sub-Saharan Africa (Ingram 2011). While equally ambitious, the intimacy of population management in Afghanistan has deepened at a much faster pace since 2001, as the PRT-ANSF-NSP timeline and missions suggest. That any 'lessons' have been 'learned' is an affirmation of the productivity of weakness – of the fact that Afghanistan can be claimed as a space of experimentation, a mega-laboratory of sorts. It is a testament to the utility of inequality more than a tribute to a smooth design of government by experimentation.

The Rationality of Government through Experimentation

Even if experimentality is consequential, rather than successful, there is still a rationality to its usefulness as a strategy of power. While particular logics differ across apparatuses, the last bit of this chapter outlines the underlying rationality of experimental conflations of external/domestic and public/private spaces. I will discuss NATO and non-NATO troop contributing nations working with 1) Afghan recruits and officers in ANSF and 2) Afghan civilians and contractors in PRTs. Third, I examine the rationality of the World Bank, transnational NGOs, and bilateral donor agencies' operations in Herati villages alongside NSP CDCs, tribal and religious hierarchies and ordinary people. If global stability needs protection against risk, how do these apparatuses help manage it? How does this affect the Heratis?

Locating town, district, province, and countrywide equilibria between lethal tools of power and nonviolent inducements (e.g. microloans and alternative livelihood programmes) has been one of the common goals of experimentation with security and development in Afghanistan. General governance rationality drives this equilibrium. As mentioned in Chapter 2, the conduct of US, NATO, and UN policies in Afghanistan has been predicated on *efficiency* (financial, temporal, administrative, etc.) in attaining pre-defined stability and economic outcomes (Schroden 2013, CALL 2007). While efficient security provision is ostensibly pursued for Heratis, they have not defined it or designed the strategies of its pursuit. Moreover, efficiency is often sought at the expense of the very population that security governance claims to support. Herat has endured night raids, drone surveillance, erratic aid levels and conditionalities, and crossfire among the coalition forces/ANSF, warlords, the insurgency and criminal groups – all in the name of pressing security and humanitarian needs. Furthermore, NATO's efficient 'quick-impact' projects have made Afghans more vulnerable to deadly insurgent attacks and sabotage in 'contested' areas (Sexton 2016).

Therefore, the type of efficiency that Resolute Support (previously ISAF), OFS/OEF, and NSP are based upon is inward looking, intra-organizational and private to the US, NATO, and 'global' allies and donors (US Department of Defense 2017, Perito 2005). They are concerned with levels of financial, technological and human resources committed to UN, World Bank, IMF, NATO and EU missions. Beyond that, foreign governments and global institutions are wary of how their political capital is used, and how 'interoperable' international and Afghan agencies are within ANSF – and previously PRTs and NSP (Petrik 2016, 168, Szanya, et al. 2009, Rubin 2006). This puts on the backburner the needs of the Afghans who are allegedly being secured. The efficiency logic behind the funding and maintenance of NSP, PRT-Herat and ANSF is operationalized through aggregate and project, time and location-specific inputs and costs, and projected and actualized outputs and benefits. Critiqued as a work of power, however, these variables reflect *for whom* utility is sought. For instance, ANSF's mission is defined in terms of global stability (US Department of Defense 2008, 4) rather than the usual task of national defence.

Furthermore, casual descriptions of Afghanistan as dangerous and risky enable NATO and the UN to gloss over specifying *whom it is risky for*. Aided by the imaginations of a vulnerable globe, accounts of risk tacitly assume that international troops and civilian experts are the subjects in need of priority protection 'on the ground', for they are the agents and defenders of stability. Accordingly, this utility calculus neglects *lower-level* international civil servants and aid workers (Rubin 2013, 308–311, Perito 2005, 7, 9), as well as ordinary Heratis. The latter are, moreover, unequipped with racial and class privileges that could help them access better security (Fast 2014, Fluri 2009).

While interpretations of efficiency in security, development and economic reforms vary, they neglect Herati experiences of safety and well-being. Security and development metrics that operationalize the calculus of *'whether Afghanistan is worth it'* (Twining 2009) rarely – if ever – prioritize Herati deaths, losses of income and bodily injuries. A former State Department analyst even cautioned that *'the problem with the current debate over Afghanistan is that it is too focused on Afghanistan'* (Ibid). When 'Afghan' variables are included, they are not central to the ledger of success and worth, and feature only incidentally (US Department of Defense 2017, 27, US Department of Defense 2012, 31–32). While the UN is an outlier among global institutions in recording Afghan 'quality of life' statistics (UNDP 2018, UNFPA 2017), the organization makes no correlation between Afghan life chances and the effects of NATO, World Bank or IMF interventions in Afghanistan. NATO has not declassified the variables used to assess 'progress' and 'effects' of its Afghan missions. However, the Alliance's public conceptions of 'comprehensive security' privilege data on coalition troop casualties, the rates and counts of insurgency attacks, measurements of Afghan government capacity, and levels of 'legitimate socioeconomic activity' (Schroden 2013, 50). Ironically, what the Afghan government should be 'capable' of doing and what counts as 'legitimate' socioeconomic activity is pre-defined within NATO. Similarly, World Bank and IMF notions of growth and development are exhausted in aid levels, GDP, GNP and GNI statistics within the familiar frameworks of private enterprise, fiscal discipline, monetary stability, and trade liberalization (The World Bank 2018a, The World Bank 2018b, International Monetary Fund 2018). They are bequeathed to the Afghan government and economists to intuit how far along the scale of modernity their country has made it.

Moreover, hegemonic portrayals of Afghanistan's economy treat the life chances of ordinary Afghans as merely instrumental to global stability. Depicting Afghanistan as a 'sub-subsistence' and 'landlocked' economy should capture everything: the causes and effects of opium and aid dependency, the insurgency, 'market fragmentation', and an uncompetitive economy (Cordesman 2012, Ward, Mansfield, et al. 2008). Since 'growth' is apparently unrelated to politics, building an internationally competitive economy is recommended as Afghanistan's ticket out of 'poverty'. This neglects the hurdles in international trade for Afghanistan, the capture of productive resources by Western-aligned warlords, as well as the existing realities of production that are intended for household consumption and small-scale trade (rather than market competitiveness). Curiously, this discourse ignores at least one market force: the global demand that fuels the supply of Afghan opium. Ultimately, abstract commitments to market efficiency disregard evidence that subsistence farming (a cornerstone of

Afghanistan's pre-Soviet economy) can be beneficial and that imposing commercial farming practices can deepen social inequalities (Mitchell 2002).

How did operational efficiency shape the functioning of PRT-Herat (through 2014) and NSP (through 2017), and how does it still inform the work of ANSF? What learning processes should these apparatuses facilitate for the sake of global stability? In short, security apparatuses accept certain levels of risk as inevitable in the surveillance of, and learning about the postcolonial subject. This has made insurgent infiltration and insider attacks, 'ghost soldiering', and pilfering tolerable as long as security apparatuses can monitor the population: its pacification, views of the government and the 'international community', and its pathological propensities (for violence, illicit economic practices, sectarianism, religious fundamentalism, gender oppression, etc.). The frontline presence of brown bodies in ANSF, NSP's CDCs and PRT-Herat's logistics, implementation, maintenance and transportation services has made the risk-benefit trade-off less costly for global security. Therefore, the logic of operational efficiency informs the very tactical conduct of security and pacification. PRTs, ANSF and NSP did not use sovereign prerogatives to merely outlaw terrorism, poverty, insurgency or gender discrimination in government institutions. While significant resources have been mobilized to fight the insurgency, drugs and poverty, coercive measures alone are seen as insufficient in pacifying Afghanistan. Instead, global institutions recast the problem of insurgency as one of population volatility. If the population is volatile, strategies that are embedded within it are needed to pacify it. Thereby, *two steps* are crucial to the efficiency of governing from within.

First, PRT-Herat, NSP and ANSF have continuously surveilled roads, marketplaces, private homes, mosques, schools, government offices, crops, military barracks and other spaces of circulation that could benefit the insurgency as material resources, sources of recruitment or targets of attack. Beyond subjects with a criminal or militant past, surveillance has included religious and tribal leaders, distinguished politicians, warlords, and oligarchs (NDS Employee No. 1 2014, NDS Employee No. 2 2014). The United States, UN, and NATO describe the cooperation of prominent Afghans as paramount to 'stability' (Felbab-Brown 2013, Eide 2012), thereby blurring the lines between criminals, allies, deserving individuals, coalition enemies, public officials, and 'power brokers'. The population monitored through NSP, ANSF and PRTs is understood as fluid, contingent and its conduct aleatory – fluctuating between political constraints, threats and governing opportunities. The global institutions have deployed PRT-Herat, NSP, and ANSF to work within this uncertainty and normalize it through the use of warlords, and tribal, village and religious elders as allies in collecting intelligence, maintaining physical security, and suppressing poppy production, or by pitting warlords and/or Taliban leaders against one another in order to control general levels of violence. To manage the circulation of violence and illicit trade more efficiently, PRT-Herat, NSP, and ANSF have been used to observe and collect information about populations and power hierarchies across Herat Province. For instance, US SIGAR has repeatedly called on US Department of Defense (DoD) and (indirectly) NATO allies to improve the existing monitoring of ANSF capabilities, preparedness, corruption, and '*will to fight*' (Sopko 2017). Richard Holbrooke, President Obama's special envoy to Afghanistan (2009-2010), estimated that 90 per cent of US intelligence about Afghanistan came from aid organizations (Fast 2014, 117). Elsewhere, DoD acknowledged its 'monitoring' and population screening functions in the demilitarization and reintegration of former-insurgent fighters (US Department of Defense 2014, 20–21). Likewise, a high-ranking US official at the Herat PRT described his mission as *'watch[ing] the new governor'* appointed after the removal of Ismael Khan from power in March 2004 (US Foreign Service Officer in Herat 2005). According to this US official, his job entailed monitoring the relationship between the new governor, provincial government officials, local military leaders, warlords, and Khan's associates in Shindand and Herat (Ibid).

Second, PRTs, NSP and ANSF are deployed to operate within the dynamics of instability and uncertainty by recruiting ordinary Heratis into the armed forces, law enforcement, hundreds of CDCs or as PRT subcontractors. Thereby, the UN, NATO, the World Bank and the government in Kabul deliberately compete with the Taliban insurgency, Al-Qaeda, ISIS, local warlords and gang leaders for manpower and loyalty. NATO and Afghan ANSF commanders, the provincial governor and NSP governing bodies do not always know the individual criminal or paramilitary histories of recruited Heratis. However, they do know that some share of the eligible population has, in the past, fought or gathered intelligence for the insurgency, or participated in the illicit opium economy. ANSF recruits and private security sub-contracted by NATO, foreign companies, or NATO governments include populations who simultaneously pledge allegiance to warlords or the insurgency (McCain 2010). After nearly two decades of insurgent infiltration and deadly 'green-on-blue'[4] insider attacks, NATO commanders have learned that some ANSF recruits will be taking their weapons up against NATO troops or fellow ANSF service members. Likewise, the World Bank expected some NSP funding would be embezzled or spent in ways that violated gender equality (Kapstein 2017, Nixon 2008). Although some ANSF training programmes and PRT reconstruction projects were temporarily discontinued (US DoD 2012, 37), the rationality of NATO and the World Bank's engagement with the risks of mismanagement or death eclipsed such blanket solutions. As security apparatuses, ANSF and PRT-Herat have worked to learn about the profiles and patterns of insurgent and criminal 'infiltration' (Katzman 2013), as well as to determine why Afghans join and support insurgency groups and criminal gangs, what incentivizes illicit economies and aid corruption, etc. Learning through experimental trial-and-error procedures helps redesign counterterrorist and counterinsurgency strategies. However, for lessons to be learned, a degree of risk and uncertainty needs to be factored into the calculus of troop safety and financial-temporal efficiency. The probabilistic processes of ANSF funding, equipment procurement, recruitment and training remain perilous for NATO and its troops. Likewise, NSP projects fuelled corruption, conflicts over funding between NSP 'treatment' and 'control' villages, and strained gender relations during CDC elections and deliberations. Yet, these destabilizing dynamics have been governed through PRT-Herat, ANSF, NSP Steering Committee and NSP CDCs. They were absorbed into the strategy to weaken the insurgency and the illicit economy. When all risk is observable, its containment becomes feasible. Order is mapped out, if not attained.

---

[4] The term refers to insurgents who infiltrate ANSF and shoot at NATO, NATO-allied or US troops.

Conclusion: Herati Hearts and Minds

In conclusion, I will address two notions that I have tackled indirectly so far. The post-2001 attempt to reshape Herati towns into droplets of peace where '*working men don't rebel*' (Berman, Callen, Felter and Shapiro 2011) was predicated on winning the population's 'hearts and minds'. Alas, the imperatives of 'hard security' and counterterrorism have made the inaccuracies of lethal technologies (drones, jets, precision-guided munitions, and guns) more visible. As the Taliban – cruel and cannibalistic (Khamoosh 2015) – are being fought, some unintended civilian casualties, or 'collateral damage', are incurred. Thus emerges the narrative of US-led counterterrorism and collateral damage undermining the goals and popular effects of the 'hearts and minds' counterinsurgency strategies – a 'counterproductive' outcome of multiple overlapping and incoherent missions in Afghanistan (Eland 2013). Apparently, the rationale of counterinsurgency (to gain popular support) is undercut by a byproduct of counterterrorism (massacred Afghans). As state-building declined as a priority in 2014, this debate ostensibly lost steam, too.

However deprioritized, the debate is ongoing – still framed as an ill-fated binary between 'collateral damage' and 'hearts and minds' (Peña 2016). Nevertheless, it has been the implied contention of this chapter that winning over Afghan 'hearts and minds' is compatible with ignoring them as 'collateral damage'. The CIA echoed this when it found that 'effective' counterterrorist operations were integrated into '*comprehensive counterinsurgency strategies*' (CIA Office of Transnational Issues 2009, ii). (Apparently, this is another 'lesson learned'.) Both strategies objectify Afghan bodies as resources and targets in the War on Terror, as means deployable in defence of global security.

Whether the desires and truths (the 'hearts and minds') of Afghan bodies are won over or they die in the globe's pursuit of peace, both practices work to master Afghan life and calibrate the strategies of its management and pacification. While subjecting 'hearts and minds' ostensibly stabilizes Afghan volatility and 'collateral damage' incites it, these are merely different outcomes of the same game of postcolonial security. They are merely differently distributed on the graph of postcolonial calculus that captures how costly or beneficial different governing strategies can be. The rationality is still one of efficiency, the method is one of experimentation, and the goal is unchanged: to locate an equilibrium between lethal violence and coercive (but 'softer') inducements in the administration of Afghan populations. An efficient management of subaltern life correlates both strategies. At times, buying the allegiance of a 'rural community' and their elders (or of a warlord) can maximize utility. In different circumstances, smiting them with bombs and drones could be more efficient and less costly over time, even if children and women (publicly, the least acceptable victims) were to die. Echoing a violent colonial genealogy (Rahimi 2017), Herat has experienced both strategies since 2001. While winning Afghan popular support seems preferable to unintended death, to think of the two outcomes as mutually exclusive is deceptive. Thousands of Afghans who died as 'collateral damage' were sacrificed so that the US-led coalition could eliminate 'high-value targets' (CIA Office of Transnational Issues 2009). In fact, many 'communities' supportive of the military intervention in Afghanistan paid for peace with their own lives (Thier and Ranjbar 2008). They merely experienced the incidence of being re-evaluated between two points in time: their bodies travelled the distance from pacified allies with desirable hearts and minds to cherished corpses whose forced sacrifice for peace (as collateral damage) makes them the martyrs of security, Agambenian *homines sacri*. If the value of the allied subject can reach its maximum in death, then its living body already has a dark value limit. Regardless of how agreeable the pacified subject appears to the postcolonial gaze, it can always become more treasured if killed. The value of the subject is in her utility, or 'use-value', to borrow Marx's term. Then, it is no surprise that in both cases, as prized allies and cherished martyrs, Afghan lives are nameless and quantified – whether as pacified populations or lamentable civilian casualties. Either way, Afghan bodies are instrumentalized to serve the larger good and calculus of global stability.

This chapter has unpacked risk and security as power relations that designate who is risky, who is at risk, whose experience of risk is ignored, and whose risk is acted upon. I have situated this chapter in a discourse of reversed images and counter-inspection. I have presented Heratis as subjects of postcolonial security, vulnerable to its calculus of global normal life. Thus, this chapter has set the stage to *geo-graph* Heratis as imperilled by a globe terrified and scornful of brown bodies. While Afghans cannot jeopardize the globe's privileged speaking position, the following chapters show that Herati lives can frustrate the pressures of postcolonial order and counter-exploit its weight to energize a different, discordant practice of peace.

Part III

Power over Heratis and Resistances to It: Three Case Studies

4

How Pacified Heratis 'Milk the Cow': Nonviolent Resistances to Global Security

Introduction

When Safi Airways' Airbus 319 landed at the Hamid Karzai International Airport in Kabul on December 18, 2014 just before 7 A.M., I was still wondering why the gate for my flight to Kabul at the ostensibly extravagant Dubai airport – awash in jewellery stores and artificial palm trees – seemed so far out of the way, kept in a poorly lit cul-de-sac corner of the terminal. My thoughts wandered between chance as one and the reproduction of Afghanistan as Dubai's periphery as another explanation. I recalled a recent monograph by Sellers-García (2014) and wondered what contemporary technologies of micro-power could capture relations between different Afghan places and Dubai. Sellers-García focused on paper flows and mail services between Guatemala and the Iberian Peninsula in the Spanish colonial empire. I thought that focusing on the spatial orders and security procedures of airports and airliners could provide insight into the tactics of local productions of Afghan subjectivities as peripheral. As I walked through customs and immigration to collect my luggage at the Kabul Airport, its security regime and customer service struck me as oddly mirroring what I had observed in Dubai. I became a 'guest' (according to the immigration officer who checked my passport) and a prized object to be 'taken care' of, as someone who offered to help with my suitcase put it.

The purpose of my fieldwork was to understand how a cobweb of entangled governing apparatuses appropriated for and attempted in Afghanistan had affected Afghans, and how ordinary people had become security and development professionals and 'civil society members'. I wanted to explore how policy interventions predicated on 'global security' had delineated a population that needed to be described, made visible and known. Previous research had led me to view the external governance of Afghanistan as a space of power relations that utilized Afghan populations as resources of government rather than its living rationale. Once in Afghanistan, I expected to research my initial 'hypothesis' on how Afghans working in the complex 'governance' system (Kirchner and Dominguez 2011, Kirchner and Sperling 2007) – whether as civil servants or Afghan National Army (ANA) recruits – had been politically subjectivized in ways useful to NATO. I intended to explore NATO's tolerance of insurgent infiltrators in Afghan National Security Forces (ANSF) and how such recruitment practices acknowledge and factor in the risk incurred upon 'loyal' Afghan recruits and NATO troops. I wanted to understand how these and other practices of production of deployable populations reflect larger strategic calculi of governmental regulation. I was interested in how governmental power attempts to 'conduct the conduct' (Foucault 2009, Foucault 1982) of bodies and populations in spaces of death and struggle for life.

While many of my interviews would indeed maintain this line of investigation, the focus of my fieldwork and further research diversified greatly over the coming weeks and months. In retrospect, that shift seems obvious and it certainly felt spontaneous at the time. As I walked through the half-empty arrival hall of the Kabul Airport, I saw passengers who had just landed and others who were merely sitting around and waiting. ANSF were not visibly present. Vehicles hired by private security companies came and whisked away two Americans and a German while I waited for my interpreter and guide in Kabul. While the three 'Westerners' were impatiently waiting for their armoured vehicles, I managed to strike up independent conversations with them. The German seemed to have drawn a blank when I mentioned my next stop in Afghanistan – the city of Herat in the west of the country. She quickly lost interest in our conversation. One of the Americans, apparently a Florida native, observed that Kabul was a 'ratchet place'. I found it hard to make eye contact with my chance interlocutors. In any case, their tall coat collars and scarves largely covered their faces while the rest of their bodies seemed hidden behind their sizeable suitcases. When my guide, Zabiullah, arrived, I was relieved: I did not have to be a *'chatty fellow Westerner'* (as the Floridian had noted) to anyone or to be marvelled at for not intending to stay at a 'safe compound'. Ordinary Afghans have been subjected to security and development practices that at every step visibly privilege foreign career professionals and personnel. They are excluded from safe compounds, unless their bodies are temporarily needed as police officers, food suppliers, static guard, construction workers, trash collectors, pharmacists or language interpreters. My conversations with 'fellow Westerners' made me wonder about the rationalities that underwrote such entanglements of 'locals' and 'internationals'. Moreover, it took me back to conceptual notes that had shaped my expectations from fieldwork in the first place.

I remember planning my fieldwork in November 2014 and thinking how, once in Afghanistan, I would encounter more than just the overbearing weight of Western security and development apparatuses, and more than just stories of drone strikes, night raids and population censuses. My thoughts had often gone back to one excerpt from *The Subject and Power*: *'In order to investigate what power relations are about, perhaps we should investigate the forms of resistance and attempts made to disassociate these relations'* (Foucault 1982, 780). In other words, I was probably conditioned to expect encounters with nonviolent resistances to the US, NATO, and UN-led governance of the country (in addition to the violent insurgency). Yet both my prior knowledge and expectations were vague. This was perhaps due to limited Western scholarship on the topic (Fluri 2006). Over the course of the following month, I met military, police and intelligence officers, language interpreters, NGO representatives, entrepreneurs, journalists, farmers, and others as I saw the crux of my research interest expand past its original focus on the strategies of governmental power. I increasingly wondered about the tactics of 'counter-conduct' (Foucault 2009, 91–284) and resistance to power.

What makes nonviolent resistance to global security and societal violence possible in postcolonial spaces? How is everyday resistance articulated when confrontational and intentionally visible practices such as marches, sit-ins, civil disobedience or protests are foreclosed? This chapter examines some forms of nonviolent resistance (Chenoweth and Cunningham 2013) in Herat's ambivalent security conditions. First, in delineating the logic and tactics of Herati nonviolent resistances, this chapter points to ambivalent, evasive, and unstable engagement with enmeshed external/domestic security apparatuses rather than their outright rejection. The chapter sheds light on seemingly contradictory practices of ordinary Afghans who at once work to undermine postcolonial government, while also seeking to stabilize it in the short run and exploit its assets. Second, by correlating postcolonial power to contemporary security governance, I underscore power's reliance on 'weak' populations for its operation and effectiveness. Third, in drawing on de Certeau's work on micro-power and resistance and Bhabha's concept of ambivalence, I highlight how practical necessities of postcolonial power condition its relations with, and reliance on ordinary Afghans. These entanglements, in turn, allow Afghans to subject power to their own tactical responses and everyday needs. They appropriate power to maximize the possibilities of local life in ways considered unpatriotic, corrupt and wasteful by the postcolonial government apparatus. Thereby, Afghans counter-exploit power that heightens their vulnerabilities and manipulate it into fodder for personal and communal endurance.

Institutions of postcolonial government have operated across the globe without much choice or creative input from local populations. They have included military interventions and post-conflict reconstruction (Afghanistan, Iraq, Bosnia, Kosovo, Libya, etc.), trade agreements (NAFTA, Cotonou, etc.), structural adjustment programmes, poverty reduction strategies, etc. Postcoloniality has constrained and enabled ordinary people by constituting spaces of unstable contact, cooperation, conflict and myriad ambiguous relations. This chapter examines merely a sliver of these global relationships by zeroing in on nonviolent resistances to overlapping violent and regulatory authorities in Herat.

Since 2001, Herat has been contested by national and local strongmen, the government in Kabul and its provincial governor in Herat (at times competing with Kabul for primacy), US-led Operation Enduring Freedom (until December 2014) and Operation Freedom's Sentinel (as of January 2015), NATO-led International Security Assistance Force (ISAF) and Resolute Support's Train Advise Assist-West centre (TAAC-W) (as of January 2015), the Taliban, smaller insurgent groups, Daesh and armed gangs. This matrix of power is not neatly divided, since many of these formations overlap and operate as crosscutting networks rather than unitary actors with distinct boundaries. Local strongmen and warlords often control official government positions, as was the case when Ismail Khan became Herat's governor and commander of the 4th Corps in 2001. Furthermore, NATO has long depended on and aided ANSF, as well as foreign and Afghan security companies (Cordesman 2013). These linkages have necessitated spaces of shared contact, joint training, patrolling and surveillance, as well as information and intelligence pooling. Such practices have affected thousands of individuals who are at once unarmed civilians only to become insurgents, military/

police recruits, private security employees, or insurgent infiltrators in ANSF (Sieff 2012, Rivera 2011, Zaheer 2011). Afghans alternate across these points of authority, control and political economy according to various logics of necessity.

This chapter stems from my interest in the Heratis' tactical economic and political movements across the sprawling grid of power in the Province. It investigates how their social and spatial movements reflect tactics of maximization of local life and well-being. Heratis have had to cope with competing and overlapping 'Western' and 'national' authorities that have claimed to provide good governance, peace, security and development. Shifting practices of economic and intellectual resistance by ordinary Heratis have informed and complicated the competitive power matrix of the insurgency, counterinsurgency, counterterrorism, petty criminals, war and drug lords, professional kidnappers, etc. This chapter sheds light on ANSF and private security recruits, lower-ranked military and police officers, civil servants, entrepreneurs, language interpreters and others. It highlights their unstable and ambivalent professional, political, and ideological allegiances and affiliations and recounts how they use, and wrestle with the dominant hierarchies that demand their loyalty, compliance and participation in order and prosperity.

Why is economic, intellectual or artistic resistance to governance structures important? After all, nonviolence cannot threaten the performance and experience of national security the way Al-Qaeda, the Taliban or Daesh have done. The 'West' has attempted to build a nation-state in Afghanistan, *'remake it in its own image'* (Friis 2012) and cultivate secured, non-threatening and developed Afghans. Could analytics of resistance shed light on how governmental power reproduces itself in postcolonial spaces? Perhaps narratives of resistance could offer lessons for extra-juridical empowerment (Hesford and Kozol 2005) and more dissonant equality of pacified populations (Kienscherf 2011)? The following section ties this chapter to the overall conceptual framework in Chapter 2. It correlates postcolonial power in Afghanistan and the resistances it has relied on and been inseparable from.

Herat at the Limit of Power and Resistance

Chapter 2 has positioned power and resistance as mutually constitutive, embedded in and energizing one another. Bhabha's concepts of *ambivalence* and *hybridity* have helped point to their entanglements and muddled – rather than neatly oppositional – relations. Ambivalence can explain Heratis' tactical engagement and opportune cooperation with postcolonial power as techniques of its exploitation, exhaustion and destabilization rather than wholesale rejection. Furthermore, reinterpreting *security governance* as postcolonial power sheds a different light on the governance claims of, and need for, legitimacy and broad societal cooperation. The governing need for legitimacy enables Heratis to engage with security apparatuses on a tactical level and exploit their lethal, economic and financial assets. At any rate, for as long as global security can be portrayed as threatened by brown tribalism and volatility, the apparently well-govern*ed* (and, therefore, well-govern*ing*) West/North will be able to claim the status of Afghan and global caretakers.

These propositions had shaped my expectations from research in Herat. I anticipated to encounter multitudes of shifting points of contact and mutual contingence between (1) the control, discipline, policing, surveillance, and regulation by different networks of authorities, and (2) unstable and dispersed practices of nonviolent (and violent) resistances. I expected that spatial distributions, modalities, and gaps in resistances would be tactical and only partially linked to global strategic critiques and rejections of postcolonial power. Moreover, I anticipated that contacts of power and resistance would not neatly follow the needs and desires of particular actors (Foucault 1977, 206), but would be contingent upon specific, often chance events. Finally, in addition to individual and group aspirations to drive the United States, NATO or the Taliban out of Herat, I expected to encounter everyday resistances to, and negotiations of power relations geared at taking advantage of the presence and activities of entangled external/domestic security apparatuses. Indeed, I recorded accounts of everyday resistances that aimed at stabilizing the beneficial and lucrative aspects of security governance in Afghanistan.

Insofar as Herati nonviolent resistances consist of tactical uses of one's employment in security-development structures in the Province, I have analysed such practices as micro-economic exploitation – or *counter*-exploitation – of Kabul's, Afghan powerbrokers', NATO's and American financial, lethal and other resources. Therefore, local counter-exploitation is a tactic of resistance deployed to empower ordinary Heratis constrained by the precariousness of life. Examining such struggles for empowerment needs to point to how specific lives work to maximize the possibilities, measures, and modalities of own functioning amid the constraints of Afghan (in)security. Thereby, narratives of workplace resistances as specific struggles can deconstruct security governance and its claim at global effectiveness. This micro-economic focus follows from the very strategies of postcolonial power that seeks to stabilize Afghanistan by tying together its economy and security. Moreover, Afghanistan's 'governance state' (Harrison 2004) opens itself up to the distrusted local insofar as it needs to objectify him/her as a resource, recruit and a fighting body in a dangerous workplace.

Many of my interviewees portrayed the governmental practices of securing and developing Afghanistan as substantively, strategically and tactically reminiscent of Afghanistan's confined place during the colonial Great Game. I was so consumed by current-colonial and security-development linkages that I told Farid Mamundzay, Deputy Minister of the Independent Directorate of Local Governance (IDLG), that their separate analyses seemed more than incomplete. They seemed misleading. Implying that his agency was not complicit in the reinforcement of the 'security-development nexus', he responded: '*Well, there is a reason why the Directorate's approach has to focus on both security and development*' (Mamundzay 2014). He did not address my interest in colonial legacies and I did not press the issue any further.

Ambivalence in Herat

I have discussed the contingency of Herat's (in)security in Chapter 2, in particular its situation, spatial and social power dimensions. This ambiguity has enabled an array of overlapping governance apparatuses from heavily armed military units to reconstruction experts and agencies. While their attempts to pacify Afghanistan have also induced diverse tactics of resistance, I focus on nonviolent resistances as tactical maximizations of local life and renegotiations of power constraints. Tactics studied in this chapter draw on Heratis' *ambivalent (deceptive?) employment statuses* and *commitments* towards the international agencies, military and police formations in the Province. They include the exploitation of, cheating, or defection from one's employer (the coalition bloc, insurgency, etc.), as well as the locals' abilities to profit from maximizing the utility of their knowledge, professional or situational expertise and skills. Their expertise involves social, cultural, topographic, linguistic, artistic, scientific, and other skills used to extract financial and other social gains from the cobweb of foreign governments, international organizations and NGOs (Afzaly 2015, Herati Construction Company Owner 2014, Sohail 2014, Saber 2014, Chivers 2010). Drawing on de Certeau (1982, 1984) and Bhabha (1994), I focus on the micro-spatial resistance*s* as practices of *ambivalence*. While diverse in expression, they all appear equivocal and are typically considered corrupt, wasteful and nefarious by American, NATO, and other global/local governing bodies.

Ambivalent Employment as Counter-exploitation of Security Governance

Between 2007 and 2012, Afghanistan was on average the world's fifteenth deadliest country according to *Global Burden of Armed Violence* reports (del Frate, Krause and Nowak 2015). It is more than an odd paradox then that Afghan soldiers and Afghan private security personnel have been deployed to provide physical security to NATO troops and UN staff. Such relations of physical protection raise questions as to who is being secured in the Afghan chapter of the War on Terror and what lives are factored into the calculus of necessity and success of security governance in the country. Strategic deployments and exploitation of Afghan bodies, of their physical abilities and skills, and the emphasis put on the growth in their utility speak to the expanding productivity of NATO and US-led governance across the country. However, Afghans have pursued a number of tactical pathways around and through the security apparatus, extracting benefits for themselves, their families and communities at the expense of NATO, the United States, the United Nations and private contractors. Using Bhabha's notion of resistance as ambivalent and tactical engagement with power, Heratis' relations with security governance can be understood as counter-exploitation, or as taking advantage of privileged micro-economic and professional statuses and opportunities that they have acquired in an environment with double-digit unemployment rates. They have subverted the governance matrix and its operational need and ability to use the 'weak', turning it into a resource that can be deployed to maximize the possibilities of local life in ways that NATO and the UN deem inappropriate, corrupt, wasteful and threatening to peace and security. De Certeau contextualized such subversions historically by invoking resistances to Spanish colonialism:

> The spectacular victory of Spanish colonization over the indigenous Indian cultures was diverted from its intended aims by the use made of it: even when

they were subjected, indeed even when they accepted their subjection, the Indians often used the laws, practices, and representations that were imposed on them by force or by fascination to ends other than those of their conquerors; they made something else out of them; they subverted them from within – not by rejecting them or transforming them (although that occurred as well), but by many different ways of using them in the service of rules, customs or convictions foreign to the colonization which they could not escape. (1984, 31–32)

Shah Mohammad, a Herati ANA instructor, describes in detail '*the habits of fooling around*' and 'stalling' among ANA recruits in the Herat training centre (Mohammad 2015). His account of the recruits' overall commitment to training and exercise abounds with descriptions of individuals who have committed to their employer (the Afghan government and ANA) to degrees that appear limited and calculated.

A lot of the recruits are young, but there are some who are also in their thirties. I am like a father figure to them and I know a lot of them. ... Their motives to join ANA of course vary, but I would say that getting a paycheck every month and a career is generally a stronger reason than patriotism, although a lot of them love their country. (Ibid)

After asserting that financial goals primarily drive the recruits' decision to join ANA, Shah outlines the calculus behind this motivation and the accordingly measured and ambiguous commitment:

Many of them have to support families, ... parents, brothers and sisters, and their own wives and children. If you are a young man and in relatively good physical shape, this is one of the easier jobs to get if you are ready to take the security risk, know how to manage it and have no [insurgent] past. You don't need school or connections. But because the government and NATO need more of these young soldiers than they have, [the recruits] can think tactically about their job. So they don't try their hardest when it comes to physical exercises, workout routines or the battlefield. I say do a hundred pushups, they do forty, fifty and then act and cheat like they are doing more, but I see them, I see what they are doing. It is a little better when they practice with weapons or big equipment, but they are not exactly Rambos [followed by mutual laughter]. (Ibid)

Abundant policy and media reports corroborate this account. They convey practices of 'indiscipline' and 'disobedience' that include avoiding cleaning checkpoints and barracks or using drugs on military premises and grounds (Maurer and Hinnant 2009), as well as failures to provide fire support in theatre, hiding during battle or shooting carelessly past designated targets (Lardner 2011, Chivers 2010). When asked what the recruits gain by withholding their effort, Shah lowers his shoulders and voice slightly and hesitates:

Well, they are less noticeable, they stand out less if they don't show off too much, they survive, get to live, you know. And if they take it easy, they have more energy and strength to then go work their second and [a] third job. Because for a lot of them, the Army is not the only thing that they do. Maybe they think: 'Why should I do more? I do what I have to.' And I understand. The Army doesn't pay all the bills. They have families, old parents ... Someone needs to take care of them. Also, if they fool around, make jokes, don't make too much effort, they spread a different atmosphere around, and most of them feel like not trying too hard is OK, and then the whole unit is less prepared or at least less concerned with constant physical and psychological effort. At the end, they feel like not risking their lives on the job is OK as well. (Mohammad 2015)

Shah clarifies this description after I share my impression that this behaviour seems tactical, or something other than 'laziness' or immaturity:

Absolutely, some of them fool around because they want to sabotage the training for political reasons, but you don't know exactly who does that for that particular reason, so it's hard to discipline them. Others just don't want to risk their lives for something that is so distant as the nation or state, and, instead, prefer to stay alive for something more real, like their families. Also, as I already said, we can't discipline them too hard, because then we might lose some of them, we already are – hundreds and hundreds. (Ibid)

After I ask whether he thinks some of the individuals who resort to such stalling practices could be related to the insurgency, Shah adds:

Maybe, we don't know for certain. Also, they don't have to have any real connections; just this effect on the Army is enough. In reality, a lot of them don't care too much about how good the Army is. They just want to be paid and not die, unless that's why they are here – to die and take more of their fellow soldiers to death with them. So I think a lot of those sabotaging the Army have mixed ideas. (Ibid)

Shah Mohammad describes various tactics of workplace subversion integral to counter-exploitations of postcolonial power. Michel de Certeau labelled them *la perruque* or 'the wig' in the context of factory production processes. According to de Certeau, *la perruque* is '*the worker's own work disguised as work for his employer*' (de Certeau 1984, 25) or a form of 'time wasting' rather than simple theft – with which it is often combined. Shah's descriptions are also evocative of James C. Scott's account of peasant practices of nonviolent resistance to the 1970s 'green revolution' in Kedah, Malaysia, as they included '*foot dragging, dissimulation, desertion, false compliance, pilfering, feigned ignorance, slander, arson, sabotage*' (Scott 1985, xvi), as well as '*theft and, not least, cultural resistance*' (Ibid, 34). ANSF recruits may evade the military or police grid of disciplinary measures (e.g. the procedures of timely and correct exercise and other daily routines, handling of weapons, respect of hierarchy, etc.) and regulatory parameters (e.g. achieving desired margins of physical fitness, muscularity and skill in handling weapons and equipment). I did not engage with ANSF recruits themselves to examine their motivations to evade such procedures and expectations.

Nevertheless, Mohammad Shah and General Mohammad Nadir Azimi of ANA both point to the logics and effects of evasions as 'mixed' (Azimi 2016, Mohammad 2015) maximizations of the welfare of recruits, their families and communities, as the preservation and improvement of their chances to live at the expense of ANA, NATO, the US and other ANA financial contributors. Moreover, Shah and Azimi both insist on the practical consistency between one's struggle to live for a time and die at an opportune moment.

Other interviewees professionally engaged with ANSF have similarly recounted their experiences with the contingencies and tactical characters of employment. An intelligence officer from Herat spoke of financial reasons as '*perhaps the single reason why Herati men fight on the side of the government against the insurgency and bandits, whether as military personnel or police officers*' (National Directorate of Security Employee No. 2 2014). He also asserted that many Heratis who work for the 'security machine' are '*patriotic and feel dedication and love for their city and the country*', but tend to disassociate such emotions from 'serving' the country (air quotes used by the interviewee) (Ibid). When asked to explain why one would need to disassociate the two, he insisted that '*the police, army, air force, and such are all a machine that is there and doesn't depend on how well it keeps Afghans safe*', and that '*it is above all accountable to the Americans and then the strongmen around the country*' (Ibid). He finally asserted that for policemen or troops '*to remain patriotic, they need to think about this country and love it in other ways that have nothing to do with the security forces*'. I noted that his account of police and military recruits suggested that some of them saw it as precisely their job not to practice what their employer, the government, would otherwise prefer. The irony of their reasoning is that it only makes sense in an environment supposedly based on patriotism. He responded:

> It will be a great achievement for Afghanistan when one day our troops fight for the nation and the country. Now, some do that, but most first have to make sure that they bring food to their families and they stay alive so they can do other things and guarantee survival to real people, not some distant ideals of the nation. It is not noble, but it is real. (Ibid)

Both the intelligence officer and Shah Mohammad correlate the very possibility of security governance with how Heratis wrestle with it. This association speaks to Foucault's hypothesis on the impossibility of power without resistance: one's calculated engagement with security governance becomes indispensable for it to operate over its intended population. The intelligence officer, like Shah, thus narrates the vigour of the subject of security governance. *He/She* is more than a passive object of discipline and regulation. Accounts of professional commitments echo a version of 'la perruque':

> I think it defeats the purpose of having an army and a police, but this commitment to family, neighborhood, and naked life explains why many recruits try to avoid high-risk patrolling or open clashes with insurgents or even regular criminals. So they lie, evade, play stupid, sick, etc. If they do their job all the way, that will be a great loss for everyone, the government included, because they do not want

Afghans to die in the ANSF that they are still trying to build. That scares potential recruits away. (Ibid)

As Afghan National Police (ANP) Colonel Mohammad Hashim Babakarkhil applauded '*brave police recruits around the country*', he also acknowledged the government's awareness that some of them calculate how and when they commit to their jobs. Babakarkhil admitted that '*we [the ANSF leadership] obviously do not endorse this kind of dishonest behavior, but we also cannot commit too much of our resources to controlling it*' (Babakarkhil 2014). He also acknowledged that '*being too brave and committed at work*' is '*sometimes not so good*'. This is because the ANP has recruited and trained fewer personnel since 2010 when casualties on the force first increased visibly. Beyond the convenient binary between *financially* driven recruits and *true* patriots, there exist more complicated spaces of struggle. In them, ordinary Heratis articulate patriotism in self-moderating ways that enable them to improve the lives of those close to them and dependent on them. For some military and police recruits, that means experiencing the security apparatus, or 'the machine', as a life-maximizing tool for their closest ones rather than an instrument of Afghanistan's sovereignty. Measured evasion and engagement with their employer points to a calculus of maximization that is not one of neat costs and benefits. Rather, it is an ambivalent push to render life possible as patriotic and professional appropriateness meets the need to waste time, equivocate, cheat and slack off. Reminiscent of Bhabha's concept of resistance as ambivalent cooperation coupled with rejection, interplays of these necessities are never fixed. They are driven by the aleatory and shifting events-places of (in)security that render Afghan lives erratically possible, unfeasible, lost, diminishing, growing or at risk. Thus, US, EU, NATO, and UN-driven security-development and the playfulness and stubbornness of resistances to them operate as untethered to accomplished and finite strategies. Rather, power and resistance experience strategy as something to be claimed, often improvised and quickly changed. In the words of a former Italian Provincial Reconstruction Team-Herat (PRT-Herat) employee:

> There is a common assumption among my 'Western' [air quotes used by the interviewee] colleagues that Afghans here – especially ANSF recruits – are lazy, unreliable, sneaky, that they want us dead or alive, doesn't matter, as long as they get our money or steal things they can sell. And I admit, sometimes that's how it looks like, it really does. But then, due to my education, I also know that this is a stereotype, so I ask myself all the time why is it that people assume that we are rational, but that Afghans have thick heads that nothing can get into … whether it is how to take care of NATO-donated equipment, how to properly undergo training, how to behave in combat, and so on. We never assume that they, too, might be behaving rationally, but that they simply have different objectives, want different things than we do, than what we think is good for them. (Italian Provincial Reconstruction Team Employee 2014)

My follow-up question was mostly meant to be in jest, and this PRT-Herat employee did respond with a chuckle: '*Are NATO heads thick? You bet! We in the PRT were a culture of people who think that they are learning on the ground, but how can you learn anything when you question nothing?*' While insightful, this response struck me more as individual resignation than an indication of a structural 'learning curve' about the challenges of learning. The interviewee's body language was one of frustration and slight self-mockery. It did not convey much confidence in the rationality of the trial-and-error learning process.

Nonviolent resistances are possible because they are ambivalent. They work within Herat's grid of coercive, regulatory and destructive power rather than in overt opposition to it. Stories of insurgent infiltration into the ANSF (Beattie 2009) have emerged as a key element in this grid. Secretly pledging allegiance to the Taliban, Daesh or smaller groups while receiving a pay check from the government is not lethal per se. Nonetheless, recruits-insurgents assuming such risky dualities of roles are expected to embrace the death of self and other as useful. While infiltration is a non-linear process that does not necessarily lead to death, its possibility is always factored into individual calculi. In addition to being intended as risky, infiltration is also elusive insofar as it is enacted as simultaneous or quickly alternating service to mutually opposed (or, at least, formally strictly separated) armed formations including ANSF, private security firms, warlord militias, local insurgencies and the Taliban. Both the risk and elusiveness maximize the utility of infiltration to Heratis.

I asked Colonel Babakarkhil – former Deputy Commander of the ANP Central Training Center in Kabul – how individuals come to be both ANSF recruits and insurgent infiltrators. According to Babakarkhil, Afghan military and police recruits are generally *'expected to be disciplined and do their job'* (Babakarkhil 2014). This has enabled insurgent infiltration and an undisturbed influx of individuals who were once employed by private security companies and private militias. Those deemed eligible to join ANSF can easily camouflage mixed allegiances to a local strongman or the insurgency – as well as transitory or no particular allegiances – by remaining quiet and simply completing repeated, seemingly value or speech-free mechanical tasks and procedures. Thus, out of pre-existing structures, they create 'liminal' (Bhabha 1994) spaces of ambivalence and render themselves invisible to the controlling and filtering gaze of the government. Ambivalence, in turn, makes possible their pursuit of specific tasks privy to the insurgency, a warlord or their own personal calculus. Babakarkhil prides himself on having purportedly advocated for strict vetting procedures and the creation of detailed databases of recruits and known insurgents, but admits that success has been limited (Babakarkhil 2014). The interior and defence ministries ban former insurgents, employees of private militias and security companies from ever joining ANSF (unless officially 'reintegrated'). The ministries have adopted biometric technologies that help them collect and store data about the individuals who cycle in and out of ANSF. However, the biometric filter and tracking system have been a limited success, since it is much harder to know whether an individual had been an insurgent or a private militiaman before his/her fingerprints were first taken electronically (Azimi 2016, Babakarkhil 2014, Sieff 2012). Unless there are alternative sources of intelligence, there is no effective way to triangulate original biometric data. Technological and surveillance limitations, as well as self-manufactured low visibility enable individuals to circulate across the grid of armed groups in Herat. Thus, they create shifting, indefinite and self-maintained spaces of exploitation of security apparatuses. This manoeuvring has persisted in spite of Kabul's and US attempts to curb it through aggressive tactics of surveillance, performance audits by the Special Inspector General for Afghanistan Reconstruction (SIGAR), or their insistence that military and police recruits must relocate their families back from Pakistan in order to keep their jobs (Jalalzai 2014).

It is difficult to generalize or even discern individual motivations to circulate between the ANSF, private militias, security companies and the insurgency. Nonetheless, interviewees who have had insight into ANSF recruitment procedures and histories have cited similar purposes. They range from intelligence collection for the insurgency or a 'power broker', financial reasons (whereby a share of one's pay check is siphoned out to the insurgency), to buying time until recruits/infiltrators make more definitive decisions regarding their future, or until such decisions are made for them (Azimi 2016, Mohammad 2015, Babakarkhil 2014, National Directorate of Security Employee No. 1 2014, National Directorate of Security Employee No. 2 2014). At times, infiltrators would be ordered to partake in violent incursions and suicide bombings – a spectrum of different *fedayeen* (martyrdom) tactics (Hassan 2011, 122–145, Williams 2008). One former insurgent who was 'reintegrated' back into the legal security sector in Herat said that he had left the Taliban because he believed he could get a job in the ANP, but was soon disappointed by 'little progress'. He ultimately changed his mind, as he 'had no choice' but to 'become a Talib' again (Jones 2011).

Therefore, it seems that the tactic of circulation harmonizes at least two ostensibly contradictory goals. One could be to drive the coalition out of Afghanistan and Herat through repeated violence, while a second goal seems to be to keep the coalition in the country and take advantage of its many financial and other resources, or simply as one of few lucrative employment options. As Shah Mohammad put it:

> Many people in Herat, even rural rebels and warlords, do not want the Americans to go immediately, too soon or maybe at all; they want to first use them, NATO, the NGOs, etc. as cash cows that can be milked for a long time until they are tired and old. You know, it is like turning powerful drones into worn out cows. (Mohammad 2015)

Another closely related tactic of exploitation of Western governance has been 'ghost soldiering', defined in SIGAR's 2015 report as *'dead, deserted, or nonexistent soldiers [being] kept on rolls by error or intention'* (Sopko 2015, 8), a common event in the ANSF flagged as a 'major concern' (Ibid). Ghost soldiering has resulted in *'augment[ing] a superior's pay or enabl[ing] a dead soldier's family to go on collecting pay in lieu of a death benefit'* (Ibid). A section of the report refers to the incidence of ghost soldiering in Herat:

> SIGAR's audit of ANA personnel data illustrates the cause for concern. A team of SIGAR auditors made unannounced visits to the headquarters of the Afghan National Army's 207th Corps in Herat Province and the 209th Corps in Balkh

Province, and the Afghan Air Force (AAF) air wing based in Kabul. The auditors collected information on 134 service personnel present or duty. Of these, the identities of only 103 could be verified against ANA personnel data. One in nine had no ANA identification card. (Ibid, 3–4)

Shapoor Saber, a prominent Herati journalist who has worked with Radio Free Europe and the Institute for War and Peace Reporting, and Lotfullah Najafizada, director of TOLOnews, both confirmed that ghost soldiering had become one of the most persistent nonviolent challenges to ANSF in Herat and elsewhere (Saber 2014, Najafizada 2014). Shapoor added:

> Herat is especially problematic because we have a safe environment in the Province in comparison with places in the east and south. [Therefore,] people are not so busy fighting or think that when they steal from the government and NATO it is not so serious because there is no real damage to security in Herat. (Saber 2014)

Systemic ruptures, including '*weak internal controls, lack of written procedures, and classification and arithmetic errors, and use of summary data that made errors in details unidentifiable*' have enabled this tactic (Sopko 2015, 6). Numbers for ANSF units are produced based on general equation-based '*calculations on a spreadsheet, not as an input of actual observation and reporting*' (ibid). Manipulations are possible because ''*the reporting system for Afghan Security Forces personnel is still largely manual*' – relying, that is, *on piles of paper*' (Ibid, 7). Therefore, various factors (including unstable electricity supplies and low literacy rates) enable individuals in both command and lower-level accounting positions to benefit financially from skewed numbers. Data are additionally distorted in the ANP due to its use of 'trusted agents' to collect and communicate information up the chain of command. Financial flows are further altered as the same agents are also used to distribute pay checks to police officers (Rasmussen 2015).

Shad Mohammad, the ANA instructor I interviewed in December 2014, underlines the power of force commanders on the ground (lieutenants and lower levels) as one of the key '*holes in the system*' that makes such utilizations possible (Mohammad 2015). Conversely, an intelligence officer pointed to the possibility of '*small mathematical and accounting tricks that add up over time*' as crucial to ghost soldiering (National Directorate of Security Employee No. 2 2014). In his 2015 report, SIGAR Sopko notes:

> In addition to inviting and obscuring waste of money, such deficiencies can create destructive ripple effects in integrity, effectiveness, loyalty, morale, public support, and other factors that affect the likelihood of developing and sustaining a strong Afghan security force. (Sopko 2015, 4)

Prior to SIGAR's more thorough January 2015 report, I learned about ghost soldiering through earlier SIGAR findings (Brummet 2010), prior interviews (Zajc 2014, Italian Provincial Reconstruction Team Employee 2014), news (Hicks 2014), and policy reports (Perito 2009). They compelled me to inquire precisely about its potential effects on force morale, the public perception of ANSF, and its effectiveness. One answer by a Herat intelligence officer stood out:

> That phenomenon is like plague and we have some intelligence on it. But we don't know exactly why different people invent soldiers or collect dead personnel's paychecks. It looks like some do it to undermine the Forces for ideological reasons. Most people don't care about the Forces' mission, or think it is doomed, or simply that the money they take is not too much. Some think the Americans are so involved that whatever an Afghan can steal on the side is nothing compared to the wealth the Americans have. People who join the ANSF out of patriotism are often disheartened after they see widespread corruption, laziness, money grabbing, and insurgent infiltration. (National Directorate of Security Employee No. 1 2014)

Two intelligence officers from Herat emphasized a number of specific opportunity structures for ghost soldiering, such as individual discretion in data collection and manual bookkeeping within Afghanistan's Ministry of Defense. Colonel Babakarkhil's assessment captured the tactic's multiple individual necessities:

> Most people in the chain of command and most recruits would probably agree that ghost soldiering is not good ethically and not good for the country. But that doesn't matter when they need to think about feeding their children, parents, helping their cousins, paying back loans or saving up so they can change professions and do something less dangerous. (Babakarkhil 2014)

Furthermore, 'ghost workers' have been also 'found' in the national education system (Amini 2015, Sakhi 2016). As I began fieldwork in Afghanistan in mid-December 2014, I thought of ghost soldiering as a process of invention of bodies and lives in a broader matrix of welfare maximization. The interviews I conducted and subsequent SIGAR reports also highlighted ghost employment as arithmetic occupations and substitutions of once real lives and individuals rather than entirely original inventions. Therefore, much like the grid of US/NATO apparatuses of security and development, resistances to them have their own dimensions of individuation and self-regulation as micro-operative, microphysical, imperceptible and difficult to contain when identified. Whereas the individuality of ghost soldiering is central to its rationality, SIGAR suggests that NATO and the United States should deploy generalized counter-tools. SIGAR sees its ultimate leverage in the prospect of withdrawal of the international troops and financial support from Afghanistan (Sopko 2015, 11). Thus, the ultimate response to the tactic of micro-evasion and theft woven into thousands of Afghan bodies and names is a grand strategic threat itself more contingent upon US national security and NATO's global strategies.

Finally, more research remains to be done on the political effectivity of theft targeting military equipment and machine parts in Afghanistan. It seems that tactical pilfering is so resilient that ANSF officers once fired for it end up rehired and even promoted (Maurer and Hinnant 2009). Reports from ANSF outposts and installations describe the theft of US-supplied fuel, equipment, vehicles, and weapons as 'routine' (Cahn 2009). While Herat-specific numbers are hard to gauge, Pentagon officials admit *'thousands of cars and trucks intended for use by the Afghan police have been stolen and sold'*, with one asserting that *'at least half of the equipment supplied by the US' was stolen by 2007'* (Chamberlain 2007). Spare parts for Western vehicles used by ANA (Humvees, Textron armoured vehicles, and Ford trucks) are regularly unaccounted for properly. SIGAR's October 2013 report concluded that NATO *'could not account for approximately $230 million worth of spare parts for the ANSF'* (Sopko 2013a, 31). SIGAR's January report from the same year concluded that the United States had spent $6.83 million over seventeen months to maintain vehicles that had already been destroyed (Sopko 2013b, 15). Theft is often identified in the handling and storage of gas and fuel – 'liquid gold' that is *'easy to steal, easy to sell on the black market'* with *'buyers [being] local gasoline stations, roadside vendors, U.S. contractors without access to military fuel depots, or Afghan insurgents'* (Ibid, 36). Theft continues through individual and small-scale evasions of SIGAR's extensive surveillance apparatus and covert missions dispatched from SIGAR's offices in Kabul and Herat (Ibid, 34).

Formulas of stealing and sabotage worked out on micro-levels of institutional invisibility sustain what SIGAR treats as general corruption and waste. They include the regular theft of spare tyres and jacks, fuel pumps (and their replacement with older ones), entire vehicles (often Ford trucks), tools and meals, while soldiers resell TA50s (NATO and US-issued individual equipment) in open-air town markets (Thompson 2010, Sakhi 2016). The United States and NATO have pointed to high-level military leadership, lower-rank recruits and ordinary civilians as responsible for organizing, running, facilitating, and profiting from the theft of Western equipment and fuel (Sopko 2013b, 49, Chamberlain 2007). As an NDS employee commented:

> The extent of theft is subtle and common. People do it in complete disregard of the ANSDF mission or NATO. Some do it even to spite them. And some do it because that is how they help their families. (National Directorate of Security Employee No. 1 2014)

Ambivalent Resistances through Knowledge and Skills

Another way of studying Herati resistances is to focus on how the locals use their situational contextual and spatially specific skills, knowledge and expertise to render themselves indispensable and irreplaceable to the security governance apparatus. The spectrums of skills and expertise have been broad, minute and local in their attempts and deployments. They have included social, cultural, topographic, linguistic, scientific, and other knowledge used to extract financial and other gains from the cobweb of foreign governments, international organizations and NGOs. While global capitalist discourses frame these abilities as 'assets' and 'capital' (Hodgson 2015, 173–204) to be used and exploited, it seems that ordinary Heratis have tactically utilized own abilities to counter-exploit the governance apparatuses that seek to regulate the utility of Afghan lives.

Herati interpreter and pharmacist, Tariq Afzaly, recounted how he first became an interpreter for an Italian company in Kabul before moving back to his native Herat in 2005 to work for the local Italian-led Provincial Reconstruction Team (PRT) and translate from Dari to English (Afzaly 2015). He spoke in detail about his bilingual skills that made him integral to the PRT's security and development operations:

> I went almost everywhere with them [Italian and US troops]: to patrols around the Province and the different districts, to development and reconstruction sites where sewage, dams, schools, and water wells were built, to the [Herat] Provincial Development Committee meetings, even emergency meetings, ANA training sites, etc. I interacted and spoke with locals and shuras on NATO's and the PRT's behalf about the economy, insurgency, local needs, freedom, different reconstruction projects, expectations from the government and NATO, really a range of topics. … I tried my best, proved myself trustworthy, and then they started trusting me a lot and so I got to see a lot. They kept me around for almost eight years and will still probably have small tasks for me even though my contract officially ended yesterday [December 31, 2014] along with ISAF's mission. (Afzaly 2015)

When I asked Tariq to explain how his trustworthiness was beneficial to him, he pointed to a range of financial, social and career benefits. He was straightforward in his response:

> Well, if you are professional, discreet, careful, and respectful, you have your contract renewed, which is never a given, then you gain a lot of experience on the ground because they take you to all kinds of different missions. Also, new financial and business opportunities arise as you become familiar with their needs, and your respect and status grows, which is really useful for the future. (Afzaly 2015)

I asked Tariq to clarify what he meant by '*new financial and business opportunities*', which is when I learned that he is a pharmacist by training:

> I found out from my Italian superiors that the PRT needed a pharmacist. They told me because they knew my original profession. So I went through a bidding process and I won. They needed someone they could trust, and logically, when there is someone you know, you are also probably going to trust them more. Trust was important because they didn't want someone who would deliver expired medicines or medicines of poor quality, or would poison them for whatever reason. In any case, it was most probably going to be a local, so I was very fortunate, but also I know I deserved it. (Afzaly 2015)

Tariq thus laid out a twofold microstructure of foreign dependence on local expertise and skills – linguistic and pharmacological in nature. Moreover, he illustrated how an Afghan's utility to the governance and regulatory apparatus can enable him/her to gain access to otherwise restricted spaces of development and security (e.g. armed patrols and reconstruction sites). Such experiences allow Afghans to build favourable rapports with PRT or UN personnel that make them ever more useful and gradually indispensable to these organizations' quotidian activities and core missions. Tariq's experience indicates a deepening and contentious relationship:

> I have had friends and even relatives critical of my work for NATO. Sometimes it's jealousy, sometimes it's ideological, but I've heard them often say how I am not paid enough for the kind of work that I do and the risk I expose myself to, and how they are taking advantage of me for peanuts. Some of us interpreters and translators maybe feel abandoned now that NATO is withdrawing troops and equipment. But I know I managed to take advantage of NATO's presence quite a lot. I've built a good resume and have a lot of experience on the ground that makes me valuable. That is why my application to temporarily move to Italy now as a former interpreter for Italian contingents … that's exactly why it's so strong. They see what I've done and that guarantees even more professional and career opportunities for me in the future, because I want to see how it is in Italy and maybe I can make a good living there for three years [the program's duration as stipulated by the Italian government]. (Afzaly 2015)

Tariq was not the only Herati I interviewed who seemed practically unconcerned about how his experience with NATO would be labelled – 'co-dependence', 'exploitation', or 'counter-exploitation' (Sakhi 2016). However, he was acutely aware of how his relationship with Italian private companies and Italian, Slovenian, and American troops and civilian personnel evolved and how complicated and threatened their lives became when NATO started withdrawing troops and ISAF's mission ended in 2014. He was intensely cognizant of the calculus of cultural and ethical (in)appropriateness, of the costs and benefits that their mutual involvement had been and continues to be predicated on. Tariq openly spoke of 'taking advantage' of NATO governance structures. He framed it as a practical necessity integral to his space rather than an instrumental interest determined by ideology:

> My family was alright before I started working for NATO, and I didn't have to do that, but since it was there, it was a logical opportunity, there was something to be gained. It was controversial, but that doesn't matter all the time. (Afzaly 2015)

The usefulness of the locals' bilingual and multilingual skills cannot be overstated. In addition to English and/or Italian, interpreters in Herat had to be familiar with both urban and rural varieties and nuances of the local Afghan Persian dialect that overlaps with eastern Iranian Farsi dialects (roughly in the Khorasan Province) and Kabuli Persian/Dari, and is more narrowly known as 'minor Khorasani' (Ionnesyan 2009). At times, they were even practically compelled to mediate conflicts between NATO troops and ANSF recruits (Chivers 2010). However, the uniqueness and indispensability of their knowledge and skills have not worked to empower them automatically. They have not become easily deployable resources either. Instead, their situational skills have been mediated through difficulties and complexities reflected in the deaths of local interpreters and translators, physical threats against them, their social ostracization, and the obstacles they have encountered in trying to take advantage of their professional experience with NATO and receive US, Italian, UK or other emigration visas (Motal 2016, Goodman 2015). Thus, the tactical navigation of who they are as 'NATO employees', 'fathers', 'husbands', 'cousins', 'collaborators', or 'traitors' had to adapt and develop new logics of self-maintenance in function of Herat's overall contingency of (in)security.

I encountered similar complexities in the social navigation of NATO's governance system when I interviewed an owner of a large construction company from Herat. When I inquired about the risks he had had to manage because he was doing business with the USAID and PRT-Herat, he appeared surprised and defensive. Nevertheless, he responded frankly:

> I have built roads and buildings paid for by the USA and Italy, and of course, those are great opportunities that I've had to take advantage of. My company is one of the biggest in the construction business here in Herat. I am a businessman, I have expenses and bills to pay and they are willing to spend a lot here, they have a lot of money in Afghanistan. But some of my friends and relatives are very anti-Western and I can't tell them I've done business with the Americans or Italians. A lot of what I do has to be secret or my family and I will be at risk. Because people talk, gossip and so on, and a lot of the projects my company has participated in are in Herat's rural areas where the Taliban are strong. (Herati Construction Company Owner 2014)

This man's company assets and experience positioned him uniquely and favourably in bids to win coalition contracts, something that seemed to have yielded substantial profits. His tactical advantage was highlighted by NATO's need to work with local (sub) contractors, purportedly to cut costs and alleviate concerns over how the coalition's economic governance would be perceived by the locals[1] (Pan 2011, Tierney 2010, Cahn 2010). Nonetheless, this range of tactical advantages did not imply automatic business opportunities for the company owner. He still had to manoeuvre around an array of security obstacles. Once he accepted the risks, they further incentivized him to engage closely with different NATO and NATO member-state agencies. His account mirrors Tariq's logic of risk, utility, and contingent security:

> When you're in, you're in. Then you want to get every dollar from the USAID, Italians, or whatever. Otherwise, it's not worth it. And when I'm in, then they depend on me until I'm done, but then they depend on me again because they've worked with me and they know me and they need someone to trust. They all think they are here to stay, even the Taliban. That's OK. We just need to make sure we benefit as well, and then they can use us and it can last as long as they wish or as long as they can survive here. (Herati Construction Company Owner 2014)

---

[1] This pressure has repeatedly compelled the Alliance and its member governments to expedite public procurement procedures and award contracts to entities clandestinely associated with the Taliban or 'warlords' – a much-deployed tactic in the nonviolent exploitation of NATO.

Like Tariq, this man was unconcerned with abstract descriptors or ethics of his relationship with a *khaareji* ('foreigner' in Dari) or *kufar* ('infidels'). He appeared, however, sceptical of the rationality of NATO's presence in Herat and seemed to believe that the situation allowed him and, moreover, compelled him to take advantage of it. As if to mirror my first encounter with Zabiullah, my interpreter in Kabul, the construction company owner claimed: *'They need us, and if they want to be here, we have a way to make what they do our[s], because they can't do anything without us. I don't care how they see it'* (Herati Construction Company Owner 2014). Obidullah Yari, deputy head of the Craftsmen's Union of Herat, said that some Union members felt uneasy about receiving funding from the United States or Italy, as they worried how that would reflect on their business and profits. Nonetheless, Obidullah also added:

> No one is going to just reject the money because of fear, hatred of Americans, or patriotism. That's not how it works. They have already practically given it to us. We know it's not because they love us or care for us. We don't have to love them either. This is not even doing business with them. We are just trying to survive. They think this is good for them, and we are just making sure we take advantage of them as well. I heard that USAID report back when they don't spend the money that was put aside for local projects. That means they have to work with us if they want to show that they have done their job. And our members can believe in whatever they want and like whoever [*sic*] they want to like. (Yari 2015)

Therefore, organizational logics (herein, of the USAID) – and the broader necessity of postcolonial power to perpetuate own interventions – create structures predicated on a number of combined rationalities. They rest on the notion of development-*as*-security, aspirations to generate local legitimacy by winning Herati 'hearts and minds', and imperatives of surveillance of local life through funding, financial reporting, and other mechanisms (such as industrial parks, and local, national and transnational exhibitions and trade fares that the craftsmen and other entrepreneurs are incentivized to attend). Yet, these very structures both enable and constrain local life and its maximization of own chances of survival. While Heratis have to cope with the risk of engagement with the United States and other 'internationals', they also bypass the politics of 'hearts and minds'. The indispensability of the indigenous body (*'they have to work with us'*), its social functions, roles, and skills (as entrepreneurs, farmers, or interpreters) all underwrite its resistances to being 'won over' and pacified.

Furthermore, I was told about the general usefulness of the Heratis' local topographic knowledge and familiarities with landscapes and distributions of hills, mountain ranges, rivers, valleys, arid and fertile soil, animal life and flora, physical accessibility of different places (whether on foot or by various vehicle types and aircraft), and patterns of human adaptability to shifting conditions of movement, residence and habitation. Geographic Information Systems, Geoinformatics, and highly digitalized aerial surveillance have found extensive applications in military planning and 'kinetic' actions and have contributed to creating *'militarized regime[s] of comprehensive and constant hypervisibility'* (Gregory 2012, 158). Nonetheless, security apparatuses continue to deploy, incentivize, and exploit 'local human intelligence' in attempts to contextualize complex bodies of geospatial data and understand how individuals and groups make use of and navigate spaces ranging from rugged mountain terrains to flee markets. While portrayed as a source of weakness and dependence, relationships with 'local human intelligence' are regularly acknowledged by the international military coalition in Afghanistan (Brooks 2011, The United States Army Intelligence Center of Excellence 2011, Steeb et al. 2011, Azimi 2008). They are being fostered in parallel with NATO's pre-existing and evolving technologies and apparatuses of learning about the spatial tactics of Afghans' daily life. 'Human Terrain System' (The United States Army Intelligence Center of Excellence 2011) was one such project: heavily invested-in and questionably successful (Gezari 2015). Mohammad Sohail, provincial manager for the government-coordinated National Solidarity Program (NSP) in Herat, reflected on the indispensable character of the topographic knowledge that Heratis have in the domains of reconstruction, development, and security:

> Our international Facilitating Partners have significant intelligence and databases about the Province, people, places. OK, some more, others less, but they are all constantly dependent on our Ministry employees and actual CDC [Community Development Council] members, all ordinary locals and community leaders, to explain to them, advise them and guide them through the logics of how different places work. That is really important for development and reconstruction work, because people financing the projects need to know where it does or doesn't make sense to build water wells or schools, or put up solar panels or build emergency rooms. ... Knowing the customs and ways of life of people who should use these things takes knowing both the physical place and how people live in it. Maps, hydrologists, or veterinary experts cannot know the whole package. (Sohail 2014)

Tariq Afzaly added his own experience and detail to this portrayal of situational and topographic advantage:

> PRTs and NSP partners don't always know how dependent they are and how manipulated they get by the locals. They can collect all the scientifically relevant data about different places and still be fooled by the local mullah or tribal elder to build a water well or a road close to his house, sometimes to his own gain or maybe shared with a few other smart locals. Sometimes, I would warn them about what was happening, but it's also often smarter to not get involved. That is at the end again good for me. (Afzaly 2015)

Tariq was describing his own levels of topographic familiarity as a 'control variable' of sorts ('*Sometimes, I would warn them*') as he recounted forms of local knowledge in development and reconstruction. Moreover, his narrative seemed to imply that he could calibrate his own involvement as long as he mixed and combined the tactics of ethical intervention ('*Sometimes, I would warn them*') and self-preserving silence ('*it's also often smarter to not get involved*') during project implementation. He seemed to imply an intuitive equilibrium in the frequency and distribution of those two tactics, as both could end up benefiting him in certain contexts. He told me that I was 'overthinking it' when I hinted at these tactical adjustments and calculations. However, when I asked about the prevalence of the exploitation of NATO, the UN, private companies and NGOs by the locals, Tariq was quick to acknowledge that Heratis need to think tactically about their engagement with the security-development apparatus:

> Of course, in reality, even if the locals don't take advantage of them in such conspiracy kind of ways, the internationals will need them anyways because they need someone to show them the way on the ground. And that really empowers some people, maybe a limited circle, but it's still important for them since most of them are regular middle class people or maybe even poorer, struggling people. (Afzaly 2015)

He appeared reticent in his implicit sympathy for the 'struggling', but was palpably sympathetic nonetheless.

Buried in Christopher J. Chivers' casual scolding of Afghan soldiers and police officers were passages with invaluable insights into their unique situational advantages on the ground:

> Afghan soldiers have also proved, as they have for years, to be more proficient than Americans at searching Afghan homes and identifying potential Taliban members – two tasks difficult for outsiders to perform. (Chivers 2010)

Shapoor Saber is one of Herat's most prominent journalists who has investigated and reported on ANSF. I asked him to comment on the ostensible contradiction between the representations of perceptive, sharp, observant and useful Afghan recruits and images of corrupt and irresponsible freeloaders in ANSF. I quoted for Shapoor different passages from Chivers' article in *The New York Times*.

> There are some cultural stereotypes in those descriptions, they sound very typical, but also they are true for some. The point is that the West doesn't understand what they see as a lack of dedication and general laziness. People who have such special skills and kinds of knowledge about the insurgency also know that they can't be replaced so easily, especially when the ANSF is struggling to reach NATO's recruitment targets. It would take years and years to NATO troops to learn and recognize these local details in people and their orientations, their demeanor, physique, etc. Afghan troops know that and they know how it gives them power around foreign soldiers. (Saber 2014)

Given the contingency of Herat's (in)security and the locals' widespread ability to meander around it, I could not fathom how this privileged knowledge and expertise about the Taliban could be wrestled away from them other than through NATO's disengagement across the board. None of my interviewees seemed to believe that was going to happen any time soon. They all shared a sense of the 'West's' ubiquity, even as NATO troops, development workers and private security contractors had started slowly leaving the Province in 2012.

Conclusion

In a March 2015 piece, *The Wall Street Journal* described Herat as an 'opposition hub' where thousands had rallied around the local 'strongman', 'warlord' and former governor of Herat Ismail Khan to challenge the authority of Kabul, President Ashraf Ghani, and the international coalition (Stancati 2015). Furthermore, the Taliban insurgency has sustained deadly attacks across the Herat Province against the civilians and security forces alike, including an attack on Pakistan's consulate in January 2015 (Khaama Press 2015). In 2016 and 2017, the Islamic State joined in with its own deadly attacks in Herat City, targeting particularly its Shiite population and places of worship (Al Jazeera 2017a). Herat remains vulnerable to insurgent attacks from the neighbouring and more violent Ghor (Felbab-Brown 2015), while being tightly controlled through various security apparatuses. The Province headquarters one of the five US-built and supported ANA bases (Corps 207) and Shindand Airbase remains home to the 3rd Wing of the AAF aided by US Air Force advisory groups and Army trainers. In 2015, Shindand was still described as a launch site for US surveillance missions in the region (Mohammad 2015, National Directorate of Security Employee No. 1 2014, Saber 2014). Meanwhile, NATO has shifted its monitoring practices of Herat to Resolute Support Mission and US Operation Freedom's Sentinel. These structures intersect, compete, overlap, and merge with Afghan and foreign security companies (e.g. DynCorp) and militias, along with regular Afghan forces. Security apparatuses operate as both conjoined and conflicted with various development initiatives through the NSP, IDLG, Provincial Development Council, UN Assistance Mission in Afghanistan, UN Development Programme, private companies and NGOs.

This grid of governance has been sustained by NATO and facilitated by the UN in postcolonial spaces. In Herat and elsewhere, their governing necessity has been to pacify, control and regulate life. This chapter has analysed security governance in Herat by disassociating power relations that constitute it, i.e. by investigating practices of resistance to it. To conceptualize resistance, I have drawn on Foucault and de Cearteau's focus on the *microphysics* of power and Bhabha's approach to postcolonial resistance as *ambivalence*. I have studied nonviolent resistance as a strategy of maximization of Herati life within, through and against the matrix of governance apparatuses and authorities that demand exclusive loyalty, compliance and participation in the management of peace, security, development and order. I have contextualized such nonviolent maximizations as tactical micro-economic and micro-spatial counter-exploitations of governance apparatuses, and of employment relationships that sustain them. Across Herat, toying with, utilization, evasion and re-appropriation of UN, US and NATO security and development structures has unfolded through ambiguous, shifting and unstable professional and employment commitments by ordinary people. Stalling in and around the workplace, shirking of assigned responsibilities, slacking off, micro-scale sabotage, ghost soldiering, insurgent infiltration and theft of military equipment are just some tactics of counter-exploitation practised by ordinary Heratis. Moreover, efforts to drive the international coalition out of Afghanistan are intertwined with actions aimed at keeping it in the country and temporarily stabilizing it as a target of counter-exploitation. Therefore, this survey suggests that the social rationales of resistances are disjointed, ambiguous and subject to change. Such ambiguity and instability of life make its disciplining, control and regulation tempting and complicated. In conditions of contingent (in)security, Herat has operated as a space of contestation and destabilization of power, thereby cultivating arrays of entangled political subjectivities. They involve productions and policing of farmers who are police recruits, entrepreneurs who at once condemn and do business with the 'Americans', and patriots who are thieves and insurgent infiltrators. Herat is a rich space of life insofar as the shifts and transitions across these subjectivities are both tightly policed and repeatedly practised. Herati stories are not exhausted in violence and pacification. Rather, they come about through minute acts of redrawing, extension and renegotiation of spaces of safety and well-being. Paradoxically, such renegotiations both undermine and inspire the globe's protracted involvement in the government of security and development across Afghanistan.

5

Banished by Culture, Violated in Its Midst: Managing Musalla's Homeless between Minarets, Development and Security

Introduction

Just over a kilometre north of Herat's old town and citadel lies one of the largest architectural ensembles in all of Afghanistan: the Musalla of Queen Gawhar Shad and Madrasah of Sultan Hussein Bayqara, or simply – the Musalla Complex. Composed of several somewhat independent structures, the construction of Musalla lasted nearly a century, keeping busy several members of the Timurid Dynasty. Upon its completion, at the end of the fifteenth century, the entire Complex boasted an unparalleled forest of over twenty minarets, many reaching over 50 metres in height. Rising far above the green grounds of lush lawns, almond and pomegranate trees, the Complex stood out from the arid background of the Herat valley and old town's tawny walls (Abraham 2003, Golombek and Wilber 1988, Byron 1982). Nowadays, its story is usually one of architectural, cultural and social decline. Severely damaged over the past two centuries by British forces, Soviet and mujahedeen bombings, earthquakes, small and large-scale fire exchanges during the Afghan civil war, and daily traffic, the Complex now contains only five minarets. They have lost their original tops and much of the blue, white and black faience tiling. They have been damaged by shelling and other environmental factors and are now deemed unstable, at least three being visibly tilted. Archaeological studies, ordinary visitors and passers-by have repeatedly described the minarets as crumbling daily.

Thousands of ordinary Heratis still circulate around and across the Complex every day and many of their activities have remained largely the same – from the saunter of passers-by and routine haggling of local shopkeepers to the quiet work of restorers trying to save what is left of the Complex. Since the US intervention in 2001 and the overthrow of the Taliban, the national, provincial and city governments have worked to put the Musalla Complex on UNESCO's World Heritage map. Provincial and city officials in particular have claimed that, in addition to preserving Herat's historical and cultural heritage, this move would benefit the local economy, attract tourists, 'spur growth', and help '*clean up the site and the whole city and make it even more beautiful*' (Saidi 2016). Economic growth, cultural management and beautification of the site have also been rhetorically correlated. They are explicitly invoked as maximizing Herat's general welfare and seem to drive the restoration and UNESCO-focused efforts. Various restorative works have been undertaken at Musalla since 2003 under the auspices of the UN and UNESCO – from the repairs on the Gawhar Shad Mausoleum to the construction of a decorative and protective wall around the four remaining minarets at the Sultan Bayqara Madrasa.

However, throughout the process, a contradictory mix of social-economic neglect, surveillance, and physical and institutional repression has marked the governmental and public treatment of the homeless living on Musalla's grounds between the tilted and crumbling minarets. On the surface, it appears that no sustained attention has been paid to their living conditions, safety or overall welfare. Merging with the minarets' precarious state, neglect seems to dominate and define the space. To homeless families, groups of friends and individuals, the relatively quiet and isolated Complex grounds seem to offer protection. The minarets, their slabs, and many crevices in the dirt promise cover from rain, snow, wind and unbearable summer heat. They help the homeless hide from the gaze and entitlement to judgement of Heratis with homes or tourists. Yet, these very benefits eerily disguise the threat posed by the giant crumbling sandcastles. More insidiously, formal and unwritten public policies, as well as social conditions far less visible to the naked eye further constrain the survival and welfare of people already pushed to the margins. In addition to living in unsafe, degrading and unsanitary conditions, Musalla's homeless are being monitored and physically and verbally harassed by the police and ordinary Heratis.

In exploring the administration of Afghan life, always surveilled as statistically abnormal and risky, this chapter examines social marginalization through cultural management as a strategy of governmental power. It zeroes in on the Musalla Complex as a site of exemplary threat to the Afghan and Herati *normal* and a place of convergence of 'anomalous' conducts. I study the functioning of homeless vulnerabilities on Musalla's grounds because this space reflects how power can mobilize a spectrum of seemingly 'apolitical' social forces to attain political goals and maximize 'good life'. This chapter focuses on the homeless of Musalla to show that the social-political normal, social exclusion, and 'culture' do not somehow function as each other's limits. They are not mutually exclusive or unrelated. Rather, they can operate in unison and in ways that maximize each other's effects and purported general welfare. The meaning attributed to the minarets as preeminently valuable cultural artefacts – and the government's various efforts to improve their state and economic utility – ultimately disempower the homeless and undermine their lives beyond the immediately degrading and unsafe conditions. Considered deviant, dangerous and threatening to the preservation of the Complex and acquisition of the UNESCO World Heritage site status, Musalla's homeless are regularly snubbed, mocked and bullied by the locals, ignored by the authorities and produced as problematic and in need of dislocation away from the site. These representations and conducts are normalized, thereby marginalizing possibilities to see the homeless as already displaced, needing shelter, food and medical or psychiatric care. Rather than vulnerable, they are portrayed as threatening to the very survival of the minarets, as well as the safety and health of 'normal Heratis'. Stripped of any human nuance otherwise accorded to other Heratis, they are labelled, marginalized, and managed as 'drug addicts' and threats to Herat's regular life. In the social-economic extreme, they are described and excluded as addicts whose physical presence on Musalla's grounds contributes to its architectural instability and threatens 'disease' or 'insecurity' upon the rest of Herat. Their de facto access to public health and welfare resources is minimal to none and the modality of their exclusion makes them largely invisible to the welfare state. This makes them vulnerable to economic and physical violence by the civil authorities, police and locals. Socially deprived of any legitimate claims to public space or 'the right to the city', the homeless have been subject to careful neglect, up-close and remote monitoring, police harassment, banishments, dislodgment and other forms of abuse.

Thus, the governmental tactics of cultural management sustained through UNESCO, Italian and USAID assistance and the more immediate social neglect and physical brutality constrain the life chances of the homeless, refashioning them into an uncomfortable binary: either the Complex and the city will prosper or they will succumb to neglect and decay. Musalla's homeless do not explicitly appear in this equation, but they are used as an important cornerstone of its maintenance. Equated with the unfortunate prospect of decline, their lives are kept invisible in the midst of highly visible spatial and architectural transformations. This chapter invites attention to the oppressive and disempowering effects of governance, unequal communal progress, growth and public aesthetics.

What does the marginalizing treatment and abuse of Musalla's homeless tell us about the strategies of postcolonial power, or the disciplining and regulation predicated on disparate utilities of human populations? Moreover, does the misery of the homeless relate to the overall containment of the Herati and Afghan abnormal, and how so? Finally, why and how has a cultural monument become useful in this power game? This chapter draws on the conceptual framework in Chapter 2 that has outlined the operation of postcolonial power through various security apparatuses. I will *first* identify certain conceptual rifts and tensions in this chapter, and will discuss some methodological issues that researching for it has produced. *Second*, the chapter introduces a more specific framework of analysis of social forces that make the marginalization of Musalla's homeless possible and necessary. I do so by engaging C. Wright Mills' work on the cultural apparatus from a Foucauldian perspective on governmental power as productive and relational. Moreover, the chapter will revisit Foucault's genealogical work on the history of governmental power by way of *police* and the city's 'splendour' as its key object. *Third*, I will propose a twofold survey of historical secondary data (including academic, corporate, and expert reports) and own fieldwork interviews and observations on the historical decay of Musalla, as well as the origins and stories of its homeless population. On one hand, I will examine the material decline of the Complex over the centuries, as well as the degrading living conditions of its dwellers. Then, I will show that the visible architectural, material, and human decay of the Complex does not exist as a tragic and saddening reality separate from the politics of development, life and the body. Instead, I will make a twofold argument. The vulnerabilities of Musalla's homeless follow from a pervasive and de-centred oppression of bodies seen as deviant and threatening to the virtuous and normal. Moreover, discourses of culture play a critical role in that oppression. To argue that, I will detail the visible physical violence exacted upon the homeless by ordinary Heratis and the police, as well as less visible structural violence through Herat's labour market, wage regimes and its justice, welfare and healthcare systems. Therefore, this chapter points to how the discourses of civilization and culture, as well as the practices of 'caring' for culture, reinforce marginalization. Moreover, they do it in concert with the politics of distinction between the useful and useless – or dangerous – lives.

The 'Otherness' of the Homeless and the Study of It

Before I discuss how 'culture' reproduces homelessness to serve growth and normality, there are a few conceptual and methodological notes I owe the reader. These concern the *who* of homelessness and my relationship to the homeless throughout the research process. Agamben's analytic of bare life (Agamben 1995) and the contributions of Subaltern Studies (Guha and Spivak 1988) can be used to critique the production of silenced populations, as well as how 'voice' is selectively granted to them in the academia and policy making. Agamben's logic of *bare life* speaks to the quality of the body 'abandoned' by the law (Agamben 1995, 28–29) and deprived of the '*right to have rights*' (Arendt 1973, 276). However, it might not apply entirely to homelessness at Musalla. Herat's homeless are not altogether ostracized and denied citizenship or human rights. Rather, they are subject to a more probabilistic mixture of neglect, selective denial of citizenship, purposeful physical, emotional and psychological violation and socially tolerated abuse combined with situational and contingent welfare, charity, medical and juridical care. Moreover, beyond Agamben's focus on the operation of sovereign power, this chapter recounts the production of homeless vulnerabilities through a dispersed context and space-specific cultural apparatus. This kind of impact is more reflective of Foucault's notion of governmental power that directs the conduct of its subjects through infinitesimal social relations rather than an inviolable centre (Foucault 2009).

Rather than bare life, the notion of the *subaltern* (Guha 1999) may be closer to the experience of postcolonial homelessness. Subalterns are populations oppressed and silenced to the extent that their ability to speak is *questioned by* those implicated in elite and hegemonic power. The subaltern is the 'Other' that fascinates and inspires the left-wing activist, politician or intellectual, but remains always 're-presented' (as is the case in this book) and ultimately unheard (Spivak 1988b). The subaltern is the deviant body and 'radical difference' (Li 2006, 26) marginalized so profoundly that the very interest in acquiring hegemonic power is antithetical to his/her life. That makes the subaltern 'insurgent' (Spivak 1988a, 3) and invested in resistance: his/her very existence is ominous to power. Yet the subaltern is also maintained within the political-economic, juridical, and 'cultural' relations of power as an indispensable resource that can be violated, exploited, represented and tapped into anew. If the Herati homeless are framed as the subaltern, that framing challenges Foucault's notion of intentionality, desire and 'interest' as non-subjective, discursive and produced rather than authentic, owned and sovereign. Spivak critiques post-structuralist arguments as 'resistant' to the explanatory and historical role of ideology, as unable to put forward a theory of interest (Spivak 1988b, 273). While this tension is important, it is also possible to study resistance, its goals and intentions as discursive and shaped by power. However, this strategy does pose some methodological and ethical challenges.

I only spoke to one homeless person during my multiple visits to Musalla (indirectly, through my interpreter). I based this decision on the insistence of the locals who were instrumental to my fieldwork. Their view was that interviewing the homeless could risk our personal safety. While I was bound by the professional limitations of institutional risk assessment, I questioned this judgement. I also considered taking practical steps that would have reflected my doubts in the research. However, I acquiesced. One of the goals of this work is to shed light on the precariousness of homeless lives and disrupt the academic, policy, administrative and governmental practices of their erasure. Not being able to conduct more interviews with Musalla's homeless and document their voices has undermined that wider goal. That limitation has also reinforced the *expert/subaltern* divide that bell hooks and Gayatri C. Spivak critiqued in Western/Northern postcolonial research (hooks 1990, Spivak 1988b). As I regret any unintended professional role in the neglect of subaltern testimonies of domination, I acknowledge my position vis-à-vis the life chances and experiences of the oppressed. My position was one of white/Western middle-class male privilege. It was expressed through the licence to '*brandish concrete experience*' as 'the intellectual' who '*diagnoses the episteme*' or identifies the conditions of truth and knowledge (Spivak 1988b, 274). Therefore, since the situational calculus and the thralls of my subjectivity paralysed me from better highlighting the voices of the subjugated, I felt that taking pictures of them, exposing them to my prolonged gaze, and objectifying their bodies would proliferate their experience of marginalization and would caricature their lives.

'What is Splendour?' Culture as Population Management

In his account of the genealogy of governmental power, Foucault turned to its formations dating back to roughly the sixteenth century. According to Foucault, one of the key regulatory apparatuses that once made the modern state possible was an evolving practice of 'police'. Early meanings of the term are different from the contemporary designation of law enforcement. In particular, from the seventeenth century *'the word "police" ... begins to refer to the set of means by which the state's forces can be increased while preserving the state in good order'* (Foucault 2009, 313). In referring to the state's forces as *'its natural resources, commercial possibilities, balance of trade'* (Ibid, 287) and *'the population, the army, ... the production, the commerce and the monetary circulation'* (Ibid, 316), Foucault defines police as *'the calculation and technique that will make it possible to establish a mobile, yet stable and controllable relationship between the state's internal order and the development of its forces'* (Ibid, 313). In other words, police is the management of the state's growth and equilibrium. Furthermore, Foucault finds a *'rather strange word for describing the object of police'* – splendour (Ibid). He summarizes the task of police as *'ensur[ing] the state's splendor'* (Ibid) and quotes a seventeenth-century author, Turquet de Mayerne, who claimed that *'under Police must be included everything that gives ornament, form, and splendor to the city, and this is in fact the order of everything that one can see in it'* (Ibid). Similarly, Hohental defined police in 1776 as *'the set of means that serve the splendor of the entire state and the happiness of all its citizens*' (Ibid, 313–314). '*What is splendor?*' asks then Foucault and offers key parameters useful for this chapter's problem:

> It is both the visible beauty of the order and the brilliant, radiating manifestation of a force. Police therefore is in actual fact the art of the state's splendor as visible order and manifest force. (Foucault 2009, 314)

Splendour, as the object of police, is '*the good use of the state's forces*' (Ibid, 314), while '*police is the set of interventions and means that ensure that living [and] coexisting [of men] will be effectively useful to the constitution and development of the state's forces*' (Ibid, 327). Specific police tasks included activities that are contemporarily associated with *the* police (e.g. registering the population, following crime rates, etc.), but many were unrelated, such as regulating trade and markets (Ibid, 315–322). Therefore, Foucault concludes that police is '*the whole of government*' concerned with managing society and the state's forces. Yet, it is also '*a [distinct] function of the state*': '*administrative modernity par excellence*' (Ibid, 321).

There are two ways to apply the lessons of Foucault's analysis. One relates to splendour and *the* police (as law enforcement) in Herat more narrowly. A second direction of conceptualization is more properly explanatory, since it concerns the notion of *cultural apparatuses*. I will tackle first the more narrow application.

'Police' in the Study of Afghan Law Enforcement's Management of Musalla

Some of the disciplinary implications of splendour have been imparted upon *the* police as an agency enforcing, among other, 'disorderly conduct' and 'public decency' laws. Depending on the juridical order in question, they ban public nudity, inebriation, loitering, disturbance of peace, noise, damage of property (e.g. via graffiti, destruction, or theft), etc. This meaning refers to the techniques of upholding a Lockean sense of freedom, which is constraining offence or insult to another person's body or the products of its labour. Therefore, its logic is relational (disciplining conduct between multiple persons), aesthetic and utilitarian. This is because 'order' and 'the good use of forces' are narrated as beautiful, rational and socially beneficial. While the idea of 'splendour' is uniquely historical, I use it to stimulate a specific analytical point before moving on to the idea of cultural apparatuses. Namely, by claiming that the restoration of Musalla preserves Herat's historical and cultural heritage, benefits the local economy, induces growth, and helps '*clean up the site and the whole city and make it even more beautiful*' (Saidi 2016), Herat's city and provincial governments precisely convey 'splendour' as the object of restoration. Thus, they aspire to mobilize and maximize the use of public, private, community, and international resources to further induce the growth of the 'state's forces' (economic, aesthetic, security, etc.). As my analysis of fieldwork data will show, the authorities have monitored Musalla and its 'ornaments' as a resource conducive to Herat's development by utilizing surveillance and police forces. Patrolling the Complex and its surroundings, recording movements and social interactions around it from the ground and air, gathering intelligence on who frequents the site – all those measures precede immediate coercion against the homeless. Splendour and order are upheld by *securing* the Complex against desecration and theft (of mausoleum and madrasa artefacts, the invaluable faience, etc.) or against insurgency attacks. The homeless are, as will be detailed, considered a threat that ties disease, petty crime, and terrorism together and necessitates the deployment of the Afghan National Security Forces (ANSF).

Concerning the unusual insertion of disease into policing, Foucault identifies the economic management of '*the sick and disabled poor*' and interest in '*public health in times of epidemic and contagion*' (Foucault 2009, 320) as core police tasks. Staurt Elden (2003) studies the relationship between surveillance and public health, and points to Foucault's work on the historical regulation of life and population through the management of medicine and health threats (e.g. specific diseases and their geographies). Elden revisits Foucault's work to claim that medical institutions are architectures of discipline, surveillance and corporeal policing. Much like the panoptical prison, individuated surveillance comes from hospitals (Ibid). This dynamic in the maintenance of splendour-as-health will be detailed in the social production of Musalla's homeless as dangerous, unclean, and crazed 'drug addicts' seen as breeding grounds for diseases. Infections and illnesses are purportedly spread through the impurity (sexual and hygienic) of their bodies, or are tied to their risky behaviour during drug use. Scorned as a mixture of thieves, terrorists and diseased drug addicts responsible for their own failures, the homeless are abused, dislodged from the Complex, ignored and surveilled through various spatial arrangements. In other words, in upholding the Lockean values of freedom and property, the police, healthcare and welfare systems undermine a whole category of vulnerable lives. Often forcibly removed from the Complex, physically abused and generally rejected as deviants at fault for their own condition, the homeless are also excluded from the welfare and healthcare systems. Thus, the tension between their invisibility and alleged threat to society is consistent across governmental practices. Elden posits that policing and *the* police link together the disciplining of individual bodies and the conditioning of whole populations (Ibid). Each homeless individual is subject to corporeal monitoring and punishment by the police and ordinary Heratis. This possibility of individuated oppression is instrumental to the mechanics of broader systemic invisibilities in the welfare and public health systems. Homeless lives are not a useful or productive resource in the overall population, or the kind of being that should be cultivated. They are not hardworking entrepreneurs who will help Herat grow and make it more splendid. They are 'costly'. Thus, their numbers and possibilities of growth should be contained and minimized without outright extinction. Since the operation of biopolitics and governmentality are at stake here, I will briefly introduce the notion of cultural apparatuses as their extension.

The Cultural Apparatus and the Cultivation of Splendour

Decades ago, Charles Wright Mills attempted to identify sources of progressive change and resistance to war and inequality in 'overdeveloped' Western societies. Claiming that the Marxist identification of the working class as the agent of revolutionary change was misguided, he examined the potential for middle-class 'white collar' cultural elites and intellectuals to be the vanguard of a 'New Left'. He developed a concept of *the cultural apparatus* to explore the historical role of 'intellectual workmen' and 'intelligentsia', terms inspired by Central and Eastern European socialist vocabularies of the 1950s. Mills defined the cultural apparatus as made up of '*all the organizations and milieux in which artistic, intellectual, and scientific work goes on, and by which entertainment and information are produced and distributed*' (Mills 2008, 204). The apparatus '*contains an elaborate set of institutions: of schools and theaters, newspapers and census bureaus, studios, laboratories, museums, little magazines, radio networks*' (Ibid). By embedding 'cultural' practices in specific locales, Mills critiqued the artistic, academic and scientific forces that reproduce society. He indicted them as complacent perpetuations of Fordist capitalist consumerism incapable of generating subversive ideas and movements. However, he also argued that intellectual workmen could still re-appropriate the cultural apparatus. After all, the apparatus had expropriated the workmen's means of intellectual production in the first place. While sceptical about the critical potential of public institutions in the 'overdeveloped world', Mills found hope across the world in the resistances of 'young intellectuals', students, and '*young professors and writers*', who could '*break out of apathy*'. He saw their anger as socially transformative (Mills 1960, 23).

Mills did not explain why or how intelligentsia would disrupt 'apathy' and re-appropriate cultural apparatuses into agents of radicalism (Mattson 2002, 93–95). How the resisting agent *be*-comes remained unexamined. Furthermore, why would the labour, itself apparently incapable of radicalism, follow suit? Nonetheless, Mills recognized how the cultural apparatus produces its subjects:

> Our standards of credibility, our definitions of reality, our modes of sensibility – as well as our immediate opinions and images – are determined much less by any pristine experience than by our exposure to the output of the cultural apparatus. (Mills 2008, 204)

Moreover, he claimed that '*the cultural apparatus ... expropriates the very chance to have experience that can rightly be called 'our own'*' (Ibid). He understood the susceptibility of the cultural apparatus to the capitalist (or otherwise) economy and nationalism (Mills 2008, 207) and concluded that the apparatus was '*the source of the Human Variety – of styles of living and of ways to die*' (Ibid, 204).

Mills understood the cultural apparatus as a structure that moulded practices of life. However, his theory is less specific on how the revolutionary or docile agency comes about. In other words, both the apparatus and 'its' subject are pre-existing. Ideological struggle is needed to jolt the consciousness of the subject and 're-appropriate' the apparatus back to his/her needs. Yet Mills' accounts of agency, structure and power are not relational, so how ideological struggle comes about or works remains blackboxed. Therefore, it remains unclear how the apparatus is reproduced, re-calibrated or subverted. Mills' framework forecloses the ability of power to induce social conditions that make the apparatus possible and functional. Hence, it seems that capitalism or racism have no discernible role in producing their subjects, their docility or resistance.

The cultural apparatus as a concept must be re-contextualized to elucidate what and how power *does*. Said's *Orientalism* offers a clue: '*As a cultural apparatus Orientalism is all aggression, activity, judgment, will-to-truth, and knowledge*' (Said 1978, 204). The cultural apparatus' oppressive effects can be unpacked by exploring the knowledge and truths that sustain it. Nonetheless, studying how social truths articulate power (and thus govern) requires an analysis of how populations are managed, 'aroused', and 'incited' rather than simply controlled (Foucault 2009, 352). It requires analysing power as productive and creative rather than simply coercive.

Exploring the genealogy of the cultural apparatus through the productivity of power leads us back to Foucault's work on police and population. Now the notion of *police* can be used to capture governmental power and rationality. The cultural apparatus can be understood to operate within power relations as a technology of cultivating populations, i.e. of conditioning how they are to conduct themselves. Put differently, its utility is in articulating how the '*conduct of conduct*' (Foucault 1982) works. Furthermore, the cultural apparatus can be studied as a space-specific security apparatus (*dispositif*), much like the medical or juridical apparatus. Comparing Foucault's understanding of the apparatus with that of Mills, one discovers a similar sensitivity to the plurality of spaces in which power operates. Unlike Mills, however, Foucault points to how such spaces are constituted and cultivated by power (Foucault 1977, 2009).[1]

To understand how an apparatus (of cultural institutions, police forces, Heratis with homes, discourses of personal responsibility, public morality, entrepreneurialism, etc.) governs Musalla's homeless is to understand the truths that support that apparatus. It means analysing how the cultural apparatus creates an environment that maximizes Herat's strength around civilizational, historical, economic and cultural rationales and renders homelessness in certain places untenable. Studying the erasure of Musalla's homeless means identifying how certain strategies of cultural management nullify and undermine the homeless within their 'own' reality of feebleness without needing to resort to constant repression, permanent dislocation or imprisonment. My goal is to understand how culture is deployed as a means of population management, whereby the population is not limited to the homeless – they are undermined as part of the collective body. The concept of the cultural apparatus should specify how the homeless are conditioned to disappear on the grounds of their own weakness, useless as a resource to the economic and civilizational artefact such as Musalla or to the growth of the state.

Musalla and 'Its' Homeless: Visible Neglect

Queen Gawhar Shad built a domed madrasah north of Herat's old town in 1417, the first of several objects intended to give the new Timurid capital something of Samarqand's old imperial glow. It also aimed at transforming a public space already

---

[1] See Chapter 2 for a discussion on the security apparatus.

used for open-air prayer into Empire's new religious centre. Over the next century, a whole ensemble would grow and include Gawhar Shad's mosque and a mausoleum and, to the north, a madrasah built with forced labour under the tutelage of Sultan Hussein Bayqara (Byron 1982, 101). Park-i-Bihzad, *'a luxuriant haven with trees, lawns and flower beds'* (Dupree 1994, 2) was carefully maintained around the Complex. Altogether, the structure grew to encompass a surface area of around 18,500 m², reportedly matching in beauty Gawhar Shad's other grand creation of Timurid art in Mashhad, Persia (Abraham 2003). Robert Byron, once a famous travel writer of Britain's peak colonial era, wrote of the Complex as *'the most beautiful example in colour in architecture ever devised by man to the glory of his God and himself'* (Elliot 1999, 372). In *The Road to Oxiana* (1937), Byron described his first encounter with the Complex as he arrived in Herat one late November night:

Suddenly the road entered a grove of giant chimneys, whose black outlines regrouped themselves against the stars as we passed. ... The chimneys must be minarets. I went to bed like a child on Christmas Eve, scarcely able to wait for the morning. ... Their beauty is more than scenic, depending on light or landscape. On closer view, every tile, every flower, every petal of the mosaic contributes its genius to the whole. (Byron 1982, 87)

In another place, he wrote of an *'array of blue towers rising haphazard from a patchwork of brown fields and yellow orchards'* (Byron 1982, 94). By the time Byron wrote these words, Musalla had been already severely damaged for half a century. The artillery fire of combined Afghan-British forces first damaged minaret tops during the Afghan recapture of the city after over three centuries of Persian Safavid and Qajar rule (Tirard-Collet 1998). A more overwhelming episode of devastation took place in 1885 when the British military pressured the Afghan Amir to destroy the minarets. The British feared a Russian invasion of the city that, for the Raj, was a *'Gateway to India'* (Barfield 2010, 50). They needed a clear line of fire should the Russians advance on Herat. They also feared that the Tsar's army could use the Complex for hiding and tactical manoeuvring (Aalund 1990, 4, Yate 1888, 12). While the invasion, ironically, never materialized, the destruction of Musalla speaks to colonialism's inherently spatial quality. It is also a testament to the social and historical erasure that once followed the gaze and archival care of colonial-era geographers and explorers. Inaccessible by rail or good roads, Herat was only '(re)discovered' and geo-*written* earlier in 1885 and 1884 by the deceptively named 'Afghan' Boundary Commission composed of joint British, Russian and other explorers, historians, and military personnel (Yate 1888). The Commission crisscrossed the region in an attempt to survey its anthropological and geographic terrains and demarcate a border between Russia's newly acquired possessions in Central Asia and the Emirate of Afghanistan, which was at the time Britain's buffer state and de facto protectorate (Holdich 1885).

Only nine out of over twenty minarets survived Britain's preparation for war. Photos from 1915 show them ominously tilted, of 'unnatural look' (Byron 1982, 94) and decaying. Another two collapsed in a 1931 earthquake (United States Geological Survey n.d.), leaving only seven minarets standing. Byron also wrote of *'the silhouette of [the Mausoleum's] broken dome*' whose top was 'bitten off'. Another minaret collapsed during the 1951 earthquake and by the time civil war broke out in Afghanistan in 1973, there were only five minarets left. Soviet bomb shelling in 1985 claimed another one, further damaging the mausoleum and other ruins in the ensemble. The shelling also left numerous craters on Musalla's grounds (Aalund 1990, 21–28). In a 1994 email to the UN Secretary General's Special Representative in Afghanistan and Pakistan, Nancy H. Dupree remarked that the destruction of 'protective trees' of the surrounding park had '*accelerated nature's erosion, especially during the period of the 120-day wind (June through September) which picks out mosaics and flicks off faience with the precision of a dental pick*' (Dupree 1994, 3). In 1990, UNESCO's rapporteur for Afghanistan, Flemming Aalund, mourned the irreversible destruction and decay of Musalla:

> It is one of the great tragedies of fortune that only a minor part of an architecture, which elicited such admiration from its contemporaries, have survived. ... The decay of buildings has been furthered by looting and disrepair, leaving the extant buildings and ruins as an afterglow only of the former splendour. (Aalund 1990, 4)

UNESCO undertook restoration works and excavations from 1976 to 1979 (Aalund 1990, 21). After an Islamabad-based advocacy group – the Society for the Preservation of Afghanistan's Cultural Heritage – completed emergency conservation operations in 2001 (Archnet 2013), a larger international effort took the lead. Since 2002, UNESCO's work has focused on stabilizing the Gawhar Shad ('number 5') as the most tilted and heavily damaged minaret and ISMEO (*Istituto Italiano per il Medio ed Estremo Oriente*) has worked on protecting the excavations on the site. Italian architect and consultant Andrea Bruno supported both UNESCO efforts. His approach to nearly five decades of research and restoration in Afghanistan has included social-economic, socio-cultural, and anthropological projects presented to the Italian and Afghan governments and UNESCO (David 2012, Santana-Quintero and Stevens 2002, Bruno 1983). Madrassa foundations, largely excavated to date, and four minarets are all that is left of the Hussein Bayqara section of the Complex. The United States (USAID) decided to aid its restoration in 2011 (Remsen and Tedesco 2015, 106), having already assisted in restoring the Herat Citadel (Saidi 2016, Sarwary 2016).

While its descriptions and significance are embedded in discourses of architecture, civilization, history and material culture, Musalla is also integral to a number of less apparent social relations that merit critical scrutiny. One layer is most obviously related to cultural discourses and involves the management and restoration of Musalla through the work of mixed international and domestic bodies, agencies and individuals employed by UNESCO, USAID, DAFA (French Archaeological Delegation in Afghanistan), multinational research and archiving teams, or other international and bilateral agencies (Franke 2015). Moreover, the presence of US troops in the city (until 2005), of the Italian-led NATO Provincial Reconstruction Team (until 2015), and NATO's Train Advise Assist-West (TAAC-W) unit (since January 2015) has been of critical import. They have provided an environment that enables the ANSF to tactically operate on the ground marked by a controlled – and never suppressed – system of insurgency groups, warlords and criminal organizations.

But beyond the events of security, culture and civilizational imaginations, there exist a Herat and a Musalla of the homeless quite visible to any observer, yet rarely integrated into the dominant discourses of the city. This Musalla is typically disassociated from the 'civilizational' Herat whose citadel was first built by Alexander the Great (even though it was probably not) or is only associated with it as a source of threat. One's visit to the Complex might include personally thrilling stories of the mausoleum, tombs, or inaccessible ruins secretly unlocked and shown to (mainly) international visitors. (Using and bribing the guards seems to be so common that an advisor to the Mayor of Herat claimed that much of the Complex's wealth, such as tiling and inscriptions, was stolen in this precise way (Saidi 2016).) One might also be consumed by the extent of decay and destruction, comparing what is left to what was once possibly there.

Yet beyond the need to restore an object's civilizational status, there are discourses inextricably tied to its materiality, events that are narrated as subordinate to the bureaucratic, corporate, and scientific will to knowledge and progress (Baldwin 1954, Frankel 1952). In addition to being a historical site, Musalla is the crux of a growing northern and northwestern part of Herat (Loda, et al. 2013). There, the construction of residential and office spaces, shops and roads has been a daily reality throughout the 2000s. Approaching the Complex from the south by Shahzadegan Road, one sees an older mixture of two and three-story buildings on the road's southern end. It is a three hundred metre-long section mostly occupied by a mixture of businesses (banks, stores, markets, etc.). They gradually give way to residential homes of various construction qualities. They include shacks, mud-brick houses and more solid and richer ones whose facades are covered in marble, decorative bricks or those that have no visible insulation and simply show bare walls of burnt clay bricks. The same eclectic mix of residential and business structures extends to the southeast, east and west of Musalla. To the southeast of the Complex, a mere block away, one finds a locally popular furniture store and another block over is a colourful ice cream and dairy shop. A few hundred metres to the west of the Complex, there are two high schools. All of my interviewees have noted that the cluster of neighbourhoods around Musalla has mushroomed over the past two decades and its population density, while hard to estimate, appears to have increased as well. On UNESCO's webpage, a description submitted by Afghanistan's transitional government notes that there is *'a risk that the pace of inappropriate 'development' will result in the destruction of the surviving residential quarters of the old city, unless controls are introduced*' (Ministry of Information and Culture, Transitional Islamic State of Afghanistan 2004). Etienne Tellier of Iconem, a private company that has provided digital capture and visualization services to UNESCO, similarly warns:

> In the 1970s, the complex was still located in a natural environment, but it is now surrounded by dense urban development, and regular use by local inhabitants is accelerating its deterioration. (Tellier 2016)

However, shifting demographics are framed as more than linear and predictable risks. Studies and recent reports on the Complex emphasize how non-linear and less predictable movements of ordinary Heratis risk further damaging the minarets, madrasa, and other excavations: '*The Madrassah of Sultan Hussain Baiqara is constantly crossed by pedestrians, the protection wall should be repaired*' (Santana-Quintero and Stevens 2002, 14). In addition to Heratis' unrestricted access to large sections of the Complex and its valuable tiling and faience, academic and corporate experts have highlighted that a road running through the middle of the Bayqara section of the Complex must be closed to traffic (Ibid). As late as the winter of 2015, one could still see hundreds of trucks, vans, cars and motorbikes passing through the Complex every day on that road, which was itself a patchwork of worn-off asphalt overlays, potholes and dirt. The noise of vehicles bouncing off the road clearly suggested that its highly damaged state and uneven surface only magnified the countless ground vibrations produced by pedestrians, bicycles and motor vehicles. The road's strategic location and role in connecting the city centre to the suburbs further north explains why the government's various attempts in the 1990s and early 2000s to close it to traffic all failed (Dupree 1994, Santana-Quintero and Stevens 2002). Rarely are these urban events discussed on their own terms as meeting certain population needs or fulfilling a purpose. If mentioned, their logics are subordinate to the necessities of Musalla's management. They are dismissed as urban nuisances and architectural safety hazards. As if to resist the government's restrictive measures and spatial regulation, small shops and side alleys in the Complex's immediate proximity, and a canal flowing through the Complex – all seem to be expanding.

While these urban events and structures are privileged in the narrative of a threatened Musalla, there are precarious lives who depend on its minarets and foundation walls, but are rarely spoken of. They have not found their way into UNESCO's, governmental or corporate feasibility studies. Paradoxically, it might even seem that their impact on the Complex is negligible. Invisible to the archives of the governmental, expert and corporate apparatus, they do not appear as an explicit variable in broader urban and more specific restorative projects in the same manner that the problematic pedestrians, homes, businesses and cars do. The official scientific, bureaucratic and cultural scripts omit them and to a distant reader, they indeed do not exist. But every morning, they wake up underneath the minarets, by the madrasa's foundation walls, or in the holes, dents and coops in the dirt and wasteland of Musalla's grounds. Some leave and others come to take their place by the foundation slabs, under the occasional abandoned tent or, more often, plain nylon rubble. There, they eat, quietly talk to one another, walk around the Complex, sleep, play, seek shelter from the sun, rain or snow, fix old bicycles, have sex, try to strike up conversations with passers-by and tourists, relieve themselves or tend to a distressed infant. The canal that flows through the Complex seems to play an important, if unfortunate, role. In it, adults and children would bathe on a warm summer day or wash their clothes no matter the weather. The canal's steep banks of dirt, plastic rubble and discarded construction material are likewise used for various purposes. On certain parts, people rest and sleep, while elsewhere within the Complex or at other times, they use them to defecate and urinate. They also use corners of the wall that delineates parts of the Complex to find a sense of privacy, relieve themselves and masturbate. Some of Musalla's homeless arrive alone, but entire families, too, populate the Complex. Sometimes, as many as three generations live together. Musalla is where they live or stay temporarily before moving on to a different neighbourhood, an overcrowded homeless shelter or a different town altogether. If

Musalla were their home with the kind of privacy that private property accords, none of their daily practices would seem inordinate or unusual. But what undermines it as a home, improper and inadequate as it is, is not so much that they do not own a single inch of it; it is rather that their right to is not socially acknowledged. During a very brief exchange with one of Musalla's homeless – a man whose age I struggled to surmise – my interpreter translated only a few lines, one being: '*It is not bad here, but I hate it*' (Bazgar 2016).

All of my interviewees have confirmed that there have been homeless individuals and groups on Musalla's grounds for as long as they can remember. '*I can't think of the Complex without picturing them as well*', said Feridun Sarwary, Dean of the Herat Urban Development and Housing Department (HUDA). British photographer Peter Loud photographed Musalla in the early 1970s. His pictures, too, show numerous homeless families. Like in the 1970s, their clothes still include varieties of *qameezes*, *partugs*, *chadars* or *chadris* for women, and *shalwar qameezes* for men, usually black or different shades of brown. Then and now, children might wear bright blue, green or red dresses. Their makeshift tents still look largely the same; however, they are not a permanent presence at the Complex. On his webpage, Loud explains that his photography is about '*recording social history, the way people live, in the belief that it will be fascinating in years to come when things have changed*' (Loud n.d.). As a source of qualitative and quantitative data, photography can also help observers, researchers and students of power understand how things at times remain much the same. Nancy H. Dupree mentions Herat's general homeless population in her writings in the 1990s and 1970s (Dupree 1994), thereby confirming that the phenomenon is not entirely new or even predominantly tied to the 1990s civil war, Taliban regime or the post-2001 insurgency. A USAID education project report produced in 1994 criticized the closing of the Afghanistan USAID office precisely on the grounds of the Agency's unfinished work for '*the homeless and vagrant people*' (Boardman 1994, 53).

If Musalla once stood out from its environment due to the lush lawns and trees of Park-i-Bihzad around it, that has not been the case in decades, perhaps longer. Other than relatively small patches of greenery around the Gawhar Shad Mausoleum, the Complex now mostly blends in with the generally dry and dusty tawny and grey-coloured hills, mountains and houses. Affected by Herat's overall desertification through the decades of successive conflicts, Musalla looks like it has been abandoned and given up on. Its grounds, home to its homeless, are a wasteland of sand, gravel, dirt, discarded plastic bags, broken plastic furniture, the occasional dead cat or a dog, and small piles of unidentifiable trash. On a windy day, which is fairly often throughout the summer, gusts of wind carrying sand and dirt only deepen the feeling of thirst. The dry dusty wind also makes it hard to keep one's eyes open. Yet children play between the minarets every day and, moreover, spend entire weeks or months there before their parents decide to move on. While expert reports say nothing about the homeless of Musalla, their analyses are replete with warnings of the minarets' instability, staggering tilt and overall precariousness. A University of Pavia study quantified the tilt of 'Minaret number 5' prior to the 2003 restorative intervention and underlined the vulnerability of the entire Complex, including its susceptibility to earthquakes (Macchi 2005). The risk of any serious seismic shock in the earthquake-prone Herat valley is emphasized insofar as it may contribute to the collapse of one or more remaining minarets. The threat that these difficult spatial circumstances pose for Musalla's homeless is not described, quantified or even mentioned. If Musalla's rich appearance once distinguished it from its poorer and more arid environment, nowadays, the Complex is ironically surrounded by a fair amount of new, solid homes, with opulent gardens, glass and marble facades, often painted pink or blue, and belonging to Herat's more affluent families. Dupree suggested in 1994 that they could be a source of donations and a way to preserve Herat's cultural sites scattered across the city. In her email to Sotirios Mousouris, UN Secretary General's Special Representative in Afghanistan and Pakistan, she even noted:

> In all conscience, I cannot suggest that the UN consider the restoration of historical monuments in Herat a high priority for the use of major funds at this time. … There is much wealth in Herat. The building of mosques and repair of shrines seems to be a popular means of expressing religious piety and fulfilling community obligations. … It would be best to set up some mechanism to capitalize on this trend while at the same time making sure that appropriate scientific preservation techniques are utilized. (Dupree 1994, 4–5)

While insensitive given the extensive damage that various sites in Herat had sustained, this remark speaks to the implied wealth of Herat relative to most other cities in Afghanistan. However, Dupree seems to have conflated one's interest in building new mosques with a more general willingness to commit private resources to the broader restoration of Herat's cultural and historical heritage. Either way, she, too, ignored homeless lives in her recommendations. Asked why wealthier Heratis and entrepreneurs do not contribute to the restoration of the Complex, or help initiate a fund-raising campaign, an Afghan employee of the United Nations Development Programme in Afghanistan responded:

> People here, rich too, prefer to pass the buck and generally expect someone else to do it, preferably the government. Unless their personal interest is at stake, they will only maybe care about their street, otherwise, they won't do a thing or give a dime of their own. (UNDP-A Interviewee 2016)

When asked why Ismail Khan or other prominent Heratis who had held public office did not contribute or use their influence to arrange funding for Musalla, he added: *'It is not profitable for them, in particular, it was never profitable for Khan's popularity. People don't care about that stuff'* (UNDP-A Interviewee 2016). This correlates to Abdul Rahim Saidi's thoughts on the issue:

> Most people don't care about cultural heritage. It's old. People here like new stuff: new roads, new shops, new brand names, new clothes, new wedding halls, new apartment buildings. 'If there is an old building in the way, take it down, we need room.' That's the attitude. Even the mullahs have a very limited interest, mostly in the Masjid-i-Jami[2]. (Saidi 2016)

[2] The *Great Mosque of Herat*, or the *Friday Mosque*

In addition to wartime bomb shelling and earthquakes, Musalla seems to have fallen victim to a broader social practice of neglect of most historical monuments in the city. While some individuals and families around the Complex seem to be affluent – enough to build homes and businesses in its vicinity – their evolving concepts of entrepreneurialism (UNDP-A Interviewee 2016) have not included discourses of public goods. Nonetheless, the apparent culture of passive neglect seems to be at odds with the government's declarative insistence on mobilizing own budgetary, local, and international resources for Musalla (UNESCO Office in Kabul 2012). Moreover, it is at odds with the practice of continuous police surveillance of the Complex and haphazard forced removals of the homeless. Most importantly, it is in stark contrast with the incidence of police and civilian violence and verbal abuse of the homeless. Therefore, if Musalla's homeless are not physically invisible in the sense typically discussed in the literature on rural and urban geographies (Langegger and Koester 2016, Cloke, Milbourne and Widdowfield 1999, Milbourne and Widdowfield 2000), why are their conditions not recognized as urgent, disempowering and marginalizing? What makes the visible social neglect and violence possible?

How Do Visible Misery and Violence, and Invisible Pain Work?

The social tensions, discontinuities, and contradictions in the treatment of Musalla's homeless and the homeless in Herat in general are stark and reflect the politics of untethered marginalization. However, to be seen as such, the discourses of threat (criminal, terror, and medical), laziness and industry, charity, personal responsibility, splendour, growth, and ethnic/tribal superiority need to be brought out as vocabularies *of power* and *politics* rather than mere social misfortunes. To understand how the production and management of the homeless as dangerous, useless and unwanted operate via a unique cultural apparatus, it is necessary to identify the discursive strategies and truths that work to assemble and hold together said apparatus. They help to show that the misery of homelessness is a public policy, an arrangement of power relations. This section will shed light on the public imagination of homelessness in Herat gathered through my interviews. It will problematize the public truths of the origin of homelessness and its character by focusing on three key domains: (1) the social and spatial origins, backgrounds, and stories of the homeless, (2) Herati community perceptions of the homeless, and (3) the homeless' sources of income and survival strategies. Furthermore, the section will elaborate on the abuse the homeless are subjected to.

Three Questions

The methods of societal physical and structural violence that the homeless have been exposed to correlate with social imaginaries, representations and institutionalized regimes of truth that have produced them as social threats and problems. Until the late 1970s and the flaring up of conflict across the country, homeless populations in Herat and on Musalla's grounds were composed of a smaller number of Herat's urban poor and relatively larger groups of Pashtun Kuchi nomads who would temporarily occupy public spaces or abandoned private property before moving on to a different location. The rationales behind their temporary settlement were related to established nomadic practices (and this varied across groups within the Kuchi designation), lower-scale intra-Kuchi conflicts, or more specific economic reasons: droughts, desertification, and loss of agricultural land (Loda, et al. 2013). Overlapping and successive conflicts since the 1980s have added a safety and conflict component to the rationales of their displacement, further heightening its economic drivers and complicating the dimensions of their vulnerabilities. They quickly began to be seen as disturbing Herat's local ethnic balance or, worse yet, as importing Taliban allegiances alien to the city. They have also been feared as a strain on the city's limited financial resources, land, and residential infrastructure (Sakhi 2016, Stanikzai 2016, Immigration and Refugee Board of Canada 2004). Conflict and a pervasive sense of insecurity throughout the country both prior to and since 2001 have compounded the stories of homelessness in Herat. Many of them are victims of secondary displacement. Namely, they have returned to Afghanistan from (mainly) Iran after 2001, but cannot return to their homes in the south of the country, provinces around Herat (mostly Badghis and Ghor), or to the rural districts within the Herat Province. Virtually all of my interviewees agreed that the origins of homelessness are mixed. They are related to nomadic migration patterns, indigenous poverty, economic reasons (compounded by the destructiveness of air raids and drone attacks), multifaceted urbanization, fluctuations in security, ethnic animosities (between the Kuchi nomads, Tajiks, Hazaras, and others), intra-Pashtun conflicts, evasions of Taliban recruitment, destruction of property, loss of land, blood feuds, etc. Furthermore, they recognized that homelessness in the city is fuelled by local socioeconomic inequalities, instability of income, volatile employment opportunities and conflict dynamics that lead to one's loss of spouse, parent or all of family. However, the interviewees differed sharply in the way they described the homeless and community perceptions of homelessness.

A group of interviewees described Musalla's and other homeless populations in Herat as children, orphans, widows, single mothers, deprived Kuchi nomads, landless refugee returnees from Iran, rejected opium users (who have recently returned from Iran), internally displaced persons (IDPs) from Badghis and Ghor, victims of tribal conflicts, land and livestock-dependent farmers whose resources are depleted, Hazaras from central Afghanistan, abandoned youth, domestically abused women and children, mostly men, etc. (Ayoubi 2016, Stanikzai 2016, Q. S. Rahimi 2016, UNODC Interviewee 1 2016, Monib 2016, Amiri 2016, Neekzad 2016, Naseri 2016, Osmani 2016, Pakzad 2016). While the dynamics of poverty and vulnerability of each of these groups should be appreciated on their own terms, what makes this list extraordinary is the level of sensitivity and attention to its sociological diversity displayed by the interviewees. While different interviewees emphasized distinctive orders in the enumeration[3] of the various categories, the overlap in their responses was substantial. Conversely, another group of interviewees described the homeless as 'mostly Pashtuns', beggars, drug addicts, and IDPs (Sakhi 2016, Dehzad 2016, Sarwary 2016, Arimi 2016, Saidi 2016). In other words, their approach to describing the homeless was more homogenizing and less sociologically sensitive to their diversity of backgrounds and stories. Unlike references to 'landless farmers', the homogenizing approach did not include spatial references to the experience of homelessness other than the extensively used term 'IDP'. Furthermore, this latter group of interviewees used the acronym itself rather than the whole phrase. Finally, most interviewees who tried to heterogenize and specify Musalla's homeless also emphasized that they are integral to the larger phenomenon of homelessness across the city and represent only one curious subset of it. In contrast, the interviewees who homogenized their descriptions did not make such remarks.

The question on the origins and backgrounds of Musalla's (and generally Herati) homeless was immediately followed by a question on community perceptions of homelessness in the city. Amrulhaq Ayoubi from the Afghanistan Human Rights Organization highlighted a distinction that ordinary Heratis seem to insist on: that between 'the real homeless' and 'drug addicts'. Upon my insistence to explain how one distinguishes between the two, he pointed to their appearances: '*You need to look at their face. Homeless people are usually clean. Drug addicts are dirty and look sick*' (Ayoubi 2016). I followed up with three questions. Asked to explain *where this supposed difference in appearances came from*, Ayoubi said that it was thought that homeless people frequented government shelters, showered and sought medical assistance, whereas drug addicts 'didn't care'. *Prompted*, he then explained that a key distinction between the homeless and drug addicts was that the former had lost their homes due to war, structural poverty or misfortune, whereas the latter had '*only themselves to blame*'. He claimed that most drug addicts were teenagers and young adults who had left for Iran to work and 'gain independence', taking up drugs there. He said: '*Socialization in Iran rather than some situation of despair in Afghanistan led them down the path.*' Finally, when I asked *if he personally and professionally agreed with these characterizations*, he hesitated: '*No, not really. I mean, it's complicated, but there is something there*' (Ayoubi 2016).

Sanyee Development Organization Regional Office Manager in Herat, Abdul Khaliq Stanikzai, was more explicit: '*A majority of homeless people at Musalla are drug addicts. The community doesn't care about them, nor do their families. In fact, their families are ashamed of them*' (Stanikzai 2016). Qader Sayed Rahimi, Afghanistan Independent Human Rights Commission's Regional Program Manager, however, was more explicitly sympathetic, insisting on '*an odd paradox*' (Rahimi 2016), whereby

---

[3] For instance, Amrulhaq Ayoubi from the Afghanistan Human Rights Organization first spoke of children, orphans and unaccompanied minors, married and unmarried women, single mothers, widows and victims of domestic abuse (Ayoubi 2016).

most Heratis allegedly cared more about the minarets than the homeless. '*And they don't even care about the minarets*', he added (Ibid).

> People were even seen demolishing old city walls close to the Citadel and no one reacted or did anything. That tells you how much the public really cares about history, heritage, or Musalla. They steal tiles and decoration from the complex every day and try to sell it. And then, you can imagine how little they care about the homeless, whatever the reason of their homelessness ... drug addicts or not. Combine that with the fact that the city can offer only two proper shelters with a couple hundred beds and you will understand why there are so many people just sitting or sleeping on the street, or why they urinate in the canal by the minarets. (Rahimi 2016)

What seemed like Rahimi's mixed feelings of anger, frustration and disappointment with the public and, perhaps, the government was palpable. A UN Office on Drugs and Crime (UNODC) Herat official described community perceptions of the homeless as 'markedly negative', whereby '*most are seen as drug addicts*'. He insisted that the conditions in the government's single treatment centre for 'drug addicts' had deteriorated so much that when a UNODC mission visited it, all their shoes were apparently stolen (UNODC Interviewee 1 2016).

> There is very little order and discipline there. They come in and out as it pleases them and no one can really treat them. One day on the street – and Musalla is a good hideout – and then the next day back at the center. These people are ill and need help. But generally, Heratis think that if they are addicts, they got other diseases, and they will get them sick somehow, too. (UNODC Interviewee 1 2016)

When I asked him to explain what that belief entailed in terms of the public treatment of the homeless, he responded by way of example:

> If you have a house or a shop and you don't like them standing in front of it, you don't want them to be there, you can freely chase them away yourself, even though it's a public space. And if you can't or don't want to do it yourself, the police will often do it for you if you say that you're scared or that they attacked you, or they look sick. (UNODC Interviewee 1 2016)

He concluded: '*International support and funds are drying up and we have to help them. But who will help them? The government doesn't seem to believe it's a priority*' (UNODC Interviewee 1 2016). A UN Development Programme (UNDP) employee working on LOFTA[4] gave a detailed response to the question of community perceptions of the

---

[4] LOFTA is an internationally funded and UNDP-administered Law and Order Trust Fund for Afghanistan.

homeless. While acknowledging negative public perceptions, verbal, and, at times, physical abuse of the homeless, he added:

> I mean, generally, you have a lot of mixed perceptions between sympathy and disregard for the most part. But more and more, people who are working hard in Herat – because Herat is mostly peaceful – people who work hard here are starting to think: 'Hey, you should work hard, you should get a job and provide for yourself and the family.' People are starting to think that even though the homeless may have lost their homes or land due to war, or they had to leave unsafe areas, but especially to the extent that they are young people, drug addicts – people are starting to think how Herat is good and safe enough and that whatever the reason of your homelessness, you need to clean yourself up, get treatment, and be responsible for yourself. Some IDPs come here even with some capital and start their own businesses, everyone comes with something, even their bare hands. (Sakhi 2016)

All of the respondents confirmed the public's negative perceptions even though their levels of demonstrated sympathy for the homeless differed. Contrary to my general expectations, the responses of those interviewees who showed greater sensitivity to the diversity of social backgrounds and stories of the homeless did not correlate with how they conveyed dominant community perceptions. Those interviewees who tended to homogenize the homeless in their responses also spoke of negative community perceptions with a tone of understanding, adding their own critical remarks on the need for the homeless to *'take responsibility for themselves'* (Sakhi 2016). Some of the interviewees who highlighted the social diversity of homelessness were more ambiguous in their responses, showing unease and articulating self-contradicting attitudes. Others acknowledged the negative social perceptions, promptly emphasizing that the vulnerable and ill 'need help', not violence and rejection (Pakzad 2016, Neekzad 2016, Naseri 2016). Overall, there seemed to be a great variety in personal and organizational attitudes. Three conclusions started to emerge following the first and the second question on the 'who' of homelessness.

First, more broadly, a discursive move to essentialize the homeless stood out. The 'homogenizers' of the homeless usually reverted to simplifying the backgrounds and stories of homelessness to drug addiction. Yet, even many of the 'heterogenizers', while trying to explain community perceptions, resorted to simplification, coalescing around the characterization of homelessness as related to drug addiction. In other words, if a respondent could not convey a more complex image of homelessness and felt compelled to, for reasons of brevity, simplify certain descriptors, he (this was a pattern common to male interviewees) would simply use the label '(drug) addict'.

Second, the interviewees conveyed a certain common sense about homelessness in Herat, a dominant mode of imagination shared by private citizens and the authorities (the police, in particular) alike. There seemed to emerge an image of what was 'obviously truthful' about the homeless more broadly, even though individual interviewees might have felt disagreement, discomfort or internal conflict with respect to some of the characterizations. *Third*, two key premises of that public truth were that the homeless were flawed in an intimately bodily way, whether as drug addicts or vaguely 'sick' and 'dirty-looking' individuals, and that they lacked in the good ethics of hard work, personal responsibility and entrepreneurial spirit that Herat had embraced as one of Afghanistan's richest and more peaceful cities.

The commonsensical status of this truth became clearer once I would pose a third question about the background of the Herati homeless. More specifically, the interviewees were asked to share their knowledge of the sources of income and tactics of survival of the homeless. Again, a roughly binary division emerged. It largely correlated to the responses that essentialized homelessness as addiction. On one hand, a group of interviewees emphasized begging, eating trash, theft, and even possible insurgent links (Saidi 2016, Sakhi 2016, Atayee 2016, Arimi 2016, Ayoubi 2016, Dehzad 2016, UNODC Interviewee 1 2016, Sarwary 2016, Amiri 2016). Conversely, a somewhat smaller group, in addition to street begging, also pointed to the Islamic norms of charitable giving and the 'kindness wall' in the city centre where food and clothes are left weekly. Moreover, they spoke about the homeless' employment in short-term and irregular menial jobs, occasional street vending of agricultural and other products, shoe polishing and factory jobs, which paid on average $2 for twelve hours of work (Pakzad 2016, Arimi 2016, Monib 2016, Naseri 2016, Neekzad 2016, Osmani 2016, Rahimi 2016). The interviewees in the latter group also acknowledged that most Heratis did not necessarily appreciate the hardship and instability of such income tactics. Instead, they thought of the homeless as vagrants. Moreover, the interviewees who highlighted begging as the homeless' source of income added that Islamic charitable giving was drying up, since people had become desensitized to the conditions of homelessness, generally expecting the homeless to take care of themselves and 'be useful' (Sakhi 2016, Arimi 2016).

Patterns of Representation of Musalla's Homeless and the Conditions of Their Pain

Fooks and Pantazis' (1999) research articulates how the notion of *risk* operates in society in two ways. On the one hand, risk explains the inherent vulnerability of the homeless and their victimization through rough sleeping, malnutrition, poor health, lack of personal safety, etc. Conversely, risk also works to turn the various vulnerabilities against them and produce a new agency of the homeless as risky for society at large. Risk is deployed to invert victimization and recast the victim as threatening. Emphases and tactics of representation shift: from victims of crime, the homeless become dangerous beggars and criminals themselves, and from individuals vulnerable to illness, they become its dangerous source. In particular, Fooks and Pantazis underscore:

> the most widely reproduced image of homelessness and crime, especially in the news media, not only involves the depiction of the homeless person as an architect, rather than an object, of crime but, more significantly, as a victimizer, and not a victim, of the 'respectable' population. (Fooks and Pantazis 1999, 124)

My interviewees in Herat precisely acknowledged that public perceptions of homelessness at Musalla and the city more generally seemed to be shifting away from sympathy, charity and recognition of vulnerability to lamentable risk. Public truths of homelessness seemed to increasingly reflect a more hurtful imagery of lazy beggars, filthy and sick drug addicts, petty criminals, treacherous Pashtuns, terrorist supporters and potential insurgents. The local economy and security remain precarious nearly two decades into the US-NATO intervention in Afghanistan and Herat. Yet the 'respectable' Herati population is shifting in its understanding of homelessness. In different ways, ordinary Heratis are converging around a truth that is decreasingly premised on the social conditions that render populations vulnerable, homeless and roofless. Rather, the unfolding truth is based on the assumption that the homeless are themselves a condition of risk and threat to Heratis with homes. Musalla's and Herati homeless are undergoing a politics of individual and group pathologies (Fooks and Pantazis 1999). They are being socially differentiated into 'real homeless people' on the one hand, and categories of irresponsible beggars, addicts, thieves and perhaps even terrorist sympathizers who spread anything from crime and disease to outright death. The social status of this representation as truthful rests in its apparent commonsensical appeal. It has reshaped the subjectivity of the police, of law and order, of risk and splendour in Herat in a way that expresses care for the 'respectable' Heratis and their cultural heritage as opposed to the risk and threat posed by the homeless.

However, this representation operates in an environment that once enabled perceptions of the homeless as victims of systemic conditions, or at least made such perceptions prevalent. Unemployment rates in Herat, while lower than elsewhere in Afghanistan, are nonetheless considerable, with nearly 25 per cent unemployed and not gainfully employed, and as many as 15.5 per cent underemployed in inadequate jobs in 2011 (Leslie 2015, 19–20). Since then, the unemployment rate has grown due to the partial pull-out of US and NATO troops, and the retreat of past and decline in new investments that has followed. Some sources cite unemployment rates (as of 2015) as high as 40 per cent (Karimi 2016). Herat, along with Kabul, is one of the largest recipients of IDPs in Afghanistan, and the strengthening of the insurgency in Herat's rural districts, neighbouring provinces (Badghis and Ghor) and provinces to the north (Jawzjan and Balkh) has increased IDP flows into the city since NATO and the United States started withdrawing troops in 2011/12 (Jabeen and Pulla 2014). Official government data from 2014 pointed to between 6,000 and 6,500 families (around 31,000 individuals) living in three IDP camps and informal settlements around the city's peripheries – Maslakh, Shaidayee and Minaret. The settlements' informal status has grown in importance as most IDPs face inadequate housing, landlessness, or insecurity of land tenure (Rao and Turkstra 2014, Howard and Madzarevic 2014). The settlements themselves operate in untenable conditions, with irregular power supplies and limited access to water (Esser 2005, 5–6). Such instability of local conditions pushes IDPs to leave the camps and informal settlements and attempt to find better-paid (or any) jobs closer to the city centre, or maximize gains from begging. Due to Musalla's tactical proximity to Herat's key commercial areas and traffic routes, as well as its relative isolation – the Complex is the preferred choice for many trying to mitigate the conditions of homelessness. While at Musalla, IDPs have to cope with rooflessness (unless they own or somehow acquire a tent). Yet their situational opportunities for subsistence are typically better at Musalla than elsewhere outside the city centre, according to two local shopkeepers (Shopkeeper

1 2016, Shopkeeper 2 2016). Regardless, the willingness of Herati business owners to offer well-paid and reliable jobs is generally limited (Amiri 2016). On average, when given a job, a homeless person would make around 300 AFN (just under $5) for twelve hours of work (Ibid). Since certain international organizations, like the World Food Programme, still have assistance programmes for Maslakh, Shaidayee and Minaret, families sometimes tactically split. They usually keep one parent or a grandparent with a few (grand)children in the camp to collect food and other donations and act as 'placeholders', while the rest of the family temporarily lives and works in the city centre (Amiri 2016). '*Some of them sometimes almost have normal lives when they get a job, so they come back here [to Musalla] from work in the evening*' (Shopkeeper 2 2016). A small number, according to IFRC's Basir Ahmad Amiri, join the insurgency or become insurgent informants: '*The police and the government make a big deal out of that whenever there are revelations, but this number is generally exaggerated for political reasons*' (Amiri 2016). Finally, the homeless and IDPs are also deprived of political representation, even though they are Afghan citizens (Esser 2005, 6).

This brief and incomplete snapshot suggests that contemporary socioeconomic conditions in Herat enable an environment of great vulnerability and deprivation for a whole spectrum of populations, the homeless and Musalla's roofless included. Nonetheless, original interviews, news, and expert reports (Rao and Turkstra 2014, Howard and Madzarevic 2014, Shukran and Kohistani 2014) suggest growingly negative perceptions and discriminating physical treatment of the homeless. For instance, eleven interviewees were quoted an excerpt from a Jabeen and Pulla (2014) academic article: '*These IDPs often do not have enough skills to compete and lead a life in their new environments and continue to remain a second priority within their own country*' (Jabeen and Pulla 2014, 40). Eight of them agreed with this statement as 'factual' and most added that they regretted such conditions. However, three interviewees (Amiri 2016, Dehzad 2016, Sakhi 2016) pointed out that the statement could also be interpreted as an indictment of IDPs who had failed in life and had failed to acquire necessary minimum skills to provide for themselves and their families. They also emphasized that this was a growing understanding of the origins of IDP poverty and homelessness in Herat and that ordinary Heratis were '*losing patience with people who expect a handout, can't do anything, and are too lazy and too high to learn and be productive*' (Sakhi 2016). In other words, they attested to a form of homeless pathologization that stripped them of their right to be acknowledged as victims or as populations at risk.

Furthermore, women and children are particularly vulnerable and exposed to insidious degrees of physical violence and poverty. This is intimately bound up with what Rajeswari S. Rajan identifies as women being the 'sites' of postcolonial relations rather than 'participants' in them (Rajan 1993, 6). It is a relationship that locks in their multiple class, gender, racial and sexual vulnerabilities and makes their compound subalternities objects of analysis, policy, and academic 'liberation' (Spivak 1999, Rajan and Park 2000). In other words, their misery is not simply mindless and tragic. Rather, it is a product of overlapping public policies and social discourses loaded with purpose. Homeless children are being exploited as cheap labour, recruited by the various insurgency groups, warlords and gangs, or outright sold as slaves (Shukran and Kohistani 2014, International Organization for Migration 2004, Jabeen and Pulla 2014). Their educational rights are not enforced or are denied (Majidi 2011). Women are repeatedly victimized and abused physically and sexually throughout their homeless experience, and are likewise vulnerable to human trafficking and forced labour, as well as poorly paid jobs (Amiri 2016, Ayoubi 2016, Naseri 2016, Neekzad 2016, Pakzad 2016, Rahimi 2016, International Organization for Migration 2004). Even when not abused physically, their attempts to improve own living conditions and find tactics to escape homelessness are often stifled, frustrated, or sabotaged by official male community representatives (*wakils*) and elders (Esser 2005, 6–8). Since women's creative skills and education are societally constrained and discouraged, their vulnerability 'explodes' if they become widows or otherwise single mothers (Pakzad 2016). Some are compelled to rely on their children for additional low-paid labour and financial contribution to their homeless 'households'. When they do acquire relatively stable jobs, homeless women in general work for about $2 for 12 hours nearly every day, often in subpar conditions. Suraya Pakzad gives an example of pashmina factories where women work in unsanitary and hazardous conditions. They ingest toxic chemicals, often contract tuberculosis when working with goats, and are regularly exposed to poor factory lighting. This, furthermore, incurs medical expenses that the employer is reluctant to cover, ultimately reinforcing their poverty and vulnerability to sudden crises (e.g. their children's illness) (Pakzad 2016). '*It is unsurprising*', insists Suraya '*that they despair and lose hope and many of them turn to opiates to numb the pain in their arms, legs, feet, head, and lungs, since they are cheaper than actual medicines*' (Ibid). That, however, opens up a plethora of problems, especially if they lose regular jobs and are forced to turn to prostitution (Pakzad 2016). According to Jamila Naseri, head of Medica Afghanistan's Herat Regional Office:

> Many in the homeless community or even their 'normal' relatives then abandon them, or even worse, want to punish them physically for becoming drug addicts and neglecting their children. Sometimes, they are punished by no one, but they are physically weak and sick and incapable of defending themselves against rapists. So many of our women spiral down into suicide, often self-immolation. (Naseri 2016)

One of the interviewed shopkeepers confirmed that he had seen 'a few' instances of sexual intercourse on Musalla's grounds and he was '*never sure what it was*', implying that some or all of them might have been cases of rape (Shopkeeper 1 2016). A 2007 Medica Mondiale study indicated thirty-seven cases of female self-immolation in Herat, with hundreds more left unreported every year (Medica Mondiale 2007, 11).

Moreover, Musalla's homeless (like the homeless throughout the city) are exposed to haphazard and seemingly premeditated physical abuse, such as spitting, torture, beatings, forced removals from the site, and casual verbal insults involving offensive expletives about one's imagined profession or source of income, sexual proclivities, and bodily appearances (Shopkeeper 1 2016, Shopkeeper 2 2016, Dehzad 2016). In other words, the methods and discourses of abuse tend to target the social and biological utility of the homeless. Even more alarmingly, many of these instances are abuses of public office committed by the Afghan National Police and the National Directorate of Security personnel (Naseri 2016, Neekzad 2016, Osmani 2016, Pakzad 2016). According to the single homeless person that my interpreter and I briefly spoke to, he had never personally experienced beatings, forced removal or verbal violence, but he had '*once see[n] a police officer patrol the grounds and kick a guy who was asleep by the canal banks, and then tell him to leave*'. A second time, he added, '*four or five people who were sitting by the [southern] entrance were made to leave and the police, around ten of them, stayed there to guard it*'. After a while, '*a group of men in suits came and looked around*' (Bazgar 2016). Two interviewees and indirect reporting suggested that the homeless were at times beaten by drug dealers for not wanting or not being able to purchase drugs or repay old debts – all while ANP officers stood by and did nothing to protect the victims (Shopkeeper 1 2016, Shopkeeper 2 2016, Latifi 2013). Most interviewees confirmed that ANP rarely investigated crimes against the homeless. More care was shown only if a homeless person was severely injured or murdered, or if the victim came from a notable Herati family and had previously left home or been expelled. Due to a generally tense atmosphere during the interview and my interpreter's clear discomfort, I decided not to ask Mohammad Nader Arimi about this, even though his professional experience with ANSF was unparalleled among all of my interviewees. Basir Ahmad Amiri, IFRC Field-Office Manager in Herat, remarked that violence perpetrated against the homeless was '*tricky to observe*', and that while he was aware of the generally negative perception and occasionally poor treatment of the homeless, he '*personally never noticed major infractions, or differences in infractions against them as opposed to the wider populace*' (Amiri 2016). However, he also added that daily snubs and disregard of the homeless by regular Heratis and tourists amounted to '*forms of structural violence and dehumanization*' (Ibid). Feridun Sarwary, Dean of the Herat Urban Development and Housing Department, denied allegations of violence against the homeless, emphasizing that '*there [was] barely any proof of that in the police or other public records*' (Sarwary 2016). He did add, however: '*There are sometimes tensions in the community due to the IDPs' poor education and their children's frequent involvement in petty crime*' (Ibid). It should be noted that expert analysis, nongovernmental reports, and my interviews confirm accounts of ANSF human rights violations, in particular against more defenceless populations, such as (unmarried) women, children, returnees, and IDPs (The United States Department of State 2016, The United States Department of State 2014, Jabeen and Pulla 2014, Samiem 2014, Medica Mondiale 2007, International Organization for Migration 2004).

The police abuse at Musalla draws on more endemic community violence against the vulnerable. It is justified by the supposed necessities of progress, development, and growth and it is consistent with similar strategies of urban population management observed elsewhere in the world (Samara 2010, Smith 2002). Most importantly, it is not a phenomenon of random and 'senseless' police violence even though some of its specific occurrences may be best described in such a way. It is a type of governmental power that systemically and in the long run conditions the behaviour of the social body, of its 'useless' and 'useful' elements. In other words, its causes are not in unaccountable government agencies or branches of power. Law enforcement is merely one of the many technologies used to condition the self-conduct of the homeless who should 'know better' how to look and dress, where to sleep, where to live and spend time, and what skills and education to acquire and when. If they fail to conduct themselves in ways that maximize general community welfare, the hammer of 'natural' negative selection (via social exclusion) will fall upon them and minimize their cost to society.

'Better Not Talk to Them': Pathologizing Musalla's Homeless

One of the reasons I only spoke to one homeless person at Musalla is that some of the individuals I logistically relied on during fieldwork showed great reluctance to engage with the homeless verbally. After I received a few 'better not' responses, I was finally told that the homeless were probably all 'mentally unstable', 'not (mentally) good', *also sick, who knows what diseases they have* and *really filthy, so they might get you dirty and pass on some infection*. Furthermore, some of the people I closely interacted with in Herat suggested: *'They might also have weapons, ... a knife or a screwdriver'*. While I did not necessarily agree with the level of concern and caution, I complied given various situational, logistical and ethical constraints.

Over the course of fieldwork, I travelled around Herat with a number of locals, and drew two key conclusions from their attitude towards Musalla's homeless. First, they were entirely focused on self-protection and preferred not to engage with the homeless. Second, that preference itself was predicated on a pathologized imagination of the homeless and their broader representation as dangerous to the 'normal' and 'healthy' body, a body that takes care of itself. In addition to reproducing the normal/abnormal and healthy/sick binaries, this pathology was also informed by economic representations of the homeless as 'irresponsible', 'not taking care of themselves', 'lacking entrepreneurial spirit', and 'lazy'. This chapter has already discussed the predominant framing of the homeless as dangerous 'drug addicts' at fault for their own situation. They are said to threaten Herat's 'honourable' and 'normal' people (UNODC Interviewee 1 2016, Rahimi 2016) by spreading the temptation and availability of opiates on the streets. Surely, between 60,000 and 70,000 drug users are thought to be living in Herat in informal settlements. A variety of drugs are available to them and are relatively cheap. Furthermore, stories of how individuals initially take up drugs vary, but all have strong roots in modes of socialization and shared experience. Typically, they have to do with ill treatment and social isolation in Iran while on a temporary work visa there or as undocumented migrants. Other broad conditions include poverty and declining health. Therefore, opium, heroin and other drugs become coping mechanisms against loneliness, physical pain and hunger, or simply a method to socialize with other Afghans toiling in Iran. Nonetheless, the rise in substance abuse also strongly correlates to ample supply and relative affordability, particularly in an environment of high youth unemployment (Latifi 2013, Ahmed 2013b, Ayoubi 2016, Stanikzai 2016, UNODC Interviewee 1 2016). For those most desperate and poorest, even glue will do.

However, in isolation or combined, these conditions do not necessarily point to the homeless, former guest workers in Iran, or IDPs as the drivers of widespread drug addiction. To be interpreted as such, they need to be embedded in a system of social representation that relegates certain populations to the status of natural costs for society (in terms of welfare, healthcare, crime, safety and security). The calculation of those costs is so tightly associated with the ethically and aesthetically unacceptable quality of displaced and homeless bodies that they become loathed, feared and rejected. They are feared as a threat to Herat's children and youth (since they may supposedly be tricked into using drugs), and a risk to the city's 'healthy' future. Asked what health meant here, Feridun Sarwary (HUDA) said: '*Well, both medically, biologically, and as a healthy community that is doing well, that is happy and prosperous. There is no wealth with drugs*' (Sarwary 2016). Basir Ahmad Monib, a West Regional Office Representative for his NGO,[5] described drug users in globally familiar, medicalized, and pathological terms: '*Drugs are a cancer on society, and sometimes, unfortunately, so are the drug addicts*' (Monib 2016). Three of Monib's co-workers, who quietly attended the interview, nodded their heads in vigorous approval.

Therefore, discourses of the economy, personal responsibility, capitalist entrepreneurialism, community well-being, wealth, and the pseudo-medical discourse of personal and community health all converge to enact the homeless as multifarious threats. In other words, 'health' becomes a concept, a societal preference and equilibrium point that explains how one is to conduct her or himself, and how a population is to conduct itself in order to enjoy wealth, communal stability and security and bodily vigour. 'Health', therefore, becomes a condition and a technique of population management, a medical and biopolitical instrument. Moreover, it incorporates other discourses integral to governmentality: the economy and security. To be healthy in Herat means to be well off, live in a safe, opium-free, clean and disease-free neighbourhood. Health is the natural equilibrium point, much like *splendour* was for German and French intellectuals preoccupied with the guidance of men, or the problem of 'police' in the seventeenth and eighteenth centuries. More importantly, governmentality highlights how power comes to define the conduct that is seen as 'natural', clean and healthy. To understand this, the chapter will turn to the notion of the cultural apparatus and explore how it conditions population self-management through health.

Becoming a UNESCO World Heritage Site: Herat's Cultural Apparatus and its Noble Cause

The discourse on Musalla's homeless appears coherent in the representation of destitution as useless and threatening. Furthermore, it appears to be an effective justification to marginalize the homeless. However, this discourse rests on many endogenous contradictions, series of gaps and material incongruities. The gaps are abridged in the public imagination through a repeated process of essentialization, homogenization and simplification of the homeless' social backgrounds and stories. The simplified image of homelessness is one of local youths who turn to addiction. However, the homeless are mainly nomadic Kuchi Pashtuns, deeply distrusted by the

---

[5] Norwegian Project Office/Rural Rehabilitation Association for Afghanistan

majority Tajiks and Farsiwan and minority Hazaras, Uzbeks and Turkmens for their ethnic otherness and supposed support for the Taliban. Furthermore, my interviewees claimed that rhetorical juxtapositions of 'Musalla' and 'homelessness' elicited dichotomous sentiments. They prompted *sympathy* for the decaying cultural treasure followed by expressions of *enmity* and loathing for the homeless (seen as contributing to Musalla's decline). If the interviewees depicted the homeless as a threat, they also referenced the homeless' aesthetically and hygienically repellent presence on Musalla's grounds, including their dangerous effect on the integrity of the ruins and minaret slabs. Nonetheless, there is no evidence of philanthropic or communal investment in Musalla's restoration, and various interviewees claimed that the national, provincial and city governments did not prioritize Musalla's protection and repairs. Instead, they openly prefer that international organizations and NGOs bear this burden (Stanikzai 2016, Rahimi 2016, Amiri 2016, Saidi 2016). Restoration records since 2001 show only minor government investments in the Complex's regeneration with mostly international donors footing the bill (Remsen and Tedesco 2015, UNESCO Office in Kabul 2014, UNESCO Office in Kabul 2012, Santana-Quintero and Stevens 2002). Moreover, the homeless are portrayed as lazy and irresponsible, preferring to rely on welfare, theft and begging instead of own hard work that befits Herat's entrepreneurial environment. Nevertheless, as my analysis of their real social conditions has shown, the homeless are economically exploited, underpaid or outright denied higher-paying jobs and opportunities for professional development. They are relegated to menial and rough factory jobs in hazardous conditions that degrade their health. Finally, the homeless are pathologized and rejected through a popular pseudo-medical truth: their living conditions are so suboptimal that their bodies are inherently ill and threatening to the 'healthy' community. Yet, as foreign aid is drying up and the government is citing a lack of resources, the homeless are de-prioritized or outright denied regular access to health clinics, hospitals, hospices, urgent care centres, emergency rooms, and, unless treated pro bono, cannot afford access to private practice (Stanikzai 2016, Osmani 2016, Neekzad 2016, Naseri 2016, Donati and Harooni 2014). There are only two homeless shelters in Herat, around sixty beds for homeless women and children, and two addiction treatment centres with about 300 beds (which falls woefully short of Herat's needs). They are deemed inadequate and underfunded. Both centres offer very limited healthcare services to their patrons and the same dire situation is found in IDP camps (UNODC Interviewee 1 2016, Stanikzai 2016, Naseri 2016, Neekzad 2016). Bizarrely, many homeless Afghans are denied healthcare services simply because they cannot provide a *tazkera* (proof of citizenship) (Kuppers 2014).

Concurrently, charitable giving (especially during Ramadan), sympathetic views of homelessness that at times prevail, and the government's attempts to provide certain resources for the homeless (e.g. by running and co-funding shelters) contribute to a complex landscape of the politics of homelessness and social utility. They highlight the contradictions in the representation of homelessness and help explain how the homeless can be both ignored and treated as a threat. They help explain how the victim/threat binary defines bodies, lives and political struggles and animates the politics of Herati displacement. While compassion for the humanity of the weak remains, the politics of danger de-emphasize benevolent representations to sustain a heightened and effective dichotomy between the 'drug addicts' and the 'minarets'. Within the world of that dichotomy, the survival of one is incompatible with the other. But how are representations, meagre private and public funds, police forces, governmental agencies and historical-civilizational narratives mobilized and solidified to seemingly protect one and diminish the other? How are they assembled to sustain the addicts/minarets binary and its social effects? I argue that the erasure of the homeless and their reduction to 'drug addicts' (imbued with only certain deplorable characteristics) is the product of a specific cultural/security apparatus assembled to maintain and escalate the pain of the abnormal.

The operation of the apparatus intensified in 2007 when the government in Kabul – in concert with Herat's provincial and city authorities – decided to include the Musalla Complex in its application for the status of a UNESCO World Heritage site. The importance of this measure was immediately communicated both domestically and internationally as a way to financially secure the site's conservation and use it as a tool to spur local economic growth and development (Ministry of Information and Culture 2006, Qalanawi 2010). A consortium of government agencies, including Herat's governor's office, the national Ministry of Information and Culture, its regional Herati department, the Department of Historical Monuments, Institute of Archeology, and Afghanistan's embassy to UNESCO have since advertised this application as an expression of Afghanistan's progressive desires and ambitions. They have each staked out a strategy and a claim to manage the civilizational and cultural importance of Musalla, each focusing on the various aspects of Musalla's and Herat's 'sustainable development' (Ministry of Information and Culture 2006, UNESCO Expert Working Group on the Preservation of Jam and Herat ICCROM 2012, UNESCO 2016). Their decision was embedded in earlier international pressures and appeals to the Afghan government to commit to Musalla's restoration and protection rather than leaving it to decay any further (Qalanawi 2010). Some of the international actors who became closely involved in the management of Musalla's restoration include UNESCO and its Kabul office and a number of academic experts from universities in Italy and Germany who have kept pressuring the government to adopt a range of restorative and protective practices. Furthermore, included early in the process were corporate representatives bound to profit from consulting on, and monitoring the protective works necessary to acquire the World Heritage site status. An array of donor governments (including Italy and the United States) became involved as well, expeditiously demanding accountability and efficiency in protective and restorative works on the ground (UNESCO Expert Working Group on the Preservation of Jam and Herat ICCROM 2012). The involvement of the broad range of international actors has created pressure and added external controlling mechanisms upon the government in Kabul. Nonetheless, the decision to submit the application to UNESCO has also generated their political, technical and financial support to acquire the desired status for Musalla. This has relieved the government of much of the operational burden (Sarwary 2016, Saidi 2016). As the various levels of government in Afghanistan keep portraying the process as transformative for the whole city, the international actors – led by UNESCO – insist on presenting Kabul and Herat with specific demands that should be met before the status is granted. Those include the closure and removal of the road running through the Complex, the construction of an alternative road, the reinforcement and reconstruction of the protective wall around Musalla, as well restrictions on residential and commercial construction around the Complex (UNESCO Expert Working Group on the Preservation of Jam and Herat ICCROM 2012). Additionally, UNESCO and other donors have requested that the government regulate '*both human and vehicular traffic ... in the area to protect the site*' and introduce '*anti-vandalism measures*' (Ibid, 11–12). Unsurprisingly, UNESCO did not specify how measures directed at regulating human behaviour were to be achieved. In our June 12, 2016 interview, Abdul Rahim Saidi, Senior Advisor to the Mayor of Herat, reiterated UNESCO'S demands to '*secure order and who does what*' (Saidi 2016) at and around Musalla, adding that the homeless '*[had] been responsible for the damage and theft of faience and other things from the former madrasa*' (Saidi 2016). That was his response to my question about law enforcement's use of physical force to remove the homeless or simply harass them. Mr Saidi denied any abuse of power, but seemed to imply that a mandate for coercive measures existed nonetheless.

Following the government's decision to try to put the Complex on UNESCO's World Heritage map, there has been a range of analyses of Musalla's condition. Not a single one factors in the site's very specific human landscape beyond the cars running through it or the homes and businesses around it. This omission has taken place in a broader political and social context. The absence of comprehensive governmental, 'civil society', policy, or academic studies of homelessness in Herat speaks to the social invisibility of the problem beyond conflict displacement (which is certainly important). However, the operation of an unequal and discriminatory system of power can be rendered visible through its procedures, strategic games and effects. Therefore, spotlighting the work of the cultural apparatus as a technology of inequality can shed light on the exclusionary effects of care for culture. As it works to maximize Musalla's utility and 'splendour', the apparatus relies on the mobilization of degrading representations and the maltreatment of the homeless. Paradoxically, that is what makes it tangible: both oppressive and susceptible to subversion. Moreover, to incite the marginalizing representations and practices, to set them in motion, and focus them on a specific goal – Musalla's economic, security and hygienic splendour – governmental power needs to mobilize spaces and relations seemingly extraneous to the link between homelessness and culture. The cultural apparatus thus comes to encompass a vast array of international 'state' and 'non-state' actors, Herat's justice, healthcare and welfare systems, law enforcement, regional labour market, cultural and religious centres, narratives of civilizational projects and goals, urban planning, etc.

Constrained by these power relations, the homeless in Herat are marginalized in ways that comprehensively minimize their life chances and spaces. They rarely receive police protection from theft or bodily harm, and even when certain measures are taken in the short run, law enforcement follow-up is 'unheard of' (Monib 2016) or is at least 'highly improbable' (Naseri 2016). Herat's homeless do not get to see a judge in a civil or criminal case unless they are brought to one as suspects. Their access to the local juridical system usually involves a single door: the central Herat Province jail unit. Even when they make attempts to access the legal system and seek compensations, it is the very fact of homelessness that is used to introduce additional obstacles. For instance, court clerks have arbitrarily used one's inability to provide a home address to decline to register their lawsuit (Monib 2016). While my interviewees generally recognized serious obstacles to a homeless person's access to justice, they also echoed the attitude of the local police regarding the role of law enforcement on Musalla's grounds. '*There is only one response for them from the police: 'You shouldn't be here in the first place, this is not where you should sleep.' That is all they get*' (Naseri 2016).

Thus, the denial of protection and justice at Musalla works like in few other places in Herat. Its justification is not that a homeless life is not worthy of protection or justice. While that ultimately remains the core assumption of coercion, Musalla's apparent cultural meaning and value help obscure the operation of biopower. In other words, the rationale of cultural preservation can be activated and used to safeguard the life-segregating logic of unequal protection. This quiet and largely unchallenged denial to uphold life correlates with the practices of active police abuse of the homeless. This correlation escalates the marginalizing potential of the 'homeless-as-a-drug-addict' representation and maximizes the ability to oppress beyond immediate physical violence. Ignoring vulnerability, cultivating it actively, exploiting it, and refusing to ease its pains are strategies reinforced by the commonsensical notion that the homeless body is worthless and dangerous. On one hand, Musalla is seen domestically and internationally as requiring a clean-up and restoration, and such measures can conveniently benefit from the pre-existing politics of differentiation between useful and useless lives. On the other hand, Musalla can be iterated as a governing rationale to empower the denial of space and right to equal life and justice to the homeless. There is abundant evidence that Musalla's social value is contingent upon context and is otherwise poorly upheld by Herat's citizenry and government. However, its preeminent civilizational meaning can be resorted to, and deployed when needed to justify violence predicated on a deeper politics of life. Regardless of whether the homeless are being abused, forcibly removed, and humiliated in order to create an environment of civilizational splendour, or the imaginary of civilizational duty to Musalla is used to justify violence against the weak – their marginalization is predicated on the exceptional spatial logic of the Complex. Such extensive structural opportunities for loathing, neglect, physical abuse and minimization of life cannot be replicated elsewhere in Herat. This is because the cultural apparatus is tied to a specific space that is crumbling and withering before the world's eyes. Without the discourse of urgency and unquestionable, intrinsic value of cultural artefacts, the steady diminishment of life that takes place on Musalla's grounds would be impossible. Practices of neglect and violence elsewhere in the city and across the country indicate that the need to discourage homeless existence as useless and dangerous is real. Nonetheless, the effectiveness of exclusion on those 18,500 m^2 of space would be inconceivable without the drama of tilted minarets and fading faience. The productive power of splendour heightens the utility of colourful tiles and solidifies grounds for a sweeping politics of growth and development. Furthermore, the exceptional significance of Musalla extends beyond its limited space and marks the bodies of the homeless and thieves who try to sell faience or other artefacts in bazaars across and beyond Herat. The situational utility of their bodies within the city (as opposed to elsewhere) is unmatched, because there, they animate the operation of the cultural apparatus. A homeless person arrested or harassed for trying to sell Musalla's faience is far more useful in the city proper. Within its bounds, he/she serves to reproduce the apparent need to 'clean up' and 'protect' the historical complex and the city more broadly.

What makes the weakening of homeless life at Musalla worth scrutinizing is that it reveals the sweeping character of governmental power supported by civilizational and cultural imaginations. Thereby, a number of productive links are created, involving a historical site, a piece of land, the land's valuation as cultural and civilizational, social truths about the uselessness and threat of homeless bodies, etc. This set of productive links also includes the presence of the homeless, their normalized exclusion from the justice, healthcare and welfare systems, their appraisal as an expendable and low-yielding labour force, and the 'care' of international bodies, NGOs, corporations and expert-consultants. The cultural apparatus that initiates and sustains the unequal politics of life in the name of splendour is none of these links and sequences on their own. It is rather a self-assembled, self-regulated and self-perpetuating field of calculations, rejections and discouragements. These practices of subjection are fundamentally spatial, much like one's home (or lack thereof), the bazaars where faience is sold, or Musalla itself. The spatiality of subjection perpetuates its productivity. Namely, for as long as the marginalization of the homeless is tied to Musalla and its cultural import, 'normal' Heratis can participate in the politics of neglect and rationalize it as 'care' for a cleaner and developing Herat. The cultural apparatus mobilizes space and meaning, thereby making the gradual displacement of homeless lives guaranteed to prosper. Ultimately, prosperity reaffirms the rationality of postcolonial power and its entitlement to differentiate and calibrate the utility of life. For if the bad and perilous is curtailed, the good can breathe.

Conclusion

There was a near-unanimous agreement across the interviews I conducted in Herat: the provincial and city governments did not want IDPs and Pashtun nomads to settle in the city permanently. The goal was '*to have as many as possible go back to where they came from*' (Amiri 2016). Insurgency attacks and Taliban offensives have intensified across the country since the NATO/US troop withdrawal. Moreover, many IDPs had been refugees in Iran for a long time before they returned to Afghanistan and eventually wound up in Herat. Hence, it is unclear where the government imagines these places of origin to be or how to 'have' people 'go back'. Beyond this, it is important to critique the social truths that have hurt some and elevated others throughout Musalla's restoration. Many of Musalla's homeless are IDPs, former refugees and nomads. This makes them foreign to the 'locals' and problematic to the government. Their otherness helps explain why they do not feature in any of the studies on Musalla's restoration or Herat's development. An assemblage of international expectations and Herati aspirations to elicit growth have converged around a fairly small patch of dirt and historical artefacts. In their convergence, they have tapped into an easily available and sprawling imagination of costs, opportunities, risk, resources and benefits in the local politics of development. Integral to that imagination of growth and wealth has been a calculation of useful and useless economic and social practices, a thinly veiled biology of development. The calculus rests on the notion that the utility of life and body differs across spaces and populations. One space is populated with useless, costly, filthy, and hazardous 'drug addicts', sexually crazed women, prostitutes, 'Pashtuns', and terrorists, whereas the other place includes normal, entrepreneurial, industrious and responsible Heratis. This differentiation serves the deserving and eliminates the undeserving without much drama or blood. It shatters the experience of homelessness as oppression and reduces it to deplorable addiction, laziness, crime, theft and terrorism.

As Musalla began the slow and winding road to a 'clean up', conditions have been created to minimize vagrancy. They have involved ordinary citizens, governmental institutions, labour markets, wage calculations, welfare, justice and healthcare systems, public intellectuals, etc. In that sense, they resemble other places across Afghanistan where costly or useless lives are being weeded out incrementally through a managed process of natural selection. Yet, Musalla is deployed in a way that offers a richer display of the sweeping force of governmental power. This is because Musalla offers a tempting, enabling, and comforting rationale of civilizational and cultural preservation to anyone with a home who has experienced the necessity to insult, hurt or dislodge the homeless. The discourse of civilization and culture – enmeshed with the dirt, tiles and bricks of the Complex – has electrified a whole range of conducts, strategies and tactics. They have worked to improve Musalla as a social resource and have, in the process, drowned out the kind of life whose value is 'naturally' shrinking. Governmental care for material culture and development has set in motion spatial transformations seen elsewhere in the world. In the historical, cultural, and economic West/North, they have acquired levels of technological, spatial, and regulatory sophistication that has warranted them a long and contrite name: gentrification. According to Neil Smith:

> The process of gentrification, which initially emerged as a sporadic, quaint, and local anomaly in the housing markets of some *command-center* cities, is now thoroughly generalized as an urban strategy that takes over from liberal urban policy. No longer isolated or restricted to Europe, North America, or Oceania, the impulse behind gentrification is now generalized; its incidence is global, and it is densely connected into the circuits of global capital and cultural circulation. (Smith 2002)

While the story of Musalla and its homeless differs from Western or even East Asian events of modernity, it reflects a similar vulnerability of life to the strategies of postcolonial growth and security. When I returned to Musalla in May of 2016, the road through it had largely been removed. Only patches of asphalt remained. The protective wall around the Complex was reinforced and the site seemed busy, swarming with construction and conservation workers. I saw a large truck and at least two cement block machines at work, but could not discern what the cement would be used for. The canal running through the Complex was still dark brown, its banks covered with rubble and construction material, but the grounds seemed largely cleaned of piles of trash and nylon. Occasionally, locals would still ride their motorbikes through the Complex, inviting no reaction from the workers or the police who casually patrolled the site. I noticed about two-dozen people sitting or lying down along the canal banks.

They did not seem to be working on the site, but I could not determine their status. Instead, I spoke to two shopkeepers nearby. They conferred that, in their opinion, there seemed to be fewer homeless persons on Musalla's grounds.

> But many come at night when all these people leave, and it looks like they have started hiding more. And you just can't see them as well anymore from all the machines and construction stuff. (Shopkeeper 2 2016)

Ironically, the homeless have appropriated the tools deployed to make Musalla less accessible to them. The weight of power energizes its own resistances. Its materiality enables the subject to transform oppression into fodder for endurance.

6

Experiencing Self as the Periphery: Heratis at the Iranian-Afghan Border

Introduction

Afghans have been kept isolated from the world since the early 1990s and the collapse of the communist regime in the country. The combined notions of Afghans as security, welfare, demographic and health threats have made it difficult for ordinary people to leave Afghanistan for work, education, leisure, family reunification or to escape conflict, poverty and violent persecution (ethnic, religious, gender, sexual, etc.). International Air Transport Association data consistently show that Afghan passport holders experience the most extensive legal and administrative restrictions on cross-border mobility *in the world* (Henley & Partners 2018). Moreover, from Iran and Turkey, to Greece and across the EU, Afghans face policy, bureaucratic, and physical obstacles to claiming internationally recognized refugee and asylum rights (Dimitriadi 2017, Ruttig 2017, Amnesty International 2016).

Much academic and policy work has focused on the '*push-and-pull*' factors behind Afghan migrations to Iran, Europe, and the Persian Gulf (Stigter 2005, Cuno and Desai 2009, Monsutti 2016, Monsutti 2008, Mahdavi 2011), or the difficult conditions of life along the migration route (Harpviken 2009, Schuster 2011, Tober 2007, Monsutti 2007). Nonetheless, little attention has been paid to the experiences of Afghans at the difficult borders of their immediate west, or to how those borders shape Afghan conducts, aspirations, and truths about Self and the wider world.[1] More scholarship is needed to understand how Afghans cross borders and how the spatial, security and normative orders of the border affect ordinary Afghans. This chapter zeroes in on the production of peripheral (subaltern) subjectivities at Islam Qala, one of only two border crossings along 590 miles of the Iranian-Afghan border.

A number of factors make Islam Qala stand out from other Afghan border outposts: the sheer volume of crossings and Islam Qala's significance in the regional flows of migrants, traded goods and repatriated refugees. Furthermore, Iranian and Afghan popular, practical, and formal geopolitical imaginations (Ó Tuathail 1996) of spatial dominance, economic (inter)dependence, enemy surveillance, and security

---

[1] For a tangential treatment of the topic, see: Marsden, Magnus and Benjamin D. Hopkins. *Fragments of the Afghan Frontier*. London: Hurst & Company, 2011.

emphasize Islam Qala's 'key' and 'strategic' location (Bobin 2009, Favre 2004, Alamgir, Patel, et al. 2004). Islam Qala is part of the Afghan frontier of 'free' movement, already constricted by the Taliban, Daesh, smaller armed gangs, local economic disparities and unemployment rates, ethno-religious enmities and private warlord armies. Islam Qala is one of the largest land border crossings in Afghanistan and the largest one leading into Iran. The growth in human and commercial flows through it since 2001 has led to an expansion of the zone functionally associated with the border crossing, which now also includes a busy bazaar. Few other experiences of the border can quite compare to Islam Qala in the eyes and memories of Afghans. Only Torkham and Chaman (at the Afghan-Pakistani border) rival the volume of Islam Qala's commercial and human flows (Alamgir 2006) or its privileged place in the geopolitical imaginations of Afghan borders and neighbours. It is Afghanistan's 'door' to the West that, moreover, lies within Afghanistan's *own* 'West', or within Herati self-perceptions as the culturally, historically, and economically most progressive and advanced part of the country (Gammell 2016). Furthermore, Islam Qala has attracted unparalleled foreign (particularly US) infrastructure investments. The United States Army Corps of Engineers have led the construction of a passenger-processing hall, customs offices, temporary accommodation, and other facilities (Alamgir 2006).

Yet, like all of Afghanistan's international borders and border crossings, Islam Qala is merely one instance of the postcolonial administration of Afghan life. The array of technologies, methodologies, calculations and rationalities designed for Islam Qala, put in place and overseen by the US, EU, UN, World Bank and concomitant transnational networks is comprehensive in scope and intrusive in depth. They include the design, provision and maintenance of software and biometric data systems, communication equipment, and physical infrastructure, including the strategies of their long-term development and financial sustainability. They also involve the training, funding, and monitoring of the Customs Police (ACP), Border Police (ABP), National Police (ANP), National Army (ANA), and National Directorate of Security (NDS), including their codes of conduct; the development of customs codes, organizational schemes, financial auditing procedures, analyses of trade flows, the registration of returnees from Iran, etc. Therefore, transnational forces (ideas, material capabilities, and institutions) (Cox 1981) invested in the confinement of Afghans to Afghanistan are also involved in the management of Afghanistan's international borders. This correlation enables experimentations with the circulations of humans and social, cultural, and economic forms of capital (Bourdieu 1986), as well as iterative calculations of equilibria in their inflows and outflows. I have discussed in Chapter 2 how the rationality and effects of such calculations lie in the defence of 'global stability' and '[Our] way of life', or the optimization of postcolonial power along the axes of class, race, gender, sex, religion, etc.

Nonetheless, Afghans see their western neighbours in Iran and across the Persian Gulf as cherished and culturally familiar labour markets and travel destinations that restrict, monitor and control their movement and access to workplaces, streets, bureaucracies, mosques, schools, roads, shopping malls, or entire administrative regions (e.g. in Iran and Dubai). While Afghans see Iran, Dubai or Abu Dhabi as sources of income, luxury, stability, hope, survival, leisure and order, they also experience the violence and marginalization that stem from said order and its security apparatus. In addition to strict, and for many unattainable visa requirements, Afghans are exposed to sequences of control, surveillance, examination and disciplining at and around borders. These practices of subjection, and the wider geopolitical conditions in which they unfold, indicate that strategies and technologies of sovereign, disciplinary, and governmental power work to create a spatial and discursive continuity in the representation and treatment of Afghans as risky and marginally useful. There has emerged a consistency in popular and institutional imaginations of Afghans as sources of uncertainty in the domains of security, public safety, finance, labour markets and even public health and hygiene. These conceptions of Afghan lives shape how spaces of liminal contact between sovereignties (e.g. border checkpoints) are designed and enacted. They inform the rationalities and strategies of control of Afghan bodies. In other words, they condition how Afghans experience the frontier space.

This chapter argues that broader socioeconomic, racial, gendered, medical, sexual, and geopolitical discourses of the Afghan as inherently risky and perilous constitute border crossings as sites of subjection and reproduction of Afghan bodies as geo-corporeal peripheries. They recreate Afghan lives as margins of human utility. Borders remake them into expendable and hazardous 'kinds of people' to ordinary Iranians, Kuwaitis or Emiratis. Frontier orders and security apparatuses do so by iterating disciplining, punishment, and regulation as exceptional practices *at* and *of* the border that Afghans then internalize and pass on across their networks as reasonable expectations. Such logics are enmeshed in the arrangements of space around the border crossing, in security and surveillance procedures, and technologies of body/population management. They shape Afghan experiences of Self as peripheral vis-à-vis the perceived prosperity and orderliness of Iran or Dubai. Insofar as power reinforces the discourses of suboptimal and bare utility of humans through the truths of race, class, language, gender or sexuality, it also replicates familiar legacies of geopolitical domination. In other words, the contemporary strategies of discipline and government reproduce colonial discourses of white supremacy (Spencer 2014, Bush 2006, Chambers and Curti 1996). Colonial legacies are exploited by the ongoing containment of terrorists and migrants in the Global War on Terror. As long as Afghans are kept at bay, anyone can perform that task and the West need not be even visibly involved. If power is not white, militarized dominance and superiority in the relative shade of brownness and wealth will do. Iranian and Turkish security apparatuses have shown as much in their treatment of Afghan refugees. The continuous subjection of Afghan life shows that postcolonial power is dispersed, ubiquitous and untethered to the United States, NATO or the wider historical-cultural 'West'.

As I continue to zero in on Heratis as subjects of the postcolonial frontier, I use this chapter to examine the exclusionary effects of a power apparatus that I call 'border zone'. The literature on 'borderlands' has burgeoned in anthropology, political geography, international political economy, geopolitics, and studies of 'great power' borders (Boesen and Schnuer 2017, Kolossov 2012, Newman 2011, Balibar 2009, Armstrong and Anderson 2007), contributing to the emergence of *border* or *borderlands studies*. Analysing 'borderlands' allows for wider considerations of how power – guided by differentiating self/other logics – regulates populations far beyond discrete interstate borders (e.g. via the operation of EU Frontex in the Mediterranean or of US Border Patrol across New England). Examining 'land' (as opposed to a 'line') enables thicker research into social practices affected by boundaries, or practices that are boundary reproducing. I primarily use the term 'zone' (or 'area') to describe a space of postcolonial self/other differentiations, particularly those population differentiations that are intensified by encounters of unequal sovereignties.

I refer to Islam Qala as a border zone for two reasons. First, the notion of the 'border zone' connotes an Agambenian liminality of '*zones of indistinction*' (Agamben 1995), or spaces that blur differences between the *law* and the *exception*, life and death, *political* and *bare life*. Zones of indistinction are the 'slippery slopes' between the kind of life that enjoys rights, protections, and the assumption of belonging to society and humanity, from the form of life that is stripped of such qualities, that can be taken with impunity, that is dispossessed, and excluded from the '*fraternity of the social sphere*' (Downey 2009). Insofar as such zones of indistinction advance power's control over life, I argue that Islam Qala accentuates Afghan vulnerabilities precisely by rendering their bodies imminently *at risk* of being labelled a risk. Second, Islam Qala as a border *zone* evokes what Mary Pratt calls 'contact zones' or

> social spaces where disparate cultures meet, clash, and grapple with each other, often in highly asymmetrical relations of domination and subordination – such as colonialism and slavery, or their aftermaths. (Pratt 2008, 7)

It is the connotation of encounter and negotiation, of postcolonial juxtaposition and inequality that I want to capture by understanding Islam Qala as a *contact zone*. In focusing on Afghan experiences of the border *zone* and of border *crossing*, this chapter proposes a more heterogeneous picture of Afghan frontier subjectivities. It points to diverse experiences of the periphery and differently peripheral (gendered, classed, racialized) Selves. Yet, across all those experiences, Islam Qala betrays the tragedy of being Herat. Herat's distinctiveness derives from its unique position in regional geopolitics as a space that seeks domestic and foreign recognition as Afghanistan's 'most developed', 'most peaceful', and 'most civilized' province, yet one that is always considered a threat to the desired and veneered Other.

The chapter unfolds over five steps. First, the remainder of this introduction provides a brief historical overview of Afghan migration to Iran. The following section reflects on how postcolonial geopolitical differentiations marginalize Heratis (and Afghans more broadly) and how they heighten their vulnerabilities. I thereby draw on a rethinking of the World-Systems Analysis and core-periphery relations via Foucault's concepts of biopower and biopolitics. Exploring how Afghans are made into *biopolitical peripheries* will also help grasp the concomitant practices of their exploitation and violation as barely useful or useless. Third, the chapter proceeds to detail Herati experiences of postcolonial power at the Islam Qala border post, including their everyday nonviolent resistances to bodily and population management. Thereby, I will explore how Herati subjectivities are reproduced as peripheral, while being rejected and eluded through the practices of mockery, pilfering and counter-surveillance. Fifth, I conclude by emphasizing how the disciplining and regulation of Afghan circulations heightens their vulnerabilities.

Afghans in(to) Iran

Attempts by millions of ordinary Afghans to reach Iran, feel safe, form families, and earn livelihoods are tied to the dramatic events of the 1970s: a 1978 *coup d'état* that led to the creation of a Soviet-sponsored 'Democratic Republic of Afghanistan' and the ensuing Soviet Union invasion of Afghanistan in December 1979. Afghanistan's vague sense of statehood and nationhood made the notion of 'Afghans in Iran' meaningless up until the mid-nineteenth century. Yet the border between these geo-culturally and geo-politically proximate spaces on the Khorasan plateau hardened over several decades of colonial politics. Events that led to the enduring geopolitical and cartographic differentiation of Afghanistan and Iran included the 1857 Paris Treaty, Anglo-Afghan-Persian and Russo-Persian border commissions, and the conclusion of the Second Anglo-Afghan War (1878–1880), which remade Afghanistan into a political satellite of the British Raj (Kashani-Sabet 1999). As Sunni Pashtun influence grew in Afghanistan in the late nineteenth century and Emir Adbur Rahman Khan waged wars in Afghanistan's Hazara-dominated lands (Hazarajat), an exodus of Shia Hazaras to Iran followed. By the beginning of the twentieth century, there already existed a group of *Barbari* or *Khavari* Afghan Iranians who had largely integrated with the local populace (Mousavi 1998, 148–150).

Contemporary Afghan migration to Iran increased in the 1960s for largely economic reasons and intensified again after the 1971–2 drought in northwest Afghanistan. Following the 1979 coup, the number of Afghan refugees in Iran (mostly Hazara Shias and Farsi-speaking Tajiks) increased fast and peaked at around 2.8 million in 1992 (Adelkhah and Olszewska 2007, 141). Throughout this period, Afghans enjoyed the status of *mohajerin* or 'involuntary (religious) migrants'. This was an elevated refugee status allowing Afghans to receive healthcare benefits, limited employment opportunities, access the Iranian education system, and enjoy freedom of movement and property rights. In practice, however, much of the status and benefits were precarious and difficult to claim (Hyndman and Giles 2017, 59–60). As the Soviet-supported government in Kabul was toppled in 1992, the treatment of Afghan refugees quickly worsened. Police and administrative harassment, increased pressure and exploitation in the workplace, confiscation of refugee ID cards, and forced deportations were on the rise (Hyndman and Giles 2017, 63, Harpviken 2009, 79). Yet, as the Afghan civil war picked up pace, and particularly in the aftermath of the Taliban victory (1996), refugee outflows intensified anew (Adelkhah and Olszewska 2007, 142). Soon after the United States invaded Afghanistan in October 2001, the Iranian government rushed to add pressure on Afghan refugees to leave the country. Tehran also called on the UNHCR to support this strategy and endorse a repatriation programme. The UNHCR obliged and, in 2002, co-signed a tripartite refugee repatriation agreement with the government in Tehran and the Afghan Interim Authority in Kabul (Tan and Colville 2002). Simultaneously, Tehran started implementing a new refugee registration system (*Amayesh*), which revoked Afghan refugees' 'blue' residence cards and replaced them with temporary (3-9 months) IDs (UNHCR 2004). Applicants are charged each time they reapply for an Amayesh card, which is a significant financial burden given the precariousness of their generally low-paid jobs (Human Rights Watch 2013). This undermines the refugees' legal status, economic welfare and sense of personal and communal safety. It leaves them vulnerable to the Iranian state's inscrutable administrative decisions on which particular Afghan provinces, districts, cities and towns are safe for return given a refugee's ethno-religious profile.

I will return later to how Afghan vulnerabilities in Iran shape the experiences of persons attempting to cross the border at Islam Qala. At this point, it suffices to say that, since 1992, imaginations of 'the Afghan' in Iran have taken a turn that enables the physical, administrative, police, and economic abuse of Afghan refugees and undocumented migrants (the latter category referring to most post-1992 arrivals). Adelkhah and Olszewska describe the pathologizing character of contemporary Iranian imaginations of Afghans as 'afghanophobia' (2007, 153). Around a hundred thousand Afghans have been deported and 'voluntarily' repatriated from Iran each year since 2002. In 2015, there were over 950,000 Afghan refugees remaining in Iran, and over a million undocumented migrants (UNHCR 2015). Once referred to in familial terms (as 'brothers' and 'sisters') across Iran, Afghans are now disparaged as 'trash', 'filthy animals', 'dirty' health hazards who *pollute the water*' (Christensen 2016, Evangelista 2017), or are *'criminals, lazy, uneducated, stealing jobs, driving up the rent*', etc. (Al Jazeera 2016). In addition to being barred entry into twenty-eight out of Iran's thirty-one provinces, Afghans experience administrative and legal obstacles to owning and inheriting property in Iran. For instance, Afghans cannot own mobile phone cards in Iran. Afghan men cannot be naturalized as Iranian citizens through marriage, and children born in Iran to Afghan parents cannot apply for Iranian citizenship. Afghans also face numerous and arbitrary restrictions on education at all levels (from elementary school onward), including limits on what higher education degrees they can pursue (Human Rights Watch 2013). Their access to healthcare is restricted and subject to ethno-racial prejudice, and the quality of its provision remains subpar relative to their Iranian counterparts (Bisaillon, Gooshki and Briskman 2016). This is generally the case even if some services are more accessible to refugees and regular migrants (Tober 2007, 270).

Harsha Walia argues that insecurities in legal and social status and '*the state denial of legal citizenship ... ensure legal control over the* disposability *of the laborers, which in turn embeds the* exploitability *of their labor*' (original emphasis) (Walia 2013, 70). The precariousness and disposability of life produced by diminishing Afghans as 'working bodies' (Baron and Boris 2017), or rather as workplace bodies, is a perverse equilibrium of state-market governmental strategies. They devalue and reproduce subaltern life (e.g. by consistently depreciating the price of Afghan labour) while maintaining bare incentives for Afghans to seek access to an unequal labour market that strictly differentiates them from more privileged Iranians. The Iranian state has imposed restrictions that undermine the Afghans' ability to acquire higher-paid jobs; including quantitative limitations on work visas, administrative hurdles to the renewal of work permits, consecutive spikes in the costs of work visas, and legal restrictions on the sectors of the labour market that Afghans are allowed to access (limited to manual jobs). To Aníbal Quijano, racialized distributions of labour precisely constitute modernity and *'coloniality of power'* (Quijano 2000), as I have argued in Chapter 2. Combined, these measures exclude Afghans from the labour market, allowing them access to a limited class of jobs. This is where juridical limitations align with market-driven conceptions of profit: large populations of Afghans (effectively, over a million) compete for a limited amount of jobs in three Iranian provinces. This depreciates the wages of legally employed Afghans already locked in low-paid jobs. Moreover, these pressures generate a perverse spill over dynamic and a dichotomy between the 'legal' and 'illegal' Afghan workforce. The dichotomy enables employers to further depress the wages of undocumented migrants by threatening them with deportations and substitution for 'legal workers'. Simultaneously, Iranian employers use the existence of undocumented (lower-paid) migrants as a bargaining chip to compel those with valid work permits to accept lower wages. Both groups are utilized to depress the wages of working-class Iranians (employed in construction and farming). Finally, normalized wage theft by employers (Human Rights Watch 2013, Franklin 2011) disciplines all Afghan labourers into complying with postcolonial exploitation.

Since Afghans are confined to manual and high-risk jobs, the precariousness of work (as both *access to* and *safety at*) intensifies the larger precariousness of life constricted by mutually reinforcing corporate and sovereign forces. The corporate-market rationality of utility/profit maximization (and its downward pressure on wages) normalizes the state's interest in protecting the 'national' labour force, as opposed to 'economic migrants' (documented or not). Likewise, the many restrictions imposed on Afghans' access to the Iranian labour market and loose workplace safety protections reinforce the employers' ability to minimize wages and maximize profits. Therefore, a combination of differentiations enables the expansion of postcolonial power through the exploitation of undervalued and unprotected Afghan bodies. The differentiations are sovereign ('domestic' *versus* 'foreign' populations), political-economic and class ('labour'/'capital', 'wage'/'profit'), ethno-racial ('Iranian'/'Afghan', local'/'migrant', 'clean'/'dirty'), juridical ('legal'/'undocumented', 'law-abiding'/'law-breaking') and disciplinary ('obedient' *versus* 'disobedient' or 'criminal'). This confluence of strategies degrades Afghan lives to the paradoxical point of amplifying their utility to postcolonial power. Afghan lives are minimized through a disregard for their 'labour power' and they are cared for only as 'variable capital' (Marx 1906). According to Marx:

> The maintenance and reproduction of the working-class is, and must ever be, a necessary condition to the reproduction of capital. But the capitalist may safely leave its fulfilment to the labourer's instincts of self-preservation and of propagation. (Marx 1906, 627)

Therefore, Afghans in Iran are left to care for self-preservation and recuperate own 'labour power' through rest, nutrition, and self-care in hazardous workplaces (from construction sites to urban sewage systems). However, their utility to power cannot be allowed to dwindle to the point of extinction, precisely because Afghans are needed as 'variable capital' in the production process. Drawing on James Mill, Marx correlates this lower bound of the capitalist's care for labour power (and for the price of labour) with the '*labourer's productive consumption*',

> which is required for the perpetuation of the class, and which therefore must take place in order that the capitalist may have labour-power to consume; what the labourer consumes for his own pleasure beyond that part, is unproductive consumption. (Marx 1906, 627–628)

Yet, I question how much the current inhumane treatment of Afghans (including their subpar access to healthcare) in a postcolonial context meets the minimum prerequisites for the '*perpetuation of the class*'. The distinctly Afghan labour class (as markedly low-paid) is maintained despite continuous *attrition* (including high suicide rates, opium addiction, and zealous deportations) through *replenishments* from Afghanistan. The supply of Afghan labour has been controlled and allowed to fluctuate since the early 2000s: 'old' bodies are deported or temporarily leave the labour market to recuperate, and 'new' – ostensibly stronger – ones arrive from Afghanistan (some are returnees who had been deported or repatriated). Naturally, this crude calculus is contingent upon the overall demand for low-paid labour in the Iranian economy (itself a function of transnational forces), as well as other racial-demographic, welfare and public health concerns about Afghan populations in Iran. As Walia stresses:

> The noncitizen status of these [migrant and undocumented] workers *guarantees* that they fall outside the realm of the state's obligations; they can be paid less than minimum wage, prevented from accessing social services, and deported during recessions without the elite having to worry about unemployment rates or social unrest. (Walia 2013, 71)

Thus, the postcolonial utility of Afghan life lies in its Agambenian 'bareness'. That 'bareness' of life and its lower limit of human strength sufficient for work (and reflected in wages) correspond to life's maximum utility for postcolonial power. In other words, bareness must be preserved on both its upper and lower ends if postcolonial power were to benefit from it. On the upper end, the price of Afghan labour should not overtake the lowest of wages for Iranian nationals. Likewise, Afghans should not be allowed to be too strong – physically (that would indicate the employer's foolish complicity in the Afghan labourer's unproductive consumption) or in terms of collective bargaining and political organization. On the lower end, the price of Afghan labour may asymptotically approach *zero*, but it should not equal it. If it did, it would disincentivize Afghan employment in Iran, or would entail a diminishing 'labour power', understood as '*the aggregate of those mental and physical capabilities existing in a human being*' (Marx 1906, 186). In that case, the postcolony would lose a cheap resource for self-perpetuation. The resource, the Afghan body, remains low-cost and easily accessible as long as there exists a generalized regime of diminished life chances for Afghans *everywhere* (in Afghanistan, Pakistan, Europe, etc.). Overall, while experienced and embodied by vulnerable individuals, *bareness* as a racialized and classed power (in)equilibrium is only sustained and calculated at the level of the population. Therefore, I turn to the intersections of biopolitics and transnational divisions of labour to describe precarious life at the postcolonial frontier.

Conceptual Reflections

The Periphery in the 'World as a System'

In conceptualizing the experiences of Afghan travellers and migrants, this chapter recognizes an economic push-and-pull dynamic in their movements (Rajan 2017). Such framings insert migrants into conversations about the international division of labour between capital and labour-intensive production processes. By extension, this associates Afghan lives with the resultant disparities in the redistribution of surplus value from labour-rich (and low-income) social spaces to those populated by capital, higher incomes and larger corporate gains. Labels for the spaces of wealth redistribution have varied, but a vocabulary of surplus value flowing from the 'periphery' to the 'core' through 'semi-peripheral' societies has dominated the debate. Variations of this discourse have been developed within the Dependency and World-Systems Analysis (WSA) schools of thought. My argument stands closer to the WSA proposition that global reproductions of inequality include transnational, cross- and 'within' societal processes rather than operating at the interstate core/periphery level privileged by the Dependency Theory (Kearney 2004, 220). Moreover, in studying Afghan practices of border crossing, this chapter seeks to understand how socioeconomic cleavages among Afghans may lead to divergent experiences of the frontier. However, I will also argue that the WSA and Marxist notions of the 'productive' and 'production' need to be expanded. They must encompass multiple strategies that power uses to shape human experience. A core/periphery matrix should examine the extent to which power itself is changed, obstructed and made to regroup in the process. Therefore, while the notion of the periphery is useful in capturing the geographies of Afghan vulnerabilities, it needs to be reworked from within to articulate them more fully. An attempt to revise internally the meaning of the core/periphery relationship also heeds Wallerstein's appeal for a 'unidisciplinary' social science (Wallerstein 2004, 19) that overcomes the 'fixing' (Mitchell 1998) of separate 'economic', 'political', 'legal', and other social domains.

But before I suggest an expansion of Wallerstein's conception of the world system and tie it to the body as a space and target of power, his overall framework should first be explored and tied to Afghanistan and Herat. Since Wallerstein stipulates that a system is '*an area less than the entire globe*' (Wallerstein 2004, 98) and that its crucial marker is the flow of profits from the periphery to the core, one can analyse smaller-scale transnational relations that operate according to this logic. Such relations would include capital-labour interactions and transfers of surplus value among households, classes, 'status-groups', and 'identities' (including races, ethnicities, genders, and 'sexual preferences') (Wallerstein 2004, 35–36) within and across multiple societies. A set of core-periphery relations can be hypothesized across Iranian-Afghan transnational relations. In engaging this hypothesis, it is important to ask why Iran (as well as the Arab Persian Gulf) functions as the 'core' relative to Afghanistan? In broader geopolitical terms, Iranian society might be better described as a 'semi-periphery' or even the periphery (Piana 2006). However, if disaggregated, such hierarchies appear simplistic. Afghan dependence on and subordination to Iran and the Arab Gulf states as sources of capital and hope emerges as a regional configuration of forces.

Wallerstein offers a grid of tripartite economic dominance of core societies over peripheries and semi-peripheries, including their dominance in *productivity*, *trade*, and *financial* flows (Wallerstein 2011). Productivity dominance allows the prevalence of capital (versus labour) intensive products of higher quality and comparatively lower price. Thereby, domination in trade reflects a core society's positive balance of trade, which reinforces its net positive financial flows, wealth accumulation and control of system-wide financial markets. While the Iranian economy has struggled since the UN Security Council imposed sanctions on the country in 2006, Iran enjoys much higher GNI per capita incomes than Afghanistan and has a more diversified economy with larger manufacturing and services sectors (Cammett, et al. 2015, Bazoobandi 2013). Furthermore, Iran has enormously lopsided trade relations with Afghanistan. Iran is Afghanistan's third largest export market and the largest source of imported goods and services, whereas Afghanistan is not Iran's top trading partner (The World Bank Group 2017). This is partly because Afghan exporters face tariffs, quotas, and non-tariff barriers (through technical, sanitary, and health standards) in attempts to sell livestock, foodstuff, or construction material in Iran (Shirdelian 2017). While foreign direct investment inflow and outflow data are unreliable for Afghanistan, local media describe Iran and the UAE as some of the largest investors in the country (along with China, India, Pakistan, the United States, and some EU nations), especially in the construction, agriculture and healthcare sectors.

Further to this, Chirot (1986) adopts the WSA method and summarizes five key unequal benefits that core societies receive from their relations with peripheral nations, including low-cost raw materials, low-wage labour, high profit margins from direct capital investments, export-market opportunities, and 'high-skilled' labour attracted through selective migration policies. Again, while the data for Afghanistan are inconsistent, they indicate Iran's preponderance over its neighbour to the east. 'Core' investors from Iran have shown interest in placing their capital in Afghanistan's extractive industries (still largely unexploited) and water resources under the combined pretexts of international cooperation, aid, and development (Mehr 2017, Acquah and Ward 2017). Meanwhile, since 2001, Afghanistan's (including Herati) politically protected business and government elites have siphoned billions of US dollars of foreign aid and domestic profits into bank accounts, businesses, and real estate around the Persian Gulf (Ulrichsen 2017). While the siphoning out of aid and national wealth has worked through a mixture of money laundering and legal financial transfers, all such practices have been predicated on rational 'incentive structures'. Afghan 'investors' and 'entrepreneurs' blame the country's lack of security, weak rule of law, and investment volatility for the '*drain of wealth*' (Bagchi 2010) and loss of surplus value, while crediting the Gulf states with favourable fiscal systems (low taxes) and 'investment climate' (lax regulation) (Johnson and Leslie 2004, 192). Afghanistan also remains dependent on Iran for consumer and capital goods (Ignatiev 2014, Pajhwok 2015).

Finally, the Gulf states (as the regional core) continue to attract Afghanistan's highly educated labour in capital-intensive industries and specialized 'white-collar' sectors, particularly engineers, IT experts and medical doctors.

The continued interest of Iranian, Emirati, Chinese and US investors in Afghan natural resources, consumer markets, and white-collar labour is at odds with the claims that Afghanistan's political instability precludes the country's immersion in transnational capital accumulation. While the Afghan government celebrates 'foreign investors' as a strategy of development, the outflows of financial assets and the legalized theft of aid are normalized as 'capital flight'. However, both processes involve transfers of surplus value to corporate, financial and state actors abroad, particularly those in Iran and the UAE. Currently under construction, a railroad between Iran's northeastern Khorasan Razavi Province and Herat encapsulates this relationship. Funded by the government in Tehran, it is meant to intensify Iranian exports to Afghanistan (Eghtesad Online 2017). Thereby, it aims to reinforce Iran's disproportionate benefits from mutual trade, while remaining largely inaccessible to Afghan travellers due to Iran's highly restrictive bilateral visa regime. This chapter precisely explores attempts of ordinary Heratis and other Afghans to travel to, or acquire poorly paid, physically and psychologically hazardous jobs in Iran in brutal construction sites, mines and farms. Reports typically cite the figure of over two million Afghans (documented and undocumented) working in low-waged jobs in Iran.

I also want to challenge this generic picture of transnational capital forces. While Wallerstein acknowledges the operation of genders, classes, ethnicities, races, and 'sexual preferences' (Wallerstein 2004, 35–36) in the modern world system, he also stipulates that their role is contingent upon '*the logic of a capitalist system*' and the division of labour that underwrites it (Ibid, 36). WSA has been criticized for reproducing an Enlightenment-Marxist bias towards materialist and economistic ontologies of the social at the expense of meaning and knowledge production and contestation. This is often seen as the neglect of 'culture' in WSA (Aronowitz 1981). While gender and other social categories play a role in Wallerstein's narrative, theories of power need to examine how they are differentiated and formed in specific social relations. How are their desires, conducts and truths reproduced beyond the deterministic positionality in transnational divisions of labour? Broader analyses of these social subjectivities would historicize and situate Wallerstein's concept of social change in everyday power struggles. This would make WSA's critique *imminent* and more relevant to the subaltern in her felt social context *from within* the specific relations of power that work to circumscribe her (Herzog 2016, Antonio 1981). For instance, a grounded critique of how power targets Heratis at Islam Qala should also consider them as subjects oppressed *as* Muslims (Ahmad 2017). This position implies engaging the complexities of identities, desires and social imaginaries that Muslim subjectivities may be invested with. Aronowitz argues:

> It is clear that Wallerstein implicitly ascribes all mass action to economic self-interest that is oblivious to ideological influences such as religion, cultural ideas that may infuse the hearts and minds of the bureaucracy or the bourgeoisie itself, or indeed, aspirations that may involve such possibilities as universal suffrage, self

rule, etc. Since in *The World System* there is no concrete examination of daily life within core or periphery societies, but merely an account of various economic, climatic, geographic and demographic factors that operated on a fairly high level of abstraction, Wallerstein could not explore the specificity of politics and culture within the underclasses to find how and why they acted, or whether their actions severely modified or constituted an aspect of the determination of the direction of history. By confining his analysis to exogenous structures, ... Wallerstein cannot but devalue the influence of these endogenous relations. (Aronowitz 1981, 516–517)

Authors committed to analysing periphery/core relations as inherently unequal have taken on board some of this criticism. Hall (1996) offers an excellent overview of expanding directions in world-systems research since the late 1980s, including the endogenous role of gender, cities, slavery, colonized and postcolonial peasantry, etc. While much of the post-Wallerstein world-systems research replicates the often-critiqued emphasis on the impact of exogenous factors (cycles, secular trends, etc.) on social change (Chase-Dunn and Grimes 1995), analyses of endogenous social forces as drivers of change have spurred, critically drawing on anthropological and ethnographic works in the process (Kardulias 1999). However, they often conclude that systemic forces, or the '*inherited differential structural place in the world system*' (Frank 1999, 280), inform the '*political and productive responses*' (Ibid) of specific subjects.

Structural analysis can deliver accounts of power and transformation that go beyond the reification of human nature or explanations rooted in the accidental and contingent. Nevertheless, it is difficult to apply it to lived experiences if the conditions of structural change are extraneous to the model and if the logic of human action is near immutable (e.g. embedded in the division of labour). In drawing on anthropological re-evaluations of WSA, this chapter extends the experience of the periphery/core from secular economic trends and structures to spaces of felt and intimate power struggles, strategies, tactics and resistances that are lived, subject to negotiation, dispersed in operation and whose meanings and rationalities are in flux. It therefore understands the periphery not as a *longue durée*, stable Euclidian geography, but as a social subjectivity produced through power relations that are globally and locally about more than divisions of labour, and whose unequal exchanges are not singularly economic. In other words, in drawing on Foucault's work on power and discourse (Foucault 1982), I use the notion of 'productivity' to include the production of desire, knowledge and identity that make ideas such as surplus value meaningful.

The Body as a Peripheral Space: Experiencing Self as the Periphery

To develop an experiential and power-based understanding of the periphery, this chapter builds on the ideas of biopolitics and biopower outlined in Chapter 2. These concepts allow one to study the (multiple) body as a site of power and eventfulness, but one that is not passive or reactive. Biopolitics and biopower can show that transnationally unequal economic structures draw on strategies of power that invest certain populations and bodies with discourses of utility. Yet, beyond just 'surplus value' or 'profits', that utility is reflected in the discourses of noble heritage, 'good genes', heroic war-fighting culture, masculinity/femininity, queerness, etc. The periphery is not merely an element of the economic system kept uncompetitive through exploitation. It is not limited to the 'economy' as an autonomous sphere of life. Afghan experiences of border crossing show that the periphery is a *process* of subjectivization or hierarchical reproduction of lives as inherently hazardous and conditionally useful. The periphery is not merely in narrow capital forces and flows; it is a political space of bodily forces, functionalities and evaluations. It is therefore rendered upon the body in a simultaneously individuating and generalizing manner (since the body is the flipside of the population). At border crossings, it is enacted through calculated orders to stand, to move only so far, show personal belongings, respond to personal questions, wait in a separate detention room, leave one's fingerprints or not use the restroom just yet. It is the internalization of these codes and calculations, one's hyper-cognizance of power, as well as the practices of their tactical evasion that intensify the felt process of self-periphery. While the unequal gaze of power (Foucault 1995, 174) (e.g. via technologies of border surveillance) heightens the experience of the periphery, the peripheral self is already operational before the physical boundary is even encountered in person. It is induced by previously lived traumas or stories passed on by family members, friends or through the media.

Yet this process is neither automatic nor haphazard. The discourse and subjectivity of Self as peripheral is only effective within certain parameters. For one's knowledge and care of Self to correlate so highly to an anticipated experience, disciplinary power has to be internalized and normalized with great efficiency. While the body is targeted insofar as it constitutes the larger population of interest, biopolitical regulation co-operates with, and co-accentuates, the anatomo-politics of docility to contain the aspirations and circulations of ordinary Afghans. Biopolitical regulatory practices can include the specifications and evaluations of desirable migrant profiles rather than simple bans of specific Afghan individuals or groups (these measures are combined habitually). They also involve the creation of biometric databases that can be recombined and reused in junction with other types of data (e.g. individual and population-level education statistics, health records, analyses of naturalization tests, etc.) (Ajana 2013, Amoore 2006). Ultimately, biopolitics re-places borders as governmental opportunities to regulate and control, and invests them in the body. Thereby, biopolitics shapes corporeal geographies as maps of the postcolonial gaze.

Finally, why and how are Afghan lives at Islam Qala (and beyond) imagined as perilous in domains of security, welfare transfers, labour markets, finance and 'free' enterprise, and public health and hygiene? What are the parameters and conditions of possibility of the discourse of a peripheral Self? Chapter 2 has addressed the work of 'dividing practices' (Foucault 1982, 777–778) that contribute to the production of Afghans as the threatening and undesirable Other. To reiterate, they constitute differentiations, polarizations, and hierarchies '*between the normal and the pathological*' (Foucault 2003a, 41) 'inside' the object of power, or between him and others (Foucault 1982, 778) and, therefore, operate as practices of exclusion. Such divisions effectuate binary hierarchies '*between the mad and the sane, the sick and the healthy, the criminals and the 'good boys*"' (Ibid). More generally, they reconstruct normal-abnormal binaries that Foucault exploits in *Society Must Be Defended* to critique colonial and modern state racism as a form of biopolitics and normalization of genocide. Therefore, hierarchical divisions are deployed across multiple superficially associated discourses that constitute the Other (Foucault 1972, 76). They include relatively stable racial, gender, class, sexual, geographic, linguistic, tribal or ethnic truths. Each truth reifies the Afghan body and Afghan populations as somehow (ab) normal (e.g. poor and filthy brown men *versus* lighter-skinned and clean brown men, docile *versus* threatening Afghans, lazy/useless *versus* hardworking/useful, feminine/harmless *versus* masculine/menacing, etc.). Given the interlocking histories of modern-day Afghanistan and Iran, there are multiple discourses that these dividing practices can rearticulate and tap into. From the shared experiences of the colonial 'Great Game' and Afghan refugee flows in the 1980s and 1990s to the geopolitics of the War on Terror and US-led government of Afghanistan, there is a rich reservoir of imaginations, rhetorical devices, scripts and vocabularies that can be deployed to represent the risky brown body of the Afghan.

The remainder of this chapter studies the periphery not so much as a geo-economic region in the world system, but as a tactical micro-space of social struggles, of microphysics of power (Jessop 2008) that constitute the marginalized body. I walked by one such display of Afghan corporeal periphery on a daily basis. In downtown Herat, there is a relatively large graffiti composite (approximately 25 ft^2/2 m^2 in size) painted on the fence wall of the Inqalab High School. On its left-hand side, it depicts seven black hands jutting out of stormy waters, struggling to stay afloat. They also reminded me of hands raised by students in a classroom. On the right-hand side, it shows a family of three expressionless black bodies behind a bright-red barbed wire, the male body carrying a small sack. Between the two drawings, there are two lines of text written in black ink against a white background. The top line is a verse from the Koran (13: 28): '*Those who believe and whose hearts are set at rest by the remembrance of Allah; now surely by Allah's remembrance are the hearts set at rest.*' The bottom phrase reads: '*Defection from the country: don't put yours or your family's lives in danger*'. Combined with the drawings of blackened bodies and hands, the script warns against emigration as marginalizing, dangerous, unpatriotic and ungodly.

The Periphery and the Frontier at Islam Qala

Islam Qala: Thinking and Encountering the Periphery at the Border

I travelled to Islam Qala from Herat in January 2015 with Barialay and a friend of his who preferred his name not be used here. Barialay was my guide and interpreter in Herat and by the time I left Afghanistan less than a week later, I considered him my friend as well. We took the two-hour trip to Islam Qala because I wanted to see the regular inflow of Afghan 'repatriates' from Iran against the backdrop of hopeful travellers to the country. I wanted to see who they would be on that January morning and how their different trajectories of mobility around the border compared. In other words, I wanted to understand the operation of Afghan peripheries in a place where

I could arguably encounter them: at the point where ordinary Afghans confront the enmeshed Iranian, Afghan and global border security apparatuses. I would come to learn that Islam Qala sharply articulated how Afghan populations were made into human peripheries. However, it also became clearer to me that the hierarchical differentiation that devalues Afghan bodies (as opposed to the apparent humanity of middle or upper-class Iranians and Arabs) unfolds every day across Afghanistan. Hierarchical differentiation is enacted whenever and wherever Afghans are asked *where* they are *from, when* they *arrived* or *where for* and *when* they are *leaving*. Whether the inquirer is a border agent, an Iranian or Emirati employer, or a fellow Afghan matters, but often less than one would imagine. Claiming Afghan non-belonging to – and intrusion into whichever 'normal' place – is a ubiquitous and productive strategy that displaces and marginalizes Afghans with great effectivity. More than just one's geo-economic situation in the world, the periphery is the cruel subjectivity that consumes specific bodies and excludes entire populations as undeserving and menacing. The periphery also involves the equally surgical separation of the useless from those who *are* risky, yet whose strengths and capital are redeemable provided the right education, workplace discipline, self-care, and contribution to 'host' society. The differentiating logic of core-periphery relations reflects what Nick Vaughan-Williams has called the '*generalized biopolitical border*',

> where exceptional measures, practices and characteristics formerly associated with borders between states in the conventional sense become routinised and dispersed throughout global juridical-political space. (Vaughan-Williams 2009, 108)

Vaughan-Williams reformulates sovereign power and its spatial articulations as the reproduction of deprived and right-less bodies, or Agambenian 'bare life'. The framing of power as practice and routine speaks to the widespread vulnerability of brown bodies and the far-reaching right to invoke their suboptimal utility. When sub-optimality is invoked, the border between the normal and the aberrant is redrawn. I have previously referred to such routines as 'dividing practices', but Vaughan-Williams enables their spatial contextualization by showing that the border is '*not something pre-given, static and localised at a territorial extremity but reinscribed as a performance throughout society*' (Ibid, 145). As Claudio Minca has argued, these modes of exclusion have become geographically normalized in everyday life (Minca 2006, 388). While Minca's analysis focuses on 'Western societies', Vaughan-Williams points to Achille Mbembe's work to argue that normalized violence has also marked the colony, where its application aims to serve 'civilization' (Mbembe 2003 in Vaughan-Williams 2009, 115). As I will discuss later, it is precisely the dream and hierarchy of civilization that is cited to put Afghans in 'their place'. It is also the imaginary of *being in the civilized* that torments Herat's subjectivity as '*Afghanistan's richest and safest city*', as the city's Dean of Urban Development and Housing Department has called it (Sarwary 2016). Rethinking the border as spatialized practice and a performance of power rather than a fixed space helps understand why Afghans experience core-periphery relations and the postcolonial 'frontier' long before they reach Islam Qala or the Kabul airport. Their periphery and frontier travel with them as potentialities inscribed on their bodies.

The morning we left for Islam Qala, Barialay and his friend seemed apprehensive about travelling to the border with Iran. I had never seen Barialay so anxious, while his friend – who drove us to Islam Qala and back to Herat with his car – appeared impatient to leave. Similarly, Barialay's friend was pacing around the car, looking eagerly at the dashboard minutes before we left back for Herat later that day. As he was greeting me that morning, Barialay shook my hand more firmly than usual and, out of the ordinary, asked me: '*Are you ready for this?*' 'This' was a vague reference to an unusual experience for all of us. Barialay and his friend had never taken a foreigner, a 'Westerner' as Barialay once called me, to the Afghan-Iranian border, and I had never visited it before. I also registered 'this' as a metonym for insurgent attacks, murders, and kidnappings that had taken place on district roads outside Herat City (Ghanizada 2014, Human Rights Watch 2007) and close to the border (Zeyaratjaye 2017). As we drove to Islam Qala, I learned that 'this' also stood for Barialay's anxiety about how ordinary people around the border crossing would react once they heard us speak English and once they realized that at least one of us was a foreigner. 'Westerners' were not a rarity at Islam Qala, but their presence 'unprotected' by other foreign civilian assistants, administrators or fellow researchers was somewhat unusual. While Barialay's concern was to not draw attention to our 'odd' presence, it was also ironic that a larger group of ostensibly Western 'professionals' would have seemed less out of place at that little stretch of the postcolonial frontier. Barialay's anxieties about my role, impact on the safety of our small group, and about my own safety were also reflected in his thorough preparation for the trip earlier that morning.

Before we left for Islam Qala around 10 a.m. Barialay had lent me a pair of sandy brown shalwar qameez commonly worn by both men and women in Afghanistan (with gender-tailored adjustments). We had discussed previously whether I should wear more locally common clothes during fieldwork and our joint trips around Herat. We had agreed that it was not necessary since many male Heratis wore jeans, khakis and wool or polyester sweaters. This time around, he thought that extra caution and 'blending in' would be helpful on the road and around the border crossing itself. As we spoke of 'caution' and 'self-protection' on the way to Islam Qala, I thought about how this trip in general, and with me in particular, tested the more predictable calculus of personal safety within Herat City. Confronted with a vague possibility of abduction for ransom, my body became financially lucrative and exploitable in this context. More importantly, the conversation and my new attire prompted me to think about the risk I posed for Barialay and his friend on this trip. My place of residence, institutional belonging, language and my linguistic mannerisms tied me to the United States at that time. In the context of Herat's district roads and the border crossing at Islam Qala, those stubborn facts drew a boundary across and around my body and pulled in the bodies of my fellow travellers. Exposed to similar physical risks, we, nonetheless, inhabited the opposite sides of the postcolonial divide. Like Islam Qala itself, this divide meant different things for Barialay (and his friend) and me. Barialay's anxiety that morning, *versus* my academic curiosity, reflected how the palpability of the border was different for us. Etienne Balibar understood this as the 'polysemic character' of borders, or the '*fact that borders never exist in the same way for individuals belonging to different social groups*' (Balibar 2002, 79). The road to Islam Qala and its ambiguous security regime impressed itself differently upon Barialay, his friend and on myself. While they spoke of our physical safety and Iran's social influence in Herat, I kept wondering how much risk my research incurred upon them. Did it reproduce their lives as expendable while the commercial worth of mine grew perversely? I could also afford to escape temporarily the feeling of discomfort by reminding myself that we '*just* needed to get to the town of Islam Qala' and then we '*just* needed to get to the border crossing', etc. Yet these estimates were inapplicable to two men whose bodies would become relevant in a whole new way once we reached the interstate border. 'Voluntary' Afghan repatriates from Iran, returning religious pilgrims and tourists, seasonal workers with temporary entry permits, truck drivers, family members of the returnees, small-business owners around the border crossing, bazaar vendors, Afghan police and military officers, NGO workers, UNHCR officials, Afghan customs officers and others felt the immanency of this postcolonial divide in different – sometimes dramatically different – ways. Yet the dividing line itself was pervasive and solidified by their – our – dissimilar racial, class, gender and sexual subjectivities.

As we parked the car about two hundred metres (close to 220 yards) from the outermost edges of the border zone, Barialay reminded me that I should speak softly. Not drawing attention remained our priority. Walking from the car towards the border, I was reminded that thinking of Islam Qala as a 'border crossing' or a 'line' was misleading. The Islam Qala border area struck me as much larger and more crowded than the sparsely frequented regional road leading to it might suggest. According to Farrukh, who at the time worked as a server at a café/restaurant within the border zone, the 'thickness' of the zone varied on any given day, but tended to be around 1.2 kilometres (0.75 miles). It consisted of spatial fragments bound together by the notion that Islam Qala is one of Afghanistan's two crossings into Iran, a country economically, politically and culturally central to everyday life in Herat. This, in turn, reinforces the importance of Islam Qala to Iranian-Afghan commercial and human flows, including those of migrants, returnees and other travellers. Therefore, Islam Qala's unique role as a rare point of physical opening between two sharply unequal sovereignties shapes its spatial order as well. Visual, physical and functional fragmentation and densification mark the area of around 1.5 km^2 (or 0.6 mi^2) prior to the very crossing. Its outermost edges consist of multiple commercial compounds and outposts, including at least two parking lots (crammed with automobiles) on both sides of the main A1 road, improvised flea markets and several clusters of orderly parked trucks. When I asked Barialay if we could take a walk around the various parking lots, he advised against it, saying '*we have no business walking around there*'. I asked whom he would expect to see there and he responded: '*Just the drivers [in the trucks] and maybe some passengers sleeping in the cars. But we shouldn't just walk around.*'

However, we walked around one of the makeshift bazaars with about twenty vendors who were selling their goods strewn on the ground. Those included car and machine parts, water and soda bottles and occasional Iran-made candy. Hundreds of people walked hurriedly past the vendors. Occasionally, someone would stop to inquire (mostly in Farsi) about a certain item or buy a bottle of water. Even though it was January, the day was relatively warm (around 11°C/52°F) and the omnipresent fine sand in the air ensured that people felt thirsty. While the whole picture seemed rushed and somewhat chaotic, it quickly occurred to me that it was only our little group that stood out visually: we did not seem like we were in a hurry; we were moving in no particular direction and with no apparent purpose. Since Barialay and his friend also seemed uncertain as to why we were moving slowly among the vendors, I realized that the increasing number of suspicious looks that we were receiving seemed logical. I could not know for sure as to why we were suddenly attracting attention, but in a crowded place with a history of suicide attacks (Watson 2012), our awkward behaviour could reasonably alarm the vendors and passers-by.

Moving beyond the bazaar, we walked through a series of checkpoints operated by ANA, ANB and ANP. Once we would reach a security gate (one of which was a tall turnstile), we would find four or five officers around us. To my surprise, this made me anxious. Islam Qala is a place where thousands circulate each day either because they are thrown out of Iran or because different sorts of desperation – even masculine adventurism – draw them into poorly paid and unsafe jobs across the border (Monsutti 2007). Unlike the white employees of the UNHCR or the IOM, I had no immediate sense of utility to the thousands of ordinary people who surrounded me there. Was that feeling any different for the business owners within the border zone? They profited off this conglomerate of hope and desperation, off the place where the periphery was on full display. While I did not benefit financially from Islam Qala, I was clearly approaching it as an under-researched and, therefore, invaluable object of academic – of *my* academic – gaze. Therefore, in addition to race, my socioeconomic and professional background set me apart from thousands around me. Each time an ANA or ABP officer asked for and checked my passport, they would consult with a colleague, therefore signalling that my otherness required a second opinion and an extra pair of eyes. Each time they asked Barialay why I was there, I felt like I was intruding in on the experiences of thousands of people who preferred not to be there, but had to. What was pain and uncertainty for them was a privileged choice for me. This sense of intrusion made me anxious and it affected my ability to observe the security officers, especially since I was reluctant to look at them for prolonged periods of time to avoid awkwardness or appearing suspicious. Barialay later described the ANA and ABP officers we had seen as merely '*normal, OK... guys in their twenties and thirties*'. Given the sensitivity of questions about border security, I decided not to raise them further with my interlocutors that day.

At any rate, each checkpoint included chest-to-toe pat-downs and brief examinations of our IDs. In my case, this entailed showing my passport before we could be allowed through. Each time, I was shown a precise spot where I should wait until officers checked my passport. Apart from spurring my angst, the fact that we went through this same procedure at each of the three checkpoints indicated ANSF's heightened surveillance and disciplining in the border zone. After nearly two hours without seeing a single ANSF vehicle on the Herat-Islam Qala road, their intense presence around the border signalled its significance to sovereign power.

Most people circulating through the checkpoints (both towards and away from the border crossing) were males between around twenty and forty years of age. Some wore variations of the shalwar qameez and others sported jeans and colourful sweatshirts or coats. Together, they formed murmuring and orderly flows of bodies whose faces and pace of walking reflected anxiety, hope, hopelessness and crushing disappointment. Much of their manifest emotion correlated with the direction of their circulation: those walking towards the border crossing generally seemed more resolute and upbeat, if nervous. However, I would occasionally notice male refugee 'repatriates' and returning seasonal workers in their twenties or thirties coming in from Iran, carrying duffle bags and walking with surprising vigour in their steps. They stood out from among dozens of others who merely seemed to wobble and dawdle along with their heads down. Nodding in the direction of one of the 'energetic' returnees, I asked Barialay why he thought this particular man in his early twenties seemed different. *'That one is going back [to Iran] for sure, or maybe really wants to go back,'* he said. Most returnees, however, seemed exhausted, some emaciated. Most wore clothes and shoes that looked dusty, old and often frayed.

Being a Child, Being Afghan, Being a Woman at Islam Qala

As we walked through the first of the three gates, I noticed that some returnees boarded a clearly marked IOM bus parked at around 50 metres (55 yards) from the first checkpoint. According to Najibullah, who operates a van transportation business between Herat and Islam Qala, the IOM helps some of the most vulnerable and most desperate youths ('unaccompanied minors') deported from Iran. We talked to Najibullah at the same café where Farrukh worked as a server, and both recounted stories of Afghan children taken from their families in Iran and deported to Afghanistan with no adult supervision or care. Najibullah and Farrukh never spoke to the minors who sought the IOM's help, since they would quickly board the buses provided by the organization and would continue on to an IOM transit centre in Herat. Yet some deported minors regularly decide to not seek official (IOM or UNHCR) assistance and instead try to find food, shelter and transportation from Islam Qala on their own. Herat is their first stop and often just a temporary destination. Najibullah said that he would give them a free ride to Herat every now and then, especially to the youngest among them, and Farrukh shared with pride that they would often give unaccompanied minors free meals at the restaurant. *'Life is bound to be horrible for them once they arrive in Herat and many of them end up homeless there,'* added Najibullah. Why do so many of the unaccompanied minors deported from Iran decide to forgo institutional support?

Amrulhaq Ayoubi (AHRO[2]), Farrukh and Najibullah said that many youths did not trust the government and international agencies. Deportees know that the organizations offering help and care will also collect some of their personal information (including biometric data in the case of ABP). They suspect that this information could be further exchanged across different agencies and used to restrain their movement in Afghanistan or even ban them from returning to Iran to look for their families or jobs. Their fear is inflated by widespread perceptions that the Afghan government has been intent on showing 'cooperativeness' since 2002 in helping Iran fight 'illegal immigration', even as Kabul has protested against the inhumane treatment of Afghan refugees and temporary workers in Iran (Bezhan 2015, Mehregan 2010). Iran has

---

[2] Afghanistan Human Rights Organization

arrested and deported thousands of Afghans – including entire families – after they agreed to register with local authorities and apply for Iranian refugee documents, temporary residence permits, and Afghan passports (Christensen 2016). Therefore, to preserve 'tactical' manoeuvring room (de Certeau 1984), these teenagers sacrifice a few days worth of meals and free transfer to Herat. The border is where Iran's sovereign gaze dissipates and the regulatory need to 'care' takes over for a brief moment until their 'case' is archived and administrative knowledge of their predicament is created. Thereafter, they are released, indeed abandoned, until the next time they are said to have posed a threat to Iran's labour market, child welfare services, or even Iranian-Afghan diplomatic relations (Christensen 2016, Ferris-Rotman 2012).

It seems implausible that economically and juridically excluded, exploited and undernourished bodies are generating the multiplicity and severity of threats and concerns that require violent deportations, constraints on movement, and involuntary biometric data collection (by Iranian and Afghan authorities). Yet the perilousness of Afghan bodies is not something that requires proof. It is axiomatic in a postcolonial system of meaning where the weak struggle to live is always more disconcerting and disruptive than legitimate. Returning to Balibar's notion of polysemic borders, these 'unaccompanied minors' do not experience Islam Qala as a clash between two sovereignties with conflicting geopolitical agendas. The way the border presents itself to these youths is as a *'nexus of systems of oppression'* (Walia 2013, 9), a more concordant space. They are passed on between two sovereignties and across mixtures of (interstate and non-state) regulatory power. While some may treat them with brutality and others with neglect or apparent kindness, all power relations objectify them and constrain their choice. Thus, these youths hide and try to avoid ABP's and UNHCR's human and video surveillance around the border (Ayoubi 2016). Instead of being subjected to yet another iteration of *order*-ly procedures of law and care, they accept potential homelessness and the assistance of other strangers *ostensibly less* interested in monitoring them.

I write *ostensibly*, because the stories that Najibullah and Farrukh conveyed reminded me of the perpetual interest of power in the life and body of the vulnerable. Najibullah prided himself on wanting nothing in return for the free rides that he gave to unaccompanied minors. Yet he also claimed that those were rare moments of respite that these youths could expect. He and Farrukh talked of rape and forced labour that had apparently befallen some of the youth returnees. *'Desperation sometimes makes you trust the wrong kind of people',* said Najibullah and, upon my insistence, explained that he was referring to the deportees' *'desperation to escape capture and move freely, even if it means going back to Iran'.* News, government, and civil society reports confirm that the physical (economic and sexual) abuse of Afghan minors is widespread and engulfs their bodies from Pakistan to Greece (Kamminga and Zaki 2018, Neslen 2017, Radio Free Europe – Radio Liberty 2015). Therefore, these children and teenagers experience the border as a continuity of human devaluation. The border frustrates the needs of ordinary Afghans to reach more ample labour markets and safer towns, or experience cultural, socioeconomic, gender, and sexual difference on their own terms (Monsutti 2007). The border regime of separation is not allowed to control, frustrate and regulate life merely because two sovereignties occupy distinct spaces. The border is divisive because it is taken for granted that Afghans and Iranians are different, deserving of *difference* in the context of work, well-being, travel and safety. But more than 'less deserving', Afghans are 'more dangerous'. In whichever direction an Afghan walks – into or out of Iran – he or she is constrained to reproducing the postcolonial order of disparate human value. Walking out of Iran, Afghans are *again* shown that they have no say in what is done to their 'freedom of movement' or 'refugee rights': individuals with valid residence permits have been regularly deported, regardless of their status, since 2002 (Human Rights Watch 2013). Likewise, those few allowed into Iran – and most travellers are made to cross the interstate boundary on foot – are explicitly reminded of the temporality of their privilege to enter the country. Moreover, they are exposed to exhaustive pat-downs, intrusive security checks and meaningless long hours of waiting to be allowed in. For them, the border reflects the paradox of their situation: the very experience of fortune to be let in unfolds through the games of anxiety, relief, humiliation, and uncertainty initiated by Iranian border guards, or 'temporary sovereigns' (Vaughan-Williams 2009, 121) at the Dogharoon border crossing just opposite Islam Qala. The experiences of Afghans both entering and leaving Iran reflect the differentiations made between their bodies and the bodies of Iranian security guards, civil servants and occasional tourists or businessmen. Worse yet, lines are drawn between the contemptible Afghan bodies and the physical objects and architecture at the Dogharoon crossing: the guards warn them and – if 'need' be – yell at them to keep off the walls and signs along the corridor into Afghanistan to avoid damaging them. Harsha Walia reminds us that analysing 'embodied borders' – or boundaries that inscribe themselves onto our skins, movements, emotions and affects – exposes '*how we are not just spatially segregated but also hierarchically stratified*' (Walia 2013, 9).

Walia's 'hierarchical stratification' speaks to the postcolonial core-periphery relationship that I have tried to elucidate here by reformulating Wallerstein's matrix of the transnational exploitation of labour. For the body is reproduced as peripheral when it is underpaid, whenever its pay is stolen, or when life is arrested and ostracized from the privileged space because its worth is understood as inferior. The periphery is enacted when- and wherever Afghans are denied entry into Iranian mosques, schools, government buildings, and entire provinces (Human Rights Watch 2013, Moosakhail 2014, Esfandiari 2012, Adelkhah and Olszewska 2007). Rejection is indispensable because the presence of 'filthy' (Christensen 2016, Evangelista 2017, Olszewska 2015, 47) Afghan bodies might shrink the distance needed to maintain the core's self-avowed cleanliness, normality, spirituality and citizenship in the face of wretchedness on its eastern frontier. As an Iranian border guard apparently asserted according to a Herati NGO activist, '*the civilized have to be separated from filthy animals*' (Anonymous NGO Activist 1 2016).

Azad, a patron at the café where Farrukh worked, captured the experience of *becoming* the periphery as he reminisced about the times he crossed the border at Islam Qala. He repeatedly referred to the entire timespan between leaving his home in Herat and entering Iran on short-term work visas as 'traumatic' and filled with both 'hope' and 'dread'. Barialay asked him to clarify his feelings and Azad simply explained: '*No one likes being called a "bastard"* [Persian: ḥarām-zāde] *by another man*

[Dogharoon border guards], *especially if we share the language and faith*.' News reports show the attractiveness of Farsi-speaking populations from Afghanistan (Hazaras and some ethnic Tajiks) to the Iranian government and the Islamic Revolutionary Guard Corps (IRGC). They are recruited to boost Iran-affiliated troops in Syria's civil war. As of January 2018, over 2,000 Afghans fighting in IRGC-trained Liwa Fatemiyoun brigade had reportedly died in Syria (MEMO 2018). However, cultural, religious, ethnic and linguistic affinities between Iranians and certain Afghans, as well as the utility of Afghan bodies to Iran's *raison d'état*, do not necessarily translate into humane treatment of Farsi speakers at the border. Disdainful and instinctive associations of specific humans with 'their' geographies of proper belonging disintegrate the discourse of historical-cultural 'commonness'. This strategy reinforces the hierarchy of alienation, or one's marginalizing and crippling 'otherness'. Within this hierarchy, one's Afghan geography anchors him/her firmly to the bottom of the scale. It thereby offers pleasure to the border agent, who is not merely a (civil or law enforcement) servant anymore, but an Agambenian 'temporary sovereign' elevated by the right to exceptionalize and embody sovereign exclusion. The Afghan body is laid bare and its desires, truths, and relationship to Self (Foucault 1980d, 59, Foucault 2017) are repressed. Simultaneously, her/his body is infused with reified geopolitical imaginations of hazardousness and instability inflated by Afghanistan's threatening 'vastness' (Kaplan 2012). Accounting for how identities are mediated by power, Wendy Brown invokes the sociological notion of 'ascriptive' identification, or the production of '*subjects who carry the group identity*' (Brown 2006, 45). Thus, the excluded body is circumscribed as properly belonging to a different space and group – to that of other 'Afghan bastards' like Azad. A bastard body is a treacherous periphery to be kept at bay. Indeed, Azad added that the feelings of angst and dread are 'always there' when he travels to Iran, even before he leaves his Herati home for Islam Qala. They are stirred whenever he visits the Iranian consulate in Herat to apply for a visa, when he packs for the trip, or talks to friends and relatives about it. He *becomes* the periphery whenever his desires, memories and Self become targets of security, stability and order.

As we walked through the consecutive checkpoints, I watched crestfallen men and children walk into Afghanistan. Iraj, an elderly man in the wheelchair – all by himself, in a thin brown jacket and a dusty pink beanie – embodied the frontier's facile dehumanization. We stopped to ask him why he was returning to Afghanistan and he simply said: '*They don't want me anymore. I used to be a brother, now I'm a leech. They tore up my refugee card, kept me in a detention center overnight, and then put me on the bus to Islam Qala yesterday*.' Yet, in the midst of these flows of angst into and out of Iran, the presence of about a dozen women stood out for me. Clearly a minority in crowds of men, the women I noticed walked alone or with children; most around 50 metres (approximately 55 yards) away from us. The distance made it harder for me to grasp their gesticulations, facial expressions, age or the directions of their gaze. Yet they stood out visually due to the chadors they wore, while two or three also wore face-covering burqas. My attempt to guess their age was a superficial effort at engagement with their lives in that space, having known all along that conversations or closer interaction would be very difficult. Yet the question of age would re-emerge later on as we listened to men's tales of women's experiences at the border. Recalling the women we saw that day, it seemed to me that only two were girls under ten and the rest could have been anywhere between young adults and sixty or so years of age. Speaking quietly with Barialay, I nodded in the direction of a person I thought was an elderly woman; I was wondering whether she was travelling to Iran or welcoming someone back. But Barialay quickly responded that she seemed much younger to him and '*only walked hunched down like that*'. Apparently, the vaguely abstract floral pattern of her chador was 'very youthful', according to Barialay. The women were walking in the direction of the border crossing (i.e. towards Iran), but by the time we reached the border checkpoint, I could no longer see any of them. I do remember their brisk pace of walking; some seemed like they were marching ahead. I wanted to understand that movement, but it struck me how impenetrable the wall around their experience was to me. It was hardly conceivable that the three of us could approach them and strike up a conversation. Many of the same boundaries would exist if those had been men instead.

As I was watching them, I thought all of us were separated by the congealed discourses and customs of gender and sexual boundaries in a 'conservative' and 'patriarchal' part of Afghanistan, as virtually all of my interviewees between December 2014 and June 2016 described Herat. Yet, as I recalled Barialay's heightened caution throughout the trip, and as we continued to walk through the border zone, I realized that much of the boundary I thought of as gendered and sexualized actually reflected the amplified sense of risk and angst around the security apparatus. In other words, what stood in my way were moods and sensitivities common to many people there. I again felt that being peripheral vis-à-vis Iran was an engulfing status that in some circumstances transcended my whiteness, maleness and my intimate Western geography. I had to abide by the dictates of security tensions, risks, caution and business-like focus on the purpose of my trip much like everyone else. Otherwise, I was bound to heighten my companions' and my own vulnerability. The subtlety of the core-periphery relationship placed yet another boundary around me, and Barialay tried to make sure that I obliged.

At any rate, as we talked to a few men at 'Farrukh's café' later on (and Farrukh himself), I realized that gender norms merely facilitated my conversations with men more than they frustrated my access to the 'female experience' at Islam Qala. This is because such norms regulated how and when one should interact with women that *he* did not personally know; but they also allowed, and perhaps encouraged, casual exchanges and banter between men in certain social spaces (e.g. cafés, flea markets, waiting lines, etc.). In other words, I could imagine Barialay and myself cautiously striking up conversations with women we did not know in spaces that were less marked by heightened sensitivities around one's safety. In fact, the precise thing happened as we lined up at one of the ATM machines in Herat. Either way, the farther the women were from me on that January day, the harder it was to glean their practices of the border. I interpreted the way that two women kept tugging their girls and boys ever tighter to themselves as making sure they did not lose them in the smothering crowd. But it also seemed to me that they wanted to make sure their children did not slow them down as they rushed ahead. I asked Barialay whether he agreed with me that the women within the border zone walked a little faster than men. He agreed hesitantly, vaguely adding: '*Who knows ... Women ...*'

I mentioned that observation to all of my interlocutors that day and none of them could interpret it for me, even though most agreed with it upon brief reflection. Azad, however, went a step further: '*No one here feels totally comfortable and because women are different, they will behave even more differently than normal in a place like this.*' I later wrote down in my notes that rather than being naturally different, one could argue that women everywhere had internalized experiences and expectations of differential treatment. Practices of masculine gaze and bodily responses to them constitute what Foucault called 'anatomo-politics' (Foucault 1977). None of my interlocutors seemed particularly concerned that the way women moved, carried themselves and walked in the vicinity of the border might be mediated by the disciplinary power of masculinity. While Azad spoke about the apparent feminine 'difference' in behaviour, two male friends of his at the café nodded along in agreement. Such androcentric conceptions of difference, however, produce felt bodily consequences that uphold the feminine/masculine rift. Denaturalizing the notions of '*the female body*' and 'femininity', and rethinking them as social discourses, Moira Gatens posits: '*If [these] discourses cannot be deemed 'outside', or apart from, power relations then their analysis becomes crucial to an analysis of power*' (Gatens 1996, 71). I will return to the embodied reality of femininity as I discuss the accounts of abuse of women at the border.

Ultimately, we walked by four women at close enough distance and exchanged brief looks and head nods. They did not walk together; nonetheless, they shared the focus and fast pace in their motions. Two of them were hauling along two boys each and, at this proximity, a number of things struck me about their demeanour. I saw facial expressions of tension: frown lines across the forehead, eyebrows pressed slightly down and together, a wrinkling nose and a stiff upper lip. Given the context, my observations remained constrained to the apparent. I was also aware of how oddly unrepresentative these encounters were, since Barialay and my other interlocutors that day confirmed that women would typically frequent public spaces accompanied by men. Farrukh added that some of the women were probably in the company of 'their men'. I could not observe that since men usually keep their distance from the 'female company' and walk a few steps ahead of them. As I thought of this spatial hierarchy, I wondered how much of it was an entrenched expectation and stereotype rather than dominant everyday reality (Es 2016). However, as I pondered the renegotiation of this 'natural' practice, the conversation moved on quickly.

I had long followed media and NGO reports about the pervasive corporeal abuse of Afghan migrants in Iran for work and sex, or through senseless police brutality (Evangelista 2017, Human Rights Watch 2013). I asked Barialay and his friend, Azad and his two friends (whose names I did not catch), Najibullah, and Farrukh whether they were aware of any stories of bodily abuse at the Afghan-Iranian border, on either side. I posed this question twice (once primarily to Najibullah, and then a second time to Azad and his friends) and both times my interlocutors at first hesitated or showed incredulity. Yet at the risk of letting the awkward silence linger on too long, I kept quietly looking at them to signal that they could still think about my question and offer more specific responses.

Najibullah broke his silence by bringing up his transportation business. He explained how he sometimes talked to his customers and spontaneously learned details about their lives. He sounded subdued as spoke about a middle-aged man – once a refugee in Iran – whose wife had been allegedly abused by ABP at Islam Qala. Allegedly, the Iranian police had picked her up in Shiraz outside the house where she lived with her husband. She was purportedly a legally residing refugee there, but when her husband was at work, she was arrested while cleaning the front yard. She spent nearly three weeks in two detention centres and was raped twice by guards there. Subsequently, she was deported to Afghanistan, wearing only a t-shirt, a pair of old jeans she was given after her chador had been torn up, and flip-flops. Her deportation allegedly took place in the middle of the winter. Purportedly, her misery did not end there. As she crossed into Afghanistan, two ABP officers approached her and asked her to follow them so they could take her fingerprints and personal information. Then, one of them raped her again in an improvised ABP office close to the final Islam Qala checkpoint for non-commercial traffic. As her husband recounted to Najibullah, the couple reunited after he voluntarily left Iran. He had since been back in Iran several times to take up seasonal jobs in construction. Then, to my surprise, Najibullah told us about his cousin who tried to enter Iran with her husband. They were accused of using false passports.

The two of them allegedly tried to enter Iran in April 2014. ABP waved them through, but the questioning on the Iranian side – first by the roadside and then in a separate office – was much more detailed. Eventually, a uniformed police officer came into the room claiming that their passports were forged and did not belong to them. They were told that they could either pay a fine on the spot and be immediately deported to Afghanistan (Islam Qala), or otherwise be taken to a detention centre. According to Najibullah, his cousin and her husband managed to pay the fine, which left them bankrupt. Nonetheless, Najibullah's cousin was still raped by two Iranian officers that same day. '*At least they didn't make her endure that humiliation in front of her husband. Her husband didn't have to see her breasts or ears exposed by another man*,' Najibullah added. Iran's visa restrictions for Afghan nationals have pushed many to attempt to enter the country with forged passports or falsified visas (Monsutti 2016, Koelbl 2015). Yet, this practice amplifies their vulnerability. If caught by the Iranian guards, they are invariably arrested and subjected to degrading detention, often accompanied by physical or verbal abuse and humiliation. But the border is particularly cruel to Afghan women. Moreover, as the Iranian security apparatus reasonably expects *some* Afghans to be in possession of falsified documents, it chooses to treat them *nearly all* as transgressing. *Nearly* – because Afghan 'entrepreneurs' and 'investors' regularly receive Iranian visas to conduct business in the country, or to attend trade fairs and exhibitions.[3]

To conclude the point on the intersection of gender, race and class at the border, I want to emphasize that what makes space meaningful or important are its social-political functions. To understand the vulnerability of ordinary Afghan women at the border, we should heed Foucault's advice to study space (Islam Qala) and its organization as intertwined disciplinary, security and regulatory functions of

---

[3] For how this practice aligns Iranian state and corporate needs, see the work of an Iranian company that specializes in the organization of international trade fairs and expos at https://en.iranfair.com/ (Accessed August 16, 2017).

government. Islam Qala points to why Foucault saw politics of the body and that of the population as conjoined, describing the population as the 'multiple body'. Islam Qala, as a micro-locus of core-periphery relations, generates illegality and criminality by cordoning off Afghans and restricting their life chances. In that sense, forged passports and criminality are merely tactics used in defence of life. Nonetheless, criminality does not hurt or break all bodies quite the same. For Afghan women, girls, and boys, criminality is more than a new juridical status (of the 'law breaker'), and more than confinement and a humiliating deportation. Even weaker than adult Afghan men, these classes of brown bodies can be exploited further and with perverse intimacy. Postcolonial (core-periphery) relations do not stop merrily at trade inequalities, unfair investments, poor labour rights or free movement restrictions. Because they are always about the utilization of the body, core-periphery relations go deeper. Postcolonial power engenders intimate vulnerabilities by rummaging through black and brown bodies, by consuming each conceivable weakness. It enables assault on them through violent acts that expose carefully tabooed spaces: the breasts, the mouth, the penis, the vulva, the anus, the muscles of the auricle, the thighs, etc. (McClintock 1995).

Azad and his friends could not share any personal knowledge of abuse at the border. They also said that they were generally unaware of it. Numerous media, NGO and IGO publications have reported on the widespread sexual abuse of Afghan women, girls and boys by the police in Afghanistan and Iran, as well as by Afghan government-affiliated militias (Nordland 2018, Poyesh, et al. 2015, Thorson 2013). Azad did, however, say that he had heard of beatings and other forms of physical abuse of Afghans by the Iranian border police. Yet, he also added that it was all hearsay and he had no specific knowledge to share. News, NGO and IGO reports corroborate what appears to be common knowledge among Afghans about the inhumane treatment of their fellow nationals by the Iranian state and private employers alike (May 2016, Barr and Sanei 2013, Adelkhah and Olszewska 2007).

International Agencies and Their Spatial Effects on the Normalization of Islam Qala

Yet there is more to the controlling and regulatory effects of space at Islam Qala. In addition to the multiple checkpoints (with a separate border crossing for commercial vehicles) and their organizing, disciplining and regulatory purposes, the presence of international (state and non-state) agencies and their offices contributes to the workings of Islam Qala as a space of postcolonial control. The UN's refugee body (UNHCR), the International Organization for Migration (IOM), Afghan Border Liaison Office (funded and supported by the UN Office on Drugs and Crime (UNODC) and occasionally monitored by their staff), and a varying number of mostly Western NGOs (e.g. British War Child) all are present physically at Islam Qala. The breadth of rationalities of these various agencies – whether they are there to maintain ABP's IT system, stop transnational opium trade or assist the deportees – is to normalize the border, control how different classes of humans, goods, and vehicles circulate through and around it, and to reduce disruptions in its operation as a limit of sovereign space.

Whether food, water, diapers, or medicines are urgently delivered to those in need, or new biometric entries are made into the national (and international) database of Afghan nationals, an array of agencies, safety and bureaucratic procedures, scientific tools and security assessments are invested in its smooth functioning. Sovereign control and geopolitical management are inherent to all interstate borders. Yet, Islam Qala's variety of normalizing technologies reflects geopolitical conceptions that posit one space as self-contained and normal, and its opposite as deviant. There is no such array of normalizing tools at border crossings across the Global North. Comprehensive instruments that manage misery and risk are deemed appropriate only in those rare places where global stability has to encounter aberration. The Iranian-Afghan border is in that sense zealously postcolonial. As a political space, it resembles less the borders between the states of the Global North and, curiously, operates more like their heavily surveilled brown and black neighbourhoods in Paris, Baltimore or Birmingham. For a border emerges as an encounter with the aberrant only when the metropolis, order and normalcy gaze at *difference* that resists their triumph. The cultivated image of deviancy both explains and justifies the practices of exclusion and containment of the abnormal.

Furthermore, all of these international bodies communicate daily with Afghan state agencies (usually with their functional counterparts in the executive). That implies circulations of Afghan government staff across parts of the border zone that otherwise might not be immediately exposed to the sovereign gaze. For instance, as an Afghan police officer was sauntering by the bazaar on his way to the IOM office, he caused almost all of the vendors and passers-by that I could see to slow down as they walked and lower their voices, as if to acknowledge the exceptional sovereign and disciplinary presence in their midst. Moreover, the professional, legal, and ideological commitments of foreign professionals Islam Qala are not easily penetrable to the local traveller and he/she cannot know how suspicious one might appear to a UNHCR, UNODC or an IOM employee. Therefore, a hopeful traveller to Iran has to cope with how the human parts of the security apparatus at the border move, since such circulations heighten security-related anxieties, constrain opportunities for vagrancy, and complicate the 'counter-surveillance' of the terrain (e.g. to facilitate illegal crossings in the future).

Islam Qala's Fluctuating and Inflated Spatiality

The tight regime of controls around Afghan populations in Iran and the international policy of containment of Afghans within Afghanistan have pushed people of diverse ethnic, religious and socioeconomic backgrounds from Herat, Badghis, Faryab and other provinces in the west and north – and as far east as Kabul – to attempt to enter Iran through Islam Qala by using forged passports and visas. They have also tried to cross the Iranian border illegally beyond the 'ports of entry' in defiance of the intertwined Iranian, Afghan and global security apparatuses. Islam Qala's technologically sophisticated surveillance apparatus is large and functionally entangled with that of Iran. This makes crossing irregularly into Iran much easier through the more porous and less fortified border in Afghanistan's southwest Nimroz Province (Ramin 2017, Koelbl 2015). Nonetheless, many prefer to cross the border in Herat for reasons of geographic proximity, personal familiarity or Herat's relative security compared to Nimroz. Thousands slip into Iran every month via Herat in search of jobs, personal safety, independence, 'modern lifestyles' (Ruttig 2017), or en route to Europe. They tend to use stretches of the border north and south of Islam Qala and thereby avoid the patrols and surveillance of ABP, ANA, ANP and their Iranian counterparts around Dogharoon. Yet, the regional importance of Islam Qala inflates its spatiality and affects irregular migration. Cross-border trade with Iran, migration flows, tourism, shipping routes from Central Asia to Pakistan and India, transnational opium trade, etc. all make Islam Qala a security, surveillance, logistical and geo-economic priority for the governments in the region and far beyond it, for importers, exporters and ordinary people. The logic of compounding economic, communication, transportation, and security interests (Alamgir 2006) renders Islam Qala's spatiality unstable and expansive. This seeming boundlessness expands the ability of the security apparatus to reinforce the outer bounds of Afghanistan and assist Iran in warding off Afghan populations. Therefore, eluding ABP, ANP, ANA, and others is fraught with practical risks as far as dozens of miles away from the border posts between Iran and Afghanistan. The utility of Islam Qala for the security apparatus goes beyond its specific location and function. Since constraining the movements of the Afghan body reinforces the virility of postcolonial power, Afghans can *expect* every element of the security apparatus to be incentivized to operate at maximum capacity, regardless of its *actual* functioning or purpose. Thus, the *dispositif*'s sovereign, surveillance, disciplinary and security purposes combine effortlessly. Their amalgamation subjects Afghanistan's unruliness to a travelling *panopticon* tasked with protecting 'stability' jeopardized by poor brown bodies. Why? Because, from Vienna to Ankara, they are imagined to belong to the east of the normal.

Examples of the security apparatus' fluctuating and unpredictable spatiality abound. Speaking on the condition of anonymity, a Herati NGO activist recounted a number of testimonies from locals who have tried to cross irregularly into Iran. He claimed that remaining invisible and '*keeping a low profile*' trumped most other feelings and personal priorities around the border (Anonymous NGO Activist 1 2016). He relayed that the intense need for caution makes Heratis distrust even the British NGO engaged in demining programmes – the HALO Trust (Ferrie 2018). According to Anonymous NGO Activist 1, many fear the organization's coordination with the National Police around Islam Qala. Running into them in any of the unpopulated areas around the border crossing would raise immediate suspicion.

More violent examples of the boundless and mobile border include arrests and shootings of civilians – including unaccompanied minors – by Iranian border guards and arrests by the increasingly militarized Afghan police forces (Saif 2017, Nazar and Recknagel 2011, Bendiksen 2008, 16–17). Often, violence inflicted by the border's 'temporary sovereigns' at Islam Qala and Dogharoon appears uncoordinated or in conflict with the higher ranks of sovereign hierarchy in Tehran, Kabul, or Herat City (TOLOnews 2017). I have argued in Chapters II and III that power strategies need not be tactically consistent or directed by a central 'mastermind'. Regardless, this disconnect does not explain why border rationality regularly violates life without due process or any evidence of intent at illegal crossing.

The Exceptionality of Commerce. Commerce as a Window into Border Surveillance

I have noted earlier that Afghan 'entrepreneurs' and 'investors' enjoy privileges when applying for Iranian entry visas. While enduring arduous working conditions, Afghan truck drivers, too, experience marginally greater cross-border mobility relative to most ordinary Afghans due to their utility to international trade (International Labour Organization 2006, Alamgir 2006). Reflecting Wallersteinian accounts of transnational upper-class coalitions across core and peripheral societies in the capitalist world system (Bornschier and Chase-Dunn 1985, 23, 119–120), Afghan entrepreneurs seek to integrate with Iranian and regional bourgeoisies. For a moment, they have the privilege to perform their 'core' belonging at the border by eschewing long pat-downs and ID checks. Often, they are allowed to use a separate checkpoint for commercial vehicles, thereby avoiding the main pedestrian corridor destined for most other Afghans.

In accounting for the disciplinary functions of space, Foucault claimed that its *'axis of symmetry'* – herein, the evenness of operation of checkpoints on *all* travellers – is *'framed by and functions thanks to well-calculated dissymetries'* (Foucault 2009, 31), such as exceptional crossings guaranteed to only *some* deserving Afghans. In other words, for the security apparatus to treat a series of Afghans as if they posed a risk (in terms of security or the forged documents they carry), it must allow 'normal' and 'legitimate' travellers to select themselves out of the risky series. They do so by signalling their worth and harmlessness to the imbalance of power (e.g. transnational trade or the Iranian welfare state). Their class, gender and ownership of useful assets precisely perform this signalling function. Expecting different classes of Afghans to all undergo the same experience of the border and periphery would mean carelessly lumping the useful with the useless, thereby dis-incentivizing the growth of beneficial social forces. Instead, 'investors' (men travelling alone or in small groups) are enabled to leave the periphery and perform who they deserve to be – the well-to-do core. On the other hand, *'the well-calculated dissymmetry'* sorts out millions of other Afghans into marginally useful labour and easy targets for varieties of physical assault. Those Afghans face steeper obstacles when applying for visas, when crossing the border, while working in Iran, and upon their (in)voluntary return to Afghanistan. Of course, these class distinctions between Afghans are tenuous and tested in practice whenever suspicion towards the Afghan body arises (whether in Iranian hotels, industrial parks, or mosques), but the fragility of distinction does not negate its social utility.

Walking around the border post, I also noticed a spatial distinction and 'dissymmetry' in the placement of commercial content at Islam Qala. We saw a few customs buildings with one prominent one-story structure in close proximity to the final checkpoint on the Afghan side. Long rows of commercial trucks extended contiguously across the border zone. They, as I have mentioned, had their own regime of checks, import-export, shipping and security procedures to comply with. These commerce-related processes took place separately from the flow of returnees from Iran and other non-commercial travellers. According to Barialay, trucks regularly come into the country full, carrying construction material, household appliances, clothes, industrial machinery, candy, steel, carpets, soap, ceramic and other tiles, fuel, etc. Even '*Coca Cola and Pepsi*' come in this way (Alamgir 2006, 10). In all, a range of things that make up everyday life enters Afghanistan through Islam Qala. As I listened to Barialay enumerate the consumer and industrial goods that Afghans acquire via Iran, I recalled scholarly and policy research that described commercial flows between the two countries as heavily misbalanced in Iran's favour. Barialay agreed and added that trucks '*come full from Iran and leave empty from Afghanistan*'. This echoed almost verbatim an Asian Development Bank description of the relationship (Alamgir 2006, 6). Barialay also commented on the A1 road that Iran had helped repave, as well as the railroad to Herat that the government in Tehran was building. He said that both pieces of infrastructure had a clear commercial purpose. '*Iran is more than fine with throwing Afghans out and then selling us all kinds of shit*.' Afghan exporters, on the other hand, use the Islam Qala customs to sell '*fresh and dry fruits, medicinal plants, cumin, wool and animal skins*' (Alamgir 2006, 10). Exporting unprocessed agricultural products and raw materials, while importing a whole spectrum of processed consumer and industrial goods creates millions of dollars in trade imbalances. Such disparities correlate with the images of thousands of Afghans anxious to be allowed into Iran or determined to enter the country by any means necessary. Inequality, trade-enabled wealth transfer, Afghan migration to Iran, Iranian unilateral visa restrictions and the inhumane treatment of Afghans both at the border and in Iranian towns far beyond it, all reflect Wallerstein's logic of core-periphery relations. Yet more than that, the effortless correlation of these realities is what Afghan life is allowed to be at every turn in the shadow of, not so much Iran itself, but wider global relations of imagination-as-power. The chokehold of this power claims to keep the ever-abstract 'world' safe from Afghans and millions of other brown and black lives. Yet even the wretched should be empowered to drink Coca Cola and smoke Marlboro, or have their bodily strength exploited for work. Hence the seductive rhetoric of gradual transnational opening, normalization of trade, industrial fairs, and promises of 'mutual benefits' (Harshé and Tripathi 2016, Mobariz 2016). However, the promise of international trade as a tool of development is a familiar and problematic technology of the postcolony (McEwan 2009, Kapoor 2008).

This special place accorded to trade in the grand promise of Afghan progress is reflected in its exceptional positioning in the border zone. Aihwa Ong has analysed '*market-driven strategies of spatial fragmentation*', or how profit-maximizing rationality structures space and demands distinct treatment for capital flows through '*zones of exception*', even in ostensibly non-capitalist societies (Ong 2006, 7). Such zones reflect a distinct right to mobility enjoyed by capital goods (a 'freedom', in fact) and privilege humans functionally associated with them (investors and entrepreneurs, truck drivers in limited circumstances). At Islam Qala, commercial trucks and customs offices are located beyond the core southeast-northwest axis formed by the main road (A1). This spatial compartmentalization puts commercial practices of the border out of reach for most ordinary travellers. Moreover, it contributes to a 'thickening' of the borderland (Rosas 2006), to which I will return below. The spatial exceptionalism of commerce adds to the numerous restrictions upon travellers' movement around and throughout the ever-shifting border zone. Why would one walk around a separate commercial area if he/she is not a truck driver or a business owner visibly interacting with other drivers or entrepreneurs? Verbal and nonverbal communication that conveys the mutual recognition of 'belonging here' is important in this space. It legitimizes one's presence in it. One can wait for hours on end to cross the border and that time might be best spent sleeping in the truck, reading or chatting with others who are travelling to Iran for work. But specific material parameters are key to this casual banter or a nap: to be spoken with as someone who belongs or to be able to sleep within the commercial area, one has to signal that he is justifiably using a truck or another vehicle. While this condition seems somewhat obvious, its blatancy is important for two interrelated reasons. First, it is efficient at screening out outsiders. Second, this ability to monitor underscores the exclusionary effect of the border. Namely, unless a person meets the high bar of appropriateness for their presence in this sector of the border (e.g. owning a truck, being a licensed truck driver, or owning a business that trades with Iran/Afghanistan), they should not be there and they can be held accountable if they are. The police can be called on them and those who apparently belong can even physically expel them from the area.

I learned more about these surveillance and monitoring dynamics from Barialay and his friend, and Najibullah later confirmed their account though a personal remark:

> I own a small business – actually one that, in a way, has to do with transportation, but I wouldn't dare just show up there [with] the rest of the truck drivers. I mean, I have no reason to be there, but I also wouldn't want them to look at me weird like I'm a criminal or a terrorist because I don't exactly do what they do.

Trucks have been used across the Herat Province for cross-border human and drug trafficking, as well as insurgent attacks both before and since my visit to Islam Qala in January 2015 (BBC News 2013, Al Jazeera 2017b). Those who 'belong' in the commercial zone do not want to be around persons who cannot demonstrate their equivalent belonging and can make them feel unsafe. However, the leap from one's allegedly odd presence to its lurking association with terrorism and crime impressed upon me the force of security and surveillance discourses at Islam Qala. Moreover, it occurred to me that being surrounded by 'criminals' must happen occasionally around the border, precisely because commercial trucks are regularly used for drug and human trafficking between Afghanistan and Iran. I tried to raise this issue with Barialay, but I was unsuccessful. Since discussing this topic felt contentious so close to the border, I decided not to broach it with any of my other interlocutors that day.

In addition to different practices of 'belonging', I was interested in the dispersion of power across the border zone. Animated by a rationality that categorizes commerce as exceptional, trucks parked a little off the main road produced a monitored space, but also a space of security risks and concerns for the police, the truck drivers and businessmen, the cargo, the passers-by, etc. Therefore, the surveillance apparatus at Islam Qala far transcended the guards and the video surveillance capabilities at their disposal. The need to minimize one's exposure to sovereign control and discipline at the border induced countless micro-monitoring practices directed by everyone at everything circulating within the zone: from humans to cars, text messages, animals, etc. According to Nikolas Rose:

> Surveillance is 'designed in' to the flows of everyday existence. The calculated modulation of conduct according to principles of optimization of benign impulses and minimization of malign impulses is dispersed across the time and space of ordinary life. (Rose 1999, 234)

The regime of mutual surveillance was generalized insofar as anyone's actions could be threatening to everyone else. While performing the meticulous work of government over multiple bodies, this apparatus worked to repress and drown out opportunities for resistance. Thereby, it made any act of seemingly purposeless circulation or loitering within the zone oppositional. Being seen as lethal or otherwise dangerous for anyone within the logic of the border is contingent upon a number of probabilistic factors. Barialay warned me multiple times that day how easily I could transgress, appear suspicious, or walk into places where I *'had no business being'*. This could be as simple as asking provocative questions or walking too slow, too fast or in areas that were inappropriate given my identity. My lighter skin tone and the language I spoke made me a 'Westerner' at Islam Qala, which inoculated me from the suspicion that I was – or could ever be – lethal. Most other bodies circulating around and through the border area are not afforded the same benefit of the doubt: they are too dark to be trusted or to trust each other. They are induced to feel anxious – their brownness is the condition of their anxiety.

The security, surveillance and sovereignty of the border effortlessly infuse space with psychologies of angst that – having generated suspicious behaviours – justify the existence of the power apparatus with stunning ease. Anxiety and insecurity need to be relieved. Having internalized the presence of surveillance, threat and risk, and having subjected everyone to own watchful eye, everybody at the border becomes an extension of the security apparatus. The meticulousness of subjection and the peace of the border, however, make every eccentricity and divergence appear disruptive and, by necessity, operate as resistant. I will return below to the tactics of resistance. At this point, I want to stress that – local specificities notwithstanding – risk management structures space, subjectivity, and social practice around all borders (Muller 2010). The postcolonial border is different insofar as it constitutes an expanded calculus of risk and worth. It factors in *race* and *class/caste* filtered through brown and black oriental imaginaries. This 'inclusive exclusion' (Agamben 1995) shapes the self-expressions and vulnerabilities of oriental subjects (Proglio and Odasso 2018, Nayel 2017). Moreover, the ability of the border apparatus to expand its exclusionary gaze points to the manufactured genealogy of risk. In François Ewald's words: '*Nothing is a risk in itself; there is no risk in reality. But on the other hand, anything can be a risk; it all depends on how one analyzes the danger, considers the event*' (Ewald 1991, 199). The postcolonial border stands out in terms of *how* it analyses danger and *what* it considers dangerous: racial and class differences which are outside the limits of economic or geopolitical *utility* as cheap labour or a noble savage in need of saving from other barbarians. Born out of Eurocentric calculi of utility and worth, racial-cum-class difference operates at the point of naked exploitation, including slave trade, chattel slavery, forced labour of 'free' subjects, limited access to food, shelter and other resources, etc. In other words, ascribed difference produces the racialized and dispossessed body as bare life and, thereafter, toys with its exploitability. At those heightened points of abuse, race-cum-class subalterns reinforce their own perilousness when they are pushed to counter-mobilize. Resist or not, they remain risky to governmental power shrouded in the dream of stability. Managing them does not unsettle light-skinned bourgeois power. It is a welcome strategy, a self-serving response to perceived threat. As a power strategy, risk management elevates the optimization of *good life* at the expense of the wretched.

Overall, one of the implications of the racial calculus of who should and should not be *let* in is that it makes the border more rather than less effective or somehow distracted by yet another variable of surveillance. If the postcolonial border is not a finite or linear location but a biopolitical mechanism of marginalization that emerges through and upon the menacing body, this means that any border – in fact, any social space anywhere – can be fitted for the postcolonial mission as long as it administer racialized and classed risk. Drawing on Agamben and Foucault, Vaughan-Williams captured this contingence and mobility of the border as a social field that is enacted whenever exclusion is necessary to assess and govern risk:

> Bodies do not simply encounter pre-existing borders as if they were timeless territorial artefacts. Rather, borders are continually (re)inscribed through mobile bodies that can be risk assessed, categorised, and then treated as either trusted citizen travellers or bare life. In this way border/body performances depend upon movement and are played out at sites across everyday life. (Vaughan-Williams 2009, 134)

One's relative deprivation and brownness is imagined as threatening to the life chances of another aspiring or struggling human, as well as to the welfare of entire *normal* populations. At Islam Qala, this biopolitical imagination transpires through the generalized practice of mutual surveillance. One person *could* blow up dozens. One truck smuggling or trafficking in humans or drugs *could* bring the entire border post to a halt for hours, all of which makes Iran that much farther. *Homo homini resicum est*. Man is *risk* to man (rather than a *wolf*). In other words, the postcolonial border is productive in its exclusion because it reproduces the calculi of costs, benefits, opportunities, threats, chance and hazard. This calculation perpetually problematizes the periphery and reproduces it as the spatial and civilizational negation of the worthy core. It preserves the periphery as dangerous for everyone, including the periphery itself. Thus, the postcolonial border incentivizes a generalized practice of control and containment of the peripheral, including through self-control, i.e. by other subaltern bodies *from within* the margins.

Other risk-managing restrictions on movement around the Islam Qala post include requirements for car owners to acquire special – relatively expensive – authorizations if they wish to cross the border in their vehicles. This partially explains why hundreds of people simply walk across the interstate line, carrying, pulling or dragging their belongings stuffed into duffel or large plastic bags. Naturally, this exposes their bodies more efficiently to generalized surveillance throughout the border zone. To power, 'bare' is 'safe'.

The Fragmentation and Inflation of a 'Fine' Violent Border

I have described throughout this chapter the marked mobility, spatial fluctuation, enlargement and intensification of security, administrative and surveillance procedures of the border. Elsewhere, similar developments have been referred to as the 'thickening' or 'stretching' (Casas, Cobarrubias and Pickles 2011) of borders, especially in relation to the increase in racial/migration concerns in the West, the war on terror and outward extensions of border controls within the EU, across the Mediterranean, in North Africa, etc. (Ramraj 2012, Muller 2010, Rosas 2006). Islam Qala is Afghanistan's technologically most sophisticated border crossing (Alamgir 2006) and Iran has, on its end, deployed drones to monitor the long borders with Afghanistan and Pakistan. However, Islam Qala's 'thickening' is not so much about advanced surveillance supported by drones and sophisticated cameras, about biometric 'dataveillance' (Clarke 1988), or even the outward relocation of checkpoints deep into contested sovereignties. Its security-advancing 'thickening' or 'stretching' beyond the very border crossing struck me more as strategic fragmentation that rendered space functionally and physically more complex. This complexity was structured in such a way that it constrained, enabled, and directed movement via a series of local binaries: possible/impossible, logical/illogical, meaningful/meaningless, allowed/banned, purposeful/purposeless, etc. The border zone works as an elaborate arrangement of the various checkpoints, commercial and passenger sections, Afghan National Army and (Border) Police premises, stretches of offices of international governmental and nongovernmental organizations, and cafés and restaurants – many of which are spatially intertwined in often unpredictable ways. Each element generates its own controlling, surveillance and governing effects. Each effect is both self-driven and stimulated by the generalized objective to keep the border zone free of slowdowns, disruptions or death. At Islam Qala, a restaurateur's interest in making sure that each patron pays his/her bills naturally aligns with the sovereign interest to eliminate risky behaviours, things and bodies around the border. While the restaurateur needs to *minimize* the security apparatus' gaze at him (which includes the attention of other business owners or NGO workers in the area), the security apparatus (including the Afghan and Iranian state apparatus in the zone) needs to maximize the reach of its watchful eye. Even though they appear contradictory, these necessities often cooperate with one another, even if their correlation is imperfect. This imperfection allows for and is driven by resistance practices in the area, a point to which I will return below.

This spatial assemblage of control, discipline and security thus combines racialized, classed and gendered conceptions of threat. Their effects are peripheral subjectivities: enduring, traumatizing and actualized in the restricted mobility of the Afghan. Islam Qala's fragmented spatiality and multilayered surveillance apparatus make illegal crossings hard – nearly impossible. Dozens of my interviewees in Herat described this border outpost as 'fine', 'secure', and 'normal'. However, some of my anonymous informants recounted that individuals and small groups do attempt to cross illegally at points further north and south of Islam Qala. When spotted and pursued by the Afghan or Iranian police, those travelling with firearms will at times shoot (back) at the security forces. Iranian guards have allegedly shot unarmed civilians at the border, as well as miles deep into Iranian territory (Koelbl 2015, Sharfyar 2013, Nazar and Recknagel 2011). If caught alive, undocumented migrants are made to endure degrading incarceration, physical and verbal abuse and financial extortion. Those who cannot afford to pay their way out of prison – and be deported back to Afghanistan – are put through expedited and questionable trials, often with no legal representation. Sometimes, Afghans are kept in custody for months without having their case heard by a judge (Human Rights Watch 2013, Daiyar 2013). According to two civil society activists whom I interviewed in Herat, the situation is similar on the Afghan side. The Afghan police and army are reluctant to use lethal force against unarmed civilians apprehended at the border. However, the juridical process is riddled with corruption, nepotism, bribes, forced confessions, and physical, verbal and psychological torture in jails and prisons. The treatment of 'conflict-related' detainees accused of cooperating with the Taliban is particularly violent (Anonymous NGO Activist 1 2016, Anonymous NGO Activist 2 2016, United Nations Assistance Mission in Afghanistan and Office of the United Nations High Commissioner for Human Rights 2017).

Manoeuvring the Periphery by Evading, Co-opting and Counter-Surveilling the Border

Writing about everyday resistances that are not overtly political, but undermine relations of domination, James C. Scott associated them with the dignity and humanity of subjects (Scott 1990, xi). Drawing on the discussion of everyday resistances in Chapter 2, I want to briefly develop a link between Scott's *infrapolitics* and *hidden transcripts* with everyday life at Islam Qala. Attempts at illegal crossing into Iran precisely constitute the infrapolitical or *'low profile forms of resistance that dare not speak in their own name'* (Scott 1990, 19). So do the attempts to enter Iran on falsified visas or passports, especially by minors.[4] Nevertheless, I will focus on less obvious – yet more widespread – cases of ostensibly apolitical practices akin to *'foot dragging, dissimulation, desertion, false compliance, pilfering, feigned ignorance, slander, arson, sabotage'* (Scott 1985, xvi), as well as the acts of 'counter-surveillance' (Monahan 2006). In doing so, I will also draw on de Certeau's notion of tactics (de Certeau 1984) and Bhabha's work on the practices of cultural ambivalence of colonial subjects (1994) to show that life produced as peripheral or subaltern never quite complies with the caricature of a broken and obedient serf to order and stability. For its unsettling presence is microphysical and too ubiquitous for the strategies of power to overwhelm. As long as the bondage of discipline under international cooperation, development and security hurts, resistance endures. My intent is to move away from

[4] However, thousands of Afghan minors who cross the border with Iran illegally are victims of human trafficking.

the academically and institutionally privileged focus on the Afghan body as risky and perilous to narratives of Afghans *at risk* and *in peril*. As a function of that peril and out of '*awareness of the balance of power*' (Scott 1990, 183) in favour of the security apparatus, I keep anonymous some of the conversations that have informed my understanding of resistant practices at Islam Qala. Therefore, I am referring to some of my informants here as *Man A* through *D*, or *Anonymous NGO Activist 2*. I also decided to leave out most other markers of their identities, except for some basic facts. In addition to their gender and wide age range (between 25 and 46 years old), I specify that they were all residents of Herat City at the time of my visits (December 2014–January 2015 and May–June 2016). Our conversations allowed me to focus on the quiet subversion of power and life's inconspicuous resilience.

Nonetheless, two remarks are in order. First, repeated visits to Islam Qala, extended observation, and further conversations would improve the depth and scope of findings on the tactics of resistance in the border zone. Second, while I probed the issues of nonviolent resistance at the border with my interviewees in Herat and Kabul, by and large, I have not been able to extract valuable information that would advance the discussion here. This second caveat only highlights the need for additional visits to the field.

Since Barialay and his friend had to leave the café and 'quickly run an errand', I spent some time there on my own. I stayed at the café and their absence (as 'knowing locals') made me feel apprehensive at first. However, a group of four men (enumerated here as A through D), who had been sitting nearby, took an interest in me soon after Barialay and his friend had left. They all spoke English and our conversation started with the usual questions about where I was from and how I liked, first, Herat City and, then, Afghanistan. A proclamation habitual for Herati locals followed, asserting the city's unmatched wealth, cultural achievements and beauty in Afghanistan. In contrast to Herat, Man A called Kabul a 'shithole'. I smiled hesitantly. The remark caught me off guard and made me nervous, yet I did not want to alienate my interlocutors by appearing judgemental. The split second of my hesitation was enough to make Man B in the group pull back and ask why I was in Herat and, more curiously, at Islam Qala. My response about my academic interest in the area was somewhat generic. Yet, I did use one ambiguous phrase to try to elicit a more critical discussion without putting the nascent conversation at risk: '*I am generally interested in what NATO and the UN have done in the Province*.' Man A, who had previously made the 'shithole' joke, repeated my statement as a direct question, tweaking it in the process: '*What have NATO and the UN done to the Province?*' I was not sure whether his use of a different preposition was wordplay intended to connote a different meaning (of implicit harm *to* the Province), but the question did pique his and his friends' curiosity. They claimed that NATO's and the US presence in the country was inadvertently helping Iran interfere in Afghanistan's domestic politics. What followed was a fifteen-minute explanation of Iran's purportedly pernicious influence in Herat. The four men's accounts oscillated between conspiracy theories and verified news reports on Tehran's role in aiding the insurgency (Gall 2017).

Just as I was preparing to ask how the palpability of the Iranian border affected the four men, their families and friends, the conversation took a turn I had not expected. Man B said that Afghan authorities, too, played a role in the '*daily humiliation of Afghans*'. '*The government in Kabul, Iran's friends in Herat,*[5] *these bastards [haramzadeha] patrolling the border … they all put us last and playing nice with Iran comes first*', said Man C. They proceeded to share stories that painted a picture of a 'security system' (as Man B called the Afghan border security apparatus) that was slow, unthinking, poorly organized, readily used by Iran to do its bidding at the border, and, nonetheless, effective in its oppression of ordinary Afghans. They chuckled and 'fat shamed' an ABP officer who was strolling (or patrolling?) around the 'restaurant strip' in the zone. It began as a joke among the four of them, but soon, three other patrons at the café joined in their laughter as they kept nodding in the guard's direction and exchanging (in Farsi) apparently unflattering references to him. This exercise in mockery switched back to English when Man B whispered rather loudly: '*He is so fat I bet he can't even see his dick!*' Man A joined in: '*He is so fat they can just put him at the gate and no one will be able to get into Iran! That can be their 'security policy'*'. It seemed that everyone at the café who could hear this joke laughed. While uttering the phrase 'security policy', Man A changed the inflection in his voice and tone to convey sarcasm. Less jokingly, however, he added: '*It is like we are animals in a cage and if they let us out, it's just to use us. But these morons [nodding his head in the direction of the nearest checkpoint] help them in that.*' The fifteen-or-so seconds of silence that followed felt much longer. Man A, who had led the way with crude jokes, interrupted it to say: '*They too [referring to Afghan border guards] are just people, they also work to get paid. We can't blame them. They, too, do what higher powers make them do.*' Man D then interjected:

> I understand that, but I don't agree when they arrest people who are just desperate to leave the country. I don't agree when they expect bribe, or beat up people in jails, or when they're disrespectful to mothers and older women here.

I asked what they thought they could do about it and Man D first snickered, adding: '*What can we do? We can joke and make fun of them. That's it.*' I followed up: '*Does that feel like it is not enough?*' Perhaps irritated by my question, Man A intervened:

> It will not change the system, but it helps us to feel less like shit. If we can talk about them and laugh at them, it means that we have some freedom; it means that this land is not Taliban land and, then, this government … It means that – yes, this government can be corrupt and can think that relations with Iran are more important than how Iran treats our brothers and sisters in their country – but they can't make us believe that this is how it should be, that we should be treated like the worst in the world and like we are nothing and like anyone can call us 'trash'.

---

[5] Perhaps a reference to the political and business networks of Ismail Khan, former warlord during the Afghan-Soviet War (1980-1989), Governor of Herat (1992-1995 and again 2002-2005), and Minister of Water and Energy (2005-2013).

I asked Man A why it was important to demean the guard. He responded:

> I can call him fat, or stupid, or uneducated, or illiterate, or a government puppet. It's not about him. I don't know him; he could be a nice guy and the smartest guy. He is just the face of something we can't see. And if he is all that we see, we need to say to each other that we don't accept the 'security system' that he works for. I am a patriotic Afghan and I would like to have the police I could trust and that would be 'mine'. But these guys, they are there to make sure Kabul looks like a strong government, and to make sure that Iran isn't angry, and to make sure that Afghan migrants can't make it far … to Greece and Germany … because Europeans don't like that, and to make sure that we are not carrying drugs, because that bothers the Americans. They are there to make everyone happy, but us? Fuck us.

'*Do you often make fun of ANSF?*' I asked. Man C interjected:

> I don't know; we always talk about the stuff we heard about them – it's difficult not to when they're parading here like little kings. Now it's a little different because you are here. Sometimes, we recognize some of them; we know some of their neighbors in Herat or Shindand, Ghourian, or Islam Qala, or we know their relatives. And yes, it's always about how foolish they are to work for the government and all of their international donors and bosses. People say 'women talk', but everyone talks.

Self-deprecation through emasculation, another joke and chuckling resumed. At any rate, the four men articulated a broad argument shared by many Afghans, certainly by many of my informants: Afghan security forces serve various 'foreign relations' rather than their citizens. In the framework of that argument, Afghan 'citizens' or 'people' (often an 'us') stand in for what should be the purpose of the Afghan state. However, in practice, the Afghan government exists to mollify a network of geopolitical relations (Iranian-Afghan, German-Afghan, US-Afghan, EU-Afghan, etc.) or '*international donors and bosses*', as Man C put it. The notions of 'service', 'the people', or 'the citizen' are problematic from the perspective of power analysis insofar as they obscure the hierarchical, oppressive, violent, exploitative, and paternalistic relations that constitute postcolonial and Eurocentric politics across the world (Isin 2015, Mooers 2014). More pertinently, I saw and heard in Herat and Islam Qala how the discourses of 'serving' and 'caring' inspire resistances. Since December 2014, a number of my interviewees have described their goals for a different Afghanistan as being 'left alone' (or a version thereof) (Najibullah 2015), being 'equal' (Saber 2014, Ayoubi 2016, Neekzad 2016), or '*ending Afghan humiliations*' (Amiri 2016). In many ways, all of these scripts of a different Afghanistan are vague and contested. Through a Foucauldian lens of political struggles as relationships of subjection, transgression, and resistance (Simons 2002), these quests for a more just, equal, or dignified Afghanistan are transformative, unfinished, and open-ended (Dyrberg 2014, 56). Therefore, discourses of resistance are not important because they are indisputably liberating, but precisely because they make the political possible. That is what I took the four men's framing of the Afghan state – as meant for 'foreign relations' – to mean. The representation of the state as both negligent and oppressive energized the four men. That was the view of Afghan politics that they struggled with, which they refused to comply with, or be subject to. But how did their rejection work?

As I reflected on my conversation with the four men later that day, I first focused on the role that mockery and gossip had in fostering group cohesion and their sense of shared identity. Counter-objectifying the 'other' by creating shared vocabularies of transgression against the limits of 'normal' or 'legitimate' social practice deepens the sense of common struggles, grievance and common definitions of obstacles to better life chances. Insofar as they are not *'openly avowed to the other party in the power relationship'*, Scott refers to such transgressive practices as 'hidden' or 'offstage' discourses and 'transcripts' (Scott 1990, 2). Thereby, *'subordinates may gather outside the intimidating gaze of power'* (e.g. in the shaded restaurants and cafés around the border), practice *'sharply dissonant political culture'* (Ibid, 18), and *'insinuate a critique of power while hiding behind anonymity or behind innocuous understandings of their conduct'* (Ibid, xiii). Had I not been there to provoke the surfacing of hidden political talk by referring to my background and research, their encounter at the café would have remained as ostensibly *a*political as the 'fat jokes' when taken out of context. That is how I interpreted Man C's explanation that my presence made their talk '*a little different*', although the four men '*always talk about the stuff [they] heard about [regarding ANSF officers]*'. In other words, my presence made the political script overt within the group. While understated in its subversive ambitions, their apparently regular ridicule of ANSF is political and inspired by the fact that the guards '*work for the government and all of their international donors and bosses*', as Man C put it. It is also stimulated by the guards' performances of privilege as they 'parade' around the border '*like little kings*', in Man C's words. Even his insistence on minimizing their physique (emphasizing '*little* kings') is resistant because it constructs a power oxymoron: real kings are normally imagined as grand, and referring to ANSF officers as 'little' reconstitutes them as *false* or inauthentic kings. Be-*littling*, therefore, minimizes their intimidating materiality and diminishes the Hobbesian substratum of their legitimacy as the '*flash of sovereign power*' (Massumi in Vaughan-Williams 2009, 121). The guards' 'parading' may be intended to impress (or, indeed, *op*press) and clearly, across the human landscape of Islam Qala, it has that disciplinary effect. ANSF officers carry guns and they can arrest any of these civilians for the smallest infractions. But dissent and the disruption of discipline are still possible since he who 'parades' is 'little'. He enacts weak sovereign power preoccupied, according to Man A, with 'making sure' that various greater authorities ('Iran', 'the Americans', 'Germany', 'Europeans', etc.) are not antagonized by any of the infractions ascribed to the Afghan body (e.g. opium trade, terrorism or migration). While kings and guns 'parade', the body maximizes the space of power destabilization that cannot be shot or even entirely heard: that of casual banter rather than 'private conversation', which is always more interesting to the gaze of power. To reconstitute this space and toy within it, the body mobilizes its already-available abilities like chuckle, laughter, eye and head movement, jargon, hand motions, etc. Tactical re-combinations of these bodily technologies show that resistance is not merely reactive. It is productive inasmuch as it refashions the 'parade' (of 'little kings'), not as something grand or awesome, but as a comical performance of feigned sovereignty, theatrically disproportionate in size (*little* king/*fat* border guard) and thoughtless in conduct (Man A referred to them as 'morons' incognizant of why they were there). Between the five of us, sitting on a carpet that covered the concrete, the ANSF officers at the border were undone as authoritative 'guards'. They were more akin to lethal and poorly trained labourers who instinctively defended the will of distant sovereigns. That was their job and it did not matter who paid them as long as they could feed their families and themselves. This counter-representation was purposely tragicomic: it accorded the four men both the freedom to mock and the maturity and generosity to understand the guards' everyday lives. If the guns and the stories of trauma and violence at the ANSF detention centres intimidated and disciplined the four men, this counter-image gave them respite and empowered them. It made their group meaningful and its talk regenerative. It allowed them to acknowledge that their imagination of the guard is playful in their narrative, that, in fact, '*he could be a nice guy and the smartest guy*', as Man A put it. In discussing the discursive intertwinements of political activism and theory, Bhabha insists that social critique

> does not *contain* the truth (in polar opposition to totalitarianism, 'bourgeois liberalism' or whatever is supposed to repress it). The 'true' is always marked and informed by the ambivalence of the process of emergence itself, the productivity of meanings that construct counter-knowledges *in medias res*, in the very act of agonism, within the terms of a negotiation (rather than a negation) of oppositional and antagonistic elements. (Bhabha 1994, 33)

In other words, the simultaneity of representation of the guard as both '*a fat moron*' and '*the smartest guy*' does not reflect emotional or intellectual inconsistency, since neither of the two positions seems outright truthful. Rather, it conveys the four men's ambivalent relationship with the situational 'other'. The *o* in 'other' is a small Lacanian *o*, since the guard is different from – and even dangerous for – the four men, but he is also much like them. They share similar ethno-racialized and classed anxieties of survival and well-being in a country kept isolated from the 'world' and targeted by many aspiring powers. The guard's qualities in their narrative (as *both* and *not quite either*) capture the four men's struggle with, and renegotiation of a counter-knowledge about the burden of the postcolony. Namely, postcolonial 'dividing practices' produce subjects by drawing borders and limits around humans. The subjects engage with the postcolony, give in to its lure of hierarchy, status and employment, while rejecting it all the same. They might reject the postcolony's seduction and discipline, while learning its language, admiring its musical harmonies, and empathizing with the struggles of US-funded ANSF recruits and officers, or *brown skin, white masks*, to paraphrase Fanon. Again, drawing on Lacan, Bhabha asserts:

> Identification is initiated in the textual performance that displays a certain 'difference' *within* the signification of any single political system, prior to establishing the substantial differences *between* political beliefs (emphasis original). (Bhabha 1994, 34)

The four men recognize a process of *alterity* (othering) within their politics of 'rejection' (of '*the government and all of their international donors and bosses*') even before they encounter ANSF guards. They spoke English and made several references to American pop culture to denote personal attitudes towards its aesthetics ('*Britney Spears is very beautiful*') and its supposed ethical failings ('*but she is a little crazy; she has a porno, right?*'). At least two of the four men had worked for US-funded employers, adding that they had left their positions as the '*democracy bullshit talk*' was winding down.[6] Either way, encountering the ANSF guard and his differentness reproduces their ambivalent subjectivities. It is the 'agonism' of ambivalence that allows them to mock, undermine, empathize with, resist and understand the ANSF guard. Ambivalence, ultimately, makes them less visible, or 'infrapolitical', and capable of wrestling with the daily effects of being in the postcolony.

That is a second tactical function and effect of mockery that I want to describe. Namely, mockery expressed as an event of joy, rather than overt anger, makes the four men appear innocuous and unthreatening to power, rather than conspiratorial and subversive. The joy they draw from ridicule appears to an outsider as innocent delight. Of course, in being untethered and quirky for a fleeting moment, laughter and chuckling incite suspicion on the part of the surveillance apparatus. Yet due to its subversively vernacular articulation among the 'insiders', mockery remains impenetrable to the non-belonging. Moreover, each body, each element of the security apparatus experiences alterity within itself, an antagonistic desire and necessity (Bhabha 1994, 75) to inspect and watch. It continuously questions the practical and ontological purpose of surveillance: '*How likely is it that the worst will happen? Everyone here looks like me. Who am I even watching? What am I afraid of?*' This *split within* exhausts and undermines the surveillance apparatus. Many give up and move on, shifting their gaze towards another similar object. Therefore, small resistant obstructions (such as the kind of laughter and mockery that *both* detest and empathize) frustrate the security apparatus. Ultimately, the ambivalent chuckle ensconces the four men from the gaze of power and sustains their resistances. In a circular move, by playing itself out as infrapolitical and ambivalent, resistance guarantees own survival. It renegotiates its own status as liminal and *in between* 'being free' and 'being a subaltern' in a hegemonic structure (Ibid, 85). Put differently, nonviolent resistance remains possible due to its near-impossibility.

A third tactical function of mockery is that ridicule and gossip reinforce resentment against the forces that ordinary Heratis experience as removed from their daily lives and '*something [they] can't see*', according to Man A. Thus, mockery works as an exceptionally efficient resistance tactic: it enables the four men to remain 'offstage' and 'infrapolitical' in Scott's words and maintain *low* visibility while rendering the mechanics of power at the border *more visible*. To extend Scott's metaphor, mockery makes power's hidden transcript *public*, even if the scale is micro-social. Mockery exposes power relations that seem safely tucked into various ANSF discourses: that of 'Afghan' security (nonetheless accused of serving Iran, the United States, or regional 'strongmen' instead), 'the nation'

---

[6] Perhaps a reference to diminishing funding for 'civil society' and 'free enterprise' projects post-2014.

(while consistently marginalizing certain ethnic, gender, age, and sexual groups), a 'security provider' (while ANSF's rationale for existence, planning for troop generation, strategies, doctrines, tactics, rules of engagement, equipment, training, and funding are controlled by NATO and the United States), 'modern training' (which remains perceived as substandard in ethical, physical, and combat aspects), etc. While all of these relations are complex, their critique easily travels through the capillaries of society via the subtle technologies of the body, including inflections in speech, vernaculars, eye motions, etc. That makes the infrapolitics of mockery and laughter insurgent: they undermine power by reinforcing alternatives to the dominant order and they bring to light strategies of control that are removed from ordinary Afghans, that are 'faceless' and invisible. Mockery and laughter subvert by being intimate with the technologies of power (e.g. ANSF or any of its elements), by embodying them (in an ANSF guard), and showing that power can be spoken about, gazed at, objectified, analysed (*'He is so fat they can just put him at the gate and no one will be able to get into Iran! That can be their 'security policy''*), contextualized (in terms of who 'wields' it, where, and how), and therefore rendered knowable. That which can be mocked is tangible and not entirely beyond the subject's grasp.

As I waited for Barialay and his friend to return to the café, I also noticed when a boy, probably in his early teenage years, stopped by the establishment and bought three bottles of water from Farrukh (the server). They exchanged a few brief sentences before the boy turned to leave. Farrukh, wearing a grin on his face, slapped the back of the boy's head lightly and shouted a few words as the boy dashed away. I asked Farrukh if he was disapproving of something the boy had done and he came up to where the four men and I were seated on the floor. He explained his playful interaction with the boy as a ritual. Namely, the boy would sometimes buy water or soda for the guards, always overcharging them. He would separate the change he received from Farrukh into two piles: he would hand one back to the guards, while keeping the second one for himself, usually on the inside of his sweater. Farrukh never told on him and the boy kept coming back to Farrukh's café. Farrukh said he had once asked the boy whether he felt bad about stealing from the guards, to which the boy apparently responded: *'They, too, stole it from someone.'* According to Farrukh, Afghans perceive ANSF as corrupt or as a government tool that dispossesses ordinary Afghans. Varieties of *'greedy ANSF behavior'* – as Farrukh put it – include bribery, kidnappings and extortion from Afghans across the board, regardless of socioeconomic class or standing. Beyond the indices of corruption and transnational policy research (biased in favour of multilateral donor agencies and corporations), academic research corroborates the description of ANSF as a cluster of law enforcement and combat troops whose officers use predatory tools as a pay supplement or a way to maintain their position in patronage networks (Strand, Borchgrevink and Harpviken 2017, Singh 2014). The discourse of predatory government agencies, in turn, incites Afghans to evade or counter-exploit the conduct of security in their everyday lives. For Farrukh, the boy's petty theft of *'very little, peanuts, in fact'* was a tactic of claiming resources that had been wrongfully seized in the first place. However, pilfering was also a source of income for the boy, who, in Farrukh's words, would also steal soap, candy and dishwashing detergent from the trucks parked in the commercial zone. The boy's actions were perhaps not meant as conscious resistance against a political economy that ignores vulnerable Afghans. But they marked his refusal to comply with the unequal system that accorded him the role of an obedient victim. In eluding the legal expectation to acquiesce, pilfering served to increase the boy's life chances against power structures disinterested in his well-being. Thus, petty theft constitutes 'disguised, low-profile' and *'below the line'* (Scott 1990, 198) protest in circumstances when *'trading a slap for a slap, an insult for an insult'* (Ibid, xii) is denied to the 'subordinate'.

I have previously discussed how the resistant practices of mockery and laughter make power strategies and technologies more visible while aiming to remain invisible themselves. *'That they should be invisible ... is in large part by design – a tactical choice born of a prudent awareness of the balance of power'* (Scott 1990, 183). Another array of actions aimed at evading and weakening sovereign, disciplinary and governmental power at the border has similar effects; however, its tactical execution and rationales are different. Drawing on Monahan (2010, 128–144; 2006) and Gary Marx (2003), I will refer to practices that work to subvert unequal power relations through the surveillance of surveillers or 'role reversals' as *counter-surveillance*. In *Discipline and Punish* (1975/1995), Foucault correlated surveillance with power hierarchies and domination, insofar as the acts of observation enable the generation of knowledge about, and the disciplining of prisoners, students, military recruits, factory floor workers, etc. Foucault identified the very *gaze* as a differential of power relations, since only the strategies and technologies of power can perform it in a way that produces docile bodies. Surveillance is entrenched in power relations. Rather than 'inspect' or 'supervise', Foucault suggested that the French verb *surveiller* should be translated as 'discipline' in English to connote the work of power. This is even though 'discipline' hints at the effectivity of surveillance rather than the process of gazing or 'watching over'. John Gilliom relates the linguistic connotations of the term to power:

> If we think of surveillance as just watching, we err, because surveillance is never really just watching. It's not just vision, but *super*vision. It's not just sight, but *over*sight. Surveillance assumes, advances, and/or creates a relationship of domination. (Gilliom 2010, 205)

In particular, I want to focus on the dynamics of *visibility* at Islam Qala as it seems to me that the problem of visibility precisely captures the conditions of possibility of resistances at the border.

While I want to focus on the subversion of unequal power relations through counter-surveillance practices, an analytical distinction between 'anti' and 'inverse' surveillance is opportune here. Whereas the former would include acts of sabotage, such as *'destroying or disabling surveillance cameras'* (Monahan 2010, 128), I use the latter term to refer to *'mapping the paths of least surveillance'* and their dissemination (Ibid). Although Monahan's (2006, 2010) distinction between the 'technical' and 'social' counter-surveillance interventions may be more useful to Surveillance Studies more broadly, I differentiate *anti* and *inverse* counter-surveillance to highlight my fieldwork's situational insight into the latter. I draw the distinction to capture the practices that I was informed about, and that more closely reflect the acts of *'watching the watchers'*

(Welch 2011) or *'observing the observers'* (Kemple and Huey 2005). I concluded that inverse surveillance at Islam Qala constituted a performance of alternative and resistant counter-cartographies of the border zone (Counter Cartographies Collective, Dalton, Mason-Deese 2012). Thereby, inverse surveillance effectuates 'counter-maps' and migrant *itineraries* as *'alternative visual narratives'* of the border (Mekdjian 2015, 205), or cartographic practices distinct from *routes* produced by migrant management apparatuses that stem human flows (Casas, Cobarrubias and Pickles 2011, 900). My informants' sense of the border's marginalizing and panoptical presence and my interest in everyday resistance made me curious about how *'those who try to cross [the border] and who are excluded from the right of migration'* (Mekdjian 2015, 205) construct spatial representations of the Afghan-Iranian border zone. I was interested in how the weak observe the border zone's geography and different weather conditions, and in how they scope out border guards and the circulations, spatial distributions and volumes of security forces. I wondered about the guards' technological capabilities and collaboration with the NGOs and intergovernmental agencies at the border. As my day at Islam Qala went on, I also pondered how the weak disseminate their observations. Overall, I became curious about the 'vernacular mapping' of Islam Qala, or the production of maps *'of and for the everyday'* (Gerlach 2013, 2010).

One of Najibullah's stories about the *'people of the border'* – as we ended up calling the population that circulated through the zone – was about his wife's cousin and a regular Herat-Islam Qala traveller, who temporarily used Najibullah's services in the spring of 2014. Apparently, his car had broken down and he chose to ride with Najibullah three times over the course of five weeks, as he waited for his car to be fixed. During their trips, they commented on Afghan and Herati politics, shared personal stories and discussed how security and commercial traffic would be affected by ISAF's pull-out later that year. Both feared the Taliban insurgency and local gangs would expand across the Province. According to Najibullah, his cousin-in-law ('The Cousin', as he referred to him) had a stable job in Herat, but was nonetheless thinking about leaving for Iran, including illegally. *'Better pay, but also, maybe it's safer there, although everyone's stories are terrible. Maybe I can move on to Europe then,'* he said. Over the course of their three trips to-and-from Islam Qala, The Cousin told Najibullah that he had developed a *'mental, but also a real drawn map'* of the checkpoints and the wider area around them. *'He says he knows a good distance in both directions – to the south and north of the crossing – and he wants to expand what he knows,'* relayed Najibullah. According to him, The Cousin did not want to pay the 'vultures' or 'professional smugglers', as he allegedly called them (perhaps to avoid paying hundreds of dollars or out of spite). Instead, he wanted to *'learn the landscape for himself and get himself across the border without anyone's help'.* Apparently, he had written down *'dozens of pages of notes'* and had paid attention to how the weather might affect his chances of crossing the border illegally. For instance, he had concluded that the more inclement the conditions and the lower the visibility, the better his odds. For obvious ethical reasons, as well as brevity, I will not detail further The Cousin's vernacular map. Instead, I will focus on its framing (as relayed to me by Najibullah) and its key condition of possibility and success.

Regarding The Cousin's framing of own *'mental, but also a real drawn map',* Najibullah cautioned me that he was mostly interpreting his cousin's views. The

Cousin was apparently aware that he had enough free time and financial means to make occasional trips to the border and spend hours observing it and chronicling the movements of various groups (from travellers to guards), levels of security and human surveillance around the border, the landscape around it, etc. I asked Najibullah whether his cousin perhaps thought of himself as 'middle class' and 'a little more affluent than most Afghans' and Najibullah agreed emphatically.

> My cousin knows that he can do, in terms of time and money, what most people can't, even though he is, really, not at all wealthy or 'affluent', as you said. But yes, he is aware that, to accumulate this kind of information, you need resources that most people don't have. We talked about that a lot.

The link between socioeconomic class and the creation of counter-knowledges of the border struck me as a problem I had not considered much, but also as one that I was limited in probing. Doing so would require in-depth conversations with counter-surveillance 'transgressors' of various class backgrounds. I had difficulties identifying such persons due to their fear of self-exposure to law enforcement, as well as the relative brevity of my visits to Herat. At any rate, I appreciated this remark, since it pushed me to reconsider the questions of resistant, subaltern, and peripheral epistemologies (de Sousa Santos 2016). I was reminded of Spivak's caution against the assumption that the voices, desires, experiences, and knowledges of the marginalized historically 're-present' themselves as 'authentic' to the analyst: *'It is only the texts of counterinsurgency or elite documentation that gives us the news of the consciousness of the subaltern'* (Spivak 1988a, 12). While Najibullah's cousin merely had a stable job and was by no means part of Afghanistan's economic, political, entrepreneurial, religious or warlord elites, he was nonetheless sheltered enough to speak for and represent the subaltern. However, his goal was to shield his vernacular map from becoming integrated into the government's knowledge or *'texts of counterinsurgency'*. After all, migrant itineraries and counter-cartographies are specific statements and sites of struggle of interest to postcolonial power. I asked Najibullah how his cousin thought his maps should be best disseminated to other prospective migrants, particularly to those less privileged than him. Apparently, The Cousin thought of this as a 'toilet paper' tactic:

> First, he creates something … Like, finds out if there is a particular hour or a day when a certain section of the border is less watched. Then, that can be passed [on] to people closest to him, but as people keep passing it [on] and to circles who are further away from him, at the end, his notes and knowledge would hopefully reach those who really need it, and he thought of them as the center of the roll in this toilet paper idea.

The 'toilet paper' tactic sounded entrepreneurial: The Cousin thought that his notes would be more useful if shared more widely, and he had a plan to trigger the implementation of his idea. As I listened to Najibullah, I noted to myself that much of this model relied on hope, luck and the goodwill of friends, relatives and relative strangers to pass on information beyond their tightest social circles. However, I was also aware that something akin to the word of mouth was necessary as a dispersion mechanism. According to a USAID-funded report, less than 10 per cent of all Afghans have access to social media platforms (Altai Consulting 2017), where 'hidden transcripts' could be shared more widely and stealthily. A 'samizdat' diffusion of these vernacular maps is also problematic, since the intended recipients would certainly want information to remain hidden and inaccessible to law enforcement, particularly NDS. As I thought about the practical challenges to the 'toilet paper' tactic, Najibullah touched upon the issue of diffusion:

> He [The Cousin] says that he has to do this, that the Afghan government and Iran leave him no choice. People can't just accept no hope, no road ahead. And he knows that more people are doing this in their own way. No one goes to the border to just stare aimlessly or do something quickly and then go back home. Everyone knows that the more you can see and remember about how the border works, the better for you and people closest to you. He thinks that what he and others like him create is safe, that it dies with them unless the police or NDS put their hands on his notes and maps.

Therefore, the risk of repression of vernacular maps and of their incorporation into the (post)colonial archive or '*the prose of counter-insurgency*' (Guha 1983) reinforces their urgency and subversive meaning. Moreover, the weight of legal, safety, administrative, security and economic limitations on the movement of Afghans *everywhere*, the sense of vulnerability, and the force of discipline in the border zone compel travellers to the border to learn its landscapes, populations, security and surveillance regimes, or '*how the border works*', as The Cousin put it. For to carve out a space for the body, travellers have to identify the '*path of least surveillance*' (Monahan 2010, 128).

Najibullah's story of The Cousin also relayed a key condition for the operation of counter-surveillance, which reflects the parameters of infrapolitics more broadly:

> Since resistance is conducted in small groups, individually, ... it is well adapted to thwart surveillance. There are no leaders to round up, no membership lists to investigate, no manifestos to denounce, no public activities to draw attention. (Scott 1990, 200)

Scott's general characterization of infrapolitics captures the condition of counter-surveillance: it is self-sustained, fuelled by power and requires no purposeful organization or social mobilization, which makes delineating and targeting it nearly impossible. Put differently, to respond to counter-surveillance, power needs to rework the surveillance of bodies that purposefully maintain own ordinariness and unremarkable practices of circulation. To tackle inverse surveillance, power is made to use the same tools and logics developed to detect, discipline and punish dangerous behaviour. But the counter-look of resistance is not extraordinary, since it precisely unfolds as natural, undetectable and below the threshold of alarming behaviour. Of course, counter-inspection can reveal itself if it disobeys the limit of necessary invisibility, which is a testament to the resilience of power. As Gary Marx reminds us, resistance must remain covert '*to maximize effectiveness and/or to avoid suspicion and sanctioning*' (Marx 2003, 297). Yet, as long as counter-surveillance visibly complies with the border regime, it can perform its invisible work of resistance in the production of counter-knowledges. For now, the surveillance apparatus at Islam Qala is limited in its technologies of differentiation between a *compliant glance* of the subject and his/her *resistant counter-gaze*.

More than a year after my visit to Islam Qala, an NGO activist from Herat, who works with the homeless, IDPs and deportees from Iran, told me about the 'lessons' many deportees had relayed to him. They had apparently learned them through the experience of deportation, in a way that was improvised and situational.

> Many deportees have told me that arrest, detainment in Iran, and deportation feel very stressful, unsafe, and unpredictable. So, it's like time slows down and I also think deportation can take a few days and especially when you reach the border, you are excited and everything is bigger in your eyes. Anyways, probably everyone feels different, but many have told me how surprised they are that they could observe so much of the border area in Iran and how their security services work. Of course, it is incomplete, but people remember it. Some remember it because it is traumatic, others realize in the moment that knowing the border can be very useful later on ... but anyways, many deportees create small personal maps and sketches even. (Anonymous NGO Activist 2 2016)

Therefore, in asking the deportees to describe their experiences of arrest and deportation, this NGO activist triggered intimate processes of recollection that may reconfigure the trauma. Thus, in the deportees' narratives, their experience becomes an emotional mnemonic space (Erll 2011) implicated in personal micro-cartographies. In response to my questions, the NGO activist elaborated on the 'delayed' utility of such spatial recollections. They are politically useful because they make the deportees' testimonies more detailed. They are also beneficial because they can be mobilized as vernacular counter-maps to evade the guards and cameras in the wider border zone should one attempt to return to Iran without legal documents. Apparently, '*it is useful to see in person how big and wide the guarded area [around the crossing is], how security looks like. It makes returning illegally more real and also scarier*' (Anonymous NGO Activist 2 2016).

Conclusion

I have referred earlier to Azad's disappointment that someone who shares his '*language and faith*' would call him a bastard. He echoed feeling diminished by dehumanizing language. Yet he also regretted that historical-cultural affinity with Iran did not mean much for thousands of Afghans who sought to improve their life chances by looking for jobs, safer homes or education in Iran. The four men I met at Farrukh's café and virtually all of my interviewees in Herat shared with me representations of Heratis as better educated, more entrepreneurial (regarding work ethic and 'small business' ownership), and more cultured than other Afghans (referring to practices as diverse as taking up creative hobbies to close observance of Islamic norms). Likewise, they echoed depictions of Herat as cleaner, better organized and laid out, more prosperous, greener, more ancient and home to more historical-cultural monuments than any other Afghan city. Not all of my interviewees seemed to agree with these portrayals, but they voiced them as prevalent self-conceptions across Herat's socioeconomic landscape. Dozens described Herat as 'more civilized' and closer in 'lifestyle' and appearance to Iran, Turkey, or Samarkand and Bukhara (in Uzbekistan). The rest of Afghanistan 'struggles' (Sarwary 2016, Rahimi 2016) or is a 'shithole', as Man A said.

However, as this chapter has argued, Iranian corporate, welfare, security, migration, bureaucratic, medical, public health and other social discourses erase Heratis' much-cherished distinctions between Herat and Afghanistan. They lump social spaces that perform affinity with Iran (as reflected in Azad's words) with the unexceptional and ordinary, moreover – the threatening, poor, 'filthy', and 'trashy'. Thereby, the ethno-racial and classed discourses of virtuous (Iranian) life dismiss Herati dreams of recognition as cultural equals, or part of a civilized Khorasani space that transcends Afghanistan. This enables the politics of exclusion of Heratis – *much like other* Afghans – at Islam Qala, as well as their reproduction as weak and peripheral in the masculine conceptions of strong, virtuous and virile nationalisms of Iranians, Hindus, Turks and others. The gendered, racialized, and classed denial of civilization is as natural to those who inhabit 'stability' as it as painful to Heratis who aspire to be *in the civilized*. Islam Qala congeals a contradiction that seems constitutive of Herat's torn and liminal subjectivity. On one had, Heratis desire to be recognized as a prosperous population-territory of transnational import. However, postcolonial power reproduces Herat *as Afghan* and, therefore, belonging in the troubled periphery. In postcolonial relations, Heratis (like other Afghans) barely matter: they should be kept at bay, monitored, and exploited for labour and commerce (within or without Afghanistan). That crudely summarizes why Afghan life is *bare* in the global hierarchy of utility to stability and peace.

It is therefore crucial that postcolonial inequalities allow some Afghans to lend their lives to the Iran-run Fatemiyoun Division in Syria or to work for sub-subsistence wages in unsafe and legally precarious conditions in Iran. By and large, Afghans face administrative, physical, financial, and other obstacles to entering and settling in Iran and those obstacles are on full display within the Dogharoon-Islam Qala border zone. This chapter has argued that borders transcend the linear Westphalian imaginations of sovereign margins and instead operate as dividing practices possible wherever and whenever ethno-racial, class and cultural hierarchies are invoked. In other words, border crossings are spaces of heightened differentiation, but they are not unique in this role. As generalized biopolitical practices of marginalization, borders are induced and performed whenever Afghan refugees renew their registrations, whenever Afghans apply for Iranian visas or work permits, whenever they are asked by their Iranian employers or the Iranian police where they come from or when they arrived in Iran, whenever they are stared at because they do not belong, or are accused of transgressing in myriad different ways. Asserting that such events are border performances is not a literary metaphor. At any of those points, Afghans can be – and have been – judged to have violated Iran's laws. Since the bare brown body enjoys few, and precarious, legal protections, its depiction as transgressive enables its arrest, physical and verbal abuse, financial extortion and expulsion. Iranians across class, occupational, and gender hierarchies can act as 'temporary sovereigns' towards Afghan refugees and migrants. Whether they are government or corporate bureaucrats, police officers, neighbours, farmers or construction co-workers – Iranians are invested with sovereign and biopolitical rights to surveil and discipline the Afghan body. Meanwhile, the precariousness of Afghans' legal status in Iran reinforces the instability of their labour and employment. This makes them easy targets for economic and workplace exploitation, including wage theft.

Therefore, the enmeshed Iranian-Afghan security apparatuses at Islam Qala/Dogharoon maximize a more general exclusion of dispossessed brown bodies (with temporary privileges accorded to entrepreneurs). By drawing on a Foucauldian (biopolitical) reinterpretation of Wallerstein's WSA, I have argued that Islam Qala reveals how postcolonial relations produce Heratis and Afghans as geo-corporeal as well as geo-economic peripheries. Exploring Afghan lives as *peripheries* has enabled me to elucidate the incongruous discourse of their subjectivity as *useless*, perilous, and inferior to Iranian and other foreign bodies, and *useful* to transnational wealth transfers from the destitute and wretched to the affluent and virtuous. Seeing the Afghan body as peripheral has allowed me to understand both its exploitation and violation. Through participant observation and interview data, this chapter has explored how the spatial fragmentation of Islam Qala and its generalized surveillance of brownness correlate with wider discourses of Afghan inferiority vis-à-vis the splendour of Iran. Such correlations reproduce Afghans as peripheries, or bodies and populations that can be abused, exploited and killed at little to no social cost. Grounded theory has enabled me to explore how multiple axes of inequality (of ethnicity/race, gender, class, and age) interact with security and surveillance discourses to deepen the abuse of brown women and youths through sexual technologies that otherwise spare men, especially if they are aligned with commercial flows as 'investors' and 'entrepreneurs'.

Nevertheless, it would be misleading to portray Afghans at Islam Qala as obedient and timid subordinates of surveillance, security and stability. Even the habitually 'cooperative' Afghan government officials transgress in Iranian-Afghan relations. For instance, lower-level officials counter-portray Iran as a regional security threat whenever ABP, ANP, or NDS arrest Iranians on charges of drug and arms trafficking (TOLOnews 2012). This chapter has relayed narratives of mockery, gossip, pilfering and counter-surveillance as resistances of the weak. To do so, I drew on Bhabha's notion of ambivalence, Scott's concepts of infrapolitics and hidden transcripts, and scholarship on resistant surveillance or 'watching of the watchers'. Across the practices of everyday evasion, rejection, co-optation and erosion of the postcolonial border, toying with the liminal visibility of resistant tactics is crucial to their endurance. In fact, (in)visibility in its different situational gradients stood out to me as the key condition of resistance.

Based on my interviews and less formal conversations, I observed that evasion, co-optation and rejection of the border had a diverse array of purposes. They fostered group cohesion and common identities among ordinary Afghans and worked to recuperate their sense of dignity and agency. Resistance also helped cultivate strategic visions of politics *for* Afghans and of a government that 'cares' and 'serves' *them* instead of foreign powers. Furthermore, the tactics of petty theft operated as vehicles of retribution for the subaltern (*'They, too, stole it from someone'*) and instruments of day-to-day physical survival. Finally, fieldwork has allowed me to correlate counter-surveillance at the border (as 'inverse' monitoring and inspection) with the creation of vernacular counter-maps and outlines of migrant itineraries by Afghan deportees, seasonal workers and aspiring migrants. Drawing on the works of Monahan and Marx has enabled me to explore how subaltern subjects use surveillance tactics at the border to contest and defy their position as geo-corporeal periphery. The notion of counter-surveillance also sheds light on subaltern knowledges of the border, or the processes of production of counter-knowledge that subverts the security apparatus and displaces the 'normal'. While the normal relegates Afghans to risky and perilous subjectivities, insight into subversive and infrapolitical knowledges of the border recasts Afghans as lives *at risk* and *in peril*. Drawing on Foucault, Lila Abu-Lughod asserts that resistance is not 'liberatory', but it is 'diagnostic' of power (Abu-Lughod 1990, 42) insofar as it renders legible the spaces and mechanisms of its operation. Recalling that January day at Islam Qala, I am reminded that tracing genealogies of power via resistance needs to be informed by an *'ethics of responsibility'* to the subaltern (Spivak 2004). For without the subaltern's struggles, eccentricities, and catachresis (Bhabha 1994, Spivak 1993), the political would be reduced to docility. In extending Agamben's analysis, one must acknowledge that studies of power and political life itself are indebted to the excluded.

Part IV

Conclusion

7

On Postcolonial Power Equilibria

This book has issued a call to study how the ebbs and flows of global security governance have affected Herati lives in the Global War on Terror. This plea has been predicated on one simple assumption, so trivial that it appears unproblematic. I have proposed that life is vulnerable and that experiences of vulnerability vary across populations. I have politicized this proposition by taking it to mean that *how* one is *made* vulnerable marks *who* one is. This book has attempted to study the relationship between *global security* and *ordinary Heratis* by exploring how the *former* (in practice, a form of power) targets the *latter* at the level of intimate life or bodies invested with truths and desires. By extension, I have also asked the reader to consider how bodies alluring to power are reconstructed and reimagined within larger populations. For being alluring to power means being significant at the level of something that *takes place* across unrelated discourses and human relations, yet, something that is real because it relies on the lives of individuated subjects, of the single corporeal. Specifically, being appealing to arrays of stabilization, development, and security policies is only possible if one can be integrated into a larger historical truth that some lives are volatile and threatening, and that some places and populations are *fragile, failing and failed* in ways that are perilous for the normal world. I have asked the reader to consider how the 'normal', yet vague 'world' acquires tangibility and visibility by objectifying and subjecting very real humans. This book has contemplated how an abstract notion such as 'global stability' targets categories of bodies many have seen or spoken to before, unaware that they were speaking to *categories* and *subjects* as much as they were speaking to humans.

This framework has enabled a critique of security governance in Afghanistan as a postcolonial relationship, or a perpetuated distinction between useful and useless, peaceful and threatening populations. Sucked into the discourse of global stability, millions of people across the world have become brown, 'Islamic', fanatical, tribal and destitute. Among them, Afghans have been insulated, contained and pacified with nearly unparalleled global ambition. Yet among them, there are Heratis – people whom the world calls Afghan, but are not quite Afghan, who are Farsiwan, but not Iranian. They are made to contend with the constraints of postcolonial security as they try to perform this liminal Self, be it within the sovereign bounds of Afghanistan or without them. I have submitted that some of those constraints come from and work through enmeshments of external/domestic and public/private divides. Namely, Chapter 3 has argued that postcolonial security governance injects global (ostensibly external) rationalities and techniques of discipline, government, and control of threatening brown bodies into 'domestic' and 'local' Herati spaces (provincial institutions, banks, shuras, army and police training centres, industrial parks, etc.). Likewise, it inserts 'private' (corporate and NGO) into 'public' relations (intergovernmental aid programmes, security forces, etc.). Thereby, postcolonial power creates 'shared' venues of contact where external/domestic and public/private divides become irrelevant. Postcolonial security attracts and compels Heratis to engage with these shared spaces, as ordinary people attempt to maximize own life chances. Such apparatuses of global-Herati interactions (e.g. Afghan National Security Forces, National Solidarity Program, Provincial Reconstruction Team, etc.) extend the ability of postcolonial power to surveil, study, control and contain Herati populations. Nonetheless, surveillance and control make the apparatuses of security paradoxically dependent on the bodies they work to constrain. There can be no hybrid or enmeshed spaces without Afghans, and there can be no 'soft' conducting of Afghan conduct without their participation in the work of security. (I have bracketed off the question of 'willing' or 'free' participation as immaterial due to the overwhelming constraints upon Afghan lives, their socioeconomic tactics and mobility overall.) Therefore, when apparatuses funded, designed, and governed 'externally' deploy brown bodies to enact security and progress (as policemen or entrepreneurs), they open themselves up to Herati counter-exploitations, misappropriations, pilfering, mockery, sabotage and other forms of everyday resistance. Throughout, postcolonial power experiments with what 'works' in Afghan state-building, stabilization, counterinsurgency and pacification, thus fuelling a globalized, transnational production and circulation of knowledge about 'failed' or 'fragile' societies. Nonetheless, 'lessons learned' are never one-sided, for Afghan army and police recruits, pharmacists-turned-interpreters, migrants and homeless persons likewise gain insight into how the security-development nexus works upon them. They use knowledges generated through counter-surveillance to maximize own life chances and navigate the constraints of peace and growth.

Chapters 4, 5 and 6 have elaborated on these relationships through micro-spatial case studies. From everyday evasions and the counter-exploitation of ANSF and PRT-Herat, to the subsistence of the homeless, and migrant elusions of entangled Iranian, Afghan and global security apparatuses at border crossings – this monograph has attempted to grasp the *slippery* and *bruising* operation of power. I have tried to demystify postcolonial domination, which seems to come from nowhere in particular and yet appears to somehow touch every 'abnormal' life. Yet, this book has also worked to understand the very possibility of that life under the ubiquitous pressures of the postcolony. My method to go about understanding both ends of the power relationship was to understand them as mutually produced and sustained at microphysical and intimate levels. If power energizes its own resistances, and counter-conducts invite and justify more government and discipline, what does that mean for the life chances of ordinary Heratis? This point brings me to a more general conclusion about life in the postcolony.

The United States, the UN, NATO, the EU, the World Bank, the IMF and other global parties have set in motion various apparatuses to contain and pacify Afghan populations. They have coupled 'soft' and ostensibly non-coercive regulatory tools with lethal technologies, conditional aid, unequal terms of trade and restrictive economic reforms. Likewise, resistances to them have ranged from violent insurgencies and wholesale nonviolent rejections, to everyday struggles that do not aspire to heroically negate power, but rather seek to negotiate its weight and parameters. If power and Herati resistances induce each other, it is to subject one another in the name of (very differently understood) security. As Chapter 3 has argued, it is difficult to discern how 'peace' and 'security' should look like, but a centralized and 'cooperative' Afghanistan seems to count as 'peaceful'. Regarding 'cooperativeness', it may include anything from controlling emigration and opium flows to surveilling, disincentivizing, and suppressing 'extremism'. But for ordinary Heratis, security denotes different patterns of life. They range from not being deployed as a resource in terror wars, to having a home, a stable income and being able to travel abroad without sovereign bans or abuse. To practice their notions of mundane security, Heratis have used the United States, NATO and others – and not in the way they were 'supposed to'.

Yet neither vision of the 'secure' seems to be deflating or giving in. This book has tried to condense long hours of conversations with ordinary Heratis, 'civil society activists', and Afghan government officials and nearly two decades of global statements on Afghan security. All of which compels me to conclude that a strategic *equilibrium* has emerged in Herat (and Afghanistan). It involves the necessity (or demand) to contain brown bodies, on one hand, and the need (or counter-demand) to sap the energies of security governance and increase the life chances of ordinary Heratis. Postcolonial power needs the indigenous body to operate upon it until the subject is, at an indeterminate point, 'normal'. Conversely, Afghan life appropriates the weight of the postcolonial, utilizes its strength, and *'milks the cow'* (as one of my interviewees put it) until this bodiless force wanes and dwindles naturally, on its own. Power and resistances are thus both contradictory and perfectly linear, incompatible and in need of one another. They add up in the circularity of mutual demand and supply. Every spark of resistance desires a different – never quite specified – form of power (after all, what or whose domination feels 'right'?). Similarly, sovereign, governmental, and disciplinary strategies insist on producing a more docile and 'cooperative' subject, but the search is dreadful in the absence of finality or a clear vision of peace in Afghanistan. Therefore, each force justifies its counter-force at the point of contact.

Still, my intent is not to recover a vision of global stability that is somehow inevitable or normal. Nor is it my goal to indulge a resigned or romantic narrative of the postcolony, whereby its subjects are made vulnerable, but through hybridity and evasions, they nevertheless get to utilize the resources of power and endure. In fact, my disagreement with these statements is not in their materiality, but rather in what they imply for everyday politics. When I identify an equilibrium in the operation of the postcolony, I do not claim it entails felicity or tranquillity. That resistances can counter-exploit and frustrate power does not legitimize murder, control, discipline or containment. That power seems to always regroup and reinvest itself elsewhere does not imply a merry surrender to it. Arguably, a different implication of this equilibrium may follow. For all the lamentations about the failures and meagre successes of Afghan reconstruction, postcolonial strategies and brown resistances have nonetheless left material marks on one another in liminal micro-spaces of contact. As long as Afghan life is undermined, minimized, displaced or outright decimated, the politics of and struggles over security are bound to reproduce themselves. As the United States and NATO aim to cut their troop numbers in Afghanistan further and foreign aid drops even lower, academia might observe this equilibrium, confuse it for stability and lose interest in Afghanistan – much like it did in the 1990s. (Clearly, not every manner of academic attention will serve the Herati weak either.) But regardless of troop or aid levels, the parameters of postcolonial government of Afghanistan have been put in place. Containment and pacification remain the rational view of 'good [Afghan] life', regardless of the quantity of global coercion applied within the country. It is possible that the development-security apparatuses of postcolonial power that nurture and constrain Herati lives are exactly what they seem to be: incentives based in banal expectations that an employed body is appropriately political (i.e. invested in global stability) and prefers peace, or else regrettably chooses to be its target. If that is true, the task of critical scholarship is wholly independent of what global institutions and great powers consider Afghan security and growth to be.

Where, then, should critical scholarship continue to look and question the work of power upon Heratis? Postcolonial security encourages 'vetted' Herati bureaucrats, entrepreneurs and politicos to attend summits, conferences, exhibitions and instructional workshops. There, they are taught any of the garden-variety good governance skills: anti-corruption, fiscal and monetary discipline, human rights, business or public administration, sustainable development, etc. There, they are applauded, criticized, and 'cautioned' for their many success and failures in 'building' good life in Herat and Afghanistan. Elsewhere, like a *perpetuum mobile*, the superior status of global security *versus* Afghan instability becomes self-reinforcing in UN Security Council resolutions that ritualistically cite previous council and General Assembly resolutions, statements by other UN bodies, Secretary-General pronouncements, NATO declarations or reports by the Special Representative for Afghanistan. These and other power practices reproduce Afghan and Herati populations as troubling and in need of problem solving. If my fieldwork was any relevant, I have little doubt that Herat will not merely obey to being solved. However, I do wonder where the relentless process of pacification will take critical scholarship. Is the slow rectification of the abnormal brown body outrageous enough to pique the curiosity of the largely white male analyst?

References

Aalund, Flemming. *Draft Inventory of Historical Monuments: Herat Province, Afghanistan.* Report Prepared for the Government of Afghanistan by the United Nations Educational, Scientific and Cultural Organisation (UNESCO), 1990.

Abi-Habib, Maria. "Iranians Build Up Afghan Clout." *The Wall Street Journal.* October 26, 2012. https://www.wsj.com/articles/SB10001424052970204076204578078564022815472 (accessed July 25, 2018).

Abraham, Rudolf. "Introduction." In *Northern Afghanistan*, by Charles Edward Yate, ix–xv. London: Cambridge Scholars Press, 2003.

Abu-Lughod, Lila. "The Romance of Resistance: Tracing Transformations of Power through Bedouin Women." *American Ethnologist* 17, no. 1 (1990): 41–55.

Ackerman, Spencer. "Former Blackwater Gets Rich as Afghan Drug Production Hits Record High." *The Guardian.* March 31, 2015. https://www.theguardian.com/world/2015/mar/31/blackwater-gets-rich-afghanistan-drug-production (accessed July 17, 2018).

Acquah, Sarah, and Frank A. Ward. "Optimizing Adjustments to Transboundary Water Sharing Plans: A Multi-Basin Approach." *Water Resources Management* (2017): 1–24.

Adelkhah, Fariba, and Zuzanna Olszewska. "The Iranian Afghans." *Iranian Studies* 40, no. 2 (2007): 137–165.

Afghan Ministry of Finance. *Development Cooperation Report.* Kabul: Islamic Republic of Afghanistan: Ministry of Finance, 2011.

Afghan Ministry of Finance. *Development Cooperation Report.* Kabul: Islamic Republic of Afghanistan: Ministry of Finance, 2012.

Afzaly, Tariq, interview by Bojan Savić. *Interview with Herati Dari-English Interpreter and Pharmacist* (January 1, 2015).

Agamben, Giorgio. *Homo Sacer: Sovereign Power and Bare Life.* Stanford, CA: Stanford University Press, 1995.

Ahmad, Irfan. *Religion as Critique: Islamic Critical Thinking from Mecca to the Marketplace.* Chapel Hill: The University of North Carolina Press, 2017.

Ahmed, Akbar. *The Thistle and the Drone: How America's War on Terror Became a Global War on Tribal Islam.* Washington, D.C.: The Brookings Institution, 2013a.

Ahmed, Azam. "That Other Big Afghan Crisis, the Growing Army of Addicts." *The New York Times.* November 3, 2013b. http://www.nytimes.com/2013/11/03/world/asia/that-other-big-afghan-crisis-the-growing-army-of-addicts.html?_r=0 (accessed May 20, 2016).

Ajana, Btihaj. *Governing through Biometrics: The Biopolitics of Identity.* New York: Palgrave Macmillan, 2013.

Alamgir, Mohiuddin. *Afghanistan: Cross Border Trade and Transport Facilitation.* Technical Assistance Consultant Report, Mandaluyong City: Asian Development Bank, 2006.

Alamgir, Mohiuddin, et al. *Securing Afghanistan's Future, Accomplishments and the Way Forward: Transport Sector Building Connections.* Technical Report, Manila: Asian Development Bank, 2004.

Al Jazeera. "A Secret School for Afghans in Iran." *Al Jazeera.* August 12, 2016. https://www.aljazeera.com/news/2016/07/secret-school-afghans-iran-160720121238213.html (accessed July 5, 2017).

Al Jazeera. "Suicide Bombers Target Shia Mosque in Herat City." *Al Jazeera*. August 2, 2017a. http://www.aljazeera.com/news/2017/08/shia-mosque-herat-province-hit-deadly-explosion-170801163417483.html (accessed August 2, 2017).

Al Jazeera. "Taliban Attack Targets Police in Afghanistan's Herat." June 25, 2017b. https://www.aljazeera.com/news/2017/06/taliban-attack-targets-police-afghanistan-herat-170625102845231.html (accessed June 25, 2017).

Allison, Graham. *Nuclear Terrorism: The Ultimate Preventable Catastrophe*. New York: Henry Holt and Company, 2004.

Altai Consulting. *Social Media in Afghanistan: Users and Engagement*. Kabul: Internews, 2017.

Ammaturo, Francesca Romana. *European Sexual Citizenship: Human Rights, Bodies and Identities*. London: Palgrave Macmillan, 2017.

Amnesty International. *No Safe Refuge*. London: Amnesty International, 2016.

Amini, Karim. "Former Education Minister Denies 'SIGAR Report on Ghost Schools.'" *TOLOnews*. June 19, 2015. http://www.tolonews.com/en/afghanistan/20092-former-education-minister-denies-sigar-report-on-ghost-schools (accessed July 26, 2015).

Amiri, Basir Ahmad, interview by Bojan Savić. *Interview with International Federation of Red Cross and Red Crescent Societies (IFRC) Field-Office Manager* (June 7, 2016).

Amoore, Louise. "Biometric Borders: Governing Mobilities in the War on Terror." *Political Geography* 25, no. 3 (2006): 336–351.

Anonymous NGO Activist 1, interview by Bojan Savić. *Interview with Anonymous NGO Activist 1* Herat (May 28, 2016).

Anonymous NGO Activist 2, interview by Bojan Savić. *Interview with Anonymous NGO Activist 2* (May 27, 2016).

Antonio, Robert J. "Immanent Critique as the Core of Critical Theory: Its Origins and Developments in Hegel, Marx and Contemporary Thought." *The British Journal of Sociology* 32, no. 3 (1981): 330–345.

Archnet. "Masjid-i Jami'-i Gawhar Shad; Herat, Afghanistan." *Archent.org*. 2013. http://archnet.org/sites/3935/media_contents/43905 (accessed January 5, 2015).

Arendt, Hannah. *The Origins of Totalitarianism*. New York: Harcourt, 1973.

Aresu, Emmanuele. "(2014). Il Provincial Reconstruction Team (PRT) in Afghanistan. June: 5–13." *Informazioni della Difesa* (June 2014): 5–13.

Arimi, Mohammad Nader, interview by Bojan Savić. *Interview with Head Afghan National Army (ANA) Recruitment Officer in Herat Province* (June 11, 2016).

Armstrong, Warwick, and James Anderson. *Geopolitics of European Union Enlargement: The Fortress Empire*. London: Routledge, 2007.

Aronowitz, Stanley. "A Metatheoretical Critique of Immanual Wallerstein's The Modern World System." *Theory and Society* 10, no. 4 (1981): 503–520.

Atayee, Mirali, interview by Bojan Savić. *Interview with English Language Interpreter and Teacher* (June 8, 2016).

ATR Consulting. *Aid Effectiveness in Afghanistan*. Kabul: Oxfam and Swedish Committee for Afghanistan, 2018.

Avant, Deborah, and Oliver Westerwinter. *The New Power Politics: Networks and Transnational Security Governance*. Oxford: Oxford University Press, 2016.

Ayotte, Kevin J., and Mary E. Husain. "Securing Afghan Women: Neocolonialism, Epistemic Violence, and the Rhetoric of the Veil." *NWSA Journal* 17, no. 3 (2005): 112–133.

Ayoubi, Amrulhaq, interview by Bojan Savić. *Interview with Afghanistan Human Rights Organization (AHRO) Contact Person* (May 26, 2016).

Azimi, M. Brigadier General. "Video Tele Conference with a Spokesperson, Afghanistan Ministry of Defence." *NATO: International Security Assistance Force,* February 14, 2008. http://www.nato.int/isaf/docu/speech/2008/sp080214a.html (accessed November 20, 2014).

Azimi, Mohammad Nadir, interview by Bojan Savić. *Interview with Afghan National Army General* (June 11, 2016).

Azizi, Ahmad Wali, interview by Bojan Savic. *Interview with a Head Administrator at the National Solidarity Program* – Ministry of Rural Rehabilitation and Development (December 24, 2014).

Babakarkhil, Mohammad Hashim, interview by Bojan Savić. *Interview with Afghan National Police Colonel and Former Deputy Commander of ANP Central Training Center, Kabul* (December 21, 2014).

Bagchi, Amiya Kumar. *Colonialism and Indian Economy.* New York: Oxford University Press, 2010.

Baldwin, Robert. "Some Theoretical Aspects of Economic Development." *The Journal of Economic History* 14, no. 4 (1954): 333–345.

Balibar, Etienne. "Europe as Borderland." *Environment and Planning D: Society and Space,* (2009): 190–215.

Balibar, Etienne. *Politics and the Other Scene.* London: Verso, 2002.

Balibar, Etienne. *Race, Nation, Class: Ambiguous Identities.* London: Verso, 1991.

Bandow, Doug. "The Nation-Building Experiment That Failed: Time for U.S. to Leave Afghanistan." *Forbes.* March 1, 2017. https://www.forbes.com/sites/dougbandow/2017/03/01/the-nation-building-experiment-that-failed-time-for-u-s-to-leave-afghanistan/#50098bfa65b2 (accessed August 10, 2017).

Barfield, Thomas. *Afghanistan: A Cultural and Political History.* Princeton, NJ: Princeton University Press, 2010.

Baron, Ava, and Eileen Boris. "'The Body' as a Useful Category for History Working-Class History." *Labor: Studies in Working-Class History* 4, no. 2 (2017): 23–43.

Bazgar, interview by Bojan Savić. *Interview with a Musalla Homeless Person* (June 5, 2016).

Bazoobandi, Sara. *The Political Economy of the Gulf Sovereign Wealth Funds: A Case Study of Iran, Kuwait, Saudi Arabia, and the United Arab Emirates.* London: Routledge, 2013.

BBC News. "Herat Attack: Afghanistan Taliban Target US Consulate." *BBC News.* September 13, 2013. http://www.bbc.com/news/world-asia-24075687 (accessed July 24, 2014).

BBC News. "My Holiday with the Afghan Mujahideen." *BBC.* September 20, 2018. https://www.bbc.com/news/in-pictures-44469707 (accessed September 24, 2018).

Beath, Andrew, Fotini Christia, and Ruben Enikolopov. *The National Solidarity Program: Assessing the Effects of Community-Driven Development in Afghanistan.* Policy Research Working Paper 7415, Washington, D.C.: The World Bank Group, 2015.

Beattie, Doug. "Afghan Police Have Been Infiltrated at Every Level by the Insurgency." *The Guardian.* November 4, 2009. http://www.theguardian.com/uk/2009/nov/04/afghan-police-infiltrated-by-insurgents (accessed February 12, 2014).

Beckwith, Christopher I. *Empires of the Silk Road: A History of Central Eurasia from the Bronze Age to the Present.* Princeton, NJ: Princeton University Press, 2009.

Bellamy, Alex J. *Global Politics and the Responsibility to Protect: From Words to Deeds.* London: Routledge, 2011.

Bendiksen, Lise. *Situation Analysis of Vulnerable Groups of Children in Three Border Areas: Islam Qala, Zaranj and Torkham.* Consultant Report, Kabul: UNICEF Afghanistan, 2008.

Berger, Gwen. "Velied Motives: Women's Liberation and the War in Afghanistan." In *Globalizing Afghanistan: Terrorism, War, and the Rhetoric of Nation Building*, by Zubeda Jalalzai and David Jefferess, 95–116. Durham, NC: Duke University Press, 2011.

Berman, Eli, Callen, Michael, Joseph Felter, and Jacob Shapiro. "Do Working Men Rebel? Insurgency and Unemployment in Afghanistan, Iraq, and the Philippines." *Journal of Conflict Resolution* 55, no. 4 (2011): 496–528.

Bezhan, Frud. "'Stay With Me': Afghan Government Begs Citizens Not to Flee." *The Atlantic*. September 22, 2015. https://www.theatlantic.com/international/archive/2015/09/afghanistan-brain-drain-migrant-crisis/406708/ (accessed June 27, 2017).

Bezhan, Frud, and Nusrat Parsa. "Things Are So Bad in Iran That Afghan Migrants Are Going Home." *Radio Free Europe-Radio Liberty*. August 1, 2018. https://www.rferl.org/a/iran-s-economic-crisis-fuels-mass-exodus-of-afghan-migrants/29405068.html (accessed August 9, 2018).

Bhabha, Homi. *The Location of Culture*. London: Routledge, 1994.

Bhabha, Homi, David Bennett, and Terry Collits. "The Postcolonial Critic: Homi Bhabha Interviewed by David Bennett and Terry Collits." *Arena* 96 (1991): 47–63.

Bidet, Jacques. *Foucault with Marx*. London: Zed Books, 2016.

Billaud, Jullie. *Kabul Carnival: Gender Politics in Postwar Afghanistan*. Philadelphia, PA: University of Pennsylvania Press, 2015.

Bisaillon, Laura, Ehsan Shamsi Gooshki, and Linda Briskman. "Medico-Legal Borders and the Shaping of Health Services for Afghans in Iran: Physical, Social, Bureaucratic, and Public Health Conditions of Care." *International Journal of Migration and Border Studies* 2, no. 1 (2016): 40–58.

Bizhan, Nematullah. *Aid Paradoxes in Afghanistan: Building and Undermining the State*. London: Routledge, 2018.

Blavoukos, Spyros, and Dimitris Bourantonis. "Do Sanctions Strengthen the International Presence of the EU?" *European Foreign Affairs Review* 19, no. 3 (2014): 393–410.

Blunt, Alison, and Jane Wills. *Dissident Geographies: An Introduction to Radical Ideas and Practice*. Harlow: Prentice Hall, 2000.

Boardman, Gerald. *Education Sector Support Project*. End of Project Report, Peshawar: Afghan Field Office USAID/Islamabad, 1994.

Bobin, Frederic. "How Iran Is Expanding Its Influence in Afghanistan." *Le Monde*, April 2, 2009.

Boehmer, Elleke. *Colonial and Postcolonial Literature: Migrant Metaphors (Second Edition)*. Oxford: Oxford University Press, 2005.

Boesen, Elisabeth, and Gregor Schnuer (eds.). *European Borderlands: Living with Barriers and Bridges*. London: Routledge, 2017.

Bonilla-Silva, Eduardo. "Rethinking Racism: Toward a Structural Interpretation." *American Sociological Review* 62, no. 3 (1997): 465–480.

Bornschier, Volker, and Christophe Chase-Dunn. *Transnational Corporations and Underdevelopment*. New York: Praeger, 1985.

Bourdieu, Pierre. "The Forms of Capital." In *Handbook of Theory and Research for the Sociology of Education*, by John Richardson (ed.), 241–258. Westport, CT: Greenwood, 1986.

Bracke, Sarah. "From 'Saving Women' to 'Saving Gays': Rescue Narratives and Their Dis/Continuities." *European Journal of Women's Studies* 19, no. 2 (2012): 237–252.

Braithwaite, Rodric. *Afgantsy: The Russians in Afghanistan 1979–89*. Oxford: Oxford University Press, 2011.

Brill, Steven. "Is America Any Safer?" *The Atlantic*. September 1, 2016. https://www.theatlantic.com/magazine/archive/2016/09/are-we-any-safer/492761/ (accessed June 9, 2018).
Brooks, Michael. *Afghanistan Provincial Reconstruction Team: Observations, Insights, and Lessons*. Fort Leavenworth, KS: Center for Army Lessons Learned, 2011.
Brown, Wendy. *Regulating Aversion: Tolerance in the Age of Identity and Empire*. Princeton, NJ: Princeton University Press, 2006.
Brummet, John. *Actions Needed to Improve the Reliability of Afghan Security Force Assessments*. SIGAR Audit-10-11 Security/ANSF Capabilty Ratings, Arlington, VA: Office of the Special Inspector General for Afghan Reconstruction, 2010.
Brunon-Ernst, Anne. *Beyond Foucault: New Perspectives on Bentham's Panopticon*. London: Routledge, 2016.
Burnes, Alexander. *Travels into Bokhara*. London: John Murray, 1839.
Bush, Barbara. *Imperialism and Postcolonialism*. Harlow: Pearson Longman, 2006.
Butler, Judith. *Gender Trouble: Feminism and the Subversion of Identity*. London: Routledge, 1990.
Butler, Judith. "Restaging the Universal: Hegemony and the Limits of Formalism." In *Contingency, Hegemony, Universality: Contemporary Dialogues on the Left*, by Judith Butler, Ernesto Laclau, and Slavoj Zizek, 11–44. London: Verso, 2000.
Byron, Robert. *The Road to Oxiana*. New York: Oxford University Press, 1982.
Cahn, Dianna. "Corruption Leads to New Rules for Afghan Contracts." *Stars and Stripes*. June 26, 2010. https://www.stripes.com/news/middle-east/afghanistan/corruption-leads-to-new-rules-for-afghan-contracts-1.108877 (accessed April 4, 2015).
Cahn, Dianna. "Troops Fear Corruption Outweighs Progress of Afghan Forces." *Stars and Stripes*. December 9, 2009. http://www.stripes.com/news/troops-fear-corruption-outweighs-progress-of-afghan-forces-1.97195 (accessed August 29, 2013).
CALL (Center for Army Lessons Learned). PRT Playbook: Tactics, Techniques, and Procedures. Fort Leavenworth, KS: CALL, 2007.
Callard, Felicity J. "The Body in Theory." *Environment and Planning D: Society and Space* 16, no. 4 (1998): 387–400.
Campbell, David. *Writing Security: United States Foreign Policy and the Politics of Identity*. Minneapolis, MN: University of Minnesota Press, 1992.
Cammett, Melani, Ishac Diwan, Alan Richards, and John Waterbury. *A Political Economy of the Middle East (Fourth Edition)*. Boulder, CO: Westview Press, 2015.
Carati, Andrea. "No Easy Way Out: Origins of NATO's Difficulties in Afghanistan." *Contemporary Security Policy* 36, no. 2 (2015): 200–218.
Casas, Maribel, Sebastian Cobarrubias, and John Pickles. "Stretching Borders Beyond Sovereign Territories? Mapping EU and Spain's Border Externalization Policies." *Geopolítica(s): Revista de estudios sobre espacio y poder* 2, no. 1 (2011): 71–90.
Chamberlain, Gethin. "US Military: Afghan Leaders Steal Half of All Aid." *The Telegraph*. January 27, 2007. http://www.telegraph.co.uk/news/worldnews/1540831/US-military-Afghan-leaders-steal-half-of-all-aid.html (accessed July 25, 2013).
Chambers, Iain, and Lidia Curti (eds.). *The Post-Colonial Question: Common Skies, Divided Horizons*. London: Routledge, 1996.
Chase-Dunn, Christopher, and Peter Grimes. "World-Systems Analysis." *Annual Review of Sociology* 21 (1995): 387–417.
Chenoweth, Erica, and Kathleen Gallagher Cunningham. "Understanding Nonviolent Resistance: An Introduction." *Journal of Peace Research* 50, no. 3 (2013): 271–276.
Chirot, Daniel. *Social Change in the Modern Era*. New York: Harcourt, 1986.

Chishti, Maliha, and Cheshmak Farhoumand-Sims. "Transnational Feminism and the Women's Rights Agenda in Afghanistan." In *Globalizing Afghanistan: Terrorism, War, and the Rhetoric of Nation Building*, by Zubeda Jalalzai and David Jefferess, 117–144. Durham, NC: Duke University Press, 2011.

Chivers, Christopher J. "Marines Do Heavy Lifting as Afghan Army Lags in Battle." *The New York Times*. February 20, 2010. http://www.nytimes.com/2010/02/21/world/asia/21afghan.html?hp&_r=0 (accessed July 26, 2013).

Chomsky, Noam. *Making the Future: Occupations, Interventions, Empire and Resistance*. London: Penguin Books, 2012.

Christensen, Janne Bjerre. *Guests or Trash: Iran's Precarious Policies towards the Afghan Refugees in the Wake of Sanctions and Regional Wars*. Copenhagen: Danish Institute for International Studies, 2016.

CIA Office of Transnational Issues. *Making High-Value Targeting Operations an Effective Counterinsurgency Tool*. WikiLeaks, 2009.

Cienski, Jan. "Why Poland Doesn't Want Refugees." *Politico*. May 21, 2017. https://www.politico.eu/article/politics-nationalism-and-religion-explain-why-poland-doesnt-want-refugees/ (accessed July 5, 2018).

Clark, Kate. "Before Ashura: Extra Security Measures in Place for Second Year Running." *Afghanistan Analysts Network*. September 19, 2018. https://www.afghanistan-analysts.org/before-ashura-extra-security-measures-in-place-for-second-year-running/ (accessed September 22, 2018).

Clarke, Roger. "Information Technology and Dataveillance." *Communications of the ACM* 31, no. 5 (1988): 498–512.

Cloke, Paul, Paul Milbourne, and Rebekah Widdowfield. "Homelessness in Rural Areas: An Invisible Issue?" In *Homelessness: Exploring the New Terrain*, by Patricia Kennett and Alex Marsh, 61–80. Bristol: The Policy Press, University of Bristol, 1999.

CNN. "Talk of a Holy War Snarls Peace in Afghanistan." *CNN*. April 4, 1996. http://edition.cnn.com/WORLD/9604/04/afghanistan/ (accessed August 3, 2018).

Coburn, Noah. *Bazaar Politics: Power and Pottery in an Afghan Market Town*. Palo Alto, CA: Stanford University Press, 2011

Coburn, Noah. *Losing Afghanistan: An Obituary for the Intervention*. Palo Alto, CA: Stanford University Press, 2016

Coburn, Noah, and Anna Larson. *Derailing Democracy in Afghanistan: Elections in an Unstable Political Landscape*. New York: Columbia University Press, 2014.

Coffey, Luke. "What Does America Consider Success in Afghanistan?" *The National Interest*. June 1, 2017. https://nationalinterest.org/feature/what-does-america-consider-success-afghanistan-20956 (accessed July 2, 2018).

Collins, Patricia Hill, and Sirma Bilge. *Intersectionality*. Cambridge, UK and Malden, MA: Polity Press, 2016.

Colville, Rupert. *Afghanistan's Women: A Confused Future*. Refugees Magazine, Issue 108 (Afghanistan: The Unending Crisis), Geneva: UNHCR, 1996.

Conolly, Arthur. *Journey to the North of India*. Vol. I. London: Richard Bentley, 1838a.

Conolly, Arthur. *Journey to the North of India*. Vol. II. London: Richard Bentley, 1838b.

Cordesman, Anthony H. *Afghanistan: The Uncertain Economics of Transition*. Washington, D.C.: Center for Strategic and International Studies, 2012.

Cordesman, Anthony H. *Islam and the Patterns in Terrorism and Violent Extremism*. Washington, D.C.: Center for Strategic & International Studies, 2017.

Cordesman, Anthony H. *The Afghan War in 2013: Meeting the Challenges of Transition*. CSIS Burke Chair in Strategy Report, Center for Strategic and International Studies (CSIS), Lanham, MD: Rowman & Littlefield, 2013.

Costa, Antonio Maria. "An Opium Market Mystery." *The Washington Post*. April 25, 2007. http://www.washingtonpost.com/wp-dyn/content/article/2007/04/24/AR200704240 1508.html (accessed June 13, 2017).
Coticchia, Fabrizio, and Giampiero Giacomello. "Helping Hands: Civil–Military Cooperation and Italy's Military Operation Abroad." *Small Wars & Insurgencies*, 3–4 (2009): 592–610.
Counter Cartographies Collective, Craig Dalton, Liz Mason-Deese. "Counter (Mapping) Actions: Mapping as Militant Research." *ACME: An International E-Journal for Critical Geographies* 11, no. 3 (2012): 439–466.
Cox, Robert W. "Social Forces, States and World Orders: Beyond International Relations Theory." *Millennium: Journal of International Studies* 10, no. 2 (1981): 126–155.
Crampton, Jeremy W., and Stuart Elden (eds.). *Space, Knowledge and Power: Foucault and Geography*. London: Routledge, 2007.
Crenshaw, Kimberlé W. "Mapping the Margins: Intersectionality, Identity Politics, and Violence against Women of Color." *Stanford Law Review* 43, no. 6 (1991): 241–1299.
Crews, Robert. *Afghan Modern: The History of a Global Nation*. Cambridge, MA: The Belknap Press of Harvard University Press, 2015.
Crist, John T. *The Future of Afghanistan: The Taliban, Regional Security and U.S. Foreign Policy*. Washington, DC: United States Institute of Peace, 1997.
CSO. *The Afghanistan Living Conditions Survey 2016–2017*. Kabul: Central Statistics Organization (CSO) of the Government of the Islamic Republic of Afghanistan, 2018.
Csordas, Thomas J. "Introduction: The Body as Representation and Being-in-the-World." In *Embodiment and Experience: The Existential Ground of Culture and Self*, by Thomas J. Csordas (ed.), 1–26. Cambridge: Cambridge University Press, 1994.
Cuno, Kenneth M., and Manisha Desai (eds.). *Family, Gender, and Law in a Globalizing Middle East and South Asia*. Syracuse, NY: Syracuse University Press, 2009.
Dabashi, Hamid. *The World of Persian Literary Humanism*. Cambridge, MA: Harvard University Press, 2012.
Daiyar, Abbas. "Execution of Afghans in Iran." *Daily Outlook Afghanistan*. March 25, 2013. http://outlookafghanistan.net/topics.php?post_id=6932 (accessed December 7, 2014).
Daryaee, Touraj (ed.). *The Oxford Handbook of Iranian History*. Oxford: Oxford University Press, 2012.
David, Genieve. "Architect Works to Preserve History of Afghanistan." *NATO: Afghanistan Resolute Support*. October 26, 2012. http://www.rs.nato.int/article/news/architect-works-to-preserve-history-of-afghanistan.html (accessed January 5, 2015).
Davids, Christiaan, Sebastiaan Rietjens, and Joseph Soeters. "Analysing the Outputs of Reconstruction Efforts in Afghanistan." *Journal of Peacebuilding & Development* 6, no. 2 (2011): 15–29.
de Bellaigue, Christopher. "The Lost City." *The New Yorker*. January 21, 2002. https://www.newyorker.com/magazine/2002/01/21/the-lost-city-2 (accessed May 11, 2015).
de Certeau, Michel. "Micro-Techniques and Panoptic Discourse: A Quid Pro Quo." *Humanities in Society* 5 (1982): 257–265.
de Certeau, Michel. *The Practice of Everyday Life*. Berkeley, CA: University of California Press, 1984.
Dehzad, Ghulam Nabi, interview by Bojan Savić. *Interview with Handicap International (HI) Herat Base Coordinator* (June 8, 2016).
del Frate, Anna Alvazzi, Keith Krause, and Matthias Nowak. *Global Burden of Armed Violence 2015: Every Body Counts*. Geneva: Geneva Declaration Secretariat, 2015.
de Kock, Leon. "Interview with Gayatri Chakravorty Spivak: New Nation Writers Conference in South Africa." *ARIEL: A Review of International English Literature* 23, no. 3 (1992): 29–47.

Demmers, Jolle, Alex E. Fernández Jilberto, and Barbara Hogenboom. "Good Governance and Democracy in a World of Neoliberal Regimes." In *Good Governance in the Era of Global Neoliberalism: Conflict and Depolitisation in Latin America, Eastern Europe, Asia and Africa*, by Jolle Demmers, Alex E. Fernández Jilberto, and Barbara Hogenboom (eds.), 1–32. London: Routledge, 2004.

Derrida, Jacques. *Positions*. Chicago: The University of Chicago Press, 1981.

de Sousa Santos, Boaventura. *Epistemologies of the South: Justice against Epistemicide*. London: Routledge, 2016.

Dimitriadi, Angeliki. *Irregular Afghan Migration to Europe: At the Margins, Looking In*. Cham: Palgrave Macmillan, 2017.

Domonske, Camila. "Afghan Taliban Begin 3-Day Cease-Fire For Eid Al-Fitr." *NPR*. June 15, 2018. https://www.npr.org/2018/06/15/620234256/afghan-taliban-begins-3-day-cease-fire-for-eid-al-fitr (accessed September 19, 2018).

Donati, Jessica, and Mirwais Harooni. "Thousands of Afghans Face Cold, Hungry Winter as Aid Goes Missing." *Reuters*. January 17, 2014. http://www.reuters.com/article/us-afghanistan-displaced-idUSBREA0G1K220140117 (accessed January 2, 2015).

Dorronsoro, Gilles. *The Taliban's Winning Strategy in Afghanistan*. Washington, D.C.: Carnegie Endowment for International Peace, 2009.

Doty, Roxanne Lynn. *Imperial Encounters: The Politics of Representation in North-South Relations*. Minneapolis, MN: University of Minnesota Press, 1996.

Doubleday, Veronica. *Three Women of Herat: A Memoir of Life, Love and Friendship in Afghanistan*. London: I.B.Tauris, 2006.

Downey, Anthony. "Zones of Indistinction: Giorgio Agamben's 'Bare Life' and the Politics of Aesthetics." *Third Text* 23, no. 2 (2009): 109–125.

Drephal, Maximilian. "Corps Diplomatique: The Body, British Diplomacy, and Independent Afghanistan, 1922–47." *Modern Asian Studies* 51, no. 4 (2017): 956–990.

Duffield, Mark. *Development, Security and Unending War: Governing the World of Peoples*. Cambridge: Polity Press, 2007.

Duffield, Mark. *Global Governance and the New Wars: The Merging of Development and Security*. London: Zed Books, 2001.

Duffield, Mark. "Liberal Interventionism & the Fragile State Linked by Design?" In *Empire, Development & Colonialism: The Past in the Present*, by Mark Duffield and Vernon Hewitt (eds.), 116–129. Woodbridge: James Currey, 2009.

Duffield, Mark. "Racism, Migration and Development: The Foundations of Planetary Order." *Progress in Development Studies* 6, no. 1 (2006): 68–79.

Dupree, Nancy Hatch. "Email to Sotirios Mousouris, UN Secretary General's Special Representative in Afghanistan and Pakistan." *Herat After 18 Years*. Afghanistan Centre at Kabul University (ACKU). September 5, 1994. http://184.73.243.18:8080/jspui/bitstream/azu/15163/1/azu_acku_pamphlet_ds353_d874_1994_w.pdf (accessed May 20, 2016).

Dyrberg, Torben B. *Foucault on the Politics of Parrhesia*. Basingstoke: Palgrave Macmillan, 2014.

Dyvik, Synne L. *Gendering Counterinsurgency: Performativity, Embodiment and Experience in the Afghan "Threatre of War"*. London: Routledge, 2017.

Eghtesad Online. "Iran Steps In to Invest in Afghanistan Iron Ore Mine." *Eghtesad Online*. 2017. http://www.en.eghtesadonline.com/Section-economy-4/24295-iran-steps-in-to-invest-in-afghanistan-iron-ore-mine (accessed August 1, 2017).

Ehrhart, Hans-Georg, Hendrik Hegemann, and Martin Kahl. *Putting Security Governance to the Test*. London: Routledge, 2015.

Eide, Kai. *Power Struggle Over Afghanistan*. New York: Skyhorse Publishing, 2012.

Eland, Ivan. *The Failure of Counterinsurgency: Why Hearts and Minds Are Not Always Won*. Praeger Security International, 2013.
Elden, Staurt. "Plague, Panopticon, Police." *Surveillance & Society* 1, no. 3 (2003): 240–253.
Elliot, Jason. *An Unexpected Light: Travels in Afghanistan*. London: Picador, 1999.
Elphinstone, Mountstuart. *An Account of the Kingdom of Caubul, and Its Dependencies in Persia, Tartary, and India; Comprising a View of the Afghaun Nation, and a History of the Dooraunee Monarchy*. London: Longman, Hurst, Rees, Orme, and Brown, 1815.
Emmerson, Ben. *Report of the Special Rapporteur on the Promotion and Protection of Human Rights and Fundamental Freedoms While Countering Terrorism*. A/71/384, New York: UN General Assembly, 2016.
Erll, Astrid. "Travelling Memory." *Parallax* 17, no. 4 (2011): 4–18.
Ermacora, Felix. *Situation of Human Rights in Afghanistan*. UN Special Rapporteur's Report to the UN General Assembly, New York: UN Special Rapporteur on Afghanistan, 1990.
Esfandiari, Golnaz. "Iran Issues List of Banned Cities, Banned University Courses for Afghans." *Radio Free Europe – Radio Liberty*. June 3, 2012. https://www.rferl.org/a/iran-list-of-university-courses-banned-for-afghans/24602340.html (accessed July 10, 2017).
Es, Margaretha A. van. *Stereotypes and Self-Representations of Women with a Muslim Background: The Stigma of Being Oppressed*. Cham: Springer, 2016.
Esser, Daniel. *Determinants of IDP Voice: Four Cases from Sierra Leone and Afghanistan*. Working Paper, Inter-University Committee on International Migration, MIT, 2005.
European Asylum Support Office. *EASO Country of Origin Information Report: Afghanistan*. Valletta: EASO, 2017.
European Commission. *European Union – Afghanistan: State of Play, May 2015*. Brussels: European External Action Service, 2015.
European Council. *A Secure Europe in a Better World: European Security Strategy*. Brussels, 2003.
European Council. *Council Conclusions on Implementing the EU Global Strategy in the Area of Security and Defence*. Brussels, 2016b.
European Council. *Shared Vision, Common Action: A Stronger Europe. A Global Strategy for the European Union's Foreign and Security Policy*. Brussels: European External Action Service, 2016a.
Europol. *TESAT: European Union Terrorism Situation and Trend Report*. The Hague: Europol, 2018.
Evangelista, Joshua. "Afghans in Iran: No SIM Card, No House, No Rights." *Middle East Eye*. September 12, 2017. http://www.middleeasteye.net/in-depth/features/apartheid-being-afghan-iran-2007076995 (accessed September 25, 2017).
Eveleigh, David J. *Bogs, Baths and Basins: The Story of Domestic Sanitation*. Stroud: Sutton Publishing Limited, 2002.
Ewald, François. "Insurance and Risk." In *The Foucault Effect: Studies in Governmentality*, by Graham Burchell, Colin Gordon, and Peter Miller (eds.), 197–210. Chicago, IL: The University of Chicago Press, 1991.
Fairweather, Jack. *The Good War: Why We Couldn't Win the War or the Peace in Afghanistan*. New York: Basic Books, 2014.
Fanon, Frantz. *Black Skin, White Masks*. London: Pluto Press, 1986.
Fast, Larissa. *Aid in Danger: The Perils and Promise of Humanitarianism*. Philadelphia, PA: University of Pennsylvania Press, 2014.
Favre, Raphy. *Market Development, Location of Bazaars and Road Network Conditions in Afghanistan*. Business Report, Addis Ababa: Aizon, 2004.

Felbab-Brown, Vanda. *Aspiration and Ambivalence: Strategies and Realities of Counterinsurgency and State Building in Afghanistan.* Washington, D.C.: The Brookings Institution, 2013.

Felbab-Brown, Vanda. "Blood and Hope in Afghanistan: A June 2015 Update." *The Brokkings Institution.* May 26, 2015. http://www.brookings.edu/research/papers/2015/05/26-isis-taliban-afghanistan-felbabbrown (accessed June 4, 2015).

Felbab-Brown, Vanda. *Shooting Up: Counterinsurgency and the War on Drugs.* Washington, D.C.: The Brookings Institution, 2010.

Ferrie, Jared. "Afghan Province Declared Landmine-Free after 10-year Clearance Drive." *Reuters.* February 15, 2018. https://www.reuters.com/article/us-afghanistan-conflict-landmines/afghan-province-declared-landmine-free-after-10-year-clearance-drive-idUSKCN1FZ1NY (accessed February 21, 2018).

Ferrier, Joseph Pierre. *Caravan Journeys and Wanderings in Persia, Afghanistan, Turkistan, and Beloochistan.* London: John Murray, 1856.

Ferris-Rotman, Amie. "Iran Pushes out Afghans as Regional Power-Play Heats up." *Reuters.* December 2, 2012. https://www.reuters.com/article/us-afghanistan-iran-refugees-idUSBRE8B103T20121202?feedType=RSS (accessed July 5, 2016).

Flemish Peace Institute. "Firearms and Deaths by Firearms in the EU." Fact Sheet 030, Brussels, 2015.

Fletcher, Arnold. *Afghanistan: Highway of Conquest.* Ithaca, NY: Cornell University Press, 1965.

Fluri, Jennifer L. "'Our Website Was Revolutionary': Virtual Spaces of Representation and Resistance." *ACME: An International E-Journal for Critical Geographies* 5, no. 1 (2006): 89–111.

Fluri, Jennifer. "'Foreign Passports Only': Geographies of (Post)Conflict Work in Kabul, Afghanistan." *Journal Annals of the Association of American Geographers* 99, no. 5 (2009): 986–994.

Fluri, Jennifer L., and Rachel Lehr. *The Carpetbaggers of Kabul and Other American-Afghan Entanglements: Intimate Development, Geopolitics, and the Currency of Gender and Grief.* Athens, GA: University of Georgia Press, 2017.

Flynn, Thomas. "Foucault's Mapping of History." In *The Cambridge Companion to Foucault*, by Gary Gutting (ed.), 29–48. Cambridge: Cambridge University Press, 2005.

Fontana, Alessandro, and Mauro Bertani. "Situating the Lectures." In *Society Must Be Defended*, by Foucault Michel, 273–293. New York: Picador, 2003.

Fooks, Gary, and Christina Pantazis. "The Criminalization of Homelessness, Begging and Street Living." In *Homelessness: Exploring the New Terrain*, by Patricia Kennett and Alex Marsh, 123–160. Bristol: The Policy Press, 1999.

ForeignAssistance.gov. "Afghanistan Foreign Assistance." October 19, 2018. https://www.foreignassistance.gov/explore/country/Afghanistan (accessed October 23, 2018).

Forster, George. *A journey from Bengal to England, through the northern part of India, Kashmire, Afghanistan, and Persia, and into Russia, by the Caspian Sea.* London: R. Faulder, 1798.

Foucault, Michel. "Body/Power." In *Power/Knowledge: Selected Interviews and Other Writings, 1972–1977*, by Colin Gordon and Michel Foucault, 55–62. New York: Pantheon Books, 1980d.

Foucault, Michel. *Discipline and Punish: The Birth of the Prison.* New York: Vintage Books, 1995.

Foucault, Michel. "Nietzsche, Genealogy, History." In *The Foucault Reader*, by Paul Rabinow (ed.), 76–100. New York: Pantheon Books, 1984.

Foucault, Michel. "Power and Strategies." In *Power/Knowledge: Selected Interviews and Other Writings 1972-1977*, by Colin Gordon (ed.), 134-145. New York: Pantheon Books, 1980a.
Foucault, Michel. *Security, Territory, Population: Lectures at the Collège de France 1977-1978*. New York: Picador, 2009.
Foucault, Michel. *Society Must Be Defended: Lectures at the College de France, 1975-76*. New York: Picador, 2003a.
Foucault, Michel. *Subjectivity and Truth: Lectures at the Collège de France, 1980-1981*. London: Palgrave Macmillan, 2017.
Foucault, Michel. *The Archeology of Knowledge and the Discourse on Language*. New York: Pantheon Books, 1972.
Foucault, Michel. *The Birth of the Clinic: An Archeology of Medical Perception*. London: Routledge, 2003b.
Foucault, Michel. *The Care of the Self: The History of Sexuality Volume 3*. London: Penguin Books, 1990.
Foucault, Michel. "The Confession of the Flesh." In *Power/Knowledge: Selected Interviews and Other Writings*, by Colin Gordon (ed.), 194-228. New York: Pantheon Books, 1977.
Foucault, Michel. "The Ethics of the Concern of the Self as a Practice of Freedom." In *Ethics: Subjectivity and Truth*, by Michel Foucault, 281-301. New York: The New Press, 1997.
Foucault, Michel. *The History of Sexuality, Volume 3: The Care of the Self*. New York: Random House, 1986.
Foucault, Michel. *The History of Sexuality, Volume 1: An Introduction*. New York: Random House, Inc., 1978.
Foucault, Michel. "The Order of Discourse." In *Untying the Text: A Post-Structuralist Reader*, by Robert Young (ed.), 48-78. Boston, MA: Routledge & Kegan Paul, 1981.
Foucault, Michel. "The Subject and Power." *Critical Inquiry* 8, no. 4 (1982): 777-795.
Foucault, Michel. "Truth and Power." In *Power/Knowledge: Selected Interviews and Other Writings 1972-1977*, by Colin Gordon and Michel Foucault, 109-133. New York: Pantheon Books, 1980c.
Foucault, Michel, and Colin Gordon. *Power/Knowledge: Selected Interviews and Other Writings 1972-1977*. New York: Pantheon Books, 1980b.
Frank, Andre Gunder. "Abuses and Uses of World Systems Theory in Archeology." In *World-Systems Theory in Practice: Leadership, Production, and Exchange*, by Nick P. Kardulias (ed.), 275-296. Lanham, MD: Rowman & Littlefield Publishers, Inc., 1999.
Franke, Ute. "Ancient Herat Revisited. New Data from Recent Archeological Fieldwork." In *Greater Khorasan: History, Geography, Archaeology and Material Culture*, by Rocco Rante, 63-88. Berlin: Walter de Gruyter, 2015.
Frankel, Herbert S. "United Nations Primer for Development." *The Quarterly Journal of Economics* 66, no. 3 (1952): 301-326.
Franklin, Stephen. "Iran's Simmering Labor Struggle." *Working in These Times*. May 24, 2011. http://inthesetimes.com/working/entry/7334/irans_workers_problems_spiral (accessed June 23, 2017).
Friedrichs, Jörg. "Global Governance as Liberal Hegemony." In *Palgrave Advances in Global Governance*, by Jim Whitman, 105-122. Basingstoke: Palgrave Macmillan, 2009.
Friis, Karsten. "Which Afghanistan? Military, Humanitarian, and State-Building Identities in the Afghan Theater." *Security Studies* 21, no. 2 (2012): 266-300.
Gall, Carlotta. "In Afghanistan, U.S. Exits, and Iran Comes In." *New York Times*. August 5, 2017. https://www.nytimes.com/2017/08/05/world/asia/iran-afghanistan-taliban.html (accessed August 7, 2017).

Gammell, Charlie P. W. *The Pearl of Khorasan: A History of Herat*. London: Hurst Publishers, 2016.

Gatens, Moira. *Imaginary Bodies: Ethics, Power, and Corporeality*. London: Routledge, 1996.

Gerges, Fawaz A. *The Rise and Fall of Al-Qaeda*. Oxford: Oxford University Press, 2011.

Gerlach, Joe. "Lines, Contours and Legends: Coordinates for Vernacular Mapping." *Progress in Human Geography* 38, no. 1 (2013): 22–39.

Gerlach, Joe. "Vernacular Mapping, and the Ethics of What Comes Next." *Cartographica: The International Journal for Geographic Information and Geovisualization* 45, no. 3 (2010): 165–168.

Gezari, Vanessa M. "The Quiet Demise of the Army's Plan to Understand Afghanistan and Iraq." *The New York Times*. August 18, 2015. http://www.nytimes.com/2015/08/18/magazine/the-quiet-demise-of-the-armys-plan-to-understand-afghanistan-and-iraq.html?_r=0 (accessed August 19, 2015).

Ghanizada. "Ismail Khan Escapes a Suicide Attack in Herat Province." Khaama Press. January 24, 2014. http://www.khaama.com/presidential-candidate-ismail-khan-survives-suicide-attack-2722 (accessed January 30, 2014).

Gilliom, John. "Lying, Cheating and Teaching to the Test: The Politics of Surveillance Under No Child Left Behind." In *Schools under Surveillance: Cultures of Control in Public Education*, by Torin Monahan and Rodolfo D. Torres, 194–209. New Brunswick, NJ: Rutgers University Press, 2010.

Gilmore, Scott. "Afghanistan: Proof That Untied Aid Really Works." *The Guardian*. October 24, 2011. https://www.theguardian.com/global-development/poverty-matters/2011/oct/24/afghanistan-untied-aid-creates-jobs (accessed September 10, 2018).

Giustozzi, Antonio. *Empires of Mud: Wars and Warlords in Afghanistan*. New York: Columbia University Press, 2009.

Golombek, Lisa, and Donald Wilber. *The Timurid Architecture of Iran and Turan. Vol. I and II*. Princeton: Princeton University Press, 1988.

Goodhand, Jonathan, and Mark Sedra. "Bribes or Bargains? Peace Conditionalities and 'Post-Conflict' Reconstruction in Afghanistan." *International Peacekeeping* 14, no. 1 (2007): 41–61.

Goodman, Alana. "Afghan Interpreter Murdered by Taliban While Waiting for Visa." *The Washington Free Beacon*. May 29, 2015. https://freebeacon.com/issues/afghan-interpreter-murdered-by-taliban-while-waiting-for-visa/ (accessed August 7, 2015).

Government of the United Kingdom. *A Strong Britain in an Age of Uncertainty: The National Security Strategy*. London: The Stationery Office, 2010.

Government of the United Kingdom. *The National Security Strategy of the United Kingdom: Security in an Interdependent World*. London: The Stationery Office, 2008.

Government of the United Kingdom. *The National Security Strategy of the United Kingdom: Update 2009. Security for the Next Generation*. London: The Stationery Office, 2009.

Gramsci, Antonio, Joseph A. Buttigieg, and Antonio Callari. *Prison Notebooks, Volume 1*. New York: Columbia University Press, 2011.

Gray, Rosie. "Erik Prince's Plan to Privatize the War in Afghanistan." *The Atlantic*. August 18, 2017. https://www.theatlantic.com/politics/archive/2017/08/afghanistan-camp-david/537324/ (accessed August 21, 2017).

Green, Nile. *Afghan History through Afghan Eyes*. Oxford: Oxford University Press, 2016.

Green, Marcus E. "Gramsci Cannot Speak: Presentations and Interpretations of Gramsci's Concept of the Subaltern." In *Rethinking Gramsci*, by Marcus E. Green (ed.), 68–90. London: Routledge, 2011.

Green, Nile. *The Persianate World: The Frontiers of a Eurasian Lingua Franca*. Oakland, CA: University of California Press, 2019.
Gregg, Benjamin. *The Human Rights State: Justice Within and Beyond Sovereign Nations*. Philadelphia, PA: University of Pennsylvania Press, 2016.
Gregory, Derek. "Dis/ordering the Orient." In *Orientalism and War*, by Tarak Barkawi and Keith Stanski (eds.), 151–176. London: C. Hurst & Co., 2012.
Gregory, Derek. *The Colonial Present: Afghanistan, Palestine, Iraq*. Malden, MA: Blackwell Publishing, 2004.
Grenoble, Ryan. "This Daily Mail Anti-Refugee Cartoon Is Straight Out of Nazi Germany." *HuffPost*. November 17, 2015. https://www.huffingtonpost.com/entry/daily-mail-nazi-refugee-rat-cartoon_us_564b526ee4b06037734ae115 (accessed September 23, 2018).
Group of Experts and Former U.S. Officials on Afghanistan. "Forging an Enduring Partnership with Afghanistan." *The National Interest*, September 14, 2016.
Guha, Ranajit. *Elementary Aspects of Peasant Insurgency in Colonial India*. Durham, NC: Duke University Press, 1999.
Guha, Ranajit. "Preface." In *Selected Subaltern Studies*, by Ranajit Guha and Gayatri Chakravorty Spivak (eds.), 35–6. Oxford: Oxford University Press, 1988.
Guha, Ranajit. "The Prose of Counter-Insurgency." In *Subaltern Studies II: Writings on South Asian History and Society*, by Ranajit Guha, 1–42. Oxford: Oxford University Press, 1983.
Guha, Ranajit, and Gayatri Chakravorty Spivak. *Selected Subaltern Studies*. Oxford: Oxford University Press, 1988.
Hahn, Peter L., and Mary Ann Heiss. *Empire and Revolution: The United States and the Third World Since 1945*. Columbus, OH: Ohio State University Press, 2001.
Hall, Samuel. *A Study of Poverty, Food Security and Resilience in Afghan Cities*. Urban Poverty Report, Danish Refugee Council & People in Need, 2014.
Hall, Stuart. "When Was 'The Post-Colonial'? Thinking at the Limit." In *The Post-Colonial Question: Common Skies, Divided Horizons*, by Iain Chambers and Lidia Curti, 242–260. London: Routledge, 1996.
Hameiri, Shahar, and Lee Jones. *Governing Borderless Threats: Non-traditional Security and the Politics of State Transformation*. Cambridge: Cambridge University Press, 2015.
Hammerstad, Anne. *The Rise and Decline of a Global Security Actor: UNHCR, Refugee Protection, and Security*. Oxford: Oxford University Press, 2014.
Hanifi, Shah Mahmoud. *Connecting Histories in Afghanistan: Market Relations and State Formation on a Colonial Frontier*. Stanford, CA: Stanford University Press, 2008.
Haque, Tobias, Habiburahman Sahibzada, Saurabh Shome, Bernard Haven, and Taehyun Lee. *Afghanistan Development Update*. Washington, D.C.: The World Bank, 2018.
Harpviken, Kristian. *Social Networks and Migration in Wartime Afghanistan*. Basingstoke: Palgrave Macmillan, 2009.
Harrison, Graham. *The World Bank and Africa: The Construction of Governance States*. London: Routledge, 2004.
Harshé, Rajen, and Dhananjay Tripathi (eds.). *Afghanistan Post-2014: Power Configurations and Evolving Trajectories*. London: Routledge, 2016.
Hassan, Riaz. *Life as a Weapon: The Global Rise of Suicide Bombings*. London: Routledge, 2011.
Heath, Jennifer, and Ashraf Zahedi. *Land of the Unconquerable: The Lives of Contemporary Afghan Women*. Berkeley, CA: University of California Press, 2011.

Henley & Partners. "The Henley Passport Index." *The Henley Passport Index*. May 22, 2018. https://www.henleyglobal.com/henley-passport-index/ (accessed June 19, 2018).

Henty, George A. *To Herat and Cabul: A Story of the First Afghan War*. London: Blackie & Son, 1902.

Herati Construction Company Owner, interview by Bojan Savić. *Interview with a Herati Entrepreneur (Construction Company Owner)* (December 26, 2014).

Herati NGO Activist No. 2, interview by Bojan Savić. *Skype Interview with Herati NGO Activist No. 2* (March 10, 2018).

Herzog, Benno. "Discourse Analysis as Immanent Critique: Possibilities and Limits of Normative Critique in Empirical Discourse Studies." *Discourse and Society* 27, no. 3 (2016): 278–292.

Hesford, Wendy S., and Wendy Kozol (eds.). *Just Advocacy? Women's Human Rights, Transnational Feminisms, and the Politics of Representation*. Piscataway, NJ: Rutgers University Press, 2005.

Hicks, Josh. "U.S. Might Be Paying 'Ghost Workers' in Afghanistan." *The Washington Post: Federal Eye*. March 20, 2014. http://www.washingtonpost.com/blogs/federal-eye/wp/2014/03/20/u-s-might-be-paying-ghost-workers-in-afghanistan-security-forces/ (accessed March 29, 2014).

Hodgson, Geoffrey M. *Conceptualizing Capitalism: Institutions, Evolution, Future*. Chicago, IL: The University of Chicago Press, 2015.

Hodgson, Marshall S. G. *The Venture of Islam: Conscience and History in a World Civilization. The Classical Age of Islam*. Chicago, IL: The University of Chicago Press, 1974.

Holdich, Thomas H. "Afghan Boundary Commission: Geographical Notes I." *Proceedings of the Royal Geographical Society* 7, no. 1 (1885): 39–44

Hook, Derek. "Discourse, Knowledge, Materiality, History: Foucault and Discourse Analysis." *Theory & Psychology* 11, no. 4 (2001): 521–547.

hooks, bell. "Marginality as a Site of Resistance." In *Out There: Marginalization and Contemporary Cultures*, by Russel Ferguson, Martha Gever, Trinh T. Minh-ha, and Cornel West, 341–344. Cambridge: The MIT Press, 1990.

Hopkins, A. G. *American Empire: A Global History*. Princeton, NJ: Princeton University Press, 2018.

Hopkins, B. D. *The Making of Modern Afghanistan*. Basingstoke: Palgrave Macmillan, 2008.

Howard, Caroline, and Jelena Madzarevic. "Still at Risk: Forced Evictions in Urban Afghanistan." *Forced Migration Review* (May 2014): 38–41.

Hoy, David C., and Thomas McCarthy. *Critical Theory*. Cambridge, MA: Blackwell Publishers, 1994.

Hudson, Valerie. "Europe's Man Problem: Migrants to Europe Skew Heavily Male—and That's Dangerous." *Politico*. January 5, 2016. https://www.politico.com/magazine/story/2016/01/europe-refugees-migrant-crisis-men-213500 (accessed June 4, 2018).

Hulme, Peter. "Including America." *Ariel* 26, no. 1 (1995): 117–123.

Human Rights Watch. *Afghanistan: The Forgotten War: Human Rights Abuses and Violations of the Laws of War Since the Soviet Withdrawal*. February 1, 1991. https://www.refworld.org/docid/45c9a5d12.html (accessed August 16, 2018).

Human Rights Watch. *All Our Hopes Are Crushed: Violence and Repression in Western Afghanistan*. New York: HRW, 2002a.

Human Rights Watch. "'No Safe Place': Insurgent Attacks on Civilians in Afghanistan." May 8, 2018. https://www.hrw.org/report/2018/05/08/no-safe-place/insurgent-attacks-civilians-afghanistan (accessed September 6, 2019).

Human Rights Watch. *The Human Cost: The Consequences of Insurgent Attacks in Afghanistan*. New York: Human Rights Watch, 2007.
Human Rights Watch. "Unwelcome Guests: Iran's Violation of Afghan Refugee and Migrant Rights." *Human Rights Watch*. November 20, 2013. https://www.hrw.org/repor t/2013/11/20/unwelcome-guests/irans-violation-afghan-refugee-and-migrant-rights (accessed November 11, 2014).
Human Rights Watch. *"We Want to Live as Humans": Repression of Women and Girls in Western Afghanistan*. New York: HRW, 2002b.
Hummel, Stephen. "The Islamic State and WMD: Assessing the Future Threat." *CTC Sentinel* 9, no. 1 (2016): 18–21.
Huysmans, Jef. *Security Unbound: Enacting Democratic Limits*. London: Routledge, 2014.
Hyman, Anthony. "Nationalism in Afghanistan." *International Journal of Middle East Studies* 34, no. 2 (2002): 299–315.
Hyndman, Jennifer, and Wenona Giles. *Refugees in Extended Exile: Living on the Edge*. London: Routledge, 2017.
Ignatiev, Pavlo. "Afghanistan: Balancing between Pakistan and Iran." *Indian Journal of Asian Affairs* 27/8, no. 1/2 (2014): 43–62.
Ikenberry, G. John. "Liberal Internationalism 3.0: America and the Dilemmas of Liberal World Order." *Perspectives on Politics* 7, no. 1 (2009): 71–87.
Immigration and Refugee Board of Canada. *Afghanistan: Treatment of Ethnic Pashtuns, Particularly in Herat; Treatment of Perceived Supporters of the Taliban and/or the Communist Party*. Response to Information Request, Ottawa: Research Directorate, Immigration and Refugee Board, 2004.
Immigration and Refugee Board of Canada. *Afghanistan: Background Information on the Taliban Movement*. July 1, 1995. https://www.refworld.org/docid/3ae6ad3ac.html (accessed August 3, 2018).
Ingram, Alan. "The Pentagon's HIV/AIDS Programmes: Governmentality, Political Economy, Security." *Geopolitics* 16, no. 3 (2011): 655–674.
International Labour Organization. "Labour and Social Issues Arising from Problems of Cross-Border Mobility of International Drivers in the Road Transport Sector." TMRTS/2006, Geneva, 2006.
International Monetary Fund. "Third Review Under the Extended Credit Facility Arrangement and Request for Modification of Performance Criteria." IMF Country Report No. 18/127, Washington, D.C., 2018.
International Organization for Migration. "Return of Undocumented Migrants: Weekly Situation Report, 16–22 September 2018." *International Organization for Migration: UN Migration*. September 2018. https://afghanistan.iom.int/sites/default/files/Reports/iom_afghanistan-return_of_undocumented_afghans-_situation_report-_16_-_22_september_2018.pdf (accessed October 10, 2018).
International Organization for Migration. *Trafficking in Persons: An Analysis of Afghanistan*. Expert Report, Kabul: International Organization for Migration – Afghanistan, 2004.
Ionnesyan, Youli. *Afghan Folktales from Herat: Persian Texts in Transcription and Translation*. Amherst, NY: Cambria Press, 2009.
Isin, Engin. *Citizenship after Orientalism: Transforming Political Theory*. Basinstoke: Palgrave Macmillan, 2015.
Islamic Republic of Afghanistan. "Self-Reliance through Mutual Accountability Framework (SMAF)." Kabul, 2015.

Italian Provincial Reconstruction Team Employee, interview by Bojan Savić. *Interview with a Former Civilian PRT Employee* (November 12, 2014).

Jabeen, Mussarat, and Venkat Pulla. "Scourge of Internal Displacement of Afghan Refugees: Compromised Resiliency." *International Journal of Social Work and Human Services Practice* 2, no. 2 (2014): 40–47.

Jager, Siegfried. "Discourse and Knowledge: Theoretical and Methodological Aspects of a Critical Discourse and Dispositive Analysis." In *Methods of Critical Discourse Analysis*, by Ruth Wodak and Michael Meyer (eds.), 32–62. London: Sage Publications, 2001.

Jalalzai, Musa Khan. "Afghanistan: Ethnicisation of Intelligence." *Daily Times*. March 8, 2014. http://www.dailytimes.com.pk/opinion/08-Mar-2014/afghanistan-ethnicisation-of-intelligence (accessed September 14, 2014).

Jalalzai, Zubeda, and David Jefferess (eds.). *Globalizing Afghanistan: Terrorism, War, and the Rhetoric of Nation Building*. Durham, NC: Duke University Press, 2011.

Jenkins, Brian. "Will Terrorists Go Nuclear: A Reappraisal." In *The Future of Terrorism: Violence in the New Millennium*, by Harvey Kushner (ed.), 225–249. London: Sage Publications, 1998.

Jawad, Nassim. *Afghanistan: A Nation of Minorities*. A Minority Rights Group International Report, 92/2. London: The Minority Rights Group, 1992.

Jessop, Bob. *State Power*. Cambridge: Polity Press, 2008.

Jiwani, Yasmin. *Discourses of Denial: Mediations of Race, Gender, and Violence*. Vancouver, BC: UBC Press, 2006.

Jochem, Torsten, Ilia Murtazashvili, and Jennifer Murtazashvili. "Establishing Local Government in Fragile States: Experimental Evidence from Afghanistan." *World Development* 77 (2016): 293–310.

Johnson, Chris, and Jolyon Leslie. *Afghanistan: The Mirage of Peace*. London: Zed Books, 2004.

Johnson, Robert. *The Afghan Way of War: How and Why They Fight*. London: Hurst, 2011.

Johnson, Thomas H. "Ismail Khan, Herat, and Iranian Influence." *Strategic Insights* 3, no. 7 (2004): 1–10.

Jones, Colin, and Roy Porter (eds.). *Reassessing Foucault: Power, Medicine and the Body*. London: Routledge, 1994.

Jones, Seth. *Counterinsurgency in Afghanistan*. Santa Monica, CA: RAND Corporation, 2008.

Jones, Seth. *In the Graveyard of Empires: America's War in Afghanistan*. New York: W. W. Norton & Company, 2010.

Jones, Seth. *Reintegrating Afghan Insurgents*. Santa Monica, CA: RAND Corporation, 2011.

Joya, Omar, Saurabh Shome, Taehyun Lee, Bernard Haven, Christina Wieser, and Aman Farahi. *Afghanistan Development Update*. Washington, D.C.: The World Bank Group, 2017.

Kakar, Mohammed. *Afghanistan: The Soviet Invasion and the Afghan Response, 1979–1982*. Berkeley, CA: University of California Press, 1995.

Kamminga, Jorrit, and Akram Zaki. *Returning to Fragility: Exploring the Link Between Conflict and Returnees in Afghanistan*. Oxford: Oxfam, 2018.

Kaplan, Martha. "Panopticon in Poona: An Essay on Foucault and Colonialism." *Cultural Anthropology* 10, no. 1 (1995): 85–98.

Kaplan, Robert D. *The Revenge of Geography: What the Map Tells Us about Coming Conflicts and the Battle Against Fate*. New York: Random House, 2012.

Kapoor, Ilan. *The Postcolonial Politics of Development*. London: Routledge, 2008.

Kapstein, Ethan. *Aid and Stabilization in Afghanistan: What Do the Data Say?* Special Report, Washington, D.C.: United States Institute of Peace, 2017.
Kardulias, Nick P. (ed). *World-Systems Theory in Practice: Leadership, Production, and Exchange.* Lanham, MD: Rowman & Littlefield Publishers, Inc., 1999.
Karimi, Storai. "Declining Saffron Price Worries Herat Farmers."Pajhwok Afghan News. Oct 16, 2018. https://www.pajhwok.com/en/2018/10/16/declining-saffron-price-worries-herat-farmers (accessed October 25, 2018).
Karimi, Storai. "Growing Unemployment: Herat Youth Hit Out at Govt." *Pajhwok Afghan News.* May 9, 2016. http://www.subscribedevelop.pajhwok.com/en/2016/05/09/growing-unemployment-herat-youth-hit-out-govt (accessed August 11, 2016).
Kashani-Sabet, Firoozeh. *Frontier Fictions. Shaping the Iranian Nation 1804–1946.* Princeton, NJ: Princeton University Press, 1999.
Katzman, Kenneth. *Afghanistan: Post-Taliban Governance, Security, and U.S. Policy.* Washington, D.C.: Congressional Research Service, 2013.
Kavalski, Emilian. "The Complexity of Global Security Governance: An Analytical Overview." *Global Society* 22, no. 4 (2008): 423–443.
Kearney, Michael. *Changing Fields of Anthropology: From Local to Global.* Lanham, MD: Rowman & Littlefield Publishers, 2004.
Kemple, Thomas, and Laura Huey. "Observing the Observers: Researching Surveillance and Counter – Surveillance on 'Skid Row.'" *Surveillance & Society* 3, no. 2/3 (2005): 139-157.
Keohane, Robert O. *After Hegemony: Cooperation and Discord in the World Political Economy.* Princeton, NJ: Princeton University Press, 1984.
Khaama Press. "Gunmen Attack Pakistan Consulate with Hand Grenade in Herat." Khaama Press. January 4, 2015. http://www.khaama.com/gunmen-attack-pakistan-consulate-with-hand-grenade-in-herat-9202 (accessed January 4, 2015).
Khalilzad, Zalmay. "Afghanistan in 1995: Civil War and a Mini-Great Game." *Asian Survey* 36, no. 2 (1996): 190–195.
Khamoosh, Kawoon. "The Girl Who Secretly Filmed the Taliban." *BBC News.* October 24, 2015. https://www.bbc.com/news/world-asia-34541661 (accessed September 28, 2018).
Khan, Shahnaz. "The Two Faces of Afghan Women: Oppressed and Exotic." *Women's Studies International Forum* 44, no. May–June (2014): 101–109.
Kienscherf, Markus. "A Programme of Global Pacification: US Counterinsurgency Doctrine and the Biopolitics of Human (In)security." *Security Dialogue* 42, no. 6 (2011): 517–535.
King, Anna. "Islam, Women and Violence." *Feminist Theology* 17, no. 3 (2009): 292–328.
King, Laura. "In Western Afghan City, Iran Makes Itself Felt." *Los Angeles Times.* November 13, 2010. http://articles.latimes.com/2010/nov/13/world/la-fg-afghanistan-iran-20101114 (accessed July 5, 2018).
Kirchner, Emil J., and James Sperling (eds.). *Global Security Governance: Competing Perceptions of Security in the 21st Century.* London: Routledge, 2007.
Kirchner, Emil J., and Roberto Dominguez. *The Security Governance of Regional Organizations.* London: Routledge, 2011.
Koelbl, Susanne. "The Next Wave: Afghans Flee to Europe in Droves." *Spiegel Online.* October 30, 2015. http://www.spiegel.de/international/world/crisis-in-aghanistan-leads-wave-of-migrants-to-head-to-europe-a-1059919.html (accessed July 25, 2017).
Koepke, Bruce. *Iran's Policy on Afghanistan: The Evolution of Strategic Pragmatism.* Stockholm: SIPRI, 2013.

Kolossov, Vladimir. "Border Studies: Changing Perspectives and Theoretical Approaches." *Geopolitics* 10, no. 4 (2012): 606–632.
Krahmann, Elke. "Conceptualizing Security Governance." *Conflict and Cooperation* 38, no. 1 (2003): 5–26.
Krahmann, Elke. "Security: Collective Good or Commodity?" *European Journal of International Relations* 14, no. 3 (2008): 379–404.
Krahmann, Elke. "Security Governance and Networks: New Theoretical Perspectives in Transatlantic Security." *Cambridge Review of International Affairs* 18, no. 1 (2005): 15–30.
Krasner, Stephen D. "Structural Causes and Regime Consequences: Regimes as Intervening Variables." *International Organization* 36, no. 2 (1982): 185–205.
Kreutzmann, Hermann. "Afghanistan and the Opium World Market: Poppy Production and Trade." 40, no. 5 (2007): 605–621.
Kuppers, Maira. "Stateless in Afghanistan." *Forced Migration Review* (May 2014): 9.
La Piscopia, Patrizia, and Elena Croci. "Stabilizzare e ricostruire: Il ruolo della comunicazione culturale. Un progetto italiano per promuovere e consolidare l'identita nazionale afghana dopo decenni di conflitti." *Economia della Cultura* XXII, no. 3 (2012): 289–298.
Laclau, Ernesto. "Identity and Hegemony: The Role of Universality in the Constitution of Political Logics." In *Contingency, Hegemony, Universality: Contemporary Dialogues on the Left*, by Judith Butler, Ernesto Laclau, and Slavoj Zizek, 44–89. London: Verso, 2000.
Lal, Mohan. *Travels in the Punjab, Afghanistan and Turkistan, to Balk, Bokhara and Herat, and a Visit to Great Britain and Germany.* London: W. H. Allen, 1846.
Lamb, Christina. *The Sewing Circles of Herat: A Personal Voyage through Afghanistan.* London: HarperCollins, 2002.
Langegger, Sig, and Stephen Koester. "Invisible Homelessness: Anonymity, Exposure, and the Right to the City." *Urban Geography* (2016): 1–19.
Lardner, Richard. "Investigation: Afghan Troops Ran, Hid During Deadly Battle." *The Virginian-Pilot*. June 11, 2011. http://www.highbeam.com/doc/1G1-258796651.html (accessed July 24, 2013).
Latham, Robert. "Politics in a Floating World: Toward a Critique of Global Governance." In *Approaches to Global Governance Theory*, by Martin Hewson and Timothy J. Sinclair (eds.), 23–53. Albany, NY: SUNY Press, 1999.
Latifi, Ali M. "Addicted and Hopeless in Afghanistan's Herat." *Al Jazeera.* December 3, 2013. http://www.aljazeera.com/indepth/features/2013/12/addicted-hopeless-afghani stan-herat-20131269424334179.html (accessed May 29, 2016).
Latour, Bruno. "Give Me a Laboratory and I Will Raise the World." In *Science Observed: Perspectives on the Social Study of Science*, by Karin D. Knorr-Cetina and Michae Mulkay, 141–170. London: Sage Publications, 1983.
Lefkovitz, Lori Hope (ed.). *Textual Bodies: Changing Boundaries of Literary Representation.* Albany, NY: SUNY Press, 1997.
Leslie, Jolyon. *Political and Economic Dynamics of Herat.* Washington, D.C.: United States Institute of Pease (USIP), 2015.
Levi, Michael. *On Nuclear Terrorism.* New York: Council on Foreign Relations, 2007.
Li, Victor. *The Neo-primitivist Turn: Critical Reflections on Alterity, Culture, and Modernity.* Toronto: University of Toronto Press, 2006.
Lister, Tim, Ray Sanchez, Mark Bixler, Sean O'Key, Michael Hogenmiller, and Mohammed Tawfeeq. "ISIS Goes Global: 143 Attacks in 29 Countries Have Killed 2,043." *CNN*.

February 12, 2018. https://edition.cnn.com/2015/12/17/world/mapping-isis-attacks-around-the-world/index.html (accessed March 20, 2018).

Loda, Mirella, Gaetano Di Benedetto, Manfred Hinz, Massimo Preite, and Mario Tartaglia. *Herat Strategic Master Plan: A Vision for the Future*. Florence: Laboratorio di Geografia Sociale, Università degli Studi di Firenze (LaGeS), 2013.

Loomba, Ania. *Colonialism/Postcolonialism (The New Critical Idiom)*. London: Routledge, 2005.

Loud, Peter. "Photographs by Peter Loud." http://www.peterloud.co.uk/photos/photos.html (accessed May 27, 2016).

Lucarelli, Sonia. "Multilateral Governance." In *Handbook of Governance and Security*, by James Sperling (ed.), 63–81. Cheltenham: Edward Elgar Publishing, 2014.

Lund, Joshua. *The Mestizo State: Reading Race in Modern Mexico*. Minneapolis, MN: University of Minnesota Press, 2012.

Macchi, G. *Saving Minarets at Risk in Afghanistan*. Vol. 2, in *Structural Analysis of Historical Constructions*, by Claudio Modena, Paulo B. Lourenço, and Pere Roca, 1372–1382. Leiden: A.A. Balkema Publishers, 2005.

Mahdavi, Pardis. *Gridlock: Labor, Migration, and Human Trafficking in Dubai*. Stanford, CA: Stanford University Press, 2011.

Mahr, Krista. "ICRC Says Five Aid Workers Seized in Western Afghanistan." *Reuters*. August 16, 2014. https://www.reuters.com/article/us-afghanistan-kidnapping/icrc-says-five-aid-workers-seized-in-western-afghanistan-idUSKBN0GG0CE20140816 (accessed June 4, 2017).

Majidi, Nassim. *Urban Returnees and Internally Displaced Persons in Afghanistan*. Expert Report, Washington, D.C.: Middle East institute; Fondation pour la Recherche Strategique, 2011.

Maley, William, and Susanne Schmeidl (eds.). *Reconstructing Afghanistan: Civil-Military Experiences in Comparative Perspective*. London: Routledge, 2015.

Malkasian, Carter. *War Comes to Garmser: Thirty Years of Conflict on the Afghan Frontier*. Oxford: Oxford University Press, 2013.

Mamundzay, Farid, interview by Bojan Savić. *Interview with Deputy Minister of the Independent Directorate of Local Governance* (December 22, 2014).

Manchanda, Nivi. "The Imperial Sociology of the 'Tribe'." In *Routledge Handbook of Postcolonial Politics*, by Olivia U. Rutazibwa and Robbie Shilliam. London: Routledge, 2018.

Mann, Michael. *Incoherent Empire*. London: Verso, 2003.

Mansoor, Peter R. "Is Another 9/11 Possible?" The Hoover Institution. August 15, 2016. https://www.hoover.org/research/another-911-possible (accessed June 10, 2018).

Martin, Mike. *An Intimate War an Oral History of the Helmand Conflict, 1978–2012*. London and Oxford: Hurst Publishers and Oxford University Press, 2014.

Marty, Franz J. "Taliban Launch Multiple Attacks in Herat Province." *IHS Jane's Defence Weekly*. June 17, 2015. http://www.janes.com/article/52402/taliban-launch-multiple-attacks-in-herat-province (accessed June 19, 2015).

Marx, Gary T. "A Tack in the Shoe and Taking off the Shoe: Neutralization and Counter-neutralization Dynamics." *Surveillance & Society* 6, no. 3 (2003): 294–306.

Marx, Karl. *Capital: A Critique of Political Economy*. New York: Random House, Inc., 1906.

Mattson, Kevin. *Intellectuals in Action: The Origins of the New Left and Radical Liberalism, 1945–1970*. University Park, PA: The Pennsylvania State University Press, 2002.

Maurer, Kevin, and Lori Hinnant. "Corruption, Indiscipline Slow Afghan Training." *Army Times*. October 8, 2009. http://archive.armytimes.com/article/20091008/NEWS/910080310/Corruption-indiscipline-slow-Afghan-training (accessed July 13, 2013).
May, Michelle. "Anywhere but Home: An Afghan Labourer in Iran Dreams of Life in Sweden." *The Guardian*. February 3, 2016. https://www.theguardian.com/world/iran-blog/2016/feb/03/afghan-refugees-iran-greece-sweden (accessed July 7, 2017).
May, Vivian M. *Pursuing Intersectionality, Unsettling Dominant Imaginaries*. London: Routledge, 2015.
Mbembe, Achille. "Necropolitics." *Public Culture* 15, no. 1 (Winter 2003): 11–40.
Mbembe, Achille. *On the Postcolony*. Berkeley and Los Angeles, CA: University of California Press, 2001.
Mbembe, Achille. "Provisional Notes on the Post-colony." *Africa* 62, no. 1 (1992): 3–37.
McCain, John. *Inquiry into the Role and Oversight of Private Security Contractors in Afghanistan*. Washington, D.C.: Diane Publishing, 2010.
McClintock, Anne. *Imperial Leather: Race, Gender and Sexuality in the Colonial Contest*. London: Routledge, 1995.
McCoy, Alfred. "The Drug That Makes the Taliban Possible." *The Nation*. February 22, 2016. https://www.thenation.com/article/the-drug-that-makes-the-taliban-possible/ (accessed August 2, 2018).
McEwan, Cheryl. *Postcolonialism and Development*. London: Routledge, 2009.
McFate, Sean. "I Was a Mercenary. Trust Me: Erik Prince's Plan Is Garbage." *Politico*. August 31, 2017. https://www.politico.com/magazine/story/2017/08/31/i-was-a-mercenary-trust-me-erik-princes-plan-is-garbage-215563 (accessed September 1, 2017).
McNally, Lauren, and Marvin G. Weinbaum. *A Resilient Al-Qaeda in Afghanistan and Pakistan*. Middle East Institute Policy Focus 2016–18, Washington, D.C.: Middle East Institute, 2016.
Medica Mondiale. *Dying to Be Heard: Self-Immolation of Women in Afghanistan*. Research Project Report, Koln: Medica Mondiale, 2007.
Medovoi, Leerom. "Dogma-Line Racism: Islamophobia and the Second Axis of Race." *Social Text* 30, no. 2 (2012): 43–74.
Mehr. "Iran Ready to Transfer Mining Knowhow to Afghanistan." *Mehr News Agency*. July 22, 2017. http://en.mehrnews.com/news/126649/Iran-ready-to-transfer-mining-knowhow-to-Afghanistan (accessed July 25, 2017).
Mehregan, Abi. "Hard Lives for Afghans in Iran." *PBS Frontline*. November 21, 2010. https://www.pbs.org/wgbh/pages/frontline/tehranbureau/2010/11/hard-lives-for-afghans-in-iran.html (accessed August 12, 2017).
Melchior, Jillian K. "Why So Many of Europe's Migrants Are Men." *National Review*. October 12, 2015. https://www.nationalreview.com/2015/10/why-europes-migrants-are-men/ (accessed June 4, 2018).
Mekdjian, Sarah. "Mapping Mobile Borders: Critical Cartographies of Borders Based on Migration Experiences." In *Borderities and the Politics of Contemporary Mobile Borders*, by Anne-Laure Amilhat Szary and Frédéric Giraut (eds.), 204–223. Basingstoke: Palgrave Macmillan, 2015.
Memmi, Albert. *The Colonizer and the Colonized*. Boston, MA: Beacon Press, 1991.
MEMO. "Over 2,000 Iran-backed Afghans Killed in Syria." *MEMO: Middle East Monitor*. January 9, 2018. https://www.middleeastmonitor.com/20180109-over-2000-iran-backed-afghans-killed-in-syria/ (accessed January 11, 2018).
Mignolo, Walter D. *The Darker Side of Western Modernity: Global Futures, Decolonial Options*. Durham, NC: Duke University Press, 2011.

Milbourne, Paul, and Rebekah Widdowfield. "Homelessness and Rurality: 'Out-of-Place' in Purified Space?" *Environment and Planning* 18, no. 6 (2000): 715–735.

Mills, Charles Wright. "Letter to the New Left." *New Left Review* 5 (1960): 18–23.

Mills, Chalres Wright. "The Cultural Apparatus." In *The Politics of Truth: Selected Writings of C. Wright Mills*, by Charles Wright Mills and John Summers. Oxford: Oxford University Press, 2008.

Minca, Claudio. "Giorgio Agamben and the New Biopolitical Nomos." *Geografiska Annaler* 88, no. 4 (2006): 387–403.

Minh-ha, Trinh T. *Woman, Native, Other: Writing Postcoloniality and Feminism*. Bloomington, IN: Indiana University Press, 1989.

Minh-ha, Trinh T., and Annamaria Morelli. "The Undone Interval." In *The Post-colonial Question: Common Skies, Divided Horizons*, by Iain Chambers and Lidia Curti (eds.), 3–16. London: Routledge, 1996.

Ministry of Information and Culture. "Media, Culture and Youth Strategy." *Ministry of Information and Culture, Islamic Republic of Afghanistan*. 2006. http://moic.gov.af/en/page/1326 (accessed August 2, 2016).

Ministry of Information and Culture, Transitional Islamic State of Afghanistan. "City of Herat: Description." *UNESCO: Tentative List*. August 17, 2004. http://whc.unesco.org/en/tentativelists/1927/ (accessed July 20, 2016).

Mitchell, David F. "Blurred lines? Provincial Reconstruction Teams and NGO Insecurity in Afghanistan, 2010–2011." *Stability: International Journal of Security and Development* 4, no. 1 (2015): 1–18.

Mitchell, Timothy. *Colonising Egypt*. Berkeley: University of California Press, 1988.

Mitchell, Timothy. "Fixing the Economy." *Cultural Studies* 12, no. 1 (1998): 82–101.

Mitchell, Timothy. *Rule of Experts: Egypt, Techno-Politics, Modernity*. Berkeley, CA: University of California Press, 2002.

Mobariz, Ahmad Shah. "WTO Accession of Afghanistan: Costs, Benefits and Post-accession Challenges." *South Asia Economic Journal* 17, no. 1 (2016): 46–72.

Mohammad, Shah, interview by Bojan Savić. *Interview with Afghan National Army (ANA) Instructor*. (January 1, 2015).

Monahan, Torin. "Counter-Surveillance as Political Intervention?" *Social Semiotics* 16, no. 4 (2006): 515–534.

Monahan, Torin. *Surveillance in the Time of Insecurity*. Brunswick, NJ and London: Rutgers University Press, 2010.

Monib, Basir Ahmad, interview by Bojan Savić. *Interview with Norwegian Project Office/Rural Rehabilitation Association for Afghanistan West Regional Office Representative* (June 2, 2016).

Monsutti, Alessandro. "Afghan Migratory Strategies and the Three Solutions to the Refugee Problem." *Refugee Survey Quarterly* 27, no. 1 (2008): 58–73.

Monsutti, Alessandro. "Migration as a Rite of Passage: Young Afghans Building Masculinity and Adulthood in Iran." *Iranian Studies* 40, no. 2 (2007): 167–185.

Monsutti, Alessandro. *War and Migration: Social Networks and Economic Strategies of the Hazaras of Afghanistan*. London: Routledge, 2016.

Mooers, Colin P. *Imperial Subjects: Citizenship in an Age of Crisis and Empire*. New York: Bloomsbury Academic, 2014.

Moosakhail, Zabiullah. "Iran Bans Afghans in Nine Provinces." *Khaama Press*. December 23, 2014. https://www.khaama.com/43221-2596/ (accessed December 28, 2014).

Morgan, David. *Medieval Persia 1040–1797*. London: Routledge, 1988.
Morris, Sharon, James Stephenson, Ciminelli, Paul Donald Muncy, Tod Wilson, and Al Nugent. *Provincial Reconstruction Teams in Afghanistan: An Interagency Assessment*. Washington, D.C.: U.S. Agency for International Development, 2006.
Mosher, Dave, and Skye Gould. "How Likely Are Foreign Terrorists to Kill Americans? The Odds May Surprise You." *Business Insider*. February 1, 2017. http://uk.businessinsider.com/death-risk-statistics-terrorism-disease-accidents-2017-1?r=US&IR=T (accessed February 2, 2017).
Motal, Julius. "The Translators Promised Visas but Made Into Refugees by the US Army." *Quartz*. June 20, 2016. https://qz.com/702668/afghan-translators-for-the-us-army-who-were-promised-visas-but-never-got-them/ (accessed April 5, 2017).
Mousavi, Sayed Askar. *The Hazaras of Afghanistan: An Historical, Cultural, Economic and Political Study*. Richmond: Curzon Press, 1998.
Mowatt-Larssen, Rolf. *Al Qaeda Weapons of Mass Destruction Threat: Hype or Reality*. Cambridge, MA: Belfer Center for Science and International Affairs, Harvard Kennedy School, 2010.
Mukherjee, Ranjana, Mark Baird, and Ijaz Nabi. *Afghanistan – Building an Effective State: Priorities for Public Administration Reform*. Public Sector Study, Washington, D.C.: World Bank Group, 2008.
Muller, Benjamin J. *Security, Risk and the Biometric State: Governing Borders and Bodies*. London: Routledge, 2010.
Murphy, Craig N. "The Promise of Liberal Internationalism." In *Global Governance: Critical Concepts in Political Science, Volume 1*, by Timothy J. Sinclair, 145–178. London: Routledge, 2004.
Nader, et al. *Iranâ's Influence in Afghanistan: Implications for the U.S. Drawdown*. Santa Monica, CA: RAND Corporation, 2014.
Najafizada, Lotfullah, interview by Bojan Savić. *Interview with Director of TOLOnews*, Kabul (December 23, 2014).
Najibullah, interview by Bojan Savić. *Interview with a Private Transportation Business Owner* (January 2015).
Naseri, Jamila, interview by Bojan Savić. *Head of Medica Afghanistan's Herat Regional Office* (June 11, 2016).
National Directorate of Security Employee No. 1, interview by Bojan Savić. *Interview with National Directorate of Security Employee No. 1* (December 29, 2014).
National Directorate of Security Employee No. 2, interview by Bojan Savić. *Interview with National Directorate of Security Employee No. 2* (December 31, 2014).
NATO Public Diplomacy Division. "Afghan National Army (ANA) Trust Fund." *NATO Media Backgrounder*. April 15, 2018. https://www.nato.int/nato_static_fl2014/assets/pdf/pdf_2018_04/20180425_1804-backgrounder-ana-trust-fund-en.pdf (accessed September 13, 2018).
NATO Public Diplomacy Division. "Afghan National Security Forces (ANSF)." Media Backgrounder, Brussels, 2013.
Nayel, Amina Alrasheed. *Alternative Performativity of Muslimness: The Intersection of Race, Gender, Religion, and Migration*. Cham: Palgrave Macmillan, 2017.
Nazar, Zarif, and Charles Recknagel. "Shooting to Kill on the Iran-Afghan Border." *Radio Free Europe – Radio Liberty*. January 24, 2011. https://www.rferl.org/a/shooting_iran_afghan_border/2285746.html (accessed June 29, 2016).
Neal, Andrew W. "Cutting Off the King's Head: Foucault's Society Must Be Defended and the Problem of Sovereignty." *Alternatives* 29 (2004): 373–398.

Neal, Andrew W. *Exceptionalism and the Politics of Counter-Terrorism: Liberty, Security, and the War on Terror*. London: Routledge, 2010.
Neekzad, Hassina, interview by Bojan Savić. *Interview with Afghan Women's Network Regional Office Manager* (June 8, 2016).
Nemser, Daniel. *Infrastructures of Race: Concentration and Biopolitics in Colonial Mexico*. Austin, TX: University of Texas Press, 2017.
Neslen, Arthur. "'Horrific' Levels of Child Abuse in Unsafe Refugee Camps, Warns EU." *The Guardian*. April 24, 2017. https://www.theguardian.com/global-development/201 7/apr/24/eu-urgent-protection-23000-unaccompanied-child-refugees-squalid-camps-greece-italy (accessed May 15, 2017).
Newberg, Paula, and Kathleen Newland. "Politics at the Heart: The Architecture of Humanitarian Assistance to Afghanistan." *Carnegie Endowment for International Peace*. July 2, 1999. https://carnegieendowment.org/1999/07/02/politics-at-heart-architecture-of-humanitarian-assistance-to-afghanistan-pub-686 (accessed June 8, 2018).
Newman, David. "On Borders and Power: A Theoretical Framework." *Journal of Borderlands Studies* 18, no. 1 (2011): 13–25.
Newport, Frank, and Igor Himelfarb. "Americans Least Favorable Toward Iran." *Gallup*. March 7, 2013. https://news.gallup.com/poll/161159/americans-least-favorable-tow ard-iran.aspx?g_source=link_NEWSV9&g_medium=TOPIC&g_campaign=item_&g_ content=Americans%2520Least%2520Favorable%2520Toward%2520Iran (accessed September 14, 2018).
Nguyen, Vinh-kim. "Government-by-Exception: Enrolment and Experimentality in Mass HIV Treatment Programmes in Africa." *Social Theory & Health* 7, no. 3 (2009): 196–217.
Nixon, Hamish. *The Changing Face of Local Governance: Community Development Councils in Afghanistan*. Working Paper Series, Kabul: Afghanistan Research and Evaluation Unit, 2008.
Noelle-Karimi, Christine. "Afghan Polities and the Indo-Persian Literary Realm: The Durrani Rulers and Their Portrayal in Eighteenth-Century Historiography." In *Afghan History through Afghan Eyes*, by Nile Green (ed.), 53–78. Oxford: Oxford University Press, 2016.
Nordland, Rod. "Afghan Pedophiles Get Free Pass From U.S. Military, Report Says." *The New York Times*. January 23, 2018. https://www.nytimes.com/2018/01/23/world/asia/ afghanistan-military-abuse.html?ref=todayspaper (accessed May 4, 2018).
Nowrasteh, Alex. *Terrorism and Immigration: A Risk Analysis*. No. 798, Washington, D.C.: The CATO Institute, 2016.
NSIA. *Afghanistan Provincial Profile*. Kabul: Islamic Republic of Afghanistan, National Statistics and Information Authority, 2018.
Nunan, Timothy. *Humanitarian Invasion: Global Development in Cold War Afghanistan*. Cambridge: Cambridge University Press, 2016.
O'Connel, Aaron B. (ed.). *Our Latest Longest War: Losing Hearts and Minds in Afghanistan*. Chicago, IL: The University of Chicago Press, 2017.
Olszewska, Zuzanna. *The Pearl of Dari: Poetry and Personhood among Young Afghans in Iran*. Bloomington, IN: Indiana University Press, 2015.
Omi, Michael, and Howard Winant. *Racial Formation in the United States: From the 1960s to the1980s*. London: Routledge and Kegan Paul, 1986.
Ong, Aihwa. *Neoliberalism as Exception: Mutations in Citizenship and Sovereignty*. Durham, NC: Duke University Press, 2006.
Osmani, Lutfudin, interview by Bojan Savić. *Interview with Danish Afghanistan Committee Herat Office Coordinator* (June 11, 2016).

Ó Tuathail, Gearóid. *Critical Geopolitics: The Politics of Writing Global Space*. London: Routledge, 1996.

Pajhwok. "Iran Ready to Export Gas to Afghanistan." *Pajhwok Afghan News*. February 2, 2015. http://mines.pajhwok.com/news/iran-ready-export-gas-afghanistan (accessed July 3, 2017).

Pakzad, Suraya, interview by Bojan Savić. *Interview with Voice of Women Organization (VWO) Founder* (June 12, 2016).

Pan, Jonathan. "Economic Violence: It's Time to Change the Game." *Military Review* 91, no. 3 (2011): 77–82.

Pandolfi, Mariella. "Laboratory of Intervention: The Humanitarian Governance of the Post-communist Balkan Territories." In *Postcolonial Disorders*, by Mary-Joe DelVecchio Good, Sandra Teresa Hyde, Sarah Pinto, and Byron Good (eds.), 157–188. Berkeley, CA: University of California Press, 2008.

Pennington, Matthew. "Pentagon Says War in Afghanistan Costs Taxpayers $45 Billion Per Year." *PS News Hour*. February 6, 2018. https://www.pbs.org/newshour/politics/pentagon-says-afghan-war-costs-taxpayers-45-billion-per-year (accessed February 8, 2018).

Peña, Charles V. "The Unintended Consequences of Unintended Casualties." *The National Interest*, July 14, 2016.

Perito, Robert M. *Afghanistan's Police: The Weak Link in Security Sector Reform*. Special Report, Washington, D.C.: The United States Institute of Peace, 2009.

Perito, Robert M. *The U.S. Experience with Provincial Reconstruction Teams in Afghanistan: Lessons Identified*. Special Report 152, Washington, D.C.: United States Institute of Peace, 2005.

Peters, Gretchen. *Seeds of Terror*. New York: St. Martin's Press, 2009.

Petrik, Jaroslav. "Provincial Reconstruction Teams in Afghanistan: Securitizing Aid through Developmentalizing the Military." In *The Securitization of Foreign Aid*, by Stephen Brown and Jörn Grävingholt (eds.), 163–187. Basingstoke: Palgrave Macmillan, 2016.

Petryna, Adriana. *When Experiments Travel: Clinical Trials and the Global Search for Human Subjects*. Princeton, NJ: Princeton University Press, 2009.

Phillips, James. "The Growing Threat of ISIS Unleashing a Weapon of Mass Destruction." *The Heritage Foundation*. February 19, 2016. https://www.heritage.org/missile-defense/commentary/the-growing-threat-isis-unleashing-weapon-mass-destruction (accessed August 2, 2017).

Piana, Valentino. "The 'Pattern Approach' to World Trade Structures and Their Dynamics." *Observing Trade: Revealing International Trade Networks (Conference)*. Princeton, NJ: Princeton Institute for International and Regional Studies, March 9, 2006.

Piotukh, Volha. *Biopolitics, Governmentality and Humanitarianism: 'Caring' for the Population in Afghanistan and Belarus*. London: Routledge, 2015.

Podelco, Grant. "Afghanistan: Herat's Treasures Can't Compensate for Atmosphere of Fear." *Radio Free Europe-Radio Liberty*. November 29, 2002. https://www.rferl.org/a/1101533.html (accessed May 3, 2018).

Porter, Patrick. *Military Orientalism: Eastern War Through Western Eyes*. New York: Columbia University Press, 2009.

Poyesh, Naeem, et al. *Child Notice Afghanistan*. New York: UNICEF, 2015. Pratt, Mary Louise. *Imperial Eyes*. London: Routledge, 2008.

President of the French Republic. *French White Paper: Defence and National Security*. Paris, 2013.

President of the United States of America. *A National Security Strategy for a Global Age*. Washington, D.C.: The White House, 2001.

President of the United States of America. *The National Security Strategy*. Washington, D.C.: The White House, 2002.
President of the United States of America. *The National Security Strategy*. Washington, D.C.: The White House, 2006.
President of the United States of America. *The National Security Strategy*. Washington, D.C.: The White House, 2010.
President of the United States of America. *The National Security Strategy*. Washington, D.C.: The White House, 2015.
President of the United States of America. *The National Security Strategy*. Washington, D.C.: The White House, 2017.
Prince, Erik D. "The MacArthur Model for Afghanistan." *The Wall Street Journal: Opinion*. May 31, 2017. https://www.wsj.com/articles/the-macarthur-model-for-afghanistan-1496269058 (accessed June 4, 2017).
Proglio, Gabriele, and Laura Odasso. *Border Lampedusa: Subjectivity, Visibility and Memory in Stories of Sea and Land*. Cham: Palgrave Macmillan, 2018.
Puar, Jasbir. *Terrorist Assemblages: Homonationalism in Queer Times*. Durham, NC: Duke University Press, 2007.
Pusateri, Anthony E., et al. *Metrics to Monitor Governance and Reconstruction in Afghanistan: Development of Measures of Effectiveness for Civil-Military Operations and a Standardized Tool to Monitor Governance Quality*. USACAPOC Technical Report 04–01, Fort Bragg, NC: United States Army Civil Affairs and Psychological Operations Command, 2004.
Qalanawi. "Herat Bids for UNESCO Status." *The Killid Group*. August 21, 2010. http://tkg.af/english/comments/viewpoint/233-herat-bids-for-unesco-status (accessed August 2, 2016).
Qiu, Linda. "Fact-Checking a Comparison of Gun Deaths and Terrorism Deaths." *Politifact*. October 5, 2015. https://www.politifact.com/truth-o-meter/statements/2015/oct/05/viral-image/fact-checking-comparison-gun-deaths-and-terrorism-/ (accessed June 22, 2017).
Quijano, Aníbal. "Coloniality of Power, Eurocentrism, and Latin America." *Nepantla: Views from South* 1, no. 3 (200): 533–580.
Rabinow, Paul. *French Modern: Norms and Forms of the Social Environment*. Chicago, IL: The University of Chicago Press, 1989.
Rabinow, Paul. "Introduction." In *The Foucault Reader*, by Paul Rabinow (ed.), 3–29. New York: Pantheon Books, 1984.
Radio Free Europe – Radio Liberty. "Afghan Child Rape Report Prompts Outrage But No Action." *Radio Free Europe – Radio Liberty*. September 22, 2015. https://www.rferl.org/a/afghan-chld-rape-report-prompts-outrage-but-no-official-action/27261810.html (accessed January 10, 2016).
Radio Free Europe-Radio Liberty. "Afghan Government Employee Accused of Spying for Iran." *Radio Free Europe-Radio Liberty: Radio Free Afghanistan*. January 15, 2018. https://www.rferl.org/a/afghanistan-iran-official-accused-spying/28976984.html (accessed January 18, 2018).
Radio Free Europe/Radio Liberty. "Afghanistan Executes Five Convicted of Murder, Kidnapping in Herat." November 30, 2017. https://www.ecoi.net/en/document/1420249.html (accessed December 4, 2017).
Rahimi, Mujib Rahman. *State Formation in Afghanistan: A Theoretical and Political History*. London: I.B.Tauris, 2017.

Rahimi, Qader Sayed Abdul, interview by Bojan Savić. *Interview with Afghanistan Independent Human Rights Commission (AIHRC) Regional Programme Manager,* Herat (May 29, 2016).
Rajan, Rajeswari Sunder. *Real and Imagined Women: Gender, Culture and Postcolonialism.* London: Routledge, 1993.
Rajan, Rajeswari Sunder, and You-me Park. "Postcolonial Feminism/ Postcolonialism and Feminism." In *A Companion to Postcolonial Studies*, by Henry Schwarz and Sangeeta Ray (eds.), 53–71. Malden, MA: Blackwell Publishing, 2000.
Rajan, S. Irudaya (ed). *South Asia Migration Report 2017: Recruitment, Remittances and Reintegration.* London: Routledge, 2017.
Ramin. "Hundreds of Afghans Flee Country through Nimroz Border Daily." *Centre for Conflict and Peace Studies Afghanistan.* November 8, 2017. http://www.caps.af/detail.asp?Lang=e&Cat=2&ContID=17050 (accessed November 26, 2017).
Ramraj, Victor V. Cambridge: Cambridge University Press, 2012.
Rao, Shobha, and Jan Turkstra. "Enhancing Security of Land Tenure for IDPs." *Forced Migration Review*, May 2014: 15–18.
Rashid, Ahmed. *Taliban: The Power of Militant Islam in Afghanistan and Beyond.* London: I.B.Tauris, 2010.
Rashid, Ahmed. "The Taliban: Exporting Extremism." *Foreign Affairs*, November/December 1999.
Rasmussen, Sune Engel. "Afghan Police Struggle as US Watchdog Finds Holes in Payroll Data." *The Guardian.* January 12, 2015. http://www.theguardian.com/world/2015/jan/12/afghanistan-police-payroll-data-watchdog-report (accessed January 13, 2015).
Rasmussen, Sune, and Luke Harding. "Foreign Tourists Attacked in Western Afghanistan." *The Guardian.* August 4, 2016. https://www.theguardian.com/world/2016/aug/04/foreign-tourists-attacked-in-western-afghanistan-says-officials (accessed August 5, 2016).
Redaelli, Silvia. *Research Study on IDPs in Urban Settings: Afghanistan.* Kabul: The World Bank & UNHCR, 2011.
Reid, Julian. "The Biopolitics of the War on Terror: A Critique of the 'Return of Imperialism' Thesis in International Relations." *Third World Quarterly* 26, no. 2 (2005): 237–252.
Remsen, William C. S., and Laura A. Tedesco. "US Cultural Diplomacy, Cultural Heritage Preservation and Development at the National Museum of Afghanistan in Kabul." In *Museums, Heritage and International Development*, by Paul Basu and Wayne Modest (eds.), 96–121. London: Routledge, 2015.
Rhodes, Lorna. "Panoptical Intimacies." *Public Culture* 10, no. 2 (1998): 285–311.
Richter-Montpetit, Melanie. "Empire, Desire and Violence: A Queer Transnational Feminist Reading of the Prisoner 'Abuse' in Abu Ghraib and the Question of 'Gender Equality.'" *International Feminist Journal of Politics* 9, no. 1 (2007): 38–59.
Riley, Robin L. *Depicting the Veil: Transnational Sexism and the War on Terror.* London: Zed Books, 2013.
Rivera, Ray. "Afghans Build Security, and Hope to Avoid Infiltrators." *The New York Times.* June 28, 2011. http://www.nytimes.com/2011/06/28/world/asia/28infiltrate.html (accessed April 10, 2012).
Rosas, Gilberto. "The Thickening Borderlands: Diffused Exceptionality and 'Immigrant' Social Struggles during the 'War on Terror.'" *Cultural Dynamics* 18, no. 3 (2006): 335–349.
Rosén, Frederik. *Collateral Damage: A Candid History of a Peculiar Form of Death.* London: C. Hurst & Co., 2016.

Rose, Nikolas. *Powers of Freedom: Reframing Political Thought*. Cambridge: Cambridge University Press, 1999.

Rose, Nikolas. *The Politics of Life Itself: Biomedicine, Power, and Subjectivity in the Twenty-First Century*. Princeton, NJ: Princeton University Press, 2007.

Rosenau, James N. "Governance in the Twenty-First Century." In *Palgrave Advances in Global Governance*, by Jim Whitman (ed.), 7–40. London: Palgrave Macmillan.

Rostami-Povey, Elaheh. *Afghan Women: Identity and Invasion*. London: Zed Books, 2007.

Rühle, Michael. "NATO 10 Years After: Learning the Lessons." *NATO Review*. 2011. https://www.nato.int/docu/review/2011/11-september/10-years-sept-11/EN/index.htm (accessed June 12, 2018).

Rubin, Barnett R. *Afghanistan From the Cold War Through the War on Terror*. Oxford: Oxford University Press, 2013.

Rubin, Barnett R. Afghanistan: The Forgotten Crisis. *WRITENET*. December 1, 1996, https://www.refworld.org/docid/3ae6a6c0c.html (accessed August 20 2018).

Rubin, Barnett R. "Peace Building and State-Building in Afghanistan: Constructing Sovereignty for Whose Security?" *Third World Quarterly* 27, no. 1 (2006): 175–185.

Ruiseñor-Escudero, Horacio, et al. "Risky Behavior and Correlates of HIV and Hepatitis C Virus Infection Among People Who Inject Drugs in Three Cities in Afghanistan." *Drug and Alcohol Dependence* 143, no. 1 (2014): 127–133.

Ruttig, Thomas. *Afghan Exodus: Afghan Asylum Seekers in Europe (1–3)*. Research Report, Kabul: Afghanistan Analysts Network, 2017.

Ruzza, Stefano. "Italy: Keeping or Selling Stocks?" In *Commercialising Security in Europe: Political Consequences for Peace Operations*, by Anna Leander (ed.), 181–201. London: Routledge, 2013.

Saber, Shapoor, interview by Bojan Savić. *Interview with Herati Journalist*. Herat, Herat Province, (Decembber 30, 2014).

Said, Edward. "Michel Foucault, 1926–1984." In *After Foucault: Humanistic Knowledge, Postmodern Challenges*, by Jonathan Arac (ed.), 1–11. New Brunswick: Rutgers University Press, 1988.

Said, Edward. *The World, the Text, and the Critic*. Cambridge, MA: Harvard University Press, 1983.

Said, Edward. Orientalism. New York: Pantheon Books, 1978.

Saidi, Abdul Rahim, interview by Bojan Savić. *Interview with a Senior Advisor to the Mayor of Herat* (June 12, 2016).

Saif, Shadi Khan. "Afghanistan Shuffles Border Security Control." *Anadolu Agency*. December 2, 2017. https://www.aa.com.tr/en/asia-pacific/afghanistan-shuffles-border-security-control/988131 (accessed January 16, 2018).

Sakhi, Tahir, interview by Bojan Savić. *Interview with United Nations Development Program (UNDP) Contact Person in Herat* (June 2, 2016).

Salamon, Gayle. *Assuming a Body: Transgender and Rhetorics of Materiality*. New York: Columbia University Press, 2010.

Samara, Tony Roshan. "Policing Development: Urban Renewal as Neo-Liberal Security Strategy." *Urban Studies* 47, no. 1 (2010): 197–214.

Samiem, Abdul Aziz, interview by Bojan Savić. *Interview with a National Democratic Institute Program Manager in Herat* (December 28, 2014).

Santana-Quintero, Mario, and Tarcis Stevens. *Metric Survey Tools in Recording: Mussalah Complex Herat and Minaret Jam, Afghanistan*. Mission Report, Paris: UNESCO: Division of Culture, 2002.

Sarwary, Feridun, interview by Bojan Savić. *Interview with the Dean of Herat Urban Development and Housing Department (HUDA)* (June 11, 2016).

Schroden, Jonathan. "Operations Assessment at ISAF: Changing Paradigms." In *Innovation in Operations Assessment: Recent Developments in Measuring Results in Conflict Environments*, by Andrew Williams, James Bexfield, Fabrizio Fitzgerald Farina, and Johannes de Nijs (eds.), 39–67. The Hague: NATO Communications and Information Agency, 2013.

Schuster, Liza. "Turning Refugees into 'Illegal Migrants': Afghan Asylum Seekers in Europe." *Ethnic and Racial Studies*, 2011: 1392–1407.

Scott, James C. *Domination and the Art of Resistance: Hidden Transcripts*. New Haven, CT: Yale University Press, 1990.

Scott, James C. *Seeing Like a State: How Certain Schemes to Improve the Human Condition Have Failed*. New Haven, CT: Yale University Press, 1998.

Scott, James C. *Weapons of the Weak: Everyday Forms of Peasant Resistance*. New Haven, CT: Yale University Press, 1985.

Scott, Peter Dale. *Drugs, Oil, and War: The United States in Afghanistan, Colombia, and Indochina*. Lanham, MD: Rowman & Littlefield Publishers, 2003.

Sellers-García, Sylvia. *Distance and Documents at the Spanish Empire's Periphery*. Stanford, CA: Stanford University Press, 2014.

Sexton, Renard. "Aid as a Tool against Insurgency: Evidence from Contested and Controlled Territory in Afghanistan." *American Political Science Review* 110, no. 4 (2016): 731–749.

Sharfyar, Sharafuddin. "Afghanistan Says Nine Migrants Killed by Iranian Border Guards." May 11, 2013. https://www.reuters.com/article/us-afghanistan-iran-migrants-idUS BRE94A09H20130511 (accessed November 6, 2014).

Shawki, Noha, and Michaelene Cox (eds.). *Negotiating Sovereignty and Human Rights: Actors and Issues in Contemporary Human Rights Politics*. Farnham: Ashgate Publishing, 2009.

Sharifi, Shoaib, and Louise Adamou. "Taliban Threaten 70% of Afghanistan, BBC Finds." *BBC News*. January 31, 2018. https://www.bbc.com/news/world-asia-42863116 (accessed March 22, 2018).

Shirdelian, Ali. "Iran-Afghan Economies Tied by One-Way Trade." *Financial Tribune*. August 22, 2017. https://financialtribune.com/articles/economy-business-and-market s/70824/iran-afghan-economies-tied-by-one-way-trade (accessed August 29, 2017).

Shopkeeper 1, interview by Bojan Savić. *Interview with Local Musalla Shopkeeper* (June 5, 2016).

Shopkeeper 2, interview by Bojan Savić. *Interview with Local Musalla Shopkeeper* (June 5, 2016).

Shukran, Shoaib Tanha, and Hamed Kohistani. "Weak Rights Mechanisms Fail Afghan Children." *Rawa News*. February 23, 2014. http://www.rawa.org/temp/runews/201 4/02/23/weak-rights-mechanisms-fail-afghan-children.phtml (accessed August 10, 2016).

Sieff, Kevin. "Afghans to Spy on Own Troops to Stop 'Insider' Attacks." *The Washington Post*. August 20, 2012. https://www.washingtonpost.com/world/asia_pacific/afghans-to-spy-on-own-troops-to-stop-insider-attacks/2012/08/20/e9f93ea8-eafd-11e1-866f-60 a00f604425_story.html (accessed May 13, 2013).

Sieff, Kevin. "In Model Afghan City, Kidnappings Surge." *The Washington Post*. April 24, 2013. https://www.washingtonpost.com/world/asia_pacific/in-model-afghan-city-kidnappings-surge/2013/04/24/2cf88976-a6b4-11e2-9e1c-bb0fb0c2edd9_story.html?utm_term=.d5cd7824410d (accessed March 5, 2017).

Simons, Jonathan. *Foucault and the Political*. London: Routledge, 2002.
Singh, Danny. "Corruption and Clientelism in the Lower Levels of the Afghan Police." *Conflict, Security and Development* 14, no. 5 (2014): 621–650.
Sivanandan, A. "Poverty Is the New Black: An Introduction." *Race and Class* 43, no. 2 (2001): 1–5.
Smedley, Edward, Hugh J. Rose, and Henry J. Rose. *Encyclopaedia Metropolitana: Miscellaneous and Lexicographical*. London: Baldwin and Cradock, 1845.
Smith, Neil. "New Globalism, New Urbanism: Gentrification as Global Urban Strategy." *Antipode: A Radical Journal of Geography* 34, no. 3 (2002): 427–450.
Snesarev, Andrei Evgenievich. *Afghanistan: Preparing for the Bolshevik Incursion into Afghanistan and Attack on India, 1919–20*. Stroud: Helion & Company, 2014.
Sohail, Mohammad, interview by Bojan Savić. *Interview with National Solidarity Programme Provincial Manager in Herat*. Herat, Herat Province (December 28, 2014).
Sopko, John. *Afghanistan Reconstruction Trust Fund: The World Bank Needs to Improve How it Monitors Implementation, Shares Information, and Determines the Impact of Donor Contributions*. SIGAR 18-42 Audit Report, Arlington, VA: Special Inspector General for Afghanistan Reconstruction (SIGAR), 2018b.
Sopko, John. *Reconstructing the Afghan National Defense and Security Forces: Lessons From the U.S. Experience in Afghanistan*. Arlington, VA: Special Inspector General for Afghanistan Reconstruction, 2017.
Sopko, John. SIGAR Report, Arlington, VA: Special Inspector General for Afghanistan Reconstruction, 2018c.
Sopko, John. *Special Inspector General for Afghanistan Reconstruction (SIGAR) Quarterly Report to the United States Congress*. Arlington, VA: SIGAR, 2013.
Sopko, John. *Special Inspector General for Afghanistan Reconstruction (SIGAR): Quarterly Report to the United States Congress*. Arlington, VA: SIGAR, 2015.
Sopko, John. *Special Inspector General for Afghanistan Reconstruction (SIGAR) Report to the United States Congress*. Quarterly Report: October, Arlington, VA, 2018a.
Spivak, Gayatri Chakravorty. *A Critique of Postcolonial Reason: Toward a History of the Vanishing Present*. Cambridge, MA: Harvard University Press, 1999.
Spivak, Gayatri Chakravorty. "Can the Subaltern Speak?" In *Marxism and the Interpretation of Culture*, by Cary Nelson and Lawrence Grossberg, 271–313. Basingstoke: Macmillan Education, 1988b.
Spivak, Gayatri Chakravorty. *Outside in the Teaching Machine*. London: Routledge, 1993.
Spivak, Gayatri Chakravorty. "Righting Wrongs." *The South Atlantic Quarterly* 103, no. 2/3 (2004): 523–581.
Spivak, Gayatri Chakravorty. "Subaltern Studies: Deconstructing Historiography." In *Selected Subaltern Studies*, by Ranajit Guha and Gayatri Chakravorty Spivak, 3–34. Oxford: Oxford University Press, 1988a.
Spencer, Jack, and Ha Nguyen. "Are We Safer Today Than Before 9/11?" *The Brookings Institution*. September 10, 2003. https://www.heritage.org/homeland-security/report/are-we-safer-today-911 (accessed June 11, 2018).
Spencer, Stephen. *Race and Ethnicity: Culture, Identity and Representation*. London: Routledge, 2014.
Sperling, James, and Mark Webber. "Security Governance in Europe: A Return to System." *European Security* 23, no. 2 (2014): 126–144.
Stancati, Margherita. "Afghan City Rises as Opposition Hub." *The Wall Street Journal*. March 15, 2015. http://www.wsj.com/articles/afghan-city-rises-as-opposition-hub-1426463328 (accessed March 15, 2015).

Stanikzai, Abdul Khaliq, interview by Bojan Savić. *Interview with Sanyee Development Organization (SDO) Herat Regional Office Manager* (May 26, 2016).
Steeb, Randall, et al. *Perspectives on the Battle of Wanat: Challenges Facing Small Unit Operations in Afghanistan.* Santa Monica, CA: RAND Corporation, 2011.
'Steinhäusler, Friedrich. "Terrorist Threats to NATO Countries: A Bestiary." *NATO Review*. April 2007. https://www.nato.int/docu/review/2007/Reviewing_Riga/Terrorist_threads_NATO_countries/EN/index.htm (accessed June 11, 2018).
Stern, Jessica. *The Ultimate Terrorists.* Cambridge, MA: Harvard University Press, 2001.
Stigter, Elca. *Transnational Networks and Migration from Herat to Iran.* Kabul: The Afghanistan Research and Evaluation Unit (AREU), 2005.
Stoler, Ann L. *Carnal Knowledge and Imperial Power: Race and the Intimate in Colonial Rule.* Berkeley, CA: University of California Press, 2002.
Stoler, Ann L. *Race and the Education of Desire: Foucault's History of Sexuality and the Colonial Order of Things.* Durham, NC: Duke University Press, 1995.
Strand, Arne, Kaja Borchgrevink, and Kristian Berg Harpviken. *Afghanistan: A Political Economy Analysis.* Oslo: Norwegian Institute of International Affairs, 2017.
Szanya, Thomas S., et al. *Integrating Civilian Agencies in Stability Operations.* Santa Monica, CA: RAND Corporation, 2009.
Tamboukou, Maria. "A Foucauldian Approach to Narratives." In *Doing Narrative Research*, by Molly Andrews, Corinne Squire, and Maria Tamboukou, 88–107. London: Sage Publications, 2013.
Tan, Vivian, and Rupert Colville. "Key Repatriation Agreement Signed Between Iran, Afghanistan and UNHCR." *UNHCR News*. April 3, 2002. http://www.unhcr.org/news/latest/2002/4/3cab30fd4/key-repatriation-agreement-signed-iran-afghanistan-unhcr.html (accessed July 12, 2017).
Tellier, Etienne. "Herat – Musalla Complex." *Iconem: Projects*. April 18, 2016. http://iconem.com/herat-musalla-complex/ (accessed May 30, 2016).
The Telegraph. "Terrorist Groups Planning Another 9/11-Style Attack, Top US Official Warns." *The Telegraph*. October 19, 2017. https://www.telegraph.co.uk/news/2017/10/19/terrorist-groups-planning-another-911-style-attack-top-us-official/ (accessed November 23, 2017).
The United States Army Intelligence Center of Excellence. "Human Terrain System." *Military Intelligence Professional Bulletin (MIPB)*. Vol. 37. no. 4. Fort Huachuca, AZ: The United States Army Intelligence Center of Excellence, October–December 2011.
The United States Department of State. *Afghanistan 2013 Human Rights Report.* Annual Report, Washington, D.C.: The United States Department of State, 2014.
The United States Department of State. *Afghanistan 2015 Human Rights Report.* Annual Report, Washington, D.C.: The United States Department of State, 2016.
The World Bank. *Afghanistan Country Update*, Washington, D.C.: The World Bank Group, October 2018a.
The World Bank. *Economy Profile Afghanistan*. Doing Business 2019, Washington, D.C.: The World Bank Group, 2018b.
The World Bank Group. "Afghanistan Trade at a Glance: Most Recent Values." *World Integrated Trade Solution*. January 3, 2017. http://wits.worldbank.org/CountrySnapshot/en/AFG (accessed August 4, 2017).
Thier, Alexander, and Azita Ranjbar. *Killing Friends, Making Enemies: The Impact and Avoidance of Civilian Casualties in Afghanistan.* Peace Brief, Washington, D.C.: United States Institute of Peace, 2008.

Thobani, Sunera. "White Wars: Western Feminisms and the 'War on Terror.'" *Feminist Theory* 8, no. 2 (2007): 169–185.
Thompson, Carl, interview by Institute for Defense and Government Advancement (IDGA) Editorial Staff. *Winning in Afghanistan: Podcast with Captain Carl Thompson.* New York, NY, (May 11, 2010).
Thorson, Jane E. *Forgotten No More: Male Child Trafficking In Afghanistan.* Charlotte, NC: Hagar International, 2013.
Tirard-Collet, Olivier. "After the War. The Condition of Historical Buildings and Monuments in Herat, Afghanistan." *Iran* 36 (1998): 123–138.
Tierney, John F. *Warlord, Inc. Extortion and Corruption Along the U.S. Supply Chain in Afghanistan.* Report of the Majority Staff to the Subcommittee on National Security and Foreign Affairs, Committee on Oversight and Government Reform. Washington, D.C.: U.S. House of Representatives, 2010.
Tober, Diane. "'My Body Is Broken Like My Country': Identity, Nation, and Repatriation among Afghan Refugees in Iran." *Iranian Studies* 40, no. 2 (2007): 263–285.
TOLONews. "Ghani Suspends Herat Mayor over Residents' Complaints." *TOLO News.* May 28, 2017. https://www.tolonews.com/index.php/afghanistan/ghani-suspends-herat-mayor-over-residents%E2%80%99-complaints (accessed June 19, 2017).
TOLONews. "Iranian Drug Smuggler Arrested in Herat." *TOLONews.* July 5, 2012. https://www.tolonews.com/afghanistan/iranian-drug-smuggler-arrested-herat (accessed August 10, 2017).
TOLONews."Taliban Attack Herat District." *TOLOnews.* May 12, 2015. http://www.tolonews.com/en/afghanistan/19481-taliban-attack-herat-district (accessed May 16, 2015).
Toscano, Roberto. *Iran's Role in Afghanistan.* Barcelona: Barcelona Centre for International Affairs, 2012.
Toukan, Abdullah, and Anthony Cordesman. *Terrorism and WMD the Link with the War in Afghanistan.* Washington, D.C.: Center for Strategic & International Studies, 2009.
Towghi, Fouzieyha, and Kalindi Vora. "Bodies, Markets, and the Experimental in South Asia." *Ethnos: Journal of Anthropology* 79, no. 1 (2014): 1–18.
Trofimov, Yaroslav. "U.N. Maps Out Afghan Security." *The Wall Street Journal.* December 26, 2010. http://www.wsj.com/articles/SB10001424052970203568004576043842922347526 (accessed February 5, 2014).
Turner, Mandy, and Florian P. Kühn. "Introduction: The Tyranny of Peace and the Politics of International Intervention." In *The Politics of International Intervention: The Tyranny of Peace*, by Mandy Turner and Florian P. Kühn (eds.), 1–18. London: Routledge, 2016.
Twining, Dan. "The Stakes in Afghanistan Go Well Beyond Afghanistan." *Foreign Policy.* September 30, 2009. https://foreignpolicy.com/2009/09/30/the-stakes-in-afghanistan-go-well-beyond-afghanistan/ (accessed June 22, 2016).
Ulrichsen, Kristian Coates. *The United Arab Emirates: Power, Politics and Policy-Making.* London: Routledge, 2017.
UN Office on Drugs and Crime. *Afghanistan Opium Survey 2007.* Executive Summary, Vienna: UN Office on Drugs and Crime, 2007.
UN Office on Drugs and Crime. *Afghanistan Opium Survey 2015: Cultivation and Production.* Vienna: UN Office on Drugs and Crime, 2015.
UN Office on Drugs and Crime. *Afghanistan Opium Survey 2017: Cultivation and Production.* Vienna: UN Office on Drugs and Crime, 2017.
UN Office of Drugs and Crime. *Financial Flows Linked to the Illicit Production and Trafficking of Afghan Opiates.* Vienna: UN Office of Drugs and Crime, 2008.

UN Security Council. "UN Security Council Resolution S/RES/1377." New York, November 12, 2001a.
UN Security Council. "UN Security Council Resolution S/RES/1378." New York, November 14, 2001b.
UN Security Council. "UN Security Council Resolution S/RES/1383." New York, December 6, 2001c.
UN Security Council. "UN Security Council Resolution S/RES/1401." New York, March 28, 2002.
UN Security Council. "Security Council Resolution S/RES/1536." New York, March 26, 2004.
UN Security Council. "UN Security Council Resolution S/RES/1589." New York, March 24, 2005.
UN Security Council. "UN Security Council Resolution S/RES/2145." New York, March 17, 2014.
UN Security Council. "Security Council Resolution S/RES/2405." New York, March 8, 2018.
UNAMA Human Rights Service. *Afghanistan: Protection of Civilians in Armed Conflict. Annual Report 2017*. Annual Report, Kabul: United Nations Assistance Mission in Afghanistan, 2018a.
UNAMA Human Rights Service. *Midyear Update on the Protection of Civilians in Armed Conflict: 1 January to 30 June 2018*. Midyear Report, Kabul: United Nations Assistance Mission in Afghanistan, 2018b.
UNDP. *Human Development Indices and Indicators: 2018 Statistical Update: Afghanistan*. New York: United Nations Development Programme, 2018.
UNDP-A Interviewee, interview by Bojan Savić. *Interview with United Nations Development Programme in Afghanistan Employee* (June 2, 2016).
UNESCO. "Cultural Heritage and Development Initiatives: A Challenge or a Contribution to Sustainability?" Conference Proceedings. Rome: UNESCO, 2016.
UNESCO Expert Working Group on the Preservation of Jam and Herat ICCROM. *3rd Expert Working Group Meeting for the Old City of Herat and the Archeological Remains of Jam World Heritage Property*. Working Group Report, Turin: UNESCO World Heritage Centre, 2012.
UNESCO Office in Kabul. "The Gawhar Shad Mausoleum in Herat Stabilized for the Future." *United Nations Educational, Scientific and Cultural Organization*. March 27, 2012. http://www.unesco.org/new/en/kabul/about-this-office/single-view/news/the_gawhar_shad_mausoleum_in_herat_stabilized_for_the_future/#.V7oWX44iX1o (accessed May 26, 2016).
UNESCO Office in Kabul. "UNESCO, Government of Afghanistan and Herat's Community Representatives Agree to Work Together to Help Safeguard Herat's Extraordinarily Rich Cultural Heritage." *United Nations Educational, Scientific and Cultural Organization*. July 30, 2014. http://www.unesco.org/new/en/kabul/about-this-office/single-view/news/unesco_government_of_afghanistan_and_herats_community_representatives_agree_to_work_together_to_help_safeguard_herats_extraordinarily_rich_cultural_heritage/#.V8PHMI4iX1o (accessed May 29, 2016).
UNFPA. *Annual Report 2017: Afghanistan*. Kabul: United Nations Population Fund in Afghanistan, 2017.
UNHCR. *Background Report: Herat Province*. Geneva: UNHCR, 1990.
UNHCR. *Report of the United Nations High Commissioner for Refugees A/47/12*. New York: United Nations, 1992.

UNHCR. *Briefing Note: UNHCR Sub-Office in Mashhad, Khorassan Province, The Islamic Republic of Iran.* Mashhad: UNHCR, 2004.

UNHCR. *Solutions Strategy for Afghan Refugees to Support Voluntary Repatriation, Sustainable Reintegration and Assistance to Host Countries.* Portfolio of Projects, Geneva: UNHCR, 2015.

United Nations Assistance Mission in Afghanistan and Office of the United Nations High Commissioner for Human Rights. *Treatment of Conflict-Related Detainees: Implementation of Afghanistan's National Plan on the Elimination of Torture.* Annual Report, Kabul: UNAMA and OHCHR, 2017.

United States Geological Survey. "Narrative Descriptions of Earthquakes in Afghanistan 819–2000." United States Geological Survey, Pasadena Office. https://pasadena.wr.usgs.gov/office/hough/roger.html (accessed July 19, 2016).

UNODC Interviewee 1. Interview by Bojan Savić. *Anonymous United Nations Office on Drugs and Crime (UNODC) Official in Herat* (May 30, 2016).

Urquhart, Cathy. *Grounded Theory for Qualitative Research: A Practical Guide.* London: Sage Publications, 2013.

US Department of Defense. *Enhancing Security and Stability in Afghanistan.* Report to Congress, Arlington, VA: US Department of Defense, 2017.

US Department of Defense. *Report on Progress Toward Security and Stability in Afghanistan.* Arlington, VA: US Department of Defense, 2012.

US Department of Defense. *Report on Progress Toward Security and Stability in Afghanistan.* Arlington, VA: US Department of Defense, 2014.

US Department of Defense. *United States Plan for Sustaining the Afghanistan National Security Forces.* Arlington, VA: US Department of Defense, 2008.

US Foreign Service Officer in Herat, interview by Charles Stuart Kennedy. *Afghanistan Experience Project Interview* (March 22, 2005).

Vaughan-Williams, Nick. *Border Politics: The Limits of Sovereign Power.* Edinburgh: Edinburgh University Press, 2009.

Walia, Harsha. *Undoing Border Imperialism.* Oakland, CA: AK Press, 2013.

Wallerstein, Immanuel. *The Modern World-System, IV: Centrist Liberalism Triumphant, 1789–1914.* San Francisco: University of California Press, 2011.

Wallerstein, Immanuel. *World-Systems Analysis: An Introduction.* Durham, NC: Duke University Press, 2004.

Ward, Christopher, David Mansfield, Peter Oldham, and William Byrd. *Afghanistan: Economic Incentives and Development Initiatives to Reduce Opium Production.* Washington, D.C.: The World Bank Group, 2008.

Watson, Leon. "Dragged off by the Police: Afghan Insurgents Try to Evade Capture by Disguising Themselves as Women." *Daily Mail.* November 20, 2012. http://www.dailymail.co.uk/news/article-2235676/Afghan-insurgents-tried-evade-capture-disguising-womens-clothing.html (accessed June 22, 2017).

Welch, Michael. "Counterveillance: How Foucault and the Groupe d'Information sur les Prisons Reversed the Optics." *Theoretical Criminology* 5, no. 3 (2011): 301–313.

Wellman, Phillip Walter. "US Drops More Bombs in Afghanistan Than Iraq and Syria for First Time in 4 Years." *Stars and Stripes.* April 19, 2018. https://www.stripes.com/news/us-drops-more-bombs-in-afghanistan-than-iraq-and-syria-for-first-time-in-4-years-1.522810 (accessed April 27, 2018).

Williams, Brian Glyn. "Mullah Omar's Missiles: A Field Report on Suicide Bombers in Afghanistan." *Middle East Policy* 15, no. 4 (2008): 26–46.

Williams, Zoe. "Katie Hopkins Calling Migrants Vermin Recalls the Darkest Events of History." *The Guardian.* April 19, 2015. https://www.theguardian.com/commentisfre

e/2015/apr/19/katie-hopkins-migrants-vermin-darkest-history-drownings (accessed September 27, 2018).
Wimpelmann, Torunn. *The Pitfalls of Protection: Gender, Violence, and Power in Afghanistan*. Oakland, CA: University of California Press, 2017.
Woody, Christopher. "The US Is on Pace to Bomb Afghanistan More Than Ever This Year." *Business Insider*. June 20, 2018. https://www.businessinsider.com/us-bombing-afghanistan-at-record-pace-but-no-end-date-in-sight-2018-6 (accessed June 24, 2018).
Yama, Nader. Interview by Bojan Savić. *Interview with a Deputy Minister at the Independent Directorate of Local Governance* (December 23, 2014).
Yari, Obidullah. Interview by Bojan Savić. *Interview with Deputy Head of the Craftsmen's Union of Herat* (January 1, 2015).
Yate, Charles Edward. *Northern Afghanistan; or Letters from the Afghan Boundary Commission*. Edinburgh: William Blackwood and Sons, 1888.
Young, Robert. *Empire, Colony, Postcolony*. Malden, MA: Wiley Publishers, 2015.
Young, Robert. *Postcolonialism: An Historical Introduction*. Malden, MA: Blackwell, 2001.
Zaheer, Abasin. "Efforts on to Identify Insurgents Infiltrating Forces." *Pajhwok Afghan Network*. April 6, 2011. http://www.pajhwok.com/en/2011/04/06/efforts-identify-insurgents-infiltrating-forces (accessed May 5, 2013).
Zajc, Srečko, interview by Bojan Savić. *Interview with Former Slovenian Ministry of Defense Official in Provincial Reconstruction Team-Herat* (November 30, 2014).
Zakaria, Fareed. "It's Time to Get Out of Afghanistan. Here's How." *The Washington Post*. August 2, 2018. https://www.washingtonpost.com/opinions/its-time-to-get-out-of-afghanistan-heres-how/2018/08/02/afe21708-9691-11e8-810c-5fa705927d54_story.html?utm_term=.f36f288fd910 (accessed August 4, 2018).
Zeyaratjaye, Jawid. "Kidnappers Kill Three Herat Customs Officials." *TOLO News*. September 19, 2017. https://www.tolonews.com/afghanistan/kidnappers-kill-three-herat-customs-officials (accessed September 21, 2017).

Index

abnormal(ities) 3–5, 18, 24, 32, 38, 46–7, 57–8, 61, 63–4, 68, 113–14, 137, 140, 159, 172, 200, 202
abuse 12, 16, 29, 52, 55, 114–15, 118, 127–9, 131, 135–7, 141–2, 151, 165, 169–71, 178, 180, 194, 201
Afghan Air Force (AAF) 23, 72, 74, 97, 101, 110
Afghan Border Police (ABP) 74, 147, 163–5, 170–1, 173, 182, 194
Afghan Boundary Commission 8, 54
Afghani (currency) (AFN) 78, 134
Afghanistan Human Rights Organization (AHRO) 129, 164
Afghan National Army (ANA) 70, 74–7, 89, 95, 97, 100–1, 103–4, 110, 147, 163, 173, 179
Afghan National Police (ANP) 74, 98–9, 100–1, 136, 147, 163, 173, 194
Afghan National Security Forces (ANSF) 12, 16, 27, 34–5, 39, 44, 47, 69–70, 73–7, 80–1, 83–4, 89–92, 96–103, 105, 109, 118, 122, 136, 163, 183–7, 200
afghanophobia 151
Agamben, Giorgio 86, 115, 149, 153, 160, 167, 177–8, 195
agonism(s) 29–30, 45, 185–6
aid, foreign aid 4, 13–15, 34, 39, 41, 56, 62–3, 67, 75, 77, 79, 80–1, 82, 84, 106–7, 122, 139, 155–6, 200, 202
aleatory 22, 24, 83, 98
Al-Qaeda 58–9, 64–5, 67, 84, 92
Amayesh 150–1
ambivalence, ambivalent 7, 36, 40, 42–4, 52, 68, 91–4, 98–9, 103, 110, 180, 185–6, 194
American 3–4, 38, 46–8, 58–9, 61, 64–7, 76–7, 90, 93–4, 97, 100, 102, 105–7, 109, 111, 183, 184, 186
Anglo-Afghan War (First, Second, and Third) 9, 51, 150

anomalous 113
anthropology, anthropological 13, 29, 39, 47–9, 121–2, 148, 157
apparatus 3–5, 16, 18, 34–5, 37, 40–1, 43, 46–7, 49, 73–5, 77, 79–81, 83–4, 89–94, 98, 100, 102–4, 107–10, 115–20, 124, 127, 138, 140–3, 148, 160, 168, 170, 172–4, 176–7, 179, 181–2, 186, 189, 192, 194–5, 200, 202
Arab(s), Arabic 155, 160
architectural, architecture 34, 53, 55, 112, 114, 118, 121–2, 124, 166
asylum 35, 71, 146
axe(s) of difference/inequality 12, 29–31, 37, 147, 194

background (representations) 47–9, 53, 58
backward(ness) 33, 46–7, 49–51, 53–6
Badghis 71, 128, 133, 172
Barakzai, the 8, 48
bare life 115, 149, 160, 178
bareness 153
bazaar(s) 44, 54, 142–3, 147, 162–3, 172
benefit(s), beneficial 9–10, 12–14, 25, 67, 81, 83, 85, 93–4, 98, 100–1, 104–6, 108, 112–13, 117, 142–3, 150, 153, 155, 156, 163, 174–5, 177–8, 192
Bhabha, Homi 6, 36, 40, 42–4, 91–2, 94, 98–9, 110, 180, 185–6, 194–5
binary, binaries 11, 18, 24, 37, 40–3, 60, 73, 85, 98, 114, 132, 137, 139–40, 158–9, 179
biological, biology 18, 28, 32–3, 65, 135, 138, 143
biopolitical, biopolitics 22, 26, 28, 31–4, 37, 74, 80, 118, 138, 149, 154, 157–60, 178, 193–4
body 3–5, 12–15, 18, 21–4, 26–35, 42, 50, 58, 60–1, 63, 68, 70, 74, 77, 79, 86, 93, 99, 107, 114–15, 117, 120, 136–7, 142, 144, 153–4, 161, 165–7, 167–9,

169, 171, 173–4, 177–8, 184, 186–7, 191, 194, 201–2
Bonilla-Silva, Eduardo 31–3
border 5, 9, 10–14, 16, 18, 26, 38, 44, 50, 63, 75, 121, 146–51, 154, 158–82, 184–6, 188–95, 200
bourgeoisie(s) 25, 35, 156, 174, 178, 185
British 7, 9, 14, 36, 46–51, 53–5, 58–9, 61, 112, 121, 125, 150, 171, 173
British East India Company (BEIC) 7, 48
brown(ness) 4, 18, 21, 22, 33–4, 37, 39, 44, 47, 58, 63, 68, 72–3, 77–9, 83, 86, 92, 148, 159–60, 171–3, 175, 177–8, 185, 194, 199–202

café(s) 162, 164, 166, 168–9, 179, 181–2, 184, 187, 192
calculus 10, 25, 27, 34, 62, 68, 70, 82, 84–6, 94–5, 98–9, 105, 116, 144, 153, 161, 177, 178
capitalism, capitalist 13, 25, 30, 34, 37, 39, 48, 103, 119, 138, 152–3, 156, 174–5
care 10–11, 13, 15–17, 19, 23–4, 29, 35, 60, 76, 89, 96, 98, 102, 104, 107, 113, 115, 121, 126, 129–30, 132, 133, 136–7, 139, 141, 143–4, 152–3, 158, 160, 164–5, 195
chador(s) 57, 167–8, 170
checkpoint 13, 16, 26, 44, 70, 95, 148, 163–4, 167–8, 170–1, 174, 179, 182, 189
child(ren) 22, 27, 60, 71–2, 76, 85, 95, 102, 121, 124–5, 128–9, 134–6, 138–9, 151, 164–5, 167–8, 171
civilized, civilization, civilizational 5, 33, 35–6, 38, 49–51, 54, 63, 79, 115, 120, 122–3, 140–4, 149, 160, 166, 178, 193
civil society 14, 16, 73, 78–9, 89, 141, 165, 180, 186, 201
class(es), classed 4–5, 12, 14–15, 17–18, 21, 22, 25, 30–3, 35, 37–40, 44, 46, 57–8, 63–4, 68–9, 82, 109, 116, 118, 119, 134, 147–9, 152–4, 156–7, 159–60, 162, 170, 174, 177–9, 185, 187, 190, 193–4
clothes 3, 50, 124–6, 132, 161, 164, 175

coercive, coercion 27–8, 34, 48, 73–4, 76–7, 80, 83, 85, 99, 118, 120, 141–2, 200, 202
collateral damage 5, 12, 22–3, 59, 72, 85–6
colonialism, colonial, colonies, colonize, colony 3, 7, 9, 14, 15–16, 32–3, 35–9, 41–3, 47–54, 56–8, 61, 85, 89, 93–5, 121, 148–50, 157, 159–60, 180, 191
coloniality 37, 152
commerce, commercial 10, 26, 62, 83, 116, 133, 141, 147, 162, 170–1, 174–6, 179, 187, 189, 193–4
Community Development Council (CDC) 76–7, 84, 108
conditional(ity) 5, 14, 22, 34, 77, 80–1, 158, 200
conduct(s) 4, 9–10, 15–17, 22–4, 26–30, 35, 39, 50, 63, 69, 73, 74, 76, 79, 81, 83, 90, 113, 115, 117, 120, 137–8, 144, 146, 156, 177, 184–5, 187, 191
contain(ment) 9, 14, 18, 24, 30, 33, 39, 46–7, 51, 58, 60, 63, 65, 75–8, 84, 102, 112, 118, 148, 158, 172, 178, 199–202
cooperation, cooperative, cooperativeness 10, 12, 14, 16, 29, 39, 73, 77, 114, 123–4, 140, 143, 152, 154, 156, 170, 187, 193–4, 200
coordination 10–11, 80, 173
core 149, 154–7, 160, 166, 168, 171, 174–5, 178
corporate 14, 39, 73, 77, 114, 123–4, 140, 152, 154, 156, 170, 193–4, 200
corporeal, corporeality 5, 18, 22, 26, 28–30, 37, 46, 50, 60, 69, 72–3, 118, 148, 158–9, 169, 199
cost(s), costly 10–11, 13, 25–6, 28, 34, 44, 75, 81, 83, 85, 98, 105–6, 137–8, 143–4, 151, 153, 155, 178, 194
counter-exploit, counter-exploitation 4, 18, 40, 43–4, 73, 86, 91, 93–4, 96, 103, 105, 110–11, 187, 200–1
counterinsurgency 5, 11–12, 39, 72, 77, 79, 84–5, 92, 190, 200
counter-maps 189, 192, 195
counter-surveillance, counter-surveil(ling) 149, 172, 180, 188, 190–2, 194, 200

counterterrorism   5, 12, 39, 85, 92
cultivate, cultivation   4, 8, 27–9, 52, 57, 92, 111, 118, 120, 142, 172, 194
culture, cultural   4–10, 14, 26, 29–30, 33–4, 35–8, 41, 44, 52, 54–5, 57, 79–80, 94, 96, 99, 103, 105, 109, 112–20, 122–4, 126–7, 133, 138–44, 147–50, 156–8, 162, 165, 167, 180, 181, 184, 186, 192, 193
customs   29, 89, 147, 162, 174–5

Daesh   5, 65, 91–2, 99, 147
Dari   48, 104–5, 107
death(s)   21, 28, 32, 37, 66, 71–2, 82, 84–6, 90, 96, 99–100, 105, 133, 149, 179
de Certeau, Michel   41–4, 91, 94, 96, 165, 180
democracy, democratic   15, 37, 49, 60, 186
desire(s)   15, 23–4, 27–9, 43–4, 76, 79, 85, 93, 96, 115, 140, 149, 156–7, 167, 186, 190, 193, 199, 201
development   3–5, 9, 14, 16, 18, 21–2, 26, 33, 36, 39, 42–4, 46–7, 51, 55, 60, 62, 67–9, 73–82, 89–90, 92–3, 98, 102, 104, 107–12, 114, 123, 140, 142–4, 155–6, 175, 180, 199–200, 202
deviant   26, 29, 113–15, 118, 175
difference, differential, differentiate   8–9, 12, 14–15, 17, 21–2, 28, 31, 33, 36–7, 40–1, 43–4, 51–2, 60, 67, 85–6, 115, 129, 133, 136, 142–4, 149–52, 156–8, 160–2, 165–7, 169, 172, 177–8, 184–6, 188, 192–3
differentiate, differentiation   9, 14–15, 28, 31, 36, 37, 44, 51, 60, 133, 142–4, 149–52, 156, 158, 160, 166, 188, 192–3
disabled   12, 71, 78, 118
discipline, disciplinary   16, 18, 21, 22, 24–31, 34–5, 37, 39, 46, 74–6, 79, 82, 93, 95–7, 99, 111, 114, 117–18, 130, 148, 150, 152, 154, 158, 163, 169–74, 176, 179–80, 184–5, 188, 191, 194, 199–202
disease(s)   25, 51, 57, 60 67, 114, 118, 130, 133, 137–8
dispossessed   4, 22, 37, 149, 178, 187, 194

district(s)   27, 57, 69, 71–2, 81, 104, 128, 133, 151, 161
docile, docility   24, 26, 28–9, 119, 158–9, 188, 195, 201
Dogharoon   166–7, 173, 193–4
dominance, domination, dominate   4–6, 8–9, 11, 15, 18, 22–5, 29–31, 37, 40–4, 47, 49, 55–8, 63, 73, 92, 113, 116, 123, 131, 146, 148–50, 154–5, 169, 180, 187–8, 200–1
donors   5, 14, 67, 69, 77–81, 139, 141, 183–4, 186
drug addict(s)   113, 118, 129, 130–3, 135, 137–8, 140, 142, 144
drug(s)   57, 63, 67, 83, 95, 129–30, 136–8, 178, 183
Dubai   44, 63, 76, 89, 147–8
Duffield, Mark   9–10, 14, 33, 46, 76
Dupree, Nancy H.   121–2, 124–6
Durrani(s)   7, 14, 48–50, 53

East(ern)   7, 53–4, 60, 76, 173
economy, economic   3–4, 12–14, 16, 21–2, 26–8, 31, 33–6, 38, 40, 44, 47, 54, 62, 64, 69, 73, 75–84, 92–4, 104, 106, 110, 112, 114–15, 117–20, 128, 133, 137–41, 146–7, 150–60, 165, 173, 177, 188, 190–1, 194
effectivity   22, 25, 43, 102, 160, 188
efficiency, efficient   10, 28, 34, 39, 45, 61, 81–5, 140, 158, 176, 179, 186
egalitarian   11, 42
elite(s)   6, 37, 115, 119, 153, 155, 190
Elphinstone, Mountstuart   7, 48–53
Emirati   5, 14, 148, 156, 160
empire   5–7, 9, 14, 35–6, 50–1, 53, 89, 121
employment   13, 44, 71–2, 76, 80, 93–4, 97, 100, 102, 110, 128, 132–3, 150, 153, 185, 194
empower(ment)   5, 12, 17–18, 63, 92–3, 105, 109, 142, 175, 185
endurance   3, 91, 145, 194
English language, the   104–5, 161, 181–2, 186, 188
enmeshed, enmeshment(s)   5–6, 18, 25, 27, 31–2, 36, 41, 43–4, 73–4, 91, 144, 148, 160, 194, 199, 200

entrepreneur(s), entrepreneurialism 16, 18, 68, 77, 79, 90, 92, 107, 111, 118, 120, 126-7, 132, 137-9, 144, 155, 170, 174-6, 190, 192, 194, 200, 202
equality 84, 92
equilibrium, equilibria 18, 61-2, 75, 81, 85, 108, 116, 138, 147, 151, 153, 199, 201-2
ethnic(ity) 5, 7, 17, 30-2, 40, 49, 55, 60, 69, 71, 127-8, 139, 146, 154, 156, 159, 167, 172, 187, 194
ethnography, ethnographies 15, 36, 48, 157
Euclidian 157
Europe(an) 26, 32, 35-6, 48, 50-2, 54, 57-63, 65-8, 76, 119, 144, 146, 153, 173, 183-4, 189
European Union (EU) 5, 12, 14, 34, 46, 57-9, 63, 66-8, 73, 77, 81, 98, 146-7, 149, 155, 179, 183, 200
evasion(s) 5, 97-8, 102-3, 110, 128, 158, 194, 200-1
eventfulness 7, 29, 62, 157
everyday 3-5, 11, 14-16, 21, 27, 30, 39-42, 56, 63, 67, 78, 91, 93, 149, 156, 160, 162, 169, 175, 177-8, 180, 185, 187, 189, 194, 200-1
exclude, exclusion 3, 8, 10, 14, 17, 28, 34, 36, 38, 68, 77, 90, 113-14, 118, 137, 141-3, 148-9, 152, 158, 160, 165, 167, 175, 176-8, 189, 193-5
exotic, exoticize 18, 46-7, 49, 52
experiment, experimentality, experimentation 14, 21, 27, 38-40, 42, 47, 79-81, 84-5, 147, 200
exploitation, exploitative 4, 18, 22, 25, 36, 38, 40, 43, 47, 76, 91-4, 100, 103, 105-7, 109-10, 115, 134, 139, 142, 148-52, 158, 161, 165-6, 171, 175, 178, 183, 193-4
external/domestic 5, 18, 27, 35, 73-4, 81, 93, 199, 200

fail(ure) 3-5, 9, 12, 21-2, 39, 50, 59, 63, 68, 74, 77-8, 80, 118, 134, 137, 199-202
Farah 71
farmer(s) 3, 18, 68, 73, 78, 80, 90, 107, 111, 128-9, 194

Farsiwan 7, 70, 139, 199
Faryab 172
Fatemiyoun Division 29, 167, 193
female 71, 135, 168-9
feminist 15, 29, 34
filth(y) 47-8, 50, 53, 133, 134, 144, 151, 159, 166, 193
force(ful), forced, forcibly 6, 10-11, 18, 22-3, 25-8, 31, 41, 46, 55, 70, 72, 78-9, 82, 84, 86, 95, 97-8, 101-2, 110, 112-14, 117-21, 127, 135-6, 141-4, 147, 150, 152-3, 155-8, 165, 174, 176, 178, 180, 183, 186, 189, 191, 200-1
Foucauldian 16, 18, 29, 34, 39, 59, 114, 183, 194
Foucault, Michel 9, 16-18, 22-37, 40-2, 44, 47, 49, 73-5, 90, 93, 97, 110, 114-18, 120, 149, 157-9, 167, 169-71, 174, 178, 188, 195
fragile, fragility 9, 21, 51, 70, 79, 174, 199, 200
fragmentation, fragmented 32, 49, 50, 82, 146, 162, 175, 179, 194
free(dom of) movement 4, 27, 147, 150, 166, 171
frontier(s) 5, 9, 14, 17-18, 35, 51, 57, 70, 146-9, 154, 159-61, 166, 167
functionalism, functionalist 11, 46, 119, 162, 175, 179

Gammell, Charlie P.W. 6-9, 14, 53-6, 147
gender(ed) 5, 12, 14-15, 17-18, 21, 23, 25, 28-31, 33, 37, 40, 44, 46, 57, 60, 63-4, 68-9, 71, 83-4, 134, 146-9, 154, 156-9, 161-2, 165, 168, 170, 174, 179, 181, 187, 193-4
geo-corporeal 148, 194-5
geography, geographies, geographic 5-6, 8-9, 12-15, 17-18, 30, 35-6, 42, 46-9, 51-3, 71, 73, 76-7, 107, 118, 121, 127, 148, 154, 157-60, 167-8, 173, 189
geopolitics, geopolitical 5-7, 13-15, 33, 35-7, 44, 55, 57, 68, 76, 146-50, 155, 159, 165, 167, 172, 177, 183
German(y) 13, 58, 77, 90, 138, 140, 183-4
Ghor 71, 110, 128, 133
Ghourian 69, 183

global, globe   3–6, 9–14, 18, 22, 27–8, 31, 33, 37, 38–9, 44, 46–9, 53, 57–64, 67–8, 70–4, 76–86, 91–4, 103, 111, 144, 147, 154, 160, 172, 193, 199–202
global/brown binary   33, 37
Global North   172
governance   3–6, 9–16, 18, 21–2, 24–5, 27–8, 31–2, 34, 37–41, 43–4, 46–7, 58–9, 67–9, 74–8, 81, 89–94, 97, 100, 103–6, 110, 114, 199, 201–2
governmentality   27–8, 32, 39, 42, 74, 118, 138
government of life   9, 39
graffiti   17, 117, 159
Grounded Theory   15, 194
guard(s)   72, 90, 123, 136, 166–7, 170, 173, 174, 180–7, 189–90, 192

Hazara(jat)   6–7, 29, 48, 70, 72–3, 128, 139, 150, 167
hazard(ous)   18, 33, 50, 55, 79, 124, 135, 139, 144, 148, 151–2, 156, 158, 167, 178
healthcare   11, 13, 33, 64, 79, 115, 118, 138–9, 141, 143–4, 150–1, 153, 155
health(y)   4, 9, 28–9, 31, 33, 35, 39, 50–1, 55, 66, 69, 71, 80, 113–14, 118, 132, 137–9, 146, 148, 151, 153, 155, 158, 193
hearts and minds   5, 34, 76, 85–6, 107, 156
hegemony, hegemonic   9–10, 12, 35, 38, 42, 56, 59, 77, 79, 82, 115, 186
Herat Urban Development and Housing Department (HUDA)   125, 136, 138
heroin   67–8, 137
hidden transcript(s)   180, 184, 186, 191, 194
hierarchy, hierarchies, hierarchical   4, 9, 23–5, 27, 31–3, 37, 49, 68, 76–7, 81, 83, 92, 155, 158–60, 166–7, 169, 173, 183, 185, 188, 193–4
historiography, historiographies   6, 47
homeless(ness)   12, 16–18, 22, 27, 35, 38, 54, 71, 73, 78, 112–16, 118, 120, 123–45, 164–5, 192, 200
Hopkins, B.D.   5, 14, 48–9, 146
household   44, 71–2, 76, 82, 135, 154, 175

hybrid(ity)   36, 40, 43–4, 74–5, 92, 201
hypothesis, hypotheses   4, 38–9, 41, 74, 80, 89, 97, 154

identity, identities   7, 29–30, 33, 36–7, 47, 101, 154, 156–7, 167, 177, 181, 184, 194
illness   71, 118, 132, 135
imagination(s), imaginative, imaginary   3, 6, 11, 14, 15, 32, 35, 37, 44, 46–8, 50, 52–3, 58, 61, 64–5, 82, 123, 127, 131, 137–8, 142–3, 146–8, 151, 156, 159–60, 167, 175, 177–8, 185, 193
imperial   7, 9, 14, 36, 47, 52, 76, 120
in-between(ness)   6–7, 43, 49
inequality   5, 15–16, 18, 23, 30–2, 36–7, 57, 70–1, 81, 83, 118, 128, 141, 149, 154, 171, 175, 193–4
informant(s)   3, 7, 16–17, 38, 78, 134, 180–1, 183, 189
infrapolitics   180, 187, 191, 194
insecurity, insecurities   4, 9, 61, 63, 71–2, 114, 128, 133, 151, 177
instability   10, 48, 59–63, 69, 78, 84, 111, 114, 128, 132–3, 156, 167, 194, 202
insurgency, insurgent   5, 7, 11–12, 18, 35, 39, 48, 57, 64–5, 68–70, 72, 73, 75–6, 79–84, 87, 89–92, 94–7, 99–100, 102–4, 109–11, 115, 122, 125, 132–4, 143, 161, 176, 181, 189, 201
Internally displaced person(s) (IDP)   71, 128–9, 131, 133–4, 136–7, 143, 192
International Federation of Red Cross and Red Crescent Societies (IFRC)   134, 136
International Monetary Fund (IMF)   11, 47, 71, 77, 79, 81–2, 200
International Security Assistance Force (ISAF)   10, 76, 81, 91
interpreter   3, 18, 38, 78, 90, 92, 104–5, 107, 116, 125, 136, 159, 200
intersectionality, intersectional   30–1, 33, 37–8, 40, 42, 73
intervention(s)   4, 9, 12, 14–15, 18, 26, 30, 32, 34, 39, 46–50, 59, 67–8, 72–4, 76–8, 80, 82, 85, 89, 91, 107, 117, 133, 188
interview(s)   3, 7, 16–17, 90, 93, 97–102, 105–6, 109, 114, 116, 123, 125–32, 134–9, 141–3, 168, 179, 180–1, 183, 192–4, 201

investment(s)   63, 79, 133, 139, 147, 155, 171
Iran(ian)   5–8, 12–15, 18, 24–6, 29, 38, 44, 49–50, 56–7, 63, 70, 76, 105, 128–9, 137, 143, 146–56, 159–84, 186–9, 191–4, 199–200
Islam(ic)   7, 33, 50, 52, 55–8, 66, 69–70, 72, 110, 132, 199
Islam Qala   13, 15–16, 26, 146–7, 149, 151, 156, 158–68, 170–81, 183–4, 188–9, 192–5
Ismail Khan   8, 56, 91, 110, 126, 182
isolate, isolated, isolating,   4, 32, 48, 55, 56, 113, 133, 137, 146, 185
Italy, Italian   16, 33, 55, 75–6, 79–80, 98, 101, 104–7, 114, 122, 140
itinerary, itineraries   189–90, 195

job(s)   13, 16, 68, 71, 74, 77–8, 84, 95–100, 107, 131–5, 139, 151–2, 156, 163–4, 170, 173, 185, 189, 190, 192

Kabul   3–4, 7–8, 13–16, 30, 48, 50–1, 55, 69, 71, 75, 84, 89–91, 93, 99–101, 103–5, 107, 110, 133, 140, 150, 160, 164, 172–3, 181–3
Kandahar   7, 14, 48, 69
Kartids, the   7
Khorasan   6–8, 14, 51, 105, 150, 156, 193
Kuchi   30, 128, 138

labour   22, 32, 37, 80, 114, 117, 119, 121, 134–5, 141, 143–4, 147–8, 151–8, 165–6, 171, 177–8, 193–4
laughter   182, 184, 186–8
Law and Order Trust Fund for Afghanistan (LOFTA)   75, 130
law enforcement   16, 24, 67, 75, 84, 116–17, 136, 141–2, 167, 187, 190–1
learning curve   80, 99
legitimacy, legitimate   10–11, 22, 24, 33, 40, 61, 76, 82, 92, 107, 114, 165, 174, 184
lessons   4, 39–40, 47, 73–4, 79–80, 84, 192, 200
lethal   11, 40, 56, 81, 85, 92–3, 99, 177, 180, 185, 200
liberal   5, 9–11, 13–15, 34, 79, 82, 144, 185

life chances   4, 5, 12–13, 16, 28, 30, 32, 34, 37, 41, 43, 46, 67–8, 70–2, 76, 82, 114, 116, 141, 153, 171, 178, 184, 188, 192, 200–1
liminal(ity)   6–9, 43–4, 49, 53, 99, 148–9, 186, 193–4, 199, 201
livelihood(s)   13, 76, 77–8, 80–1, 150
low-paid   135, 151–3
Lund, Joshua   4

male(s), maleness   3, 5, 17, 34, 116, 131, 135, 159, 161, 163–4, 168, 169, 202
management   9–10, 26, 30, 39, 42, 46–7, 67, 73–4, 76–7, 79–80, 84–5, 110, 112–14, 116–18, 120, 122, 124, 127, 136, 138, 140, 147–9, 172, 177–8, 189
map(s)   7, 53, 70, 72, 108, 112, 141, 158, 188–9, 190–2, 195
marginalize, marginalization, marginalized   4, 12, 14, 17, 30–1, 35, 37, 60, 80, 113–16, 127, 138, 141–3, 148–9, 159–60, 167, 178, 187, 189–90, 193
market(s)   9–14, 46, 67, 70, 82–3, 103, 108, 115, 117, 123, 141, 144, 147–8, 151–3, 155–6, 158, 162, 165, 168, 175
Marx (Karl), Marxist   31–2, 55, 86, 118, 152–4, 156
Mashhad   6–7, 121
Maslakh   71, 133–4
Mbembe, Achille   4, 30, 160
microphysical, microphysics   15–16, 24, 72, 102, 110, 159, 180, 200
micro-space, micro-spatial   15, 18, 25, 26, 30, 44, 61, 75, 94, 110, 159, 200–1
Middle East   51, 60–1, 63, 66, 67–8
migrant(s)   12–13, 17–18, 24, 29, 34, 51, 57, 61, 66, 137, 146, 148, 150–4, 158, 162, 169, 180, 183, 189–90, 194–5, 200
migration, emigration, immigration   4, 9–11, 13, 22, 24, 27, 33, 39, 48, 51, 67, 89, 93, 106, 128, 146, 149–50, 155, 159, 164, 173, 175, 179, 184, 189, 201
Mills, Charles Wright   114, 118–20
Minaret   71, 133–4
minaret(s)   112–13, 121–6, 130, 139–40, 142
mock(ery), mocked   99, 149, 182, 184, 186–8, 194, 200

modern(ity)   3, 6–7, 15, 21, 28, 32, 35, 37, 39, 42, 44, 48–51, 64, 68, 79, 82, 116–17, 144, 152–6, 159, 173, 187
mohajerin   150
Mongol, Mughal   6–8
mosque(s)   53–4, 57, 70, 72, 83, 121, 126, 147, 166, 174
Musalla Complex   16, 54, 112–18, 120–30, 132–45
Muslim(s)   4, 15, 33–4, 37, 66, 156

National Directorate of Security (NDS)   16, 69, 74, 83, 97, 100–3, 110, 136, 147, 191, 194
National Solidarity Program (NSP)   74–7, 79–81, 83–4, 108, 110, 200
neglect   4, 11, 13–14, 28, 56, 71, 82, 113–16, 120, 127, 135, 142–3, 156, 165
Nimroz   172–3
nomad, nomadic   30, 128, 138, 143
Nongovernmental organizations (NGOs)   10–12, 16, 29, 55–7, 57, 59, 69–70, 73, 75, 77–8, 80–1, 90, 94, 100, 103, 109–10, 138–9, 139, 143, 166, 169, 171, 173, 179–81, 189, 192, 200
nonsubjective intentionality   24, 25
nonviolence, nonviolent   5, 8, 40, 81, 89–94, 96, 99, 101, 106, 110, 149, 181, 186, 201
normal, normalize, normalization   4, 9, 14, 16, 18, 32–3, 35, 38–9, 44, 50, 58, 61–3, 68–9, 73–4, 79, 83, 86, 113–15, 134–5, 137, 143–4, 152, 156, 158–60, 166, 169, 171–5, 178–9, 184, 195, 199, 201
normative, normativity   9, 12, 21, 25, 37, 146
North Atlantic Treaty Organization (NATO)   3, 5, 10–14, 16, 34–6, 44, 46, 57–63, 65, 67–8, 70, 73, 75–6, 81–4, 89–91, 93–5, 97–8, 100–6, 109–10, 122, 133, 143, 148, 181, 187, 200–2
North(ern)   9, 11, 26, 33, 38, 47, 52, 57, 60, 62, 64, 67–8, 76, 79, 92, 116, 144, 172

object(s), objectify, objectification   5, 18, 22–4, 26–9, 34, 45, 53, 60, 85, 89, 93, 97–8, 114, 116–17, 123, 132, 134, 158, 163, 165–6, 179, 187, 199
Office of the United Nations High Commissioner for Refugees (UNHCR)   55–6, 58, 150–1, 162–5, 171–2
ominous   4, 14, 64, 115, 121
Operation Enduring Freedom (OEF)   10, 80–1, 91
Operation Freedom's Sentinel (OFS)   10, 63, 91, 110
oppressed, oppression, oppressive   5, 18, 25, 28, 30, 34, 37–8, 41, 43–4, 52–6, 63, 83, 114–16, 118, 120, 141–2, 144–5, 156, 165, 182–4
order(ly), orderliness   9–10, 21, 25, 27–8, 33, 44, 47, 59–62, 64, 68, 74–5, 83–4, 86, 89, 92, 110, 116–18, 130, 133, 141, 146, 147–8, 158, 162–3, 165–7, 172, 180, 187
ordinary   3–4, 13–14, 16–18, 30, 34, 40–1, 43, 45, 49, 51, 57, 59, 63–4, 67–8, 70, 72, 79, 81–2, 84, 89–93, 98, 103, 108, 110, 112–14, 118, 123, 128–34, 129, 133–4, 144, 146, 148, 150, 156, 158, 160–1, 161, 163, 165, 170, 173–5, 177, 182, 186–7, 193–4, 194, 199–201
Orient(al)   47, 51, 54, 56, 120, 177
other(s), otherness   9, 14, 30, 35–9, 43–4, 52, 63, 99, 115, 139–40, 143, 149, 158–9, 163, 167, 184–6, 193

pacification, pacify   9, 25, 33, 67, 73–4, 79, 83, 94, 110, 200
Pakistan, Pakistani   15, 48, 50, 56, 64–5, 70, 74, 100, 110, 122, 126, 147, 153, 155, 165, 173, 179
Pakistan(i)   15, 48, 50, 56, 64–5, 70, 74, 100, 110, 122, 126, 147, 153, 155, 165, 173, 179
Pashtuns   6–9, 12, 14–15, 33, 48–6, 73, 128–9, 133, 138, 143–4, 150
pathological, pathologize   46–9, 53, 55, 83, 138, 158
peace   9–12, 18, 25, 28, 32–3, 37, 43, 51, 59–62, 64, 67–8, 74–5, 80, 85–6, 92, 94, 110, 117, 132–3, 149, 177, 193, 199–202
performative, performativity   17, 23, 25

peril(ous), perilousness 5, 22, 53, 56, 63, 68, 73, 78, 84, 143, 148, 158, 165, 178, 181, 194–5, 199
periphery, peripheral 5, 14, 36, 38, 46, 89, 133, 146, 148–9, 154–5, 157–60, 163, 166–8, 171, 174–5, 178–80, 190, 193–4, 195
Persia(n) 6-9, 14, 48–9, 54–5, 105, 121, 146–7, 150, 155, 166
Persianate 8
photo(s) 3, 16–17, 121, 125
police 3, 17–18, 24, 27, 66, 74, 78, 90, 92, 94, 96–101, 103, 109, 111, 113–14, 116–18, 120, 127, 130–1, 133–4, 136, 138, 140–2, 144, 147, 150–1, 162, 169–73, 176, 179–80, 183, 191, 193–4, 200
population(s) 3–7, 9, 14–15, 18, 21, 24, 26–9, 31–5, 37–40, 44, 46–52, 57, 60–2, 64–7, 70–1, 73–7, 80, 83–6, 89–92, 114–18, 120, 124–5, 128, 132–4, 136–8, 148–9, 152–3, 157–60, 167, 171–3, 178, 189, 191, 193–4, 199–200, 202
portray(als) 4, 7, 9, 11, 14–15, 34, 38, 46–7, 50–3, 55–7, 73, 76–7, 82, 92–3, 108, 113, 139–40, 193–4
positionality 17, 156
postcolonial, postcolonialism, postcolony 4–5, 9, 13–18, 21, 29–30, 32–48, 51, 68, 70, 72–9, 83, 85–6, 91–3, 96, 107, 110, 114–16, 134, 143–4, 147–9, 152–4, 157–8, 160–2, 165–6, 171–3, 175, 177–8, 183, 185–6, 190, 193–4, 199–202
power 3–7, 9, 11–12, 14–18, 21–44, 47, 51, 57–8, 67, 69, 73–9, 81, 86, 89–94, 96–9, 107, 110, 113–16, 119–20, 127, 138, 141–3, 145, 148–9, 152–4, 156–60, 165, 169, 173–9, 181, 184, 186–8, 191, 195, 199–202
power/knowledge 23, 51
power struggle(s) 6, 9, 15–16, 21, 29–30, 40, 44, 55, 156–7
precarious(ness), precarity 12–13, 22, 40, 56, 70, 93, 113, 116, 124–5, 133, 150, 151–2, 154, 193–4
probabilistic, probability 22, 34, 39, 65–6, 69, 79, 84, 115, 177

productivity, productive, production 14, 22–4, 26–9, 33, 35, 36–7, 39–40, 47, 62–3, 73, 89–90, 94, 96, 111, 114–16, 118–20, 127, 134, 142–3, 146, 152–8, 160, 167, 178, 184–5, 189, 192, 195, 200
profit(s), profitable 6, 12, 38, 94, 103, 106–7, 126, 140, 152, 154–5, 158, 163, 175
province, provincial 4–6, 8, 12–13, 54, 56–7, 69–71, 79, 81, 83, 84, 91–4, 100, 101, 104–6, 109–10, 112, 117, 128, 133, 139–41, 143, 149, 151–2, 156, 166, 172, 176, 181, 189, 200
Provincial Reconstruction Team (PRT) 16, 43–4, 73–7, 79, 80–1, 83–4, 98, 101, 104–6, 122, 200
proximate(representations) 47–51, 53, 58
public health 4, 28, 33, 39, 114, 118, 148, 153, 158, 193
public/private 18, 73–4, 81, 199, 200

Qajar dynasty; Qajars, the 8, 121
Quijano, Aníbal 37, 152

race, racial, racialize(d) 4–5, 12, 14–15, 17–18, 21, 23, 25, 31–3, 35, 37, 39–40, 44, 46, 48, 50, 63–4, 68, 82, 119, 134, 147–9, 151–4, 156, 159, 162–3, 170, 177–9, 185, 193–4
rationality, rationalities 15, 18, 29, 32, 34, 36–9, 67–8, 75–6, 81, 84–5, 90, 99, 102, 107, 120, 143, 147–8, 152, 157, 171, 173, 175–6, 199
reconstruction, (Afghan, post-conflict) 3–5, 10, 14–16, 39, 41, 47, 75–6, 79–80, 91, 94, 104, 108, 141, 201
recruitment 16, 27, 44, 57, 72, 80, 83–4, 90, 100, 109, 128
reflexivity 16–17
refugee(s) 13, 51, 56, 61, 66–7, 71, 143, 146, 148, 150–1, 159, 164–7, 170, 171, 193–4
region(s), regional 4, 6–7, 11, 14, 34, 58, 60–1, 69, 72, 74, 77, 80, 121, 147, 149, 155–6, 159, 173–4, 187, 194
regulate, regulation, regulatory 9, 14, 18, 21–2, 27–31, 34–6, 39, 44, 90–1, 93,

96–7, 99, 103–4, 110–11, 114, 116–18, 124, 141, 143–4, 148–50, 158, 165, 168, 170–1, 200
represent, representation(s)   4, 10, 12, 14–17, 21, 30, 33–4, 38, 41–2, 47–9, 51–2, 58–60, 63–4, 67, 109, 113, 115, 127, 132–5, 137–42, 148, 159, 183, 185, 189–90, 192
repress, repression   4, 11, 23, 56, 113, 120, 167, 177, 185, 191
reproduce, reproduction   4, 16, 22–5, 29–31, 36, 48, 59–60, 62, 70, 89, 92, 115, 119, 132, 137, 143, 148–9, 151–2, 154, 156, 160, 162, 166, 178, 186, 193–4, 202
resistance(s), resistant   4–5, 8–9, 12, 15, 18, 21–2, 26, 29–30, 34, 36, 40–4, 55, 73–4, 79, 89–94, 96–9, 102–3, 107, 110–11, 115, 118, 119, 145, 149, 157, 177, 179–81, 183–4, 186, 188–92, 194–5, 200–1
risk, risky   3–4, 9–11, 13, 16–17, 22, 26–7, 32–3, 36, 39, 42, 45–7, 51–3, 56–65, 67–70, 73, 78, 81–4, 86, 90, 95–9, 105–7, 113, 116, 118, 123, 125, 132–4, 138, 143, 148–9, 151–2, 159–62, 168–9, 172–4, 176–9, 181, 191, 195
rural   7, 56–7, 69–71, 75–7, 85, 100, 105–6, 127–8, 133, 138
Russia(n)   5, 9, 14, 47, 52–5, 75, 121

Sadozai   7–8
Safavid(s), the   7, 121
safety   9, 13, 27, 51, 67, 69, 71, 75, 82, 84, 111, 113, 116, 124, 128, 132, 138, 148, 151–2, 161–2, 166, 168, 172–3, 191
Sassanian   6–7
Scott, James C.   12, 15, 42, 67, 96, 180–1, 184, 186, 188, 191, 194
security   3–6, 9–19, 21–8, 31–5, 37–49, 54, 58–64, 67–86, 89–95, 97–104, 106–12, 138, 141, 144, 146, 148, 160–1, 163, 167–8, 170, 172–4, 176–7, 179–83, 186–7, 189–95, 199–202
security-development nexus   9, 14, 22, 93, 200
security provision   9–10, 13, 21, 38, 81
segregation   4, 142, 166

Self-Reliance through Mutual Accountability Framework (SMAF)   77
sexed   21, 60
sexual, sexuality, sexualize   14, 17, 28–9, 33, 37, 60, 69, 71, 118, 134–5, 144, 146, 148, 154, 156, 159, 162 165, 168, 171, 187, 194
Shaidayee   71, 133–4
shalwar qameez   125, 161, 163
shelter(s)   124, 129–30, 133, 139, 164, 178, 190
Shia   6–8, 55, 57, 70, 72–3, 150
Shindand   8, 69–70, 72, 84, 110, 183
shopkeeper(s)   16, 112, 133–6, 145
signifier, (master and empty)   63, 68, 72
site(s)   16, 30, 62, 72, 78, 104, 110, 112–13, 117–18, 122–3, 126, 134–5, 138, 140–1, 143–5, 148, 152, 156–7, 178, 190
South(ern)   47, 51, 60, 76
sovereignty, sovereign   16, 22, 24–8, 30–1, 34, 37, 46, 68, 73–5, 83, 98, 115, 148–9, 152, 160, 162–3, 165–7, 171–3, 176–7, 179, 184–5, 188, 193–4, 199, 201
Soviet   8, 47, 55, 65, 83, 112, 122, 150, 182
space   4, 8–9, 14–16, 18, 23, 25–7, 29–33, 36, 39–44, 46–7, 50–3, 55, 59–62, 64, 67, 69, 73–6, 78–81, 83, 89–92, 98–100, 104–5, 108, 111, 113–15, 120, 123, 128, 130, 141–4, 148–50, 154, 157–60, 165–72, 174–9, 184, 191–3, 195, 200–1
spatial   14–16, 18, 23, 25–9, 31, 34, 36, 41, 44, 50, 60–1, 64, 68–9, 72–7, 79, 89, 92–4, 108, 110, 114, 118, 121, 124, 126–7, 129, 142–4, 146, 148, 160, 162, 166, 169, 171–5, 178–9, 189, 192, 194, 200
Spivak, Gayatri Chakravorty   17, 32–4, 38, 115–16, 134, 190, 195
splendo(u)r   114, 116–18, 122, 127, 133, 138, 141–3, 194
stability   4–5, 9–13, 18, 21–2, 28, 31, 33–4, 37–9, 44, 46, 60–4, 67–8, 72–83, 86, 133, 147, 172–3, 178, 180, 193–4, 199, 201–2

stabilize, stabilization   10, 14, 22, 41, 50, 62, 74–6, 78–9, 85, 91, 93, 110, 199, 200
state-building   4–5, 9, 14, 39, 62, 67, 85, 200
strategy, strategies, strategic   3, 5, 6, 14, 16, 18, 21–39, 41–4, 46, 48–9, 51, 58–62, 64–5, 68, 74–7, 79–81, 83–5, 90–91, 93–4, 98, 102, 110, 113–15, 120, 127, 136, 140–2, 144, 147–8, 150–2, 154, 156–7, 160, 167, 173, 175, 178–80, 187–8, 194, 201
subaltern(ity)   17, 37–8, 80, 85, 115–16, 134, 146, 151, 156, 178, 180, 186, 190, 195
subject, subjectivity   3, 6, 8, 12–13, 15–17, 21, 23–33, 35–8, 40, 43–5, 47–50, 59–60, 63, 68–9, 72–3, 78–9, 82–3, 86, 89–90, 97, 111, 115–16, 119, 133, 145–6, 149, 156–8, 160, 162, 167, 177–80, 185–7, 192–5, 199, 201
subjectification   23, 26
subjection   23–4, 26, 41, 73, 78, 95, 143, 148, 177, 183
Sunni   6, 7, 48, 53, 73, 150
surplus value   154–7
surveillance   4, 9, 18, 23–4, 26, 29, 39, 42, 44, 65, 67, 72–3, 77, 79, 81, 83, 91, 93, 99–100, 103, 107, 110, 117–18, 127, 146, 148, 158, 163, 165, 172–4, 176–80, 186, 188–92, 194–5, 200

tactic(s), tactical(ly)   8, 17–18, 24, 29, 40–4, 79, 83, 89, 90–7, 100–3, 106, 108–10, 114, 121–2, 132–5, 144, 157–9, 165, 171, 173, 177, 180–1, 184, 186–8, 190–1, 194–5, 200
Taliban   5, 8, 29, 34, 41, 50, 56–9, 61, 65–7, 69–70, 72, 75, 83–5, 91–3, 99–100, 106, 109–10, 112, 125, 128, 139, 143, 147, 150, 180, 182, 189
technology, technologies of power   9, 16, 32, 38, 44, 89, 108, 120, 136, 141, 147–8, 172, 175, 184, 187–9, 192, 194
Tehran   7–8, 29, 57, 63, 150, 156, 173, 175, 181
territory   6, 22, 25, 42, 49, 65, 180, 193
thickening   175, 179

threat(s), threaten   3, 10–11, 14, 18, 22, 24, 27, 33, 39, 41, 44–5, 47, 49–50, 52, 57–61, 63–8, 70, 72–4, 78, 83, 92, 94, 102, 105, 113–14, 118, 123–4, 126–8, 132–3, 137–9, 143, 146, 149, 152, 158–9, 165, 167, 177–9, 193–4, 199
Timurid   8, 54–6, 112, 120–1
trade   6, 8, 13–14, 52, 57, 60, 67–8, 78, 79, 82, 91, 107, 116–17, 146–7, 155–6, 170–1, 173–6, 178, 184, 200
Train Advise Assist Command West (TAAC-W)   43–4, 91, 122
trans-corporeal   4, 45, 66
transgression, transgressive, transgressor   24, 30, 44, 72, 170, 177, 183–4, 190, 193–4
transnational   8–10, 15, 31, 36–7, 52, 58, 60, 63, 68, 75, 81, 85, 107, 147, 153–4, 156–7, 166, 171, 173–5, 187, 193–4, 200
trial-and-error   38–9, 79, 84
tribal(ism), tribe, tribesmen   5–6, 12, 15, 30, 33, 46, 48–51, 53, 55, 69, 71–2, 81, 83, 92, 108, 127–8, 159, 199
truth(s)   6, 10, 17, 21–4, 27–9, 31, 36, 38, 47, 52, 73, 85, 116, 120, 127–8, 131–3, 139, 143, 146, 148, 156, 159, 167, 185, 199

uncertain(ty)   9–10, 22, 34, 40, 42, 55, 68–9, 83–4, 148, 163, 166
unequal   5, 12, 18, 24, 37, 46, 114, 141–3, 149, 151, 155, 157–8, 162, 188, 200
ungovernable   12, 21, 49–50, 53
United Arab Emirates (UAE)   155–6
United Kingdom (UK)   51, 60–2, 75, 106
United Nations (UN)   3, 10, 12–13, 16, 34, 44, 46–7, 55, 57–63, 67–70, 73, 75, 77, 79–84, 90, 94, 98, 105, 109–10, 113, 122, 125–6, 130, 147, 155, 171, 180–3, 200 202
United Nations Assistance Mission in Afghanistan (UNAMA)   22, 72, 180
United Nations Development Program (UNDP)   58, 82, 126–7, 130
United Nations Educational, Scientific and Cultural Organization (UNESCO)   112–14, 122–3, 127, 138–41

United Nations Office on Drugs and
  Crime (UNODC) 67–8, 128, 130,
  132, 137, 139, 171–2
United States (US) 8, 25, 33, 51–2, 56–7,
  59–68, 72, 75–6, 80, 94, 103, 107–8,
  121–2, 133, 136, 140, 147, 150, 155,
  161, 186, 200, 202
United States Agency for International
  Development (USAID) 39, 47, 67,
  75, 80, 106–7, 114, 122, 125, 191
universal, universalism 29, 34, 39,
  59–61, 64
unstable 9, 18, 23–4, 29, 33, 36, 41–2,
  46–7, 49–50, 53, 80, 91–3, 101, 110,
  112, 137, 173
urban, urbanites 6–7, 38, 52, 55–6, 69,
  71, 105, 123–5, 127–8, 136, 141, 144,
  152
urban(ites), urbanization 6–7, 38, 52,
  55–6, 69, 71, 105, 123–4, 127–8, 136,
  141, 144, 152
useful 5, 14, 26–8, 33, 40, 69, 73–4,
  81, 89, 99, 104–5, 107, 109, 114–15,
  117–18, 132, 136, 142–3, 148–9, 154,
  158–9, 174, 190, 192, 194, 199
useless 12, 22, 28, 68, 74, 115, 120, 127,
  136, 138, 142–4, 149, 159–60, 174, 194,
  199
utility 4, 14, 22, 26, 28, 30, 32–3, 37–8,
  44, 81–2, 85–6, 94, 99, 103–4, 106,
  113, 120, 135, 139, 141–4, 148, 152–3,
  157–8, 160, 163, 167, 173–4, 177,
  192–3
Uzbek(istan) 6, 48, 139, 193

Vaughan-Williams, Nick 160, 166, 178,
  184
victim(s), victimize 12–13, 23, 38, 53,
  56–7, 63, 67–8, 85, 127–9, 132–6, 139,
  180, 188
violence, violent 5, 12, 13, 24, 36, 39, 42,
  47, 49, 50, 55–7, 60–1, 64, 68–9, 72, 75,
  83, 85, 91, 93, 100, 111, 114, 127, 131,
  134, 136, 142, 146, 148, 160, 165, 171,
  173, 179–80, 183, 185

vulnerable, vulnerability, vulnerabilities
  4–5, 13, 15, 16–18, 21, 22, 24, 26, 29,
  31–2, 37, 46, 53, 69–70–3, 78–9, 81–2,
  86, 91, 113–15, 118, 125, 128, 131–6,
  142, 144, 149–51, 153–4, 160, 164–5,
  168, 170–1, 177, 188, 191, 199, 201

wage(s) 13, 37, 80, 115, 144, 150, 152–3,
  155–6, 193–4
Wallerstein, Immanuel 31, 154–7, 166,
  174–5, 194
warlords 8, 12, 39, 56–7, 67, 69–70, 75,
  79, 81–5, 91, 99–100, 106, 110, 122,
  134, 147, 182, 190
War on Terror 3, 5, 10, 15, 21, 59, 66, 69,
  85, 94, 148, 159, 179, 199
weak 12, 22, 25, 34, 38, 40–3, 51, 63, 67,
  70, 80, 91, 94, 120, 135, 139, 142, 165,
  171, 181, 184, 188–9, 193–4, 202
Weapon of mass destruction (WMD)
  48, 65
welfare 4, 9, 28, 33, 39, 57, 71, 76, 97,
  102, 113–15, 118, 137–9, 141, 143–4,
  146, 151, 153, 158, 165, 174, 178, 193
wellbeing 5, 71, 82, 92, 111, 138, 185,
  188
West, Western, Westerner(s) 3, 5, 9,
  11–12, 14–15, 25–6, 33–4, 36, 38,
  44, 47, 50, 52, 55, 57–8, 60, 62, 64–8,
  76–7, 79, 82, 90, 92, 100, 106, 109,
  116, 118, 144, 147–8, 160–1, 168, 171,
  177
white(ness) 5, 17, 29–30, 33, 36, 38, 58,
  68, 116, 148, 163, 185, 202
women 12, 15, 21, 34, 37, 50, 52, 56–7,
  63, 68, 70–2, 76, 85, 125, 128–9, 134–6,
  139, 144, 161, 167–71, 182–3, 194
workplace 71, 93, 96, 110, 147, 150–2,
  160, 194
World Bank, The 47, 70–1, 75, 79, 81–2,
  84, 147, 155, 200
World-Systems Analysis (WSA) 149,
  154–7, 194

Young, Robert 4, 32, 36

www.ingramcontent.com/pod-product-compliance
Lightning Source LLC
Chambersburg PA
CBHW072140290426
44111CB00012B/1933